David Mitchell's
Post-Secular World

New Horizons in Contemporary Writing

In the wake of unprecedented technological and social change, contemporary literature has evolved a dazzling array of new forms that traditional modes and terms of literary criticism have struggled to keep up with. *New Horizons in Contemporary Writing* presents cutting-edge research scholarship that provides new insights into this unique period of creative and critical transformation.

Series Editors

Martin Eve and Bryan Cheyette

Editorial Board: Siân Adiseshiah (University of Lincoln, UK), Sara Blair (University of Michigan, USA), Peter Boxall (University of Sussex, UK), Robert Eaglestone (Royal Holloway, University of London, UK), Rita Felski (University of Virginia, USA), Rachael Gilmour (Queen Mary, University of London, UK), Caroline Levine (University of Wisconsin–Madison, USA), Roger Luckhurst (Birkbeck, University of London, UK), Adam Kelly (York University, UK), Antony Rowland (Manchester Metropolitan University, UK), John Schad (Lancaster University, UK), Pamela Thurschwell (University of Sussex, UK), Ted Underwood (University of Illinois at Urbana-Champaign, USA).

Volumes in the series

Life Lines, John McLeod
The Politics of Jewishness in Contemporary World Literature, Isabelle Hesse
South African Literature's Russian Soul, Jeanne-Marie Jackson
Transatlantic Fictions of 9/11 and the War on Terror, Susana Araújo
Wanderwords, Maria Lauret
Writing After Postcolonialism, Jane Hiddleston

Forthcoming volumes

The Contemporary Post-Apocalyptic Novel, Diletta De Cristofaro
Contemporary Posthumanism, Grace Halden
Jonathan Lethem and the Galaxy of Writing, Joseph Brooker
New Media and the Transformation of Postmodern American Literature, Casey Michael Henry
Northern Irish Writing After the Troubles, Caroline Magennis
Postcolonialism After World Literature, Lorna Burns

David Mitchell's Post-Secular World

Buddhism, Belief and the Urgency of Compassion

Rose Harris-Birtill

BLOOMSBURY ACADEMIC
LONDON • NEW YORK • OXFORD • NEW DELHI • SYDNEY

BLOOMSBURY ACADEMIC
Bloomsbury Publishing Plc
50 Bedford Square, London, WC1B 3DP, UK
1385 Broadway, New York, NY 10018, USA

BLOOMSBURY, BLOOMSBURY ACADEMIC and the Diana logo are trademarks of
Bloomsbury Publishing Plc

First published in Great Britain 2019

Cover design: Eleanor Rose
Cover image © Alice Marwick

A catalogue record for this book is available from the British Library.

A catalog record for this book is available from the Library of Congress.

ISBN: HB: 978-1-3500-7859-8
ePDF: 978-1-3500-7860-4
eBook: 978-1-3500-7861-1

Series: New Horizons in Contemporary Writing

Typeset by Deanta Global Publishing Services, Chennai, India

To find out more about our authors and books visit www.bloomsbury.com
and sign up for our newsletters.

From womb to tomb we are bound to others, past and present.
And by each crime and every kindness we birth our future.
– Sonmi 451, *Cloud Atlas* film

Compassion is the radicalism of our time.
– Tenzin Gyatso, Dalai Lama XIV

Contents

Illustrations

Preface

If you are opening these pages for the first time, you are probably expecting a book that ventures into David Mitchell's fictional world, and its relation to the shifting attitudes towards belief in the twenty-first century known as the 'post-secular'. So far, so good. There are also some extra resources to help along the way: a chronology of David Mitchell's complete fictions to date, including his novels, libretti and short stories; a list of selected critical reading to help researchers, students and teachers alike; and two substantial new interviews with David Mitchell, discussing everything from Shakespeare and Tolkien to Star Trek (and Trump).

However, what you may not be expecting to find in this book is a journey that uses a different type of map to find its way into David Mitchell's fictional world: the mandala (a type of religious art form – all will be explained in the introduction). How did this come about? Well, this book started not as an exploration into the post-secular, or the mandala, but simply as an itch to find out what made this author's works tick. When this project began, I was working long hours in London as a writer while searching for a suitable topic for my PhD, and I would spend my journey into the city wedged between fellow commuters, alternating between reading literature and criticism (my apologies to the elderly passenger who happened to start reading William Burroughs's *Naked Lunch* over my shoulder, and promptly moved carriages).

Along the way, I discovered David Mitchell's fantastically immersive fictional world – soon followed by critical essay after essay that used visual metaphors to describe his stories: fractal, kaleidoscope, web, carousel. None of these seemed to quite fit the ethical world that I was moving through, text by text, train by train. And yet I couldn't shake the feeling that each of these critics was onto something; here was a meticulously structured fictional world that felt like it was built according to some kind of overarching plan. After long evenings of researching and rereading, I remember waking at 3.00 am, grabbing a notepad and scribbling: 'DM ≠ kaleidoscope. MANDALA.'

If this sounds epiphanic, it wasn't. At this stage, my previous encounters with mandalas had been brief and perfunctory: in C. G. Jung's writings while studying psychoanalysis and literary criticism during my master's degree, and in passing in exhibitions (and later, in a blurry in-flight film of sci-fi adventure *The Last Mimzy*). Wary of adding yet another visual metaphor to an already-overflowing pot, I started tracking down more credible sources.

And yet, as I began to learn more about the mandala's history, philosophies and representations in the West, while venturing further into David Mitchell's fictions, the two worlds started to pull together, the Buddhist principles and the urgency of compassion behind both world views leading me further into the research project that would become this book.

Gathering material for this book was an adventure in itself, taking me across three continents. Researching David Mitchell's writing for opera, I met the wonderful original cast members and composer of *Sunken Garden* at the Opéra National de Lyon in France, and dined with the original Dr Iris Marinus (the lovely and incredibly talented soprano Claron McFadden). As well as interviewing *Sunken Garden*'s cast, I also interviewed *Wake*'s Dutch composer Klaas de Vries, who kindly gave his time to share his unique memories of the opera's composition and performances, and David Mitchell himself, who was as generous, fascinating and obliging an interviewee as I could have wished for.

My research also took me to the British Museum in London, the *Enter the Mandala* exhibition at San Francisco's Asian Art Museum (and the World of Coca-Cola in Atlanta, Georgia – see Chapter 4 to find out why), to the giant temple of Borobodur in Indonesia, to an unexpected Indian-Tibetan *puja* ritual at Choe Khor Sum Ling Tibetan Buddhist Meditation and Study Centre in Bengaluru and, finally, to Namdroling Monastery in Bylakuppe, India. Here, Buddhist monk and senior teacher Lopen Pema Wangdak generously gave his time to answer my questions and take me to the array of different mandalas to be found throughout the monastery and temples: in golden sculptures, painted on walls and handcrafted as teaching aids, as two-dimensional blueprints and three-dimensional temples. Before I left, I asked what, for him, was the single most important thing that I should know about the mandala. He immediately replied that the mandala is a tool – and so it could be fashioned anywhere, out of anything, and discarded once used: the real mandala lies in its effects.

What follows here, then, is the use of the mandala as a tool, but a post-secular one – repurposed to help guide you through David Mitchell's immersive fictional world. In Tibetan Buddhism, it is said that the mandala bestows benefits on all those who encounter it, at whatever level you are able to understand it. In my own post-secular way, then, I choose to believe that this is true, and hope that your voyage into *David Mitchell's Post-Secular World* helps you along your own personal journey, wherever it may take you.

Rose Harris-Birtill, April 2018

Acknowledgements

The author and publisher gratefully acknowledge the permission granted to reproduce the copyright material in this book. Every effort has been made to trace copyright holders and to obtain their permission for the use of copyright material. The publisher apologizes for any errors or omissions in the below list and would be grateful if notified of any corrections that should be incorporated in future reprints or editions of this book.

An earlier version of part of Chapter 3 appears as "'Looking Down Time's Telescope at Myself": Reincarnation and Global Futures in David Mitchell's Fictional Worlds' in *KronoScope: Journal for the Study of Time* 17.2 (2017): 163–81, reprinted courtesy of Brill. An earlier version of part of Chapter 4 appears as "'A Row of Screaming Russian Dolls": Escaping the Panopticon in David Mitchell's *number9dream*' in *SubStance* 44.1 (2015): 55–70, and is reprinted courtesy of the University of Wisconsin Press. Part of Chapter 2 appears in the edited collection *David Mitchell: Contemporary Critical Perspectives*, eds. Wendy Knepper and Courtney Hopf (London: Bloomsbury, forthcoming), and is reprinted courtesy of Bloomsbury. All reasonable efforts were made to contact the rights holders of the quotations used in the epigraph.

My heartfelt thanks to Dr Peter Mackay for all his expertise and support throughout this project, to Dr Alex Davis for his time and help in reading through an early draft, to Professor Berthold Schoene, Dr James Purdon, Professor Martin Paul Eve and Professor Paul Harris for their very useful comments and suggestions, to David Avital, Clara Herberg and all the Bloomsbury Academic team for their help in bringing this to press, and to Dr Sarah Dillon for recognizing this project's early potential.

A huge thank you to David Mitchell for so generously giving his time for interviews and for his warmth, kindness and good humour. Thank you also to Klaas de Vries, Claron McFadden, Roderick Williams and Katherine Manley for sharing their unique insights in interviews, the English National Opera and Silbersalz for access to *Sunken Garden* and *Wake*'s video footage, Michel van der Aa and Intermusica for providing access to *Sunken Garden*'s libretto, the University of Amsterdam and Donemus for providing access to *Wake*'s recording and score, Nielsen for providing book sales data, and *Prospect Magazine* for access to David Mitchell's short story 'Acknowledgements'.

Thanks also to Thomas Bergmann, videographer for *Wake*, for his kind permission to make the performance footage available to future researchers; DVDs of *Wake* are now available in the University of St Andrews Special Collections and the University of Amsterdam Special Collections.

My warmest thanks also to Lopen Pema Wangdak and Khenpo Sonam Tsewang from Namdroling Monastery in Bylakuppe, India, for their help with my mandala research.

Thanks to the Spalding Trust for their generous funding, enabling me to present part of this research in progress at the International Society for the Study of Time (ISST) Sixteenth Triennial conference in Edinburgh in June 2016, and to the ISST for their recognition of this research with their award of the Founder's Prize for New Scholars.

Finally, a huge thank you to my family, and to my wonderful David H-B, for all their love, support and encouragement.

David Mitchell's Fictional World: A Chronology

Pre-1999 – *The Old Moon* (unpublished manuscript)
1999 – Mongolia
1999 – *Ghostwritten*
2001 – *number9dream*
2003 – The January Man
2004 – *Cloud Atlas*
2004 – What You Do Not Know You Want
2005 – Acknowledgements
2005 – Hangman
2006 – *Black Swan Green*
2006 – Preface
2007 – Dénouement
2007 – Judith Castle
2009 – The Massive Rat
2009 – Character Development
2010 – *Wake*
2010 – *The Thousand Autumns of Jacob de Zoet*
2010 – Earth Calling Taylor
2010 – Muggins Here
2010 – All Souls Day
2011 – The Siphoners
2011 – Imaginary City
2011 – The Gardener
2012 – In the Bike Sheds
2012 – An Inside Job
2012 – The Earthgod and the Fox (translation of Kenji Miyazawa's short story)
2012 – *Cloud Atlas* film released, directed by the Wachowskis and Tom Tykwer
2013 – *Sunken Garden*
2013 – Lots of Bits of Star
2013 – *The Reason I Jump* (joint translation of Naoki Higashida's memoir)
2013 – *The Voorman Problem* film released, directed by Mark Gill
2014 – *The Bone Clocks*
2014 – Variations on a Theme by Mister Donut
2014 – The Right Sort
2015 – *Slade House*
2015 – I_Bombadil
2015 – Six Shorts (untitled)

2015 – From Me Flows What You Call Time (submitted to the Future Library project in 2016; publication scheduled for 2114)
2016 – My Eye On You
2017 – *Fall Down 7 Times Get Up 8* (joint translation of Naoki Higashida's memoir)
2017 – A Forgettable Story

Introducing David Mitchell's Fictional World

British writer David Mitchell (b. 1969), author of seven novels, two libretti and some twenty-six published short stories to date, is constructing an enormous fictional terrain. As the author notes in a 2010 interview with Wyatt Mason, his works together form a growing 'fictional universe with its own cast'; he asserts, 'each of my books is one chapter in a sort of sprawling macronovel. That's my life's work' ('David Mitchell: The Experimentalist'). Similarly referring to his continuous body of fiction as an 'über-novel', Mitchell remarks in a 2013 interview with Jasper Rees that his libretti for the operas *Wake* (2010), composed by Klaas de Vries, and *Sunken Garden* (2013), composed by Michel van der Aa, are also an important part of this macronovel, noting, 'I like to think of everything I do as chapters in one bigger über-novel and the libretti are also chapters in the über-novel' ('10 Questions'). Mitchell's short stories also further enlarge the boundaries of this fictional world. For example, characters that the thirteen-year-old protagonist of *Black Swan Green* (2006) encounters in childhood resurface as adults in several short fictions, including 'Acknowledgements' (2005), 'Preface' (2006) and 'The Massive Rat' (2009). However, this isn't a series of works joined by a single time or place. David Mitchell's 'macronovel' creates a cross-temporal, cross-cultural narrative world whose combined subject is the global trajectory of humanity itself – and it is this shared ethical dimension of the macronovel that this study investigates.

Mitchell's oeuvre cumulatively depicts not the world of a single individual or family, but that of an entire global community, in a body of interconnected fictions that – as well as crossing art forms – spans several continents, eras and genres. For example, *Ghostwritten*'s (1999) plot travels through Japan, Hong Kong, China, Mongolia, Russia, London, Ireland and New York; *Cloud Atlas* (2004) begins in the nineteenth century and moves forward in time to a post-apocalyptic far future; *number9dream* (2001) is a coming-of-age novel, *The Thousand Autumns of Jacob de Zoet* (2010)[1] is a historical novel, *Black Swan Green* a semi-autobiographical novel, *The Bone Clocks* (2014) is part-fantasy and *Slade House* (2015) is a supernatural horror story. Such a varied body of interconnected literary works raises a series of critical enigmas: how to critique this 'sprawling macronovel' as a continuous world; what it is – if not genre, place or time – that binds its constituent parts together; why such a complex macro-scale formal strategy is being employed in the current global context; and where to situate this body of works in relation to other shared narrative strategies emerging within other twenty-first-century fictions in English. The question, in short, is quite how to map it.

---

[1] Hereafter referred to as *The Thousand Autumns*.

To this end, this book approaches the author's fictional world in its entirety, on a wider scale than has been undertaken within existing literary criticism to date, discussing his novels, short stories and libretti as an interconnected world. Taking a similarly 'entire world' approach to Mitchell's essays and interviews as to his fictions, this study also draws on his non-fiction writings, as well as on new interviews with the author, the composer of *Wake* and the cast of *Sunken Garden*, conducted as part of the wider research for this study. The interviews with David Mitchell are included in the appendices to help researchers, students and those simply curious to know more about this fictional universe in the author's own words. This book also includes a chronology of David Mitchell's novels, writing for opera and short stories to date, as well as a list of selected further reading, reflecting a growing area of study whose critical approaches are every bit as diverse, innovative and thought provoking as the textual world that they critique.

Moving through this multi-genre macronovel, this study approaches Mitchell's interconnected works as a post-secular fictional world – a term that will be discussed later in this chapter. Of course, there are many other connecting threads and themes which join his fictions together into a self-contained unit, but this book explores the secular reworking of the religious influences that run throughout his writing, focusing on the Buddhist ethical influences that continue to resurface throughout this fictional universe. However, where this study embarks on a journey into this post-secular fictional world, it also ventures a post-secular critical approach to help map it. As such, it draws on the forms and philosophies of the Tibetan Buddhist mandala – a traditionally religious symbol that maps an ethical worldview – as the basis for a secular comparative tool, using this to help chart the Buddhist influences that are reworked in Mitchell's fictional world, and – more broadly – to help identify an emerging category within other contemporary fictions that also create their own post-secular ethical worlds.

Entering Mitchell's macronovel

Since the publication of his first novel in 1999, David Mitchell's writing has attracted substantial critical and popular acclaim. His list of literary accolades includes a World Fantasy Award, the John Llewellyn Rhys Prize, the Geoffrey Faber Memorial Prize and the Commonwealth Writers' Prize, as well as being named as one of Granta's Best of Young British Novelists. His works have appeared on shortlists for *The Guardian*'s First Book Award, the James Tait Black Memorial Prize and the Arthur C. Clarke Award, with two novels shortlisted and three longlisted for the Booker Prize. His fictional world has entered Hollywood: the 2012 film adaptation of *Cloud Atlas*, directed by the Wachowskis and Tom Tykwer, became one of the most expensive independent films ever made, with a budget of over $100 million, while the narrator's daydream from *number9dream* was made into an Academy Award- and BAFTA-nominated short film, *The Voorman Problem* (2013).[2] In 2007, the author featured in *TIME* magazine's list

---

[2]   The budget of the *Cloud Atlas* film was widely reported by the UK and the US media. See articles by Holly Williams ('Heads Up: *Cloud Atlas*' 2013), Phil Hoad ('*Cloud Atlas*' 2013), and Nicholas Kulish and Michael Cieply ('Around the World in One Movie' 2013) for examples.

of the 100 most influential people in the world; in 2011, the White House announced that the then US president Barack Obama had chosen *The Thousand Autumns* for his holiday reading. In 2014, songwriter and musician Kate Bush brought in David Mitchell to write dialogue for her first live shows since 1979, while American actress and designer Sarah Jessica Parker was photographed leaving her home with 'a large pastel handbag in one hand and Mitchell's *The Bone Clocks* in the other' – a month before the novel was released.[3] In 2017, David Mitchell served as a consultant for the second season of director Lana Wachowski's Emmy Award-nominated Netflix series *Sense8*, in which the author also made a cameo appearance; Mitchell later returned to co-write the 2018 series finale.[4] This is an author whose writing is now name-dropped in Hollywood – as it is simultaneously researched, taught and studied in universities across the globe.

However, despite this increasing momentum, no single-author study has yet analysed David Mitchell's entire body of fiction to date. At the time of writing, there is currently no published attempt to critique all of his novels, short stories and libretti as a continuous world. Growing critical interest in the writer's fictions includes three UK academic conferences on his works (the first in St Andrews in 2009, the second in Bloomsbury, London, in 2014, and a third in St Andrews in 2017),[5] two essay collections (ed. Sarah Dillon, 2011; eds. Wendy Knepper and Courtney Hopf, forthcoming), and David Mitchell special editions of the journals *SubStance* (ed. Paul A. Harris, 2015) and *C21 Literature* (ed. Rose Harris-Birtill, 2018). At the time of writing, there are over 100 published papers and book chapters in English discussing Mitchell's works, as well as a critical introduction to Mitchell's first six novels, *A Temporary Future: The Fiction of David Mitchell* (2015) by Patrick O'Donnell. However, most of the scholarly focus to date has been on Mitchell's early novels: *Ghostwritten*, *number9dream* and *Cloud Atlas*. These have received some critical attention as a group, for example in Sarah Dillon's edited collection *David Mitchell: Critical Essays* (2011), although Dillon's introduction usefully acknowledges the remaining critical gap by discussing Mitchell's following two novels, in a brief but insightful analysis of their links with his earlier works ('Introducing David Mitchell's Universe' 3). To give a brief survey of the 124 English-language essays and book chapters on Mitchell's fictions found as part of the research for this study, each published between 2002 and 2017, ninety-five (77%) focus on either one, two or all three of Mitchell's first three novels. Just twenty-nine

---

[3]　See 'David Mitchell' (2007) by Pico Iyer in *TIME* magazine at http://content.time.com/time/specials/2007/time100/article/0,28804,1595326_1595332_1616691,00.html, 'Obama's little light reading' (2011) by Guy Adams in *The Independent* at http://www.independent.co.uk/news/world/americas/obamas-little-light-reading-tales-of-spies-and-a-republican-hero-2174671.html, 'Kate to release the live album "Before the Dawn"' on the artist's official website at http://katebush.com/news/kate-release-live-album-dawn, and 'She's so VIP!' (2014) by Johnni Macke on the *Daily Mail* website at http://www.dailymail.co.uk/tvshowbiz/article-2718402/Spotted-Sarah-Jessica-Parker-leaving-home-carrying-novel-not-released-yet.html, accessed 26 September 2017.

[4]　In season 2, episode 11 of *Sense8*, Amanita Caplan, played by Freema Agyeman, can be seen reading a copy of *Slade House* at the start of the scene where she gets engaged to Nomi Marks, played by Jamie Clayton.

[5]　A video from the conference, 'David Mitchell Conference 2017: David Mitchell & Prof. Paul Harris evening reading', can be found on YouTube at https://www.youtube.com/watch?v=5L2BMBVhEos, uploaded by David Mitchell Conference 2017, accessed 2 February 2018.

(23%) feature his other works, with only two papers discussing his short stories. Of the three publications that include *Sunken Garden*, only one is dedicated entirely to this work, and while two refer to his libretto for *Wake*, there are no papers dedicated to its discussion.[6] It is understandable that Mitchell's earlier fictions have had more time to attract academic critique. However, even within this substantially larger distribution of essays on Mitchell's first three novels, this critical bias finds its apex in his third novel: *Cloud Atlas*.

If *Cloud Atlas*'s widespread popularity has made it the most well known of Mitchell's works – he wryly remarks in a 2013 interview with Elmira Kuznetsova that this novel will be on his gravestone – the same is perhaps true for *Cloud Atlas* within literary criticism, where its commercial success appears to have influenced the novel's critical legacy ('Writer David Mitchell Talks'). Nielson book sales data reveals that *Cloud Atlas* accounts for 46 per cent of Mitchell's total UK book sales as of March 2018 (see Appendix A). Perhaps fuelled by this momentum, much existing literary criticism on Mitchell's texts tends to focus on *Cloud Atlas* – so much so that when the editors of the second essay collection on his works sent out a secondary call for papers, it specifically asked for essays on topics *other* than this novel. While much more is still to be said on this structurally and temporally fascinating work, this critical focus risks creating a body of scholarship which misses productive connections with Mitchell's other writing, and his larger textual project as a whole. For example, in '"This Time Round": David Mitchell's *Cloud Atlas* and the Apocalyptic Problem of Historicism' (2010), Heather J. Hicks' perceptive reading of cyclical and linear time in *Cloud Atlas* mentions *Ghostwritten* only in passing in its footnotes, although the latter's textual cyclicality would make it a natural fit for a paper on this topic. Similarly, in Fredric Jameson's *The Antinomies of Realism* (2013), *Cloud Atlas* is the single David Mitchell novel chosen for his close reading; again, with its similarly interconnected approach to storytelling, *Ghostwritten* would also merit discussion alongside Jameson's analysis of this interwoven 'series of stories' (305). In fact, of the 124 published critical works on Mitchell's fictions mentioned earlier, *Cloud Atlas* arises with remarkable frequency: eighty-one (65%) feature *Cloud Atlas*, discussing this text either alone or in conjunction with other works. To compare this with his other novels, *Ghostwritten* features significantly in thirty-eight of the publications (31%), followed by *number9dream* (twenty-five, or 20%), *The Thousand Autumns* (sixteen, or 13%), *Black Swan Green* (fourteen, or 11%) and *The Bone Clocks* (ten, or 8%). Similarly, of the ninety-six critical studies that focus on just one of Mitchell's fictions, fifty-seven of these (59%) are on *Cloud Atlas* – followed by just fifteen (16%) on *Ghostwritten*, ten (10%) on *number9dream*, seven (7%) on *The Thousand Autumns*, three (3%) on *The Bone Clocks* and three (3%) on *Black Swan Green*, with one (1%) on *Sunken Garden*.

To venture beyond the author's fictional works, some thirty non-fiction essays by the author form a significant contribution to his wider writing that, like Mitchell's short stories and libretti, remains largely overlooked in literary criticism of his works. These

---

[6] Statistics have been rounded to the nearest percentage point. Papers in these statistics include published journal articles, books and book chapters that have substantial content on David Mitchell's works (rather than, for example, a brief mention of a novel in passing), with book reviews, unpublished conference papers, blogs and theses excluded.

essays give a valuable insight into the personal encounters and formative experiences that have shaped the author and his writing, from his time spent living as an outsider in Japan ('Japan and My Writing', 2000) and his travel writing on Iceland ('A sublime search for the ancient sagas in Iceland', 2012), to his chosen future professions as a child – which included 'milkman', 'forester' and 'lighthouse keeper' ('My life before writing', 2016). They also reveal his struggles and triumphs as a stammerer, as in 'Let Me Speak' (2006), 'Lost for Words' (2011) and in *Dreizehn Arten das Stottern zu betrachten* (2016), a bilingual German-English publication of the author's hour-long speech *Thirteen Ways of Looking at a Stammer*, given at the International Stuttering Association World Congress 2013. Mitchell also discusses the difficulties and rewards of parenting a child with autism ('Learning to live with my son's autism', 2013; 'Almost everything I'd been told about my son's autism was wrong', 2017; 'David Mitchell: What my son's autism has taught me', 2017), a topic also explored in the author's introductions to Naoki Higashida's memoirs on living with autism, *The Reason I Jump* (2013) and *Fall Down 7 Times Get Up 8* (2017), texts that Mitchell has jointly translated into English with K. A. Yoshida. Interspersing the personal with the literary, Mitchell's other essays explore topics as diverse as the purpose of dreams in literature ('What use are dreams in fiction?', 2008), the historical fiction genre ('David Mitchell on Historical Fiction', 2010), the topic of 'Asia in English Literature' (2005), and his self-confessed literary influences, Italo Calvino, Russell Hoban and Ursula Le Guin ('Enter the Maze', 2004; 'The Book of Revelations', 2005; 'David Mitchell on Earthsea', 2015).

Augmenting this non-fiction material, there are also over 200 written and recorded interviews with the author; by drawing on these often critically overlooked resources, this study also seeks to encourage wider research into this non-fiction material while the ability to interview the author – and those involved in staging his libretti – is still available. Of course, the notion of authorial intention remains problematic within literary criticism, and this study's inclusion of interview material is by no means an attempt at re-privileging the voice of the author within literary criticism.[7] However, one of the vital strengths of contemporary literature is that many of its authors are still alive and, as such, are able to comment on their own work, producing supplementary material that can suggest valuable further avenues for critical investigation. As such, the inclusion of interview material is used to augment, rather than undermine, the poststructural methodologies employed in this study.

The lack of published research on Mitchell's entire macronovel – defined for the purposes of this study as his body of fictional writing, including his novels, short stories and libretti – makes this a particularly neglected research area. Mitchell himself refers to the thematic 'indestructible whack-a-moles' that resurface across his fictional universe in a 2010 interview with Adam Begley ('David Mitchell: The Art'). Such recurring themes include, for example, reincarnation, predation and structural experimentation with the

---

[7] For more on the ongoing debates about authorial intention within literary criticism, see Roland Barthes' 1967 essay 'The Death of the Author', Michel Foucault's 1969 lecture 'What is an Author?', Seán Burke's *The Death and Return of the Author: Criticism and Subjectivity in Barthes, Foucault and Derrida* (2008), Kaye Mitchell's *Intention and Text: Towards an Intentionality of Literary Form* (2008) and John Farrell's *The Varieties of Authorial Intention: Literary Theory Beyond the Intentional Fallacy* (2017), among others.

short story form. As the macronovel continues to expand, Mitchellian literary criticism would now benefit from closer attention to the shared themes that run through his fictional network as a whole, in order to investigate why such a multi-genre fictional world has emerged in the current literary and historical moment. Mitchell's use of shared characterization also connects a realist coming-of-age novel set in 1980s Worcestershire, a historical novel set in late-eighteenth-century Japan, and a fantasy-speculative-fiction hybrid that stretches into a dystopian Ireland in 2043; the reincarnated character of Marinus also appears in seven separate works to date. By overlooking the significance of these shared factors, the failure to critique Mitchell's macronovel as a continuous whole is arguably as great a critical oversight as analysing merely a single scene of a play and failing to investigate its role within the wider performance, or only studying every fifth line of a poem. This is not to disparage stand-alone literary criticism of individual narratives as self-contained entities; such attention to individual texts on their own grounds remains a vital and necessary part of the discipline. However, the limited number of scholarly analyses on his libretti and short stories, the continued critical dominance of *Cloud Atlas* and the failure to conduct detailed analysis on Mitchell's cumulative fictional world view as a macro-scale narrative unit all risk compromising the breadth and depth of academic research on his fictions – issues which this study seeks to highlight, challenge and illuminate for future criticism.

David Mitchell's narrative cartographies

Having given a brief overview of David Mitchell's body of writing to date, its popular and literary acclaim, and a broad survey of its criticism, we now return to this introduction's opening question: how to map such a vast, varied and – when read in its entirety – critically uncharted fictional world. The author's own approaches to narrative creation as a form of map-making suggest that a similarly cartographic approach may, in fact, hold promise for analysing his works as a continuous fictional terrain. Mitchell has written and spoken extensively about his childhood map-making as an early form of world creation. For example, in his 2010 essay, 'Once upon a life: David Mitchell', he writes of finding inspiration from the fictional maps that J. R. R. Tolkien created to accompany his writings on Middle Earth: '[w]hat grabbed me were the maps [...] I burnt to imitate these maps, so imitate I did, over hundreds of hours, with endless notes about the countries, peoples and wars.' He similarly recalls his early fascination with maps in a 2010 interview with Adam Begley:

> my parents discovered they could shut me up for hours by mounting a large piece of cartridge paper [...] and leave me to draw, and name, maps of imaginary archipelagos and continents. Those maps, I think, were my protonovels. I was reading Tolkien, and it was the maps as much as the text that floated my boat. ('David Mitchell: The Art')

Mitchell's anecdotes reveal an early fascination with literature as textual geography, an approach inspired by Tolkien's fantasy worlds in which the writer's fictional maps became immersive visual paratexts, augmenting his narratives by revealing the spatial relationships between each group of characters. This early influence is also visible in Mitchell's continuous fictional terrain, across which its inhabitants move freely, and which continues to grow with each new publication. In a 2015 interview with Michael MacLeod, Mitchell confirms that his 'large-scale' macronovel is effectively his own form of Tolkiensien Middle Earth ('David Mitchell: "I have created my own Middle Earth"'). However, as Courtney Hopf notes in 'The Stories We Tell: Discursive Identity through Narrative Form in *Cloud Atlas*' (2011), Mitchell's works form 'a boundless and ever-expanding world' (106); unlike Tolkien's Middle Earth, its characters aren't contained within a single landmass, making this 'ever-expanding world' far more difficult to chart using any simple form of geographical map.

In a 2004 interview with Wayne Burrows, Mitchell again describes his own cartographic creations as 'an early form of novel writing' – and reveals his interest in 'creating an alternative road map of world literature' ('An Interview with David Mitchell'). The global ambitions of Mitchell's fictions situate these works within a much larger terrain, depicting an interconnected world-system, rather than a single realm, and thereby suggesting their own 'alternative' approach to mapping the interconnections that shape the contemporary world. Approaching Mitchell's macronovel as 'an alternative road map of world literature' also moves literary criticism of his works away from traditionally linear modes of narrative interpretation, towards the simultaneous viewpoints created by the polyphonous global narratives emerging in contemporary writing. As Sarah Dillon notes, '[t]raditional linear narratives are now being replaced by complex systems that more accurately represent our experience of the contemporary world' ('Chaotic Narrative' 2011, 29). To chart this fictional global world-system requires a suitably complex form of map, itself able to transcend the confines of a single territory or temporal dimension in order to model the relationships between the disparate parts of this textual universe.

Where, then, might such a map be found? The author's novels each suggest their own in-built form of mapping, each containing images that model the structure of the text. In a 2006 interview with Robert Birnbaum, Mitchell reveals of *Black Swan Green*:

> Another model for the novel, which I indulge myself by trying to sneak into all of my books, is provided by the postcards Jason buys […] when you put them end-to-end, the background is one continuous whole. That's the village and the background plots […] yet the foreground dinosaurs are the themes of each separate, individual story. ('David Mitchell')

Critical discussions of the miniature self-reflexive models within each of his books are often matched by the tendency to use these existing structures to map the author's textual landscapes; several literary critics suggest that Mitchell's own models reflect his body of fiction's wider structural organization. For example, Peter Childs and James Green argue that this 'sequence of individual postcards that together create one picture-string describes not just *Black Swan Green* but Mitchell's common approach to his fiction' ('The Novels in Nine Parts' 2011, 49). Similarly, Sarah Dillon compares the image of the endlessly fertile Goddess in *The Thousand Autumns* with Mitchell's entire oeuvre, each work 'pregnant with explanations of each other' ('Introducing David Mitchell's Universe' 2011, 9). This technique of embedding self-reflexive models in each work can also be seen in *The Bone Clocks*, which incorporates several embedded structural models, including the circular labyrinth, concentric circles and the spiral, reflecting the novel's fascination with rebirth and reincarnation.

While these models neatly reflect the individual narratives that they sit within, problems soon arise when attempting to use their structures to map his entire body of fiction. Applied to the author's wider works, the linear postcard sequence becomes an inadequate metaphor for the cyclical narratives of *Cloud Atlas*, *Ghostwritten* and *Slade House*, while the model of the endlessly fertile Goddess suggests multiple structural frames and nested narratives – a structure that aligns poorly with the less overtly metafictional *Black Swan Green* and *The Thousand Autumns*. Similarly, the spirals, circles and labyrinths of *The Bone Clocks* suggest narratives driven by structural games and repetition, failing to address the importance of political engagement and narrative progression within Mitchell's oeuvre. However, the fact that none of these models is able to adequately map Mitchell's entire body of work provides a new challenge: to find other critical models that can.

Mapping the macronovel

Following Mitchell's own intra-textual models, literary critics have put forward a range of structural metaphors to map Mitchell's works. To give a brief survey, a dozen comparisons used in essays and reviews to describe part or all of his works include the kaleidoscope, planetary novel, house of fiction, rabbit warren, Ferris wheel, concentric circles, Venn diagram, carousel, Chinese box, labyrinth, rhizome or networked web structure – and even the old lady who swallowed a fly. To give examples for each of these critical comparisons: in 'The Concertina of Time' (2004), Pico Iyer argues that Mitchell 'invented the planetary novel' with *Ghostwritten* (70), while Sarah Dillon notes that Mitchell's work 'can be understood […] with each novel, both those written and those yet to be written, constituting a room in the house of fiction that he is constructing' ('Introducing David Mitchell's Universe' 6). John Lopez remarks in a 2014 interview with Mitchell, 'Your fiction is almost like a rabbit hole within a rabbit hole'; the author responds, 'I do like making connecting tunnels between my books […] the analogy of a rabbit warren is not misplaced' ('Q&A with David Mitchell'). In a 2007 interview with the author, David Pilling notes that *Cloud Atlas*'s 'extraordinary structure reminds me of a Ferris wheel. Starting in the past, it moves closer to the present before arcing into the future' ('Lunch with the FT' 12). During Harriet Gilbert's 2010 interview with David Mitchell, Gilbert recounts one reader's use of a diagram of 'concentric circles' to 'make sense of […] the interconnectedness of the stories' in *Cloud Atlas* ('World Book Club'). In *The Cosmopolitan Novel* (2009), Berthold Schoene also uses the image of concentric circles from *number9dream*, noting '[a]s Mitchell's writing demonstrates, these circles need not be neatly concentric […] what matters is that they originate from the same impulse, exist within the same medium, and are bound by the same sets of laws' (99). Andrew Graham-Dixon notes in his 2010 interview with Mitchell that the structure of *The Thousand Autumns* is 'a series of Venn diagrams' ('Andrew Graham-Dixon Interviews'), while A. S. Byatt's 1999 review of *Ghostwritten* notes that when reading the novel in an airport, she 'finished at the carousel. It seemed appropriate' ('Wild World'). Jessica Winter's 2004 review describes the 'Chinese-box architecture' of *Cloud Atlas* ('Only Connect'); William Skidelsky describes 'the labyrinthine, almost Borgesian construction of his novels' ('A World of Tricks' 2004). Peter Childs and James Green note of *Ghostwritten*, '[t]he Deleuzian figure of the rhizome seems apposite here, as the novel spreads through a kind of textual diffusion' ('The Novels in Nine Parts' 31). Berthold Schoene argues that *Ghostwritten* 'creates a communal web of the world' (103), while Shawn Ballard also observes that '*Ghostwritten* models as a web' ('Complex Systems and Global Catastrophe' 2011, 5). Finally, Will McMorran suggests the lyrics to the children's song, '[t]here was an old lady who swallowed a fly [...]. She swallowed a spider to catch the fly', are apt to describe *Cloud Atlas*, noting its 'metaphor of narratological consumption and predacity fits the themes as well as the structure' ('*Cloud Atlas*' 165). This list is by no means exhaustive. Other metaphors used to describe Mitchell's works include 'wandering rocks' (Burn 2012, 440), the 'elevator' (Jameson 2013, 303), the 'boomerang' (Parker 2010, 205; and Hicks 2010, 4), the 'karmic wheel' (Jeffries 2013), the 'concertina' (De Cristofaro 2017, 5) and the 'fractal' (Larsonneur 2010, 146; Paul Harris 2015; and Visel 2016).

Of these models, the kaleidoscope has perhaps been used most extensively to describe the structural patterns in Mitchell's works. It is used by Peter Childs and James Green to describe *Ghostwritten*'s form (2011, 30), by Kathryn Simpson to describe *number9dream*'s narrative structure (2011, 52) and by Hélène Machinal to describe *Cloud Atlas*'s 'nature' (2011, 134). The kaleidoscope metaphor also resurfaces in Richard Bradford's 2007 study to describe *Cloud Atlas*'s presentation of history (62). It is used by several reviewers, including Douglas Stewart's 2004 review of *Cloud Atlas* to describe this novel; Ruth Scurr's 2006 review of *Black Swan Green*, which describes the 'kaleidoscopic plots' of Mitchell's first three novels; Ruth Franklin's 2006 *Black Swan Green* review, which likens both *Ghostwritten* and *Cloud Atlas* to kaleidoscopes; Jennifer Reese's 2006 review of *Black Swan Green*, which describes each chapter of this novel as 'kaleidoscopic'; Ursula K. Le Guin's 2014 review of *The Bone Clocks*, which highlights the novel's 'kaleidoscopic tumult of imagery'; Jonathan Barnes' 2014 review of *The Bone Clocks*, which describes the author's imagination as 'kaleidoscopic'; and Anthony Schneider's 2015 review of *Slade House*, which observes that the author is renowned for 'long, kaleidoscopic novels'.

Throughout, the metaphor of the kaleidoscope is typically briefly used as a descriptor, giving little explanation as to why this particular term appears so widely in discussions of Mitchell's works. Without clarification, this well-worn critical metaphor risks becoming a stereotype in its imprecision. However, Schoene explores the kaleidoscope more extensively, describing the cosmopolitan narrative as

quite like a child's kaleidoscope held still for only a second before collapsing into new, equally wondrous, yet perfectly plausible constellations. Cosmopolitan narration proceeds without erasing the essential incongruousness or singularity of these individual segments. (27)

Schoene's use of the kaleidoscopic, read in light of Mitchell's distinctive narrative patterning, usefully evokes the shifting textures of the author's works, as seen in the interlinked narrative 'segments' in *Ghostwritten, Cloud Atlas, The Bone Clocks* and *Slade House*. However, despite this perceptive usage for the cosmopolitan novel and the persistent resurfacing of the kaleidoscope in the wider critical literature on Mitchell's works, the kaleidoscope metaphor on its own risks oversimplification when used to encapsulate the author's wider writing. Its aimless pleasure in two-dimensional chaos and fascination with simple appearance only encompass a single facet of these works – neglecting to address their vital ethical engagement, global narrative perspectives and their sociopolitical commentaries.

However, the resilience of the kaleidoscope metaphor, combined with the other critical tropes used to describe Mitchell's works, suggests an intriguing critical congruity. To return to the dozen metaphors identified earlier, these initially seem as varied as they are incompatible. Yet their similarities indicate key traits across these works. The kaleidoscope, Ferris wheel and carousel metaphors suggest narrative circularity and symmetry, while maintaining a textual playfulness. The house of fiction, planetary novel and rabbit warren reflect a linked narrative world with a multidimensional terrain, inhabited by a global community of characters. The Venn diagram, rhizome and labyrinth reflect a fascination with patterning, interconnection and overarching structural design. Concentric circles and Chinese boxes conjure the interlinking of the micro- and macrocosmic, evoking the nested narrative format of the short story unit. The final image – the old lady who swallowed a fly – conjures the macronovel's preoccupations with individual agency and chains of linked consequences, power hierarchies, containment and mortality. Alone, each image represents discrete aspects of Mitchell's body of work. But together, these models begin to map a complex fictional universe driven by a far larger system.

Introducing the mandala

These diverse critical approaches each put forward competing visual structures and diagrams, which, even where they diverge, suggest that an illustrative approach may prove particularly useful in the quest to map this multifaceted textual universe. This study therefore introduces an unusual type of map – one which combines these attributes while allowing for a more detailed exploration of this author's oeuvre, contributing further cross-cultural perspectives that foster new approaches to the macronovel's global and ethical ambitions. The type of map that this study will employ for its critical framework is the mandala: a visual map of an entire imagined world as seen from above, whose features reflect each of the traits identified from the critical tropes discussed earlier, and suggest many more. An art form with a more complex approach to world-building than the profusion of simple critical models can suggest, this study demonstrates that the mandala can be used as a comparative framework to help navigate Mitchell's cluster of texts as an entire fictional world.

But what is a mandala – and why use it here? Meaning 'circle' in Sanskrit, the mandala is a form of ancient symbolic map and a Hindu and Buddhist meditation aid. An intricately designed geometrical religious symbol, its structures and perspectives have a secular duality that can be used to help map the macronovel's key traits, as this study will reveal in the chapters to come. Its detailed patterning and distinct ethical purpose particularly resonate with the author's humanitarian – and in some ways counter-postmodern – refusal to abandon a sense of overarching design in his fictions. From the references to a mysterious 'Script' that seems to influence the course of events in *The Bone Clocks* and *Slade House*, to the reincarnated Dr Marinus as a cross-textual healer, to the uncannily repeated narrative structures in *Ghostwritten*, *Cloud Atlas* and *Slade House*, this sense of predestination and metafictional narrative patterning remains a notable feature of Mitchell's writing, described by John Shanahan in 'Digital Transcendentalism in David Mitchell's *Cloud Atlas*' (2016) as a 'secularized transcendental' (135). The mandala, as an intricately designed map of a self-contained world-system, also offers its own superimposition of sacred and secular worlds. As Jung A. Huh states in 'Mandala as Telematic Design' (2010), the mandala depicts a world view in which 'the sacred is not viewed differently from the secular', suggesting a broader interpretative potential beyond its religious usages (20–3). As such, the mandala has already been employed by cultural geographers to aid theoretical analyses. Susan M. Walcott notes that an understanding of the mandala can usefully broaden conventional cartographic approaches, emphasizing that '[w]e sharpen our vision by seeing worlds other than those we are accustomed to viewing' ('Mapping from a Different Direction' 2006, 75). Similarly recognizing its potential secular applications, Dellios also notes that the mandala has also been adopted by contemporary historians to map Southeast Asia's political structures ('Mandala: From Sacred Origins' 2003, 2). This study therefore investigates the mandala's potential uses in mapping a different world altogether: the post-secular literary world of David Mitchell's macronovel.

Mandalas feature in many cultural traditions, from Tibetan Buddhism to Native American ceremonies. Stanley Krippner argues that their basic form appears 'throughout human history as a symbol of integration, harmony and transformation' ('The Role Played by Mandalas' 1997, 30). Of its many different forms, Walcott recognizes that the Tibetan Buddhist mandala is 'the most widely utilized contemporary form of traditional mandala', noting 'their introduction into Tibet […] in the eleventh century' (75). It is the Tibetan Buddhist mandala whose form and philosophies seem most suited to mapping Mitchell's work (see Appendix B). The theme of reincarnation is introduced into Mitchell's work through the framework of Tibetan Buddhism from his first novel; in *Ghostwritten*, the spirit of the noncorpum is revealed to be the soul of a young boy, transmigrated by a monk from 'the Sect of the Yellow Hat' whose clothing and headwear identify him as a member of the Gelug school of Tibetan Buddhism, as Chapter 3 will discuss further. In a 2014 interview with James Kidd, Mitchell notes that he was reading *The Tibetan Book of the Dead* – the translation of an eighth-century Tibetan Buddhist scripture that provides guidance through the processes of death and rebirth – while writing *The Bone Clocks* ('Time and Again'). In a 2015 interview he discusses its influence on his fictional approach to mortality, noting, '*The Tibetan Book of the Dead* is something that might be healthy for Westerners to read' because of its confrontation of this cultural taboo ('Interview by Rose Harris-Birtill'; see Appendix G). In Scene five of *Sunken Garden*'s libretto, the reincarnated character of Marinus explains, 'I'd make more sense in Sanskrit, or better yet, Tibetan.' Explicitly referring to the languages of Tibetan Buddhism to explain her supernatural realm, this enigmatic phrase prompts a questioning as to whether her cross-textual role would also 'make more sense' when interpreted through its belief systems. This study pursues these references further, using the Tibetan Buddhist mandala as the basis for an interpretive tool to help map the ethical perspectives and post-secular Buddhist influences that shape Mitchell's narrative universe.

The Tibetan Buddhist mandala presents its own highly detailed 'microcosmic' world, as Walcott notes, a universe depicted as residing within the petals of a lotus flower (75). Although their forms vary, Walcott emphasizes that mandalas are used to provide a functional mental framework for those trained to create and interpret their complex forms, offering a form of visual narrative for the participant 'following the path indicated from outer rim to inner circle and learning the lessons contained within' (77). As a form of map when viewed from above, those trained in its interpretation visualize entering the mandala and progressing from its outermost rim to its centre, encountering pre-taught symbols that give meaning to each stage of the journey. Walcott notes that the mandala therefore functions as

> an instructive space wherein [...] the individual can learn how to transcend earthly constraints and ordinary perceptions in order to realize his/her potential as a more enlightened being [...] with the central object of bringing about the acquisition of the associated virtues of wisdom, compassion and healing. (73–4)

When viewed comparatively, the ethical purpose of the Tibetan Buddhist mandala – as a form of tool that provides guidance and develops compassion – evokes the ethical exploration built into Mitchell's works, for example in *Cloud Atlas*'s narrative trajectory, in which the trope of reincarnation encourages the reader to question the possibility of a shared humanity and the individual's ability to change, or in Marinus' role as a reincarnated healer, whose compassionate acts span many lifetimes.

To briefly summarize its basic features, the mandala essentially depicts a plan of a central temple and surrounding gardens as seen from above, a form of two-dimensional map that is intended to be imagined and entered as a three-dimensional structure.[8] As Walcott notes, the 'three-dimensional imagined nature of the mandala is a key part of the visualization process', comparing the participant's imagined journey through its structures to navigating a three-dimensional terrain in a flight simulator, while its four gateways 'should be envisioned as upright structures flanked by a pair of trees underneath a pair of stylized clouds' (76–9). This can be seen in the radial lines of perspective that run from the top of each of the mandala's gateways, which emphasize that each entrance is intended to be visualized as pointing upwards (see Appendix C).[9] Ken Taylor also notes that the Buddhist mandala depicts 'a single world system where

---

[8] For a computer visualization that illustrates this shift in perspective from two-dimensional blueprint to three-dimensional structure, see 'Kalachakra Mandala in 3D view' on YouTube at https://www.youtube.com/watch?v=exZiswZt7NE, accessed 12 April 2018, uploaded by Tenzin Wangyal and created by Kavita Bala and Elizabeth Popolo in collaboration with Namgyal Monastery, Cornell University, 2007.

[9] The Tibetan Buddhist mandala also contains its own internal evocation of an 'atlas' of clouds visible above each gateway, a shifting sky above a virtual world. This motif recurs in Mitchell's work and is found not only in *Cloud Atlas*, but also in *number9dream* ('[t]he cloud atlas turns its pages over'),

relationships exist between various parts of the universe and where myth and reason coalesce' ('Cultural Landscape' 2003, 54). With its merging of 'myth and reason' across an interconnected 'world system', the mandala suggests a fitting map for the blending of these elements in the macronovel. For example, *The Bone Clocks* is a 'half-fantasy' novel that blurs the boundaries between 'myth' and 'reason' as the largely realist tale of Holly's life becomes drawn into an ancient battle against soul-eating Carnivores (348); similarly, in *Sunken Garden*, Toby's domestic film project becomes fantasy as he is lured into the supernatural garden of the opera's title. With even the semi-autobiographical *Black Swan Green* disrupted by the extra-diegetic venturing of some of its characters into supernatural situations – as Chapter 1 will discuss – this is a fictional world that stubbornly refuses to stay anchored in either the mythic or the real.

The Tibetan Buddhist mandala's world-system is organized using meticulous structural patterning, visible in its repeated sets of four gateways within a four-sided palace structure (see Appendix B). As Walcott notes of its nested structures, 'numerical sets are used to echo and contain other values that occur in the same number (three of this, four of that)' (76). Precise numerical patterning is also woven into Mitchell's structural designs, for example, around the number nine in his first three novels, as noted by Childs and Green in 'The Novels in Nine Parts' (2011). This continues into Mitchell's short stories and libretti, including the grid of nine rooms in *Wake*, and the short story 'Acknowledgements', in which Clive Pike's 900-page theory of psychomigration is born on the ninth floor of his office building, creating an uncanny sense of interconnection and overarching design that further connects these works into a continuous fictional universe. Mitchell discusses this in a 2005 interview by Richard Beard, noting: 'I don't believe in numerology, no, but I do believe in the aesthetics of numbers. The numbers 9, 36 and 64 have a particular beauty' ('David Mitchell Interview'). Such metafictional numerical patterning contributes to a sense of teleological interconnection across the macronovel – deliberately encouraging the reader to question the invisible forces that organize and regulate this fictional world.

This fascination with structural patterning predates Mitchell's published work. He reveals in a 2013 interview with Stuart Jeffries that his first unpublished book 'consisted of 365 chapters, one for each day of the year, with 20 subplots and dozens of characters, all woven around a pub that gave the manuscript its title, *The Old Moon*' ('David Mitchell'). This diurnal storytelling, with 365 chapters orbiting a single story, resonates both with the macronovel's formal preoccupation with narrative circularity – as Chapter 3 will discuss – and with the structural circularity that organizes the mandala's own self-contained world. The Tibetan Buddhist mandala's concentric circles permeate its entire structure, from its outermost border to the smaller circles embedded within it (see Appendix B). As Susan Walcott notes, this border of 'concentric rings' protects deities that are depicted as residing at the mandala's centre; '[t]he innermost mandala is thus set off and protected' with a powerful containing boundary that is simultaneously inclusionary and exclusionary, a concept that Chapter 4 explores further for the macronovel (77).

The Thousand Autumns ('[w]est to east, the sky unrolls and rolls its atlas of clouds') and in *The Bone Clocks* as Lorelei recites Shelley's poem 'The Cloud' (374; 395; 539).

At first glance, then, the mandala's structures appear to provide a more robust comparative model than the profusion of critical metaphors discussed earlier. However, its philosophies prove particularly illuminating for Mitchell's fictional world, prompting further investigation into the macronovel's secular reworking of Buddhist philosophy. This remains a particularly neglected area within Mitchell criticism, despite the author's own references to his 'interest in Buddhism' in several interviews, for example, in a 2010 interview with Harriet Gilbert ('World Book Club'). In an interview with Shanghai TV, he notes, 'Of the great world religions, Buddhism [...] strikes the strongest chord inside me, seems to suit me best' ('2012 Shanghai Book Fair'). He later reveals in a 2013 interview with Andrei Muchnik, 'I am a kind of secular Buddhist [...] Buddhism doesn't ask me to sacrifice my rationality or my common sense, it doesn't ask me to believe the impossible' ('David Mitchell Talks'). In a 2014 interview with Boyd Tonkin, he also discusses his interest in Buddhism as a philosophy, noting that 'the philosophy itself is the only one that does not ask me to believe things that the rational part of my mind finds risible' ('David Mitchell Interview'). In a 2015 interview, he again discusses his introduction to Buddhist texts and meditation while in Japan, stating: '[i]t was new for me, and it resonated more for me as a philosophy than a religion' ('Interview by Rose Harris-Birtill').

This influence of Buddhist philosophy resurfaces throughout Mitchell's fictional world, as this book will discuss. For example, Rosita Dellios notes that a crucial aim within Buddhist teachings is 'to develop compassion for all living beings and to realise that suffering arises from desire' ('Mandala-Building' 1996, 2). In a 2015 interview, Mitchell discusses the universality of the Buddhist philosophy of suffering arising from desire: 'The world is geared to [...] generate demands that can never be fulfilled. And this lack of fulfilment is a big part of human suffering, which incidentally is inevitable anyway' ('Interview by Rose Harris-Birtill'). This concept is frequently explored for Mitchell's characters, whose quests are repeatedly frustrated and only resolved as they come to terms with abandoning them. In *number9dream*, Eiji only resolves his quest to find his father when he abandons it, while *The Bone Clocks* ends with the breaking of attachment between Holly and her granddaughter Lorelei and adopted grandson Rafiq, their desire to remain together undercut by the knowledge that only their separation will ensure their survival.

Although these quests are largely thwarted, at the heart of Mitchell's textual universe lie the seeds of hope in the form of the possibility of change. The constant nature of change and impermanence is a foundational Buddhist philosophy known as *anitya* or *anicca*, and this sense of relentless change can also be seen across Mitchell's works. In *Cloud Atlas*, Sonmi may be captured, but her *Declarations* survive; in *The Bone Clocks*, the almost inescapably bleak future that Holly faces suddenly gives way to hope, when Lorelei and Rafiq are rescued by the reincarnated Marinus. It is this constant change that ensures the universe created is one of hope amid suffering; for example, in *Sunken Garden*'s libretto, the characters note that 'Clause One' of life's contract is '*You Will Suffer*', though '*Clause Two* reads, *You May Hope*', an integral realization on the path to Buddhist acceptance, as Chapter 2 will discuss (Scene 7, 24–5). This sense of the resilience of hope in spite of the inevitability of suffering underpins even the bleakest dystopic settings in Mitchell's novels, revealing an ethical dimension to his writing in which hopeful belief itself becomes an agent of change.

The foundational Buddhist concept of compassion is also evoked through the secular humanist attitudes that underpin Mitchell's writing. In a 2013 interview with Alison Flood on his joint translation of *The Reason I Jump* (2013) by Naoki Higashida, Mitchell emphasizes that understanding Higashida's perspective on autism 'will make you more patient, kinder, more compassionate' ('*Cloud Atlas* Author'), while the short story 'My Eye On You' (2016) demonstrates the far-reaching consequences of individual compassionate action, as Chapter 1 will discuss. The depiction of the practice of compassion is perhaps most fully realized in the character of Marinus, who is revealed to be a reincarnated 'healer' in *The Bone Clocks* (63). However, read through the framework of the Buddhist mandala (as is the case in Chapter 3), Marinus' role takes on a wider significance. In Buddhist teaching, a bodhisattva is a figure on the path to Enlightenment who, motivated by compassion, postpones reaching nirvana to help those around them. These figures are described by Giuseppe Tucci as 'compassionate, succouring companions […] vowed to reach illumination so that they might aid other creatures in this struggle against pain and illusion' (*The Theory and Practice of the Mandala* 2001, 57). As Richard B. Pilgrim notes in 'The Buddhist Mandala' (1989), bodhisattvas are also depicted as residing within mandalas (36). Appearing across *Sunken Garden, Wake, The Thousand Autumns, The Bone Clocks, Slade House* and the short stories 'I_Bombadil' (2015) and 'All Souls Day' (2010), Marinus becomes a form of secular reincarnated bodhisattva who similarly strives to make positive interventions in the lives of others over many lifetimes. This correspondence is hinted at in *The Thousand Autumns* when Lucas Marinus suggests he will be alive in a hundred years (241), and reinforced in *The Bone Clocks* with the revelation that Iris Marinus-Fenby has had forty previous lives of alternating genders (430). As Giuseppe Tucci notes, the mandala offers a 'geometric projection of the world reduced to an essential pattern'; by reworking these Buddhist concepts in a post-secular format, the macronovel effectively depicts its own 'essential pattern' in which the influence of these philosophies can be seen in action across an entire fictional world (25).

A small number of academic essays recognize the emergence of Buddhist themes in Mitchell's work. For example, Heather J. Hicks notes *Cloud Atlas's* 'fascination with reincarnation and the transmigration of souls', offering a brief reading of Sonmi-451's ascension as 'the fabricant equivalent of the Buddhist state of Enlightenment' (21). However, this reading focuses on *Cloud Atlas*, stating that 'the complexities of Buddhist spirituality are beyond the scope' of the essay. Similarly, Louise Economides notes that *Cloud Atlas's* treatment of time is, 'in contrast to Western, teleological accounts, profoundly iterative: a movement akin to Eastern and/or Buddhist models of time structured by "'samsara" (recurring cycles of birth, suffering, death, and re-birth)' ('Recycled Creatures' 2009, 618). George Gessert's 2005 review of *Cloud Atlas* also briefly discusses Buddhism, as Gessert notes that within the novel 'Buddhist attitudes […] provide one way for Mitchell's characters to live in a Darwinian world without falling into barbarism, denial or despair' ('Cloud Atlas' 426). While a useful beginning, the choice of novel for all three of these analyses is, again, *Cloud Atlas*. However, as this book will demonstrate, a broader and more detailed exploration of the macronovel's Buddhist influences reveals the broader impact of this belief system on the ethical perspectives underpinning Mitchell's wider fictional world.

Towards a plural post-secular

David Mitchell's multifaceted fictional world is a firmly post-secular one. As John Shanahan accurately notes in 'Digital Transcendentalism in David Mitchell's *Cloud Atlas*' (2016), 'Mitchell should be considered a *postsecular* author' [*sic*], as one of a 'growing set of contemporary writers, artists, and theorists who share a focus on [...] transcendence and spirituality beyond seemingly mutually exclusive choices of conventional religiosity or its wholesale rejection' (117). As such, before embarking on this study of post-secular Buddhist influences in Mitchell's fictional world more specifically, it's worth taking some time to discuss the post-secular itself.

John A. McClure usefully defines the term 'post-secular' in his preface to *Partial Faiths: Postsecular Fiction in the Age of Pynchon and Morrison* (2007), describing the post-secular as 'a mode of being and seeing that is at once critical of secular constructions of reality and of dogmatic religiosity' (ix). The post-secular, like the questions of secularity and religiosity that it conjures, is in turn particularly concerned with questions of morality. In 'A Curious Knot: Terrorism, Radicalism and the Avant-Garde' (2013), Peter Boxall rightly refers to 'an ethical turn in the fiction of the new century' (141). An important facet of this 'ethical turn' is the post-secular, as writers and artists respond to the increasing secularization – or assumption of it – in Western societies since the mid-twentieth century by re-examining a range of faiths and belief systems in search of a workable ethics.

The post-secular isn't an exclusively contemporary phenomenon; as McClure also notes, '[p]ostsecularism itself has been a feature of literary thinking since the romantics', and, of course, 'not all postsecular texts are alike' (3). However, the post-secular works discussed in this book respond to a contemporary sociocultural climate whose previously assumed secularity has become increasingly problematized: by the growth of religious fundamentalism and 'alternative' spiritualities, the ruthless secular 'faith' of late capitalism, and the increasingly pressing need to find a long-term global survival strategy amid impending ecological, political and humanitarian crises. Simultaneously responding to the ethical dilemmas wrought by a globalization that prioritizes the material over the moral, and to the proven human costs of religious grand narratives, the post-secular presents an attempt to search amid the ashes of secularity and religion alike for the tools to help make such regeneration possible.

This book focuses on the Buddhist influences in David Mitchell's post-secular fictional world because of their resonances with the author's overarching fictional project, their frequency across his works, and Mitchell's own documented interests in its philosophies, as mentioned earlier. However, many diverse belief systems are alluded to, reworked and unsettled in Mitchell's fictions. To give just a few examples (and there are many more): in *Slade House*, Jonah teases the ensnared Gordon, '[i]f you recite the Lord's Prayer from start to finish – Book of Common Prayer version – you win a Get Out of Jail Free card' (80). Later in the text, Marinus is wearing a keffiyeh – a type of scarf often associated with the predominantly Muslim region of Palestine – with 'tiny Stars of David' on it, fusing Islamic and Jewish symbolism (196). In *Cloud Atlas*, Sonmi sees the ruins of a seated 'giant sitting in the lotus position', later learning that the figure is called 'Siddhartha' – the Buddha's first name (345, 348) – while the inclusion of Ralph Waldo Emerson's poem 'Brahma' (1857) in *Cloud Atlas*, as one character dies and another revives, inserts traces of a reworked Hinduism into the text (451).[10] *The Bone Clocks* is replete with Anchorites (a religious role widely associated with Christianity), 'palm-chakras' (a reference to bodily energy centres, used in Buddhist, Hindu and Jain religions) and a final battle that takes place in the 'Chapel of the Dusk'. In the same novel, Hugo's frenzied sexual encounter with Mariângela takes place under a dreamcatcher – traditionally associated with Native American beliefs – while he holds his partner's crucifix in his mouth (120).

Further research is certainly needed into each of these layered religious influences and their post-secular reworkings; combined, they suggest that the concept of belief itself is central to Mitchell's post-secular fictional universe, as Chapter 1 will discuss. However, it is worth mentioning here that to treat 'the' post-secular as a singular, fixed category risks minimizing the plurality and ongoing evolution of this vibrant field. McClure rightly notes that 'while postsecular texts do share certain features, they are stylistically and thematically diverse' (*Partial Faiths*, 3) – yet the post-secular's intrinsic diversity needs far more critical attention in order to avoid minimizing its differences. There are as many different potential 'post-seculars' as there are abandoned and revisited faiths, myths, superstitions and folktales, each forged by a specific historical context that nudged its believers from sacred, to secular, to something beyond both categories altogether.

It is also vital to recognize the importance of cultural and faith diversity in shaping different forms of post-secularity. The cultural phenomenon of a post-war Anglo-American generation brought up without the predominantly Christian frameworks given to their parents, seeking ethical direction from 'alternative' spiritualities – or those who are '[r]eligiously unhoused but spiritually hungry', as McClure eloquently puts it (*Partial Faiths* 8) – is a readily identifiable facet of contemporary culture. But what about the cultural experiences of other forms of post-secularity – where the 'pre-secular' dominant religious influences and post-secular artistic outputs are predominantly shaped by non-Christian belief systems? Whether in literature, criticism or elsewhere, a specifically Christian post-secular will differ from, for example, an Islamic post-secular or a Buddhist post-secular, while still other post-secular imaginings may complicate this further by drawing on, pushing against and revisiting any number of belief systems. Far from being a singular, stable category, then, the post-secular is plural.

In particular, the analysis of Christian perspectives has long dominated critical discussion of religious ethics within literatures in English. While this remains an important and legitimate area of study, 'Western' Anglophone literary criticism must not neglect the impact of other global belief systems on the post-secular

---

[10] See John Shanahan's essay for a perceptive reading of the influence of American transcendentalism on *Cloud Atlas*, which also contains a useful list of further reading on the post-secular (140).

ethical perspectives emerging within contemporary fiction. C. G. Jung highlights the permeation of Christianity into supposedly 'secular' society, a perspective that he noted in the mid-twentieth century. In 'The Difference between Eastern and Western Thinking', published in 1958, Jung asserts that '[i]n spite of everything, the West is thoroughly Christian as far as its psychology is concerned' (482). Over half a century later, this bias remains prevalent in Anglophone 'secularized' societies, in which both the concept of religion and its assumed opposite, secularism, remain defined by dominant Christian paradigms that have shaped Western thinking for centuries. It is this that makes a Christian-dominated concept of religion broadly inadequate for discussing other belief systems, such as Buddhism; as Marcus Boon notes in 'To live in a glass house is a revolutionary virtue par excellence: Marxism, Buddhism, and the politics of Nonalignment' (2015), Buddhism 'is not a theology and has no transcendental God' (81).

Although the post-secular is generally approached as a predominantly Western world view, this too is built on a problematic secularism which is structured as an opposition to 'religion' – which itself is often still primarily discussed through the beliefs and practices of Christianity in Anglophone criticism. However, as Talal Asad notes in *Formations of the Secular: Christianity, Islam, Modernity* (2003), 'the secular is neither singular in origin nor stable in its historical identity', rightly recognizing that 'many people in the West contest secularism or interpret it in different ways' (25, 13). The theorization of the post-secular must therefore acknowledge and break away from binary assumptions that risk merely adding evermore 'posts' to a single dominant conception of religion or secularity (for example, 'post-post-Christian'), both of which continue to retain, Turin-Shroud-like, traces of Christianity. This bias has also had lasting consequences for the European critical theoretical tradition; for example, Marcus Boon, Eric Cazdyn and Timothy Morton note in their introduction to *Nothing: Three Inquiries in Buddhism* (2015) that 'the decidedly Christian turn taken by a number of contemporary European philosophers (Žižek, Badiou, Agamben) has not been matched by anything like a Buddhist turn' (9).

However, Buddhism is not the only belief system being marginalized. A wider trend of such marginalization can be seen within several studies of postmodern and contemporary literature and culture claiming the broader field of 'religion' as their focus – when their discussions often remain disproportionately biased towards Christian faiths. This can be seen in several publications in recent years. For example, *Secular Steeples: Popular Culture and the Religious Imagination* (2012) by Conrad Ostwalt takes an overtly theological approach to its study of American popular culture; the 'religious imagination' to which its title refers is a Christian imagination. The essay collection *Spiritual Identities: Literature and the Post-Secular Imagination* (2010), edited by Jo Carruthers and Andrew Tate, initially promises wider diversity as Gavin D'Costa notes in its preface that '[t]he spiritual in this collection transcends any particular religious tradition' (x). However, the claim is soon partially retracted ('although it is related to the big three [religions] of the western imaginary'), and the collection described using overtly Christian metaphor, stating that '[t]he various authors refuse to sing some single party hymn', referring to the text as 'a prayer' and asking, '[a]re we on the cusp of a new church with elegant preachers [...] the artists and writers studied here testify to a *kerygma* worthy of preaching' (xi). The overtly Christian language of the 'hymn', 'prayer', 'church', 'preachers', '*kerygma*' and 'preaching' may merely be used in an extended metaphor to introduce the rest of the collection – but it remains indicative of the dominance of Christian modes of thought which continue to structure Western criticism, even when its author's intentions are explicitly towards a pan-religious theoretical study. In the body of the essay collection, ten of the essays take a predominantly Judeo-Christian focus, while only three write from outside this tradition.

To cite other examples from the discussion of postmodern literature, *God and Religion in the Postmodern World: Essays in Postmodern Theology* (1989) by David Ray Griffin is written from an overtly biblical religious perspective; *Divine Representations: Postmodernism and Spirituality* (1994), a collection edited by Ann W. Astell, again shares a predominantly Christian approach to the discussion of 'spirituality' referred to in its title. *From Fantasy to Faith: The Philosophy of Religion and Twentieth-Century Literature* (1991) by D. Z. Phillips also employs primarily Judeo-Christian concepts of divinity. Similarly, *Faith and Doubt: Religion and Secularization in Literature from Wordsworth to Larkin* (1997) by R. L. Brett should perhaps more accurately be subtitled *Christianity and Secularization*. When it does briefly mention non-Christian religions, these are grouped within the dominant paradigm of Christianity: '[t]he three great religions which come together in *The Waste Land*, Christianity, Buddhism, and Hinduism, have much in common [...] all accept that man is sinful and requires forgiveness. They all believe in a Divinity who is merciful' (193). Even here, the Christian framework of 'sin', 'forgiveness' and a singular 'Divinity' is stretched, not entirely accurately, to encompass Buddhism and Hinduism. What becomes apparent isn't the failure of any single essay, but the larger project of literary study after literary study which claims to be pan-religious, but remains overwhelmingly Christian in its focus. Throughout these examples, a critical fallacy emerges in which belief system diversity is often inadvertently minimized in Western criticism, using 'religion' to refer almost exclusively to Christianity and 'secular' to indicate non-Christianity.

To give one final example, *Religion for Atheists: A Non-Believer's Guide to the Uses of Religion* (2012) by Alain de Botton goes some way towards productively re-evaluating the secular uses of religious belief systems.[11] However, Hinduism – widely believed to be the world's oldest major religion – is omitted from the study, as is Islam, the second largest. In de Botton's acknowledgement that this text on religion mentions 'only three of the world's twenty-one largest religions' because 'the emphasis of this book lies on comparing religion in general with the secular realm', this heavily reduced perspective is used to discuss 'religion in general' – without considering whether the Western concept of 'religion' is a singular entity that can be discussed in such terms (17). Even within this narrowed remit, which focuses on Christianity, Judaism and Buddhism, Judeo-Christian perspectives dominate throughout, with limited references to Buddhism.

---

[11] David Mitchell also discusses *Religion for Atheists* in interview; see 'Interview by Rose Harris-Birtill', 2015.

In its discussion of the latter, de Botton describes 'the complex patterns of mandalas' as 'sensuous representations of the harmony of the cosmos described in Buddhist theology' (240). However, the image of the Buddhist mandala used to illustrate this assertion – directly glossed as 'the tradition of the Buddhist mandala' – does not display the visual 'liturgy' stated. It isn't a picture of the Tibetan Chenrezig mandala, created in diaspora for its links to the Buddha of compassion, or the Kalachakra mandala, historically used in mass-initiation ceremonies. It isn't even the misprint of a Hindu yantra, or decorative rangoli. The picture of the 'Buddhist mandala' that has been reproduced in *Religion for Atheists* is a monochrome line drawing of tiny cats. Each is joined at the ears to form a circle, as if the reader is looking down a kaleidoscope. An online image search reveals that the picture features on a free-to-print colouring website, whose description is far more accurate: '[t]here are dozens of cute cat faces in this kitty kaleidoscope mandala design coloring sheet.'[12]

To date, de Botton's study has received over 200 citations on academic database Google Scholar.[13] Its publication was featured on the cover of a special issue of *New Scientist* in March 2012, entitled *New Scientist: The God Issue*.[14] That such an inaccuracy appears to have gone unnoticed is testament not only to the widespread misconceptions about Buddhist mandalas, but also to the cultural dominance of Christianity that has contributed to the ongoing marginalization of non-Christian belief systems in critical theory, however inadvertent. Although written for a popular rather than an exclusively academic audience, such a text is worth mentioning to highlight that this problematic discussion of religion continues both inside and outside the academy. Post-secular theory must now help to pluralize the assumed binaries of religion and secularity to include a far broader spectrum of approaches, and broaden the dominant critical conversation to encompass a greater diversity of religious influences and voices. As Manav Ratti notes in *The Postsecular Imagination: Postcolonialism, Religion, and Literature* (2013) – an excellent example of a literary study that approaches religion and post-secularity from a broader non-Christian perspective – '[t]his belief that religion, namely Christianity, should and *could* be made universal was of course one of the constituent features of imperialism' (135). Literary criticism must now confront such religious 'imperialism' by critiquing its own implicit attitudes towards 'religion' as well as its choice of texts, and scrutinizing the foundational assumptions that we still make about religion as an artificially singular and fixed category. By using an explicitly non-Christian comparative framework as the basis for an exploration of the Buddhist influences in Mitchell's fictions, this study aims to venture an approach to the post-secular that strives to address such Western religious 'imperialism' in practice – an issue that literary criticism must work harder to address.

---

[12] The image can also be found at crafting website Clip Art & Crafts: http://www.clipartandcrafts. com/coloring/design-posters/pages/kitty-kaleidoscope.htm, accessed 13 April 2018.

[13] See the Google Scholar search at https://scholar.google.co.uk/scholar?hl=en&as_sdt=0%2C5&q=rel igion+for+atheists, accessed 13 April 2018.

[14] *New Scientist: The God Issue* volume 213, issue 2856, dated 17 March 2012.

Mapping the mandala

Using the mandala as an interpretive tool to help investigate the author's Buddhist-influenced ethical approaches from a non-Christian perspective, then, this study reads the mandala as itself a form of map, using its philosophies and structures as a way into mapping Mitchell's textual universe as a whole. As Susan M. Walcott argues, the mandala, when interpreted as a map, provides an alternative critical approach to cartography; Walcott describes the mandala as a form of 'sacred map' whose 'spatial mapping function' exposes otherwise hidden relationships within the worldview depicted (71–2). Walcott notes:

> [m]aps serve as visualisation devices that allow geographers to see relationships revealed as patterns […]. By entering a map we enter the world of its creator(s), triggering an interaction with our own embedded, culturally contested view. (71)

To employ the Tibetan Buddhist mandala for this study is to deliberately choose – for Western audiences largely unfamiliar with its philosophies and structures – a form of map that offers a non-standard approach to mapping. The mandala's overtly culturally and historically situated forms serve as a reminder of the 'embedded, culturally contested' assumptions that determine which properties a map 'should' adhere to. Its representation of a metaphysical realm is not an attempt to depict the world as it is, but a form of intervention, suggesting a particular perspective on the way we might shape it. The Tibetan Buddhist sand mandala is deliberately impermanent; assembled from grains of sand, these mandalas are ultimately dismantled and their grains scattered. As such, the sand mandala negates the conventionally authoritarian nature of map-making by being immediately swept apart, making no claims to permanence or ownership – invaluable qualities for a twenty-first-century literary criticism still unravelling the effects of imperialism on world literature.[15] As Walcott recognizes, the mandala, when used to map out a new structure for critical analyses, 'contributes a non-Western perspective […] with its portrayal of metaphysical, multidimensional experiential space' (73), suggesting an apt framework for addressing the ethical influence of the 'non-Western' belief systems emerging in contemporary Anglophone literary fiction.

Unlike the intra-textual models described earlier – for example, *Black Swan Green*'s interlinked postcard sequence – the mandala doesn't appear in Mitchell's fictions. However, in a 2015 interview the author describes his first encounter with mandalas while travelling in the north of India, noting 'first I would have encountered them in Ladakh […] they would have imprinted themselves, obviously on my retina, but perhaps on my mind' ('Interview by Rose Harris-Birtill'). Discussing his interest in Jung's theory of archetypes, he recalls that 'around the same time I read Jung's *Memories, Dreams, Reflections* – he talks about mandalas a lot in that […] I've always had a soft spot for both Jung and that book'. The mandala has previously been interpreted by C. G. Jung as a form of universal archetype, a circular structure that spontaneously

---

[15] See Pascale Casanova's *The World Republic of Letters* (2004) for a discussion of the far-reaching effects of Western imperialism on contemporary literatures across the globe.

arises across cultures as a method of self-healing, described in *The Archetypes and the Collective Unconscious* – first published in 1959 – as 'the psychological expression of the totality of the self' (304). It is in this Jungian context that the mandala has received most of its mentions within literary criticism during the last half a century (for examples, see S. K. Heninger's 'A Jungian Reading of "Kubla Khan"' (1960), Donna Norell's 'The Novel as Mandala: Colette's *Break of Day*' (1981), Ted R. Spivey's 'The Archetype of Renewal: Mandala Symbolism in the Poetry of Wallace Stevens and Dylan Thomas' (1985), E. Deudney's 'The Archetypal Mandala: Visions of the Self in the Poetry of Coleridge, Eliot and Breytenbach' (1994), Ioana Sion's 'The Shape of the Beckettian Self: *Godot* and the Jungian Mandala' (2006) and R. Williamson's *The Writing in the Stars: A Jungian Reading of the Poetry of Octavio Paz* (2007)).

Jung's psychological interpretation of the mandala has long dominated Western approaches to this cultural artefact as an ahistorical, apolitical symbol. However, the mandala is also an important part of an evolving cultural heritage in the real world. Sand mandala displays in public exhibitions across Europe and America continue to redefine perceptions of 'Tibetanness'; as Imogen Clark notes in 'Exhibiting the Exotic, Stimulating the Sacred: Tibetan Shrines at British and American Museums' (2016), '[m]useums manufacture narratives […] Tibetanness is predominantly configured for British and American museum-goers through the twin prisms of art and Buddhism' (1–4).[16] Research into the mandala in the Anglophone world must also take into account the wider impact of its contemporary display and reception, as will be discussed in Chapter 2. This study therefore approaches the Tibetan Buddhist mandala from a post-Jungian perspective in order to reconnect its theorization with its cultural, religious and political contexts in the world at large. As such, each chapter of this book contextualizes the mandala as historically and culturally situated, rather than merely using this as an ahistorical tool for theorization alone.

While there is some recognition of the mandala's critical application outside its spiritual origins, I have only been able to find one published full-length study in English which specifically investigates the mandala's wider potential within literary theory: the little-known *Concentric Imagination: Mandala Literary Theory* by Charu Sheel Singh (1994).[17] Published in Delhi, this study focuses on Indian Kundalini-Yoga symbolism within poetic tropes, using the Hindu mandala as its framework. Singh recognizes that '[t]he concept of the whole can best be represented by the circle and literary theory cannot dispense with it', using the mandala as a diagram for understanding specific poetic tropes, alongside a discussion of the role of the poet as interpreted through the mandala (81). While the assertion that 'the whole can best be represented by the circle' is, of course, both subjective and non-falsifiable, this emphasis on the importance of using a framework capable of analysing 'the whole' resonates with a literary criticism

---

[16] While this study refers to the Tibetan Buddhist mandala, it is important to acknowledge that, as Clark also notes, 'Buddhism is not the only religion practised by Tibetans'; Islamic and Bon belief systems also assume 'important roles in Tibetan communities worldwide' (4).

[17] The 1970 anthology *Mandala: Literature for Critical Analysis*, ed. Wilfred L. Guerin et al., is a student textbook of collected short stories, poetry, drama and novellas that briefly uses the Jungian mandala as a metaphor to describe its collection of literary works ('Like the graphic symbol of the universe after which it is named, our book is a microcosm of great literature', xiii), and as such it is not included here.

that seeks to broaden critical understanding of an author's entire oeuvre as an interconnected world-system.

Singh's study is useful in its recognition of the mandala's potential within literary approaches, and in detailing the Hindu mandala's features. However, its largely theoretical argument neglects to explore the wider implications of using its framework to analyse contemporary narratives. Its explicitly religious personal perspective and focus on poetic tropes also miss its wider secular transferability. However, the author briefly notes that a non-deistic focus which 'avoid[s] all mention of God' is integral to the Buddhist mandala (65). It is this Buddhist-influenced approach to the mandala that this study investigates, whose secular duality makes it particularly useful for exploring the macronovel's function as an interconnected ethical world, as the next chapter will discuss.

Various critics have noted several of the mandala's features when discussing Mitchell's individual texts, but have neglected to further interrogate the larger pattern that it suggests. Perhaps the closest to finding this ancient map is Shawn Ballard, who reads *Ghostwritten* as 'a complex system that itself deals with a nested complex system', featuring 'a recurring quest for rebirth' and 'looped rather than linear time structure' ('Complex Systems and Global Catastrophe' 5, 10). Ballard even draws the system of interconnections in *Ghostwritten*'s chapters, resulting in a near-symmetrical, circular diagram full of interconnected diagonals (13). Yet because a few decagonal spokes are missing, Ballard unfortunately throws his mandala-like world-system out with the bathwater. He concludes, 'the actual coherence of the novel as a whole is largely imagined', and that the book's macrocosmic connections 'are not really there'; because the pattern doesn't show mathematical perfection, the entire notion is prematurely dismissed. Yet it is this variation that makes Mitchell's works more mandalic than fractal.

Before embarking on a journey through David Mitchell's post-secular world-system, it is worth differentiating this from Franco Moretti's notion of 'world text', as described in *Modern Epic: The World System from Goethe to García Márquez* (1996, 2). Moretti's 'world text', a form of 'modern epic', shares initial similarities with the macronovel as a text that presents its own form of interconnected world-system, employing a range of genres and forms to do so. As Peter Boxall also notes in 'Sovereignty, Democracy, Globalisation' (2013), Mitchell's novels certainly demonstrate their own form of 'epic global reach' (168). Yet while Moretti's 'world text' describes a unified 'totality' that ultimately reinforces the progress of Western history and legitimates the capitalist world-system, the macronovel's multiplicity of experiences resists such homogenizing totality. Instead, it depicts an interconnected system of global relations and lived experiences, whose simultaneously articulated futures and diversity of cultural perspectives deliberately complicate any notion of historical progress – and whose narrators are often used to critique the capitalist super-structures that contain them.

However, Moretti also applies the world-system to the literary world outside the text. It is this discussion of world literature as world-system – also developed in Pascale Casanova's *The World Republic of Letters* (2004) – that proves more productive for the macronovel. In 'Conjectures on World Literature' (2000), Moretti describes world literature as 'a system *of variations*' which is 'one' but 'not uniform', a single 'planetary system' which remains 'profoundly unequal' (54; 64; 56). Again, in 'World-Systems

Analysis, Evolutionary Theory, "Weltliteratur'" (2005), Moretti notes that within this system '[t]he world becomes *one*, and *unequal*: one, because capitalism constrains production everywhere on the planet; and unequal, because its network of exchanges requires, and reinforces, a marked power unevenness' (221). Refusing the limited totality of Moretti's 'world text', Mitchell's macronovel depicts this inequality of global relations as 'a marked power unevenness' in the world at large, similarly unsettling the concept of national boundaries with its global focus. As opposed to the Lukácsian concept of the novel form (see Georg Lukács' 1920 publication *The Theory of the Novel* (1971)), which interprets this as a secular quest for meaning within the individual's inner world, Mitchell's *macro*novel uses its vast scale – in its temporality, geography and forms – to embody the diversity of global experience that it presents, cumulatively decentring the individual's interior quest, and thereby making its subject the diversity of interconnected experiences that form the global multitude itself. And as Chapter 4 will discuss, the mandala also suggests a hierarchical world-system whose disparate entities are connected within a single super-structure, even as they remain – like Moretti's literary world-system – 'profoundly unequal'.

At this point, it is also worth briefly defining the concept of genre, as will be discussed further in this study. Described in the *Oxford English Dictionary* as 'a type of literary work characterized by a particular form, style or purpose', questions of genre are particularly relevant to the classification of Mitchell's macronovel and its constituent parts.[18] This complex concept has many competing approaches and will be approached in this study as a fluid entity; as Amy J. Devitt notes in 'Integrating Rhetorical and Literary Theories of Genre' (2000), 'genre can be redefined [...] as a dynamic concept' which shifts according to the interactions of readers, writers, texts and contexts, and as such, genre is 'always unstable, always multiple, always emerging' (699, 715). John Frow's *Genre* (2006) notes that genre is 'a shared convention with a social force' that 'defines a set of expectations which guide our engagement with texts' (102, 104). In light of this, what 'set of expectations' does Mitchell's wider use of genre conventions set up, and is there a cumulative 'social force' behind it?[19] Chapter 1 investigates these questions, using the broad concept of genre to identify groups of short stories with shared thematic traits, which, combined, productively suggest previously unexplored critical avenues within the macronovel. While Mitchell's use of established short story genres is mapped in the next chapter, the aim is not to restrict discussion of these hybrid literary groupings to fixed and singular categories, but to view these as dynamic clusters that, constellation-like, productively suggest new approaches to literary criticism of Mitchell's macronovel as a whole.

The composite narrative world of the macronovel itself can also be approached as a form of large-scale narrative unit which destabilizes Western expectations of the novel form as the largest unit of literary 'meaning'. While the cross-textual use of shared

---

[18] 'genre, n'. *OED Online*. Oxford University Press, March 2017. Web. 20 April 2017.

[19] For further discussion of the shifting nature of genre and its relationship with affect, see Lauren Berlant's 'Austerity, Precarity, Awkwardness' (2011), which notes that 'genre is a loose affectively-invested zone of expectations about the narrative shape a situation will take' (2), and Berlant's *Cruel Optimism* (2011), which notes, '[g]enres provide an affective expectation of the experience of watching something unfold, whether that thing is in life or in art' (6).

characters and settings has long been a feature of literary serials and genre fiction alike, Mitchell's creation of a shared world that encompasses many different global settings, time periods and art forms prompts an important question: why such a macro-scale narrative world is being employed at this particular historical moment, an issue that will be discussed further in Chapter 3. However, this study doesn't aim to 'devalue' the constituent parts of the macronovel – its individual short stories, libretti and novels – by investigating each part's role within the wider fictional universe. Each also functions as a stand-alone narrative in its own right, and, of course, may also be productively critiqued as such. Similarly, Mitchell's short fictions are grouped and collectively categorized as 'short stories' in this study in order to investigate their combined contributions to the macronovel; however, other productive categorizations are certainly possible. Future studies may wish to further subdivide and critique Mitchell's body of short fictions by using other groupings altogether, including, for example, prose-poems and novel 'spin-offs'. But with seven novels, two libretti and some twenty-six short fictions all contributing to an interconnected narrative world built over two decades, the growing continuities across this vast fictional terrain demonstrate that the macronovel must now be investigated as a cohesive critical entity.

Towards a mandalic mapping

Using the mandala as a critical tool to help map the Buddhist influences that underpin David Mitchell's post-secular world, a different aspect of this task will be addressed in each of this book's chapters. To critique the macronovel as a whole is to give much-needed scholarly attention to the author's lesser-known works – his short stories and libretti – which, as discussed earlier, have received very little critical attention to date. However, while Mitchell confirms that the libretti are part of his 'über-novel', the short story is also a particularly important form for an author who has noted in interview that his work uses the short story unit as its building block.[20] To this end, the first two chapters of this book focus on his short stories and libretti as integral facets of this fictional world.

Chapter 1 investigates Mitchell's use of the short story unit as a form of islandic narrative, whose archipelagic groupings together reveal the shared ethical approaches that resurface across the macronovel. As Childs and Green note of *Ghostwritten*:

> Mitchell writes a world where humanity lives in difference on an unprecedented scale [...] a world where no single perspective can encompass the multifaceted realities of human life. (29)

Childs and Green's comments could just as easily refer to Mitchell's ambitious textual landscape as a whole. With their profusion of extra-textual interconnections and contrasting perspectives, Mitchell's short stories together serve a vital narrative function by providing the smallest 'building blocks' of the macronovel that bridge the

---

[20] See Robert Birnbaum's 2006 interview with David Mitchell for an example of this ('David Mitchell').

fictional gaps between his novels, their shared approaches revealing that each of these discrete stories forms part of a larger continuous world. Taking a comparative approach to the mandala's depiction of an interdependent world-system as a form of ethical map, this chapter argues that the macronovel cumulatively depicts an alternative world model based not purely on global economics, but on the shared fate of humanity as a co-dependent and globally interconnected species – effectively forming an ethical map which demonstrates the vital role of individual belief in creating meaningful change within such a system.

Building on this mandalic interpretation of the macronovel as a form of ethical world-system, Chapter 2 uses the impermanent form of the sand mandala to discuss *Wake* and *Sunken Garden*'s secular redeployment of Buddhist philosophies as part of a regenerative approach to human impermanence. Interpreting the sand mandala – when created in diaspora for an unfamiliar audience – as a form of public performance, this chapter reads the mandala in parallel with Mitchell's libretti in performance, using its structures, mythologies and Buddhist ethical perspectives to inform a reading of each opera's ethical approaches to finding hope after tragedy. Identifying the shared tropes that situate these works as vital components within the macronovel, Chapter 2 discusses each opera's exploration of life and death as cyclical processes, revealing how their post-secular reworkings of Buddhist philosophies of impermanence and rebirth are used to find collective sources of hope and regeneration amid tragedy.

As a result of the scant critical attention paid to Mitchell's writing for opera and short stories, there is little sustained scholarly interrogation of the reincarnated character of Marinus. This character resurfaces in seven separate works to date – *The Bone Clocks*, *The Thousand Autumns of Jacob de Zoet*, *Slade House*, 'I_Bombadil', 'All Souls Day', *Wake* and *Sunken Garden*, as mentioned earlier – prompting further critical investigation into macronovel's recurring use of reincarnation. As such, Chapter 3 builds on the previous exploration of Buddhist philosophies of rebirth with a discussion of reincarnation across the macronovel, investigating Marinus' cross-textual role as a reincarnated healer in each of these works. Arguing that Marinus' character is a secular reworking of the Buddhist concept of the bodhisattva, Chapter 3 demonstrates that a reworked conception of reincarnation is used as the basis for an alternate temporal model within this fictional world, whose focus on cross-temporal interconnection depicts the importance of collective, future-facing ethical action in the face of ecological and humanitarian crises.

Moving its focus from the temporal to the spatial, Chapter 4 investigates the controlling power structures and hierarchies that threaten the inhabitants of this fictional world. Seemingly inescapable super-structures appear throughout Mitchell's narratives. Visible in *Cloud Atlas*'s depiction of Sonmi's confinement within a resistance movement which is manufactured by the corpocracy she fights against, and Eiji's struggles with his own mental circles of imprisonment in *number9dream*, this textual preoccupation also surfaces in Mitchell's short stories and libretti, for example, in the invisible boundaries that trap Zenna's suicidal victims in *Sunken Garden*, and the seemingly inescapable virtual prisons created by the soul-consuming killers in 'The Right Sort' (2014) and *Slade House*. Confronting the mandala's assumed holisticism, and the boundaries and hierarchies that underpin its own structure, this chapter imagines the Derridean deconstruction of the mandala's properties to suggest its dark opposite: the panopticon, itself a structure that recurs throughout *number9dream*. Critiquing the panopticon as a form of anti-mandala, this chapter investigates its inclusion in *number9dream*, arguing that the panopticon's theorization as a critical model addresses aspects of the macronovel that would otherwise remain removed from any simple comparative reading of the mandala. Taking its cue from the sinister relationship between Jason and his invisible 'Unborn Twin' in *Black Swan Green*, this chapter investigates the panopticon as the mandala's insidious twin, whose hierarchies and boundaries underpin the macronovel's dystopian super-structures, demonstrating the vital importance of the individual acts of resistance and community-building behind each Sisyphean attempt to escape the system.

Moving beyond the boundaries of the macronovel, this book finally considers whether the structures and philosophies of the mandala have broader relevance for the literary criticism of other twenty-first-century post-secular narratives in English. Chapter 5 therefore shifts its engagement with the mandala from interpretive tool to emerging category, broadening its focus to discuss the possibility of a mandalic literature. It asks if the tendencies identified within Mitchell's works are symptomatic of wider shared preoccupations within contemporary post-secular literature, discussing Michael Ondaatje's novel *Anil's Ghost* (2000), Ali Smith's *Hotel World* (2001), Yann Martel's *Life of Pi* (2002), Will Self's *The Book of Dave* (2006) and Margaret Atwood's *MaddAddam* trilogy (*Oryx and Crake* 2003; *The Year of the Flood* 2009; *MaddAddam* 2013). As such, this study finally broadens its focus to explore the possibility of a wider cultural resurgence of post-secular ethical world-building in other literary fictions – a resurgence which is also becoming increasingly visible in contemporary television and film.

John A. McClure usefully discusses the rise of spirituality in postmodern literature, noting the 'increasing popularity' of 'Hindu and Buddhist ideas' in 'Euro-American novelists like Pynchon, DeLillo [...] and Atwood' ('Postmodern/Post-Secular' 1995, 154). He rightly asks, '[d]o Westerners' appropriations of non-Western traditions represent a salutary victory for the marginalized, or are they simply one more instance of European misapprehension and expropriation?' This issue will be addressed through a wider investigation of the Tibetan Buddhist mandala's creation in diaspora, critiquing the implications of its theorization. The Tibetan mandala is perhaps the most internationally well-known form of mandala due to ongoing humanitarian struggles in the Tibetan region, and their international media coverage. As a practical means of preserving the practices and beliefs of Tibetan Buddhists in the West, as well as raising the profile of Tibetan communities living in exile, the mandala will be discussed not merely as the basis for a theoretical approach, but also as a living cultural artefact. The aim of this research is therefore not to expropriate the mandala, but to engage in a wider cultural study that asks what contemporary literature may learn from this diasporic artefact-turned-symbol, and explore the significance of its ethical world view, non-linear form and Buddhist philosophies for the study of these late twentieth and early twenty-first-century approaches to post-secular world-building.

Ultimately, there will be as many different maps for any text as there are readers. But a mandalic critical approach accepts the impossibility of total representation, preserving difference – after all, no two mandalas are the same. Similarly, although this study describes some of the documented traits of Tibetan Buddhist mandalas, ultimately there can be no single mandala that can claim representation over them all; each has its own traditional interpretations, structures, purposes and cultural variations. However, in this diversity lies strength. This book's approach is about finding new openings by expanding the critical conversation to include non-Western perspectives, recognizing that there must be more than one view of the centre within a globally aware twenty-first-century literary criticism.

Enter the 'World-Machine': Navigating David Mitchell's Narrative Islands

In David Mitchell's libretto for *Sunken Garden*, the final words are spoken by Simon Vines, a character who goes missing following the trauma of his daughter's cot death and becomes trapped in the supernatural garden of the opera's title. The garden lures in the depressed and suicidal, where they remain numbed from the pain of personal trauma. Having chosen to live with his grief, Simon finally escapes and returns to his friends in the real world, where he embarks on a parachute jump. As the audience see the vast projected film footage of Simon's first-person view of the earth from above, he describes the experience:

> you're falling, falling, falling, and you see the fields and towns and roads and rivers and factories and hospitals and all … Laid out, below, and you think, Look at this, look at this … massive, unjust, beautiful, cruel, miraculous … World-Machine. Look at it. And you think, 'I'm a part of this'. (9)

The opera begins and ends with film footage from the parachute jump, but it is only in the libretto's final moments that the footage is explained as Simon's view of the earth during his skydive. In a typically Mitchellian narrative strategy, this projected landscape which frames *Sunken Garden*'s tale encourages the audience to interpret the aerial map – and subsequently the entire performance – as depicting the inner workings of a self-contained 'World-Machine' in action.

This cartographic approach to storytelling as world creation – in which the narrative is presented as a fictional landscape, a 'machine' whose inner workings are vitally interconnected – is visible in Mitchell's novels, which function both as parts of a single macronovel with shared characters and tropes, but also as microcosmic worlds-within-worlds. The wider 'World-Machine' of his macronovel features a profusion of global geographies and narrative voices, as is clearly visible in *Ghostwritten* and *Cloud Atlas*, but also in the temporal breadth and immersive supernatural world creation of *The Bone Clocks* and *Slade House*, and even in the geographically and temporally localized micro-universes of *Black Swan Green*, *number9dream* and *The Thousand Autumns*. For example, alongside *Black Swan Green*'s profusion of contemporary references to the music, politics and 'teenspeak' of 1980s Middle England, the novel's creation of a self-contained world is embedded in its characters' names and identities. In a 2006 interview by Edward Champion, the author notes of this coming-of-age novel:

> [a]lmost all of the names are taken from Ordnance Survey map 150, which is the originally government-programmed map of the UK [...] 150 is the area of Worcestershire and a bit of Gloucestershire and a bit of Herefordshire around where the book is set. So almost all of the kids – people's – names in *Black Swan Green* are names that I found off that map. ('David Mitchell II')

This act of double mapping – using pre-existing place names for fictional characters – embeds the novel's setting into its characterization, emphasizing the importance of locality in personal identity formation, but also, conversely, the cumulative importance of individual identity in the creation of such shared localities. By using this technique, Mitchell portrays the geographical as simultaneously anonymous and intimately personal, bringing a 'government-programmed map' to life via the fledging generation that inhabits it – and, in doing so, reclaiming and animating its territories from the perspective of its imagined inhabitants.

This sense of cartographic play is visible even in Mitchell's earliest approaches to storytelling, as mentioned in the introduction. However, this project to create a microscopically detailed fictional world has become a defining feature of his adult writing. In a 2010 interview by Wyatt Mason, Mitchell notes that the aim of his macronovel is to map an entire world as extensively as possible:

> I can't bear living in this huge beautiful world [...] and not try to imitate it as best I can. That's the desire and the drive [...] to try to duplicate it on as huge a scale as I can possibly do. ('David Mitchell, the Experimentalist')

The author's use of 'as huge a scale' as the limits of fiction will allow, spanning novels, short stories and libretti, remains largely unaddressed in Mitchellian literary criticism to date. Yet the challenge of mapping Mitchell's textual universe as an interconnected terrain is narratologically irresistible: as Shawn Ballard notes of *Ghostwritten*'s ambitious narrative scale in 'Complex Systems and Global Catastrophe: Networks in David Mitchell's *Ghostwritten*' (2011), 'one simply has to map it' (11).

When approaching his narratives as a whole, several critics refer to Mitchell's oeuvre as a mappable terrain, while simultaneously noting its intangible – and therefore seemingly 'unmappable' – metaphysical dimensions. For example, Kathryn Schulz notes of the author:

> he is a pangaeic writer, a supercontinental writer. What is for geologists a physical fact – that the world is everywhere interconnected, bound together in a cycle of faulting and folding, rifting and drifting, erosion and uplift – is, for Mitchell, a metaphysical conviction. ('Boundaries Are Conventions', 2014)

In 'The Novels in Nine Parts' (2011), Peter Childs and James Green also describe an expansive geological textuality underpinned by a similarly 'metaphysical' force, noting that 'an ethics of fiction' underpins the author's 'multidimensional terrain of transmigratory dreamscapes' (44). Caroline Edwards also notes in '"Strange Transactions": Utopia, Transmigration and Time in *Ghostwritten* and *Cloud Atlas*' (2011) that Mitchell's works move 'towards a revised version of humanism as it is being played out through the spatially- and temporally-disjunct coordinates of unevenly expanding globalization', combining the ethical metaphysics of humanism with the pre-mapped coordinates of a globalized world (179). Similarly, William Stephenson's '"Moonlight bright as a UFO abduction": Science Fiction, Present-Future Alienation and Cognitive Mapping' (2011) notes Mitchell's 'new and exhilarating form of cognitive cartography', combining the geographical with the psychological (240).

While each of these critics describes Mitchell's writing in terms of its expansive narrative geographies, they also simultaneously refer to these works as replete with seemingly unmappable forces that push his fiction beyond any conventional notion of textual landscape. In each case, descriptions of Mitchell's works as cartographically navigable – a 'pangaeic', 'supercontinental' textual 'terrain', with 'spatial […] coordinates' that evidence a larger textual 'cartography' – are accompanied by a fundamentally metaphysical dimension. These non-geographical forces are variously described as 'multidimensional […] transmigratory dreamscapes', creating their own 'ethics of fiction' and 'revised version of humanism'. This is an unconventional narrative terrain built on 'spatially- and temporally-disjunct coordinates', forming a metaphysical world whose cartographic approach is 'cognitive', rather than strictly physical. Any literary study attempting to visualize Mitchell's works as a cartographic whole must therefore find a critical methodology capable of mapping both its expansive narrative geographies *and* their intangible yet deeply interrelated metaphysical and ethical dimensions.

While nearly all published Mitchellian literary criticism to date focuses on the author's novels, as discussed in the introduction, this chapter maps the breadth of this textual 'World-Machine' from an alternative perspective, focusing on the author's short stories. Discussing twenty-six of these short fictions, it asks how – and why – these narrative units operate as both self-contained islands and archipelagically linked texts, and what their significance is in light of the larger project of the macronovel. Approaching his short stories as linked narrative islands, this chapter argues that these make essential contributions that would otherwise remain absent from Mitchell's novels alone, while remaining continuous with the approaches of his longer works. As the dominant categories shared by these stories demonstrate, Mitchell's textual universe eschews the conventions of traditionally linear narrative, or even the cartographic conventions of a two-dimensional approach to genre and theme as separate narrative axes. Instead, the author's short stories effectively blur the boundaries between genre and theme, their shared preoccupations exploring the components of faith from a secular perspective. In doing so, Mitchell's short stories reflect an important post-secular dimension of his writing by cumulatively interrogating the building blocks of belief, moving beyond the Lyotardian postmodern breakdown of grand narratives in order to reimagine the secular value of their individual components in galvanizing positive humanitarian action. As this chapter argues, standard conceptions of mapping are unable to account for these metaphysical, non-linear dimensions of Mitchell's fictional world. But the Tibetan Buddhist mandala, read as a belief-centred map of a precisely structured and ethically engaged world, offers an alternative approach that can help to illuminate the world-building strategies behind Mitchell's post-secular fictions.

Mapping the metaphysical

To take up the challenge of mapping Mitchell's works – or in fact any terrain – is to create a form of representation that is entirely removed from the original. This unavoidable fictionality of cartographic representation renders the act of mapping a process by which the cartographer's decisions – including the medium, area of inclusion, method of visualization, perspective and scale – will always reflect its creator's biases and assumptions as much as the area being mapped. To this end, this book foregrounds its own methodology for approaching the author's works as a form of mapping; its mandalic approach is not a transparent theoretical 'lens', but a separate critical entity whose application unavoidably changes our understanding of this textual terrain. This study therefore aims to deliberately expose the cartographic assumptions involved in its own form of map-making, employing a map of an immaterial, belief-dependent world to chart the boundaries of a fictional one.

What shared properties might this structure bring to a comparative analysis of Mitchell's textual world? The author has already indicated in interview that the scale for a map of his works must be vaster than any physical map is able to imagine; as a cosmogram, the mandala is a diagram of a universe, its area of inclusion as large as its participant's capabilities of visualization. As Schulz, Childs and Green, Edwards, and Stephenson highlight, any Mitchellian map must be simultaneously able to represent the multidimensional, metaphysical, ethical and global; the Tibetan Buddhist mandala is merely the visible map used to guide a metaphysical visualization, its distinct ethical purpose making it a fitting tool for approaching the Buddhist influences within Mitchell's works.

Mitchell's fictional 'World-Machine' also shares the mandala's meta-spatial approach in its creation of a post-secular world whose dimensions are both geographical and ethical. Discussing the mandala's early historical uses as a 'mental model of social reality', Robert A. F. Thurman notes in 'Mandala: the architecture of enlightenment' (1997) that 'there is already a clear sense of mandala as world-model', noting its use in royal rituals as a representation of a global structure that links both the sacred and the secular (130). Susan M. Walcott also argues in 'Mapping from a Different Direction: Mandala as Sacred Spatial Visualization' (2006) that the mandala is a 'multidimensional' and 'metaphysical' map whose 'mental terrain' broadens the assumed limits of geographic representation, a 'cognitive graphic of sacred space' that can valuably 'expand […] assumptions of cartographic portrayal, space, and contestation' (71–9). Mapping their own profusion of interconnected global localities, Mitchell's fictions similarly foreground the 'contestation' of such spaces through his exploration of human power dynamics and conflicts over vast geographical and temporal scales.

The mandala also offers its own form of macrocosmic 'World-Machine' in the giant edifice of Borobudur, a Buddhist monument in Indonesia which covers over 100 square metres. Ken Taylor describes Borobudur as 'a Buddhist mandala representation' in which 'the mandala form of the monument is repeated in the wider landscape' ('Cultural Landscape as Open Air Museum' 53–4). Just as Borobudur renders the mandala into a huge physical terrain, Simon's evocation of a 'World-Machine' leaves the audience with a final visual image of his entire world from above. Simon realizes he is a mere 'part' of the 'massive' terrain that he sees, its contrasting facets forming a single world that is simultaneously 'unjust, beautiful, cruel, miraculous'. As if looking down on a two-dimensional mandala, Simon's top-down view of the landscape brings a realization of his world as an integrated system – and a realization of his wider role within it.

These distinct 'World-Machine[s]' – Simon's world, the wider macronovel and the mandala – all share a form of machine-like structural organization that makes these complex worlds into self-contained world-systems. How might the theoretical concept of the world-system, then, relate to these World-Machines? In 'The Rise and Future Demise of the World Capitalist System' (1974), Immanuel Wallerstein develops a structural framework for a world-systems theory in which 'the only kind of social system is a world-system' based on labour and production (390). While Wallerstein's theory predominantly deals with economics, its structure also provides a transferrable blueprint; he argues that there are 'three structural positions in a world economy – core, periphery and semi-periphery', forming an interlinked system that can only function as a whole (391). Read outside of its economic origins, the circularity of this structure offers a useful transferrable model for imagining an interdependent fictional world-system, its structural framework replicated within the mandala's fundamental structural points of centre, outer boundary and cardinal points, as will be discussed in Chapter 4.

Employing a similarly circular structural model for literary criticism, Charu Sheel Singh notes in *Concentric Imagination: Mandala Literary Theory* (1994) that '[t]he concept of the whole can best be represented by the circle and literary theory cannot dispense with it' (81). It is worth briefly noting that the circular model is not necessarily the 'best' or most appropriate concept for the whole in every instance; for example, applied across global economics, the core-periphery model used by Wallerstein's world-systems theory risks reinscribing problematic assumptions of Western hierarchical dominance. However, applied specifically for mapping shared outcomes, the circular world-system of the mandala provides a useful comparative model for approaching a body of interconnected narratives as a continuous fictional universe. Rather than mapping assumptions of geopolitical dominance, it allows for a transferrable focus on the unavoidably shared ethical consequences of individual actions, thereby offering an alternative world model based not on global capitalism, but on the lived experiences that impact the shared fate of *Homo sapiens* as a co-dependent and now globally interconnected species.

Like the macronovel, the mandala presents a structural world-system that is replete with divisions, as well as connections. In 'Missing Mandalas: Development and Theoretical Gaps' (2004), Rosita Dellios recognizes that the mandala's circularity and cardinal points map a 'one-world scenario' based on both 'divisions' and 'connections', its structural model emphasizing 'an awareness of the value of difference for the wellbeing of the whole', and the importance of the 'balance of global forces, between

North-South, East-West, high-tech/low-tech, agrarian-urban, tribal postmodern' (10–13). However, this is no simple world-system; as Jung A. Huh notes in 'Mandala as Telematic Design' (2010), mandalas contain 'innumerable multidimensional worlds' whose 'boundaries overlap' and 'co-exist', providing a model that preserves, rather than homogenizes, complexity and difference (23).

Giuseppe Tucci also notes in *The Theory and Practice of the Mandala* (2001) that the mandala 'is a geometric projection of the world reduced to an essential pattern' (25). To take a mandalic approach to Mitchell's 'World-Machine' is to view all of his fictions – including his short stories – as integral to this larger 'geometric projection of the world', a world in which a form of 'essential pattern' is incessantly at work. As a form of visual scripture which maps philosophical, rather than physical, spaces, the mandala – when itself 'read' as a map – allows for the spatial conceptualization of relationships between the shared themes and ethical approaches of Mitchell's universe, highlighting interconnections that would otherwise remain hidden. As Walcott notes, the mandala is a form of 'symbolic roadmap' whose meticulously structured design makes such spatial patterns, groupings and hierarchies visible, providing a valuable framework for cultural geography (71, 76) – and, as this study will demonstrate, a useful comparative tool for the literary critical task of venturing into Mitchell's fictions as a single interlinked world-system.

David Mitchell's 'World-Machine' and globalization

Critics have long remarked on Mitchell's writerly 'ventriloquism' in his easy fluidity of styles, genres and voices. However, it is perhaps their interlinked world view that makes Mitchell's works particularly 'Mitchellian' – leaving those who venture into several of his works with a sense that a shared set of ethical issues is being explored across many geographies, personae and time periods. To put it another way, to read Mitchell's 'World-Machine' as a whole is to discover an intrinsic world view which resembles the linked, continuous narrative structure of a *Choose Your Own Adventure* novel, as will be discussed later in this chapter. Each part shares its ethical perspectives with the larger whole, whether novel or short story, cumulatively demonstrating the far-reaching global consequences of individual actions, and thereby demonstrating the importance of personal ethical action in the real globalized world of the reader. While the training required for mandala interpretation within Tibetan Buddhism is highly complex and disciplined – unlike a *Choose Your Own Adventure* novel – its labyrinthine visual scripture fosters an ethical process of self-discovery for its participant, in which mentally progressing through its imagined world facilitates the realization of the ethical concepts symbolized within it, an experiential process aimed at generating real change.

At this point, it's worth considering how the shared world view created across Mitchell's fictions relates to our own globalized world. As William Stephenson recognizes, 'Mitchell's polyphonic, decentred novels are a reflection of the realities of globalization and the networked world' (239). But what version of the 'realities of globalization' does Mitchell's 'World-Machine' present? Roland Robertson usefully defines the term in *Globalization: Social Theory and Global Culture* (1992), noting that '[g]lobalization as a concept refers both to the compression of the world and the intensification of consciousness of the world as a whole' (8). Mitchell's narratives depict a fictionalized world in 'compression', its multiple interconnections fostering greater readerly 'consciousness of the world' as a single, or 'whole', unit. However, it is also worth taking a moment here to differentiate between the complex economic, political, social and cultural processes of globalization and their necessary 'compression' as part of the representation of globalization in contemporary literature. Outside of the text, any attempt to map a vast whole risks becoming problematically reductionist in its attempt to determine its inhabitants' world views. Any critical discussion of globalization as a singular phenomenon risks overlooking whose 'consciousness', as Robertson puts it, is being intensified – and who, or what, is creating this sense of global 'compression'.

To briefly delve further into this issue, in 'Three Women's Texts and a Critique of Imperialism' (1985), Gayatri Chakravorty Spivak identifies the problematic 'worlding' of the so-called 'Third World', identifying that this terminology makes the action of its 'worlding' invisible (243). As the assumptions inherent in Robertson's definition demonstrate, the theoretical 'worlding' of the global is no less problematic. For example, Kristin Veel's assertion in *Narrative Negotiations: Information Structures in Literary Fiction* (2009) that we 'find ourselves in a world globally linked by media that provide us with continuous information from the whole world about the whole world' reproduces a media-sustained fallacy behind which entire cultures and geographies remain under- or misrepresented in this global 'worlding', are excluded altogether, or violently reject such attempts at inclusion in Western assumptions of 'the' global (9). To make such theoretical assumptions about a 'whole world' is to assume – either consciously or unconsciously – a normative homogeneity, in which a neatly comparable body of cultures is taken as a pre-existing phenomenon. As Spivak notes in 'Rethinking Comparativism' (2009), 'comparison assumes a level playing field and the field is never level [...]. It is, in other words, never a question of compare and contrast, but rather a matter of judging and choosing' (609). This process of 'judging and choosing' may be more clearly discernible in artistic representations of globality, but is all too easily overlooked in theoretical discussions of the global.

To discuss globality from a predominantly 'Western' – or Anglo-European-American – standpoint is to already enter into a critical conversation in which the legacy of imperialism becomes increasingly invisible – but no less present – in light of the ubiquity of 'the global', and this implicit act of 'judging and choosing'. Discussing the concept of 'globalisation', Robertson also notes that '[d]uring the second half of the 1980s its use increased enormously' (8). It exists today as a hotly contested anthropological concept, geographical symbol, advertising tool, historical phenomenon, media buzzword, capitalist system, economic marketplace, cultural fantasy, Western label and many others. As Revathi Krishnaswamy argues in 'The Criticism of Culture and the Culture of Criticism: At the Intersection of Postcolonialism and Globalization Theory' (2002), 'corporate globalization is thriving precisely by emptying out the subversive potential in culture', the now hyper-marketed image of a global culture effectively blurring the boundaries between representation and reality in the eyes of the consumer (108). While Robertson recognizes that 'the discourse of mapping is a vital ingredient of global-political culture', more than two decades later, Robertson's vision of global mapping has arguably become so ubiquitous that it is virtually invisible (57). It is worth emphasizing, then, that in each of its many forms of representation, globalization remains a form of mapping, laying intellectual, cultural, economic or sociological claim to shared territory on a larger scale than ever before, replete with the biases of its cartographer's unavoidable decisions and priorities. After all, a 13,000-kilometre-wide map is still a map.

Perhaps the most universal, and the most urgent, grounds upon which to discuss globalization, then, are those concerning global catastrophe and the possibility of change. Regardless of any attempt at defining the global, the threat of ecological or economic self-destruction implicates all of the earth's inhabitants, by which actions inflicted by a dominant culture or group of individuals can precipitate global decline and widespread human suffering. As such, the recognition of human interdependence is a crucial step towards bringing about the global-scale co-operation necessary to attempt any meaningful positive intervention. Mitchell's self-consciously fictional worlds dramatize the experience of global interconnection as simultaneously historical and contemporary, including ancient souls reborn across different times and geographies in *Ghostwritten*, *Cloud Atlas*, *The Bone Clocks* and *Slade House*; the exploration of historical global trade in *The Thousand Autumns*; and the formative experiences of everyday consumer culture in *number9dream* and *Black Swan Green*. The global is also often addressed from the position of the global outsider – for example, *Ghostwritten*'s tea shack lady and its terrorist cult member Quasar, the traveller community in *Black Swan Green*, or Sonmi, a genetically manufactured slave in *Cloud Atlas* – in each case preventing the reader from taking for granted the not-so-universal privileges and viewpoints assumed as part of the more mainstream consumer societies depicted. Yet each of these characters are part of the same 'World-Machine', heading towards the same global collapse depicted in *Cloud Atlas* and *The Bone Clocks*, their futures both visibly authored and unavoidably interlinked.

While the mandala, as a self-contained depiction of a universe, offers 'a graphic metaphor for interdependence in a globalising world', as Rosita Dellios notes in 'Missing Mandalas: Development and Theoretical Gaps' (2004), Mitchell's macronovel serves as its own 'metaphor for interdependence', depicting a single interconnected world-system that its characters must learn to share. As Peter Childs and James Green note of Mitchell's interconnected inhabitants, '[t]hough separated from each other by enormous geographical and temporal distances, their struggle against various forms of subordination is presented as a universal impulse' (36–7). It is this global interdependence that Mitchell's world view emphasizes in the face of looming shared catastrophe, the 'universal impulse' of the struggle to survive the strongest linking factor between its inhabitants, regardless of their position within the fictional world-system. Taking a mandalic approach to mapping Mitchell's fictional 'World-Machine' is to read his individual narratives as part of a single globalized world, its dystopic trajectories envisaging the humanitarian consequences when such global 'balance' is lost within the system, and – as Chapter 4 will discuss – the power divisions and hierarchies that underpin it.

David Mitchell's narrative islands

The medium that this study employs for its literary critical map is the mandala, its cartographic method of visualization metaphysical, and its area of inclusion the author's entire fictional world to date. However, this map also has a distinct base unit: the short story. As the smallest discrete elements of Mitchell's textual terrain, his short fictions operate as interconnected yet self-contained islands within the larger archipelagos of his works, complete with internal conflicts and individual relationships with the larger narrative world in which they sit. If Mitchell's novels form the mainland within an imagined map of his textual universe, the short stories are its archipelagically linked islands, remaining related to and in constant communication with his continental novels. Approaching their groupings as part of an interrelated whole requires an act of reading that, across such an expansive textual universe, effectively becomes an act of mapping – and such cartographic methods are, of course, unavoidably complicit in imposing their own limited perspectives. However, by approaching these short stories as part of an interlinked metaphysical terrain, the act of reading becomes a discovery of complexity. Each new cross-textual connection forges extended chains of causality, showing the consequences of personal compliance or resistance across an entire world-system on a global scale.

In a 2015 interview with Lana Wachowski, the author discusses the sociopolitical nature of his own island micro-narratives from even his childhood map-making:

> I drew these islands [...] and those were my first narratives, because you have to think about who lives there, and what the people are, and then immediately you're into sociology, and anthropology, and politics, and world-making. ('David Mitchell with Lana Wachowski')

The concept of such narrative 'islands' as the 'first' units within the author's early map-making – which soon becomes 'world-making' – underpins Mitchell's structural approach to his works. In a 2014 interview with Mike Doherty, he describes himself as 'a writer of novellas' as opposed to a novelist, noting this shorter medium is his 'optimum form', foregrounding his recurring use of linked yet self-contained novella-type chapters in his novels, their borders marked by geographical, temporal, vocal or thematic shifts ('It's Stupid, It Shouldn't Work' 72).

The author's use of several different fictional dimensions – the smaller scale of the short narrative unit, the larger scale of the novel and the macro-scale of the fictional universe – raises issues of narrative hierarchy, prompting a questioning of which fictional frame assumes priority within their structural relationship. For the author, the shorter piece is always given narrative authority. Mitchell notes in a 2014 interview with Claire Fallon,

> If I feel a conflict of interest between a larger world and the smaller world of an individual novel, then my constitution of the uber-book says that the smaller state – the book – has the last say in what goes on in it, and the kind of central government of the uber-novel [...] is less important than the state capitals, has less power. [*sic*] ('"The Bone Clocks" Author David Mitchell')

The 'smaller' narrative unit is unquestionably prioritized in the writing process, assuming the dominant position within the hierarchy. As will be discussed more fully in Chapter 4, the Tibetan Buddhist mandala contains its own internal structural hierarchies, in which the central deity that occupies the smallest amount of representational space within the physical mandala is its most hierarchically prominent feature. When constructed from sand, the mandala's deities are often represented with tiny dots, each only a few grains of sand in diameter; to the untrained onlooker, their presence can be easily overlooked in an intricate diagram that can be several feet wide. The central deity is visualized by the meditating participant as residing above the structure, resting on the highest level within the centre, and hierarchically set above its surroundings. By prioritizing the smaller narrative unit as the more authoritative source, Mitchell's fictional world creates its own mandalic hierarchy in which the textual space occupied is inversely proportional to its centrality within the macronovel, reversing the assumption that the largest territory assumes dominance, and prompting a revaluing of the smallest details within such narrative cartographies.

Mitchell's assertion is a valuable indicator that his short stories, which occupy the least physical and critical space in his macronovel, hold great 'political' significance within his oeuvre. It also provides a vital structural indicator of the ethical prioritization of smaller units of cosmopolitan diversity and difference over large-scale homogenization in his works, for example, visible in *Cloud Atlas* as a single fast-food worker rises up against the 'central government' of Nea So Copros. As Berthold Schoene usefully identifies for the cosmopolitan novel:

> this turn to the small is no second-best compromise, but the actually preferred mode of representation [...] apprehending globalisation as a powerfully meaning-enforcing system whose impact can be allayed only by mobilising the entire microcosmic 'nitty-gritty' of global multiplicity. (28–9)

Alongside the structural and political significance of this narrative 'turn to the small' as the author's 'preferred mode of representation' within a wider 'global multiplicity', the concept of the island in particular has recurring thematic significance in the macronovel.

As the smallest inhabitable land mass, the island offers a potential site for the exploration of such small-scale communities. As the author notes in a 2004 interview with Edward Champion:

> [i]slands keep cropping up in my work. [...] Islands are perhaps the geological expression most similar to novels. They're both protected from and cut off from mainland reality [...] it's no accident that utopias and paradises are usually set on islands. ('David Mitchell')

Here, Mitchell compares the self-contained island structure to that of the novel. However, if the island is the smallest possible form of inhabited land mass, it is the short story, rather than the novel, which provides the most 'islandic' narrative unit. Here, the island's spatial and sociopolitical significances merge as its territory becomes a testing ground for alternate realities, in an islandic short narrative form which blurs the boundaries between form, content and political world view. Writing on *Cloud Atlas* in a 2010 essay, David Mitchell also remarks that the novel encompasses 'two of my favourite themes: islands, and the fragility of knowledge' ('Guardian Book Club'). Again, Mitchell links the cartographic to the metaphysical and – with his previous reference to the island as potentially utopian – the ethical. Mitchell's short stories, as the smallest islands in his narrative terrain, offer a condensed space in which to consider 'the fragility of knowledge' through the politicized medium of the micro-narrative. As this chapter will demonstrate, when knowledge breaks down on these narrative islands, what emerges is an ethical revaluing of faith; when certainty becomes unstuck, it is the act of belief that moves to the fore.

Belief and secularity in David Mitchell's macronovel

Mitchell's discussions of faith in interview reveal an author keenly aware of the fluidity of belief in both sacred and secular contexts, and its crucial function as a means of galvanizing personal agency. As noted in the introduction, Mitchell discusses his own relationship with faith in several interviews, calling himself 'a kind of secular Buddhist' in a 2013 interview with Andrei Muchnik ('David Mitchell Talks'). Again discussing this secular relationship with belief in a 2015 interview, the author notes, 'I'm a happy agnostic […] it works for me – with Buddhism in the background' ('Interview by Rose Harris-Birtill'). However, while Mitchell consistently describes this secular approach to belief from a humanist perspective, he doesn't dismiss religious faith. In the same interview, he also discusses its practical outcomes:

> [i]f faith helps, is faith such a bad thing? When it tends to ISIS, yes. But when there's an abused Liverpudlian Catholic woman who can keep the show on the road because she's going to church and has a decent human being in the form of a priest to confide to, is that such a bad thing? ('Interview by Rose Harris-Birtill')

In a 2010 interview with Adam Begley, David Mitchell similarly notes: 'I'm not a Christian, but I dislike the current trend in British culture to trash Christian faith, which has, and does, inspire devout people to perform acts of humanism' ('David Mitchell, The Art of Fiction').

The author's approach to this outcome-focused form of secular belief, which holds tolerance at its core, doesn't overturn the Lyotardian postmodern distrust of religious grand narrative, but builds on it, treating it as a starting ground for a re-evaluation of belief when detached from religious ideology, and demonstrating the value of its components for humanitarian ends. For example, in a 2011 interview for the British Stammering Association, Mitchell remarks on his 'non-religious […] sense of mission' in his role as its patron: '[i]f I was a religious man, I'd say this is why I was born with a stammer […]. But in my secular way, I nonetheless do want to act as if what I just said is true', highlighting the value of 'secular' belief in forging positive ethical action ('Black Swan Green Revisited' 17). This perspective can also be seen in Mitchell's fictional works. For example, in 'My Eye On You' (2016), the narrator's guide tells him of the positive humanitarian interventions made by the 'meanderers', unseen humans who devote their lives to helping others: '[o]ur acts are credited to chance, to fate, or prayers. Who cares? It's outcomes, not their origins, that count. I listened to her every word. And I believed them, every one' (5). This powerful moment of belief galvanizes the narrator's decision to embark on a course of ethical action and himself become a 'meanderer', changing his own behaviour and choosing to devote the rest of his life to helping 'anyone and all, deeds both small and not-so-small, whatever seemed to be of use' (5–6).

The author has discussed his ongoing interest in the writings of C. G. Jung in interview ('I've always had a soft spot for [...] Jung'), and a Jungian perspective is particularly useful for understanding Mitchell's approach to belief ('Interview by Rose Harris-Birtill', 2015). Jung notes in 'Psychology and Religion' (1958) that the psychological components that form religious impulse are universally present, and that an individual's relationship with these can be 'positive or negative' (81). He recognizes that this 'relationship is voluntary as well as involuntary', arguing that 'you can accept, consciously', these unconscious impulses. Jung also asserts the psychological value of religious belief, noting that the difference between an 'illusion' and a 'healing religious experience [...] is merely a difference of words' (105). Similarly recognizing their practical benefit, Jung argues these 'subjective' interpretations remain worthwhile 'if such experience helps to make life healthier, more beautiful, more complete and more satisfactory to yourself and those you love', regardless of any 'transcendental truth'.

In 'My Eye On You', Mitchell's writing extends this perspective by approaching the practical value of individual belief from a secular perspective. The narrator learns that the individual's belief system is ultimately irrelevant; whether humanitarian 'outcomes' are attributed 'to chance, to fate, or prayers', it is belief itself that drives action. His response to hearing this further reinforces the legitimacy of his guide's explanation: he hears ('I listened to her every word'), he believes ('I believed them, every one') and he acts ('[t]he following morning I started my journey along the meanderer's way [...] I've never stopped') (5–6). This re-evaluation of belief as a necessary component of meaningful action takes a metamodern approach in which, as Timotheus Vermeulen puts it in a 2012 interview by Cher Potter, '[g]rand narratives are as necessary as they are problematic, hope is not simply something to distrust' ('Timotheus Vermeulen Talks').

To venture further into the established concept of 'religion' as a method of belief system categorization is to address the problems inherent in the term itself, an issue which the macronovel addresses in its post-secular approach to belief. In 'Faith and Knowledge: The Two Sources of "Religion" at the Limits of Reason Alone' (2002), Jacques Derrida interrogates the relationship between religion and belief, noting that 'faith has not always been and will not always be identifiable with religion' (48). However, Derrida also usefully highlights the Latinate, Christianity-based origins of the concept of 'religion' itself, noting that 'there is no "common" Indo-European term for what we call "religion"', terming its global imposition a process of 'globalatinization' by which our concept of religion today '*is* [...] globalization' (72, 79, 82). The term 'religion' shares its etymological roots with the Latin *religare*, meaning 'to bind'; like the process of globalization, the Western concept of religion effectively binds many discrete entities into a single homogenized global system.[1] In 'The Difference Between Eastern and Western Thinking' (1958), Jung also recognizes the pervasive influence of Christianity on Western attitudes. He notes that 'the West is thoroughly Christian as far as its psychology is concerned', even for those 'who have forgotten, or who have never heard of, their own religion', the historical dominance of this belief system extending far beyond the realms of Christian practice (482). To build on these Derridean and Jungian perspectives, the embedded concept of religion within the Anglophone world, stemming from predominantly Christian origins, is broadly inadequate for discussing the heterogeneity of global narratives of belief.

To give a further example, the application of the single term 'Buddhism' conceals a fallacy which groups a vast number of geographically and narratologically diverse belief systems, practices and sects, whose root narratives are now widely understood as more akin to the Western concept of a philosophy than its dominant Christianity-centric concept of religion. The *Oxford English Dictionary* notes that the term 'Buddhism' itself is an English derivation, its first recorded usage in 1800; the group of belief systems to which it refers predates their English-language categorization by some 2,300 years.[2] By separating the concept of belief from its normative Christianity-based understanding and exploring its secular facets, Mitchell's unsettling of the traditional boundaries of belief forges new approaches, drawing on a range of Buddhist philosophies – as will be explored further in this book – in order to question the role of belief in creating sustained ethical action at a time of ecological, capitalistic and ethical crisis. Such crises are envisaged in the speculative near futures of *Ghostwritten*, *Cloud Atlas* and *The Bone Clocks*. As Mitchell notes of these textual warnings, each imagining a dystopian near-future 'endarkenment' across the globe, 'we're in for some kind of a crash landing. Whether that crash is hard and fatal, or relatively soft, depends on what we do now'; the importance of belief-led action is vital in galvanizing an urgently needed and 'unprecedented level of international cooperation' while there is still time to act ('Interview by Rose Harris-Birtill', 2015).

Having developed entirely outside Western Christianity-normative understandings of belief, the Tibetan Buddhist mandala provides an alternative framework by which to approach Mitchell's belief-driven textual universe. To use the world model of the Tibetan Buddhist mandala to map Mitchell's expansive textual terrain is to recognize the fundamental importance of the metaphysical, ethical, and global dimensions that underpin this fictional world, while using a non-Christianity-centric model for such belief. As a physical manifestation that provides a blueprint for a mental process of visualization, the Tibetan Buddhist mandala builds on its participant's capacity for belief, providing an apt model for understanding the author's approach to morality. Walcott notes that mandalas function as 'moral and mental maps', and that when the mandala's 'practitioner-pilgrim' visualizes entering its virtual realm, the purpose of mentally journeying to its centre is that 'insight is achieved by the voyager' while doing so (86, 78). Similarly, in 'Encountering the Mandala: The Mental and Political Architectures of Dependency' (2001), Maggie Grey recognizes that the mandala 'is a

---

[1] 'religion, n'. *OED Online*. Oxford University Press, March 2016. Web. 1 April 2016.
[2] 'Buddhism, n'. *OED Online*. Oxford University Press, December 2015. Web. 7 January 2016.

multidimensional and interactive roadmap to realms other [...] and a metaphor of ideal or divine behaviour within that space', providing its own form of ethical map (6). While Mitchell's 'World-Machine' takes a secular approach to its world creation, it builds its own post-secular ethical standpoint; like the mandala, it creates a 'multidimensional' and textual space to 'realms other' which continually poses 'moral' dilemmas for its inhabitants, fostering greater 'insight' into the importance of personal and collective ethical decisions in the face of the looming ecological and economic implosions caused by human predacity.

Walcott also notes that '[g]eographic approaches to cartography largely fall into two camps: the Newtonian-Cartesian materialist approach which asserts that mapping records the physical world' and the perception-based 'Neo-Kantian view that all reality is a projection of the mind' (83). The mandala's perspective, Walcott suggests, provides a balance between the two cartographic approaches: '[t]he Buddhist "Middle Way" (*Madyamika*) view takes a third position [...] contending that the world exists both physically/conventionally and in a non-material/ultimate sense' (83–4). Mitchell's textual universe forges such a 'Middle Way' between realist and fantastic modes. Rather than creating a purely realist textual map of the world as it is, it creates its 'World-Machine' from a textual universe of interlinked characters and the consequences of their actions, with an uncanny sense of overarching design. Its extensive metafictional patterning within an otherwise realist setting includes the 'flashbacks, foreshadowings, and tricksy devices' that Timothy Cavendish criticizes in *Cloud Atlas*, and a fascination with numerical patterns and repeating structures (152). This creates an unsettling world whose simultaneous reality and fictionality undermine one another, as in the metafictional games of Borges, Calvino and Kafka. However, Mitchell's 'tricksy devices' move beyond the realms of metafictional play to meticulously construct a realm in which the patterns of causality and ethical choices are exposed as they reverberate throughout the 'World-Machine', taking a 'Middle Way' approach which employs the self-conscious artificiality of the fictional alongside realist narrative modes to make its universe a parallel to our own, in which reality itself *is* narrative.

As Courtney Hopf notes in 'The Stories We Tell: Discursive Identity Through Narrative Form in *Cloud Atlas*' (2011), 'the reader is in a privileged position as the only figure who can connect all of the novel's intertextual references, and is thus granted a greater interpretive agency' than each of the narrators in the novel (111). This observation equally applies to the macronovel; it encourages the reader to consider not merely the individual narrative being read, but also that narrative's role in shaping the world view being created. In doing so, Mitchell's fictions feature a multiplicity of interconnected diegetic dimensions which encourage the reader to make connections between these multiple narratives and those that structure our own world outside the text. Jung A. Huh's comment in 'Mandala as Telematic Design' that mandalas contain 'innumerable multi-dimensional worlds' whose 'boundaries overlap' and 'co-exist' could just as easily apply to the multidimensionality of Mitchell's diegetic universe, whose fictional offshoots lead into Twitter, film and even radio, blurring the assumed boundaries between fiction and reality (23). Alongside the insertion of one of the characters from *Slade House* into the 'real' world of social media with 'I_Bombadil', *number9dream* has resulted in its fictional film, *The Voorman Problem*, being created as a BAFTA and Academy Award-nominated British short film in 2012, while *The Bat Segundo Show*, based on *Ghostwritten*'s radio presenter of the same name, now exists as a stand-alone podcast that has been running since 2004, with over 500 episodes to date – several featuring interviews with David Mitchell. The experience of the extra-diegetic interconnections in Mitchell's fictional society is bizarrely like our own lived experience of twenty-first-century virtuality, the ubiquity of digital media and instant communications technology allowing for everyday encounters between individuals across the globe, whether face-to-face or avatar-to-avatar.[3] Far from unsettling the fictional integrity of the macronovel, these intrusions into the 'real' world replicate its uncanny parallels between reality and fantasy, creating a multidimensional and ever-expanding world and, in doing so, encouraging the reader to question their own position in the boundless, ever-unfolding narrative dimensions in which they find themselves.

'World in a bottle': David Mitchell's short stories

Appearing in print from 2003 to 2017, the short stories discussed in the remainder of this chapter form a significant counterpoint to Mitchell's novels. These short fictions chart the macronovel's narrative development from the author's first novel to the publication of his seventh, distilling many recurring themes from his longer works. For example, predacity, in its many social manifestations, is also a recurring feature of many of these narratives. To give two examples from either end of his oeuvre, the 2003 publication of 'The January Man' depicts an early revised section from *Black Swan Green*, which describes the predatory hierarchies behind its narrator's childhood games ('I hate British Bulldogs – it turns teammates into enemies […] they pick off the least hard kids first'), while the 2017 short story 'A Forgettable Story' features its narrator's terrified flight as he is chased by 'yakuza thugs'.

However, the author's short stories also make unique contributions to Mitchell's fictional world that are not featured in any of his novels, establishing his shorter narratives as an integral part of the author's fictional world. For example, while Mitchell has written and spoken about his experiences of parenting a child with autism in his essay 'Learning to live with my son's autism' (2013) and in his essay for Radio 4, 'The Reason I Jump – Book of the Week' (2013), the short story 'Lots of Bits of Star' (2013) offers Mitchell's only published fictional writing on autism to date. This brief tale describes a single incident from the perspective of Leo, a narrator living with autism, as he accompanies his grandfather to find his mother's lost mobile phone. Leo and his sister Rose are also mentioned briefly in 'The Gardener' (2011), a moving supernatural tale narrated by Leo's late grandfather as he watches the domestic goings-on from

---

[3] The term 'avatar', now used to refer to a graphical representation of an individual in a virtual environment, comes from the Sanskrit *avatāra*, meaning descent or incarnation, an etymological link whose modern usage combines an ancient sense of otherworldly interconnection with the hyperreality of technological deification ('avatar, n'. *OED Online*. Oxford University Press, December 2015. Web. 23 February 2016).

the garden outside his home, his ashes having been dug into the roots of the family magnolia tree. With 'The Gardener' and 'Lots of Bits of Star', Mitchell not only brings the topic of autism from his non-fictional writing into the world of his macronovel, but also provides an additional family of shared characters – including Leo, Rose and their grandfather – who haven't appeared in Mitchell's novels to date. However, a further connection between the two tales adds a supernatural dimension to 'Lots of Bits of Star'. In this short story, the sudden disappearance of Leo's grandfather, combined with his reference to 'my magnolia', and his playful explanation of his presence with 'I'm only the gardener', provide extra-textual links between the two stories. In doing so, Leo's grandfather is only revealed as a benevolent ghost in 'Lots of Bits of Star' when read alongside 'The Gardener', the relationship between the tales a microcosm of the interlinked relationships between Mitchell's narratives, whose diegetic worlds function cumulatively as well as separately, each changing in light of the other.

Further instances of the short stories providing details that change the way that Mitchell's novels – and the macronovel – are read can be seen in 'I_Bombadil', a series of over 500 Twitter entries which acts as a prequel to the final section of *Slade House*. This haunted house novel narrates the repeated acts of predation by the 116-year-old Norah and her brother Jonah, who bring unsuspecting visitors to Slade House to consume their souls, and thereby artificially extend their own lifespans. In the novel's final section, an unsuspecting 'conspiracy theorist' called Mark, who goes by the name of Bombadil, is used by Norah to trap her latest victim. Although he remains physically present, she takes possession of his body and mind. The last chapter is therefore narrated by Norah from within Mark's body as she uses him to lure the psychiatrist Dr Marinus into her trap, effectively rendering Mark's own character mute. 'I_Bombadil' is therefore the only work of fiction to date in which Mark is given a voice of his own, describing the comical incidents that lead up to his role in the novel. While this short story's inclusion of Marinus – the most significant of the macronovel's repeated characters, as will be discussed in Chapter 3 – situates 'I_Bombadil' within the macronovel's shared heritage, it also adds further detail to Marinus' characterization that is unavailable from any other work. Mark, writing on Twitter under the name of Bombadil, uses an alter ego fittingly taken from J. R. R. Tolkien's expansive textual realms, using the pseudonym of a benevolent ancient spirit whose often-unexplained cross-textual resurfacings echo Marinus' own role in Mitchell's textual universe.[4]

As Bombadil, Mark reveals the source of Marinus' character as 'Marinus of Tyre, ancient cartographer', a detail that is not mentioned in any of Mitchell's other fictional works. Marinus of Tyre, an ancient Greek cartographer and mathematician who developed the system of latitude and longitude, is often credited as the founder of mathematical geography. The use of this historical link for such a frequently recurring character within Mitchell's works reinforces the significance of his macronovel as an interconnected geographical terrain, in which Marinus' global travels are as extensive as her cross-textual ones. The historical source of Marinus' name as an ancient

---

[4] J. R. R. Tolkien's character Tom Bombadil appears in *The Fellowship of the Ring* (1954), is mentioned in *The Two Towers* (1954) and *The Return of the King* (1955), and in Tolkien's 1962 poetry collection, *The Adventures of Tom Bombadil*.

cartographer also resonates with the fictional character's own 'metalife of one thousand four hundred years', as mentioned in *The Bone Clocks* (440). Marinus notes that she's had forty previous lives, including 'four Chinese lives', at least one Russian life, and her time as Lucas Marinus in *The Thousand Autumns* (430, 462). This character's name and extensive global heritage mark her as deeply invested with global histories and temporalities, as will be discussed further in Chapter 3.

This hidden detail of an ancient mathematical cartographer as the source for Marinus' name – buried in a Twitter short story based on a single chapter of *Slade House* (which itself is arguably a spin-off of a single chapter of *The Bone Clocks*) – also evokes the almost mathematical structural precision by which Mitchell's expansive narrative geographies are organized. Bombadil notes:

> most Twitter followers think I'm a nutter, or a PR stunt, or a made-up character. […] these tweets=Hansel&Gretel's breadcrumbs thru a dark&perilous cyberforest, leading to–Y beat round bush?–world in a bottle. [*sic*]

As evidenced by the far-reaching textual links in this short story – including repeated references to a mysterious 'orison' which resurfaces in *Slade House* and *Cloud Atlas* – Bombadil's comments in this social media 'cyberforest' provide the reader with a profusion of references that lead further into the author's interlinked narrative terrain. Or, as Bombadil puts it, this tweeted micro-narrative – like many of Mitchell's short stories – is simultaneously its own 'world in a bottle', which in turn fits into an even larger narrative 'world in a bottle'.

As in 'I_Bombadil', Mitchell's short stories offer additional micro-narratives that remain continuous with the author's longer narrative worlds, while forging previously uncharted connections between the macronovel's many dimensions. Many of the short stories develop characters from Mitchell's novels. For example, in 'A Forgettable Story' (2017), a short story whose narrator's wish to be forgotten quickly turns into a 'curse', the narrator describes being friends with a couple called Satoru and Ai – who also feature in *Ghostwritten* – and who now have their own music shop, and an eight-year-old son. Similarly, while 'The January Man' and 'Hangman' (2005), both narrated by Jason Taylor, are based on early drafts of *Black Swan Green*, the novel's other characters continue to age and develop within the author's other short fictions, providing a 'community' of recurring voices. In a 2006 interview by Robert Birnbaum, Mitchell notes:

> twice a year I'm writing a short story narrated by one of the characters in *Black Swan Green* in the present day. When I am in my mid-40s I'll have enough for a book of them. ('David Mitchell')

Although Mitchell's *Black Swan Green* short stories have not yet been published as an anthology, these tales depict the interlinked futures of the novel's characters, enlarging both the macronovel's diegetic universe and the significance of *Black Swan Green*'s narrative legacy. These stories experiment with alternative possibilities for Jason's peers in their adult lives beyond the novel, illustrating the difference and diversity that can develop even from such a predefined locality, as a tour through some of these tales will show.

In 'Acknowledgements', the novel's child maths prodigy Clive Pike is depicted as a psychotic adult, escaping from a local care home after developing a theory of 'psychomigration' in which souls are free to shift bodies at will. It is only when read in light of *The Bone Clocks* and *Slade House* that Clive's fantasies become part of the supernatural soul-swapping depicted in these novels, although this is also a theme present in Mitchell's writing since the introduction of the noncorpum in his first novel, *Ghostwritten*. In the supernatural tale 'What You Do Not Know You Want' (2004), the narrator travels to Hawaii to search for a highly prized ceremonial knife and involuntarily commits *seppuku* – suicide by disembowelment – after becoming possessed by Wei, a mysterious woman in his hotel. In the tale, the narrator is briefly helped by Dwight Silverwind, a mystical character whose book is mentioned in *Ghostwritten*, and who also helps Holly to find her lost daughter in *The Bone Clocks*. Yet there is also a clairvoyant named Erin Silverwind in the short story 'Muggins Here' (2010) – a tale narrated by Pearl Bundy as she helps *Black Swan Green*'s Clive Pike back into his care home – providing a fictional connection between the worlds of *Black Swan Green* and 'What You Do Not Know You Want'.

Further extra-textual interconnections develop in the prose-poem 'Preface', in which an adult version of *Black Swan Green*'s Mark Badbury reminisces about climbing the quarry described in the novel with two of its characters, Clive Pike and Gary Drake. Mark also describes having an affair with Prudence Hanson, also mentioned in Mitchell's libretto for *Sunken Garden* as the artist whose work is showing at Portia Jacquemain's gallery, as well as in *The Bone Clocks* as the famous artist seen reading Holly's memoir *The Radio People*, causing its sales to rocket. In 'Dénouement' (2007), Jason's former headmaster, *Black Swan Green*'s Graham Nixon, is suffering from dementia, haunted by the death of a former student in his care. A forty-one-year-old Clive Pike narrates 'All Souls Day' (2010); tortured by his guilt at killing the terminally ill Mr Nixon during a psychotic episode fifteen years earlier (an episode that is also described by Clive in 'Acknowledgements'), the tale is told through the unconscious narrator's dream-like memories as medics fight to save his life after his suicide attempt.

Jason's neighbour Mr Castle makes an appearance in 'Judith Castle' (2007) as his daughter Judith returns to visit him and his new wife Marion. The tale also reveals the death of Judith's agoraphobic mother Mrs Castle, who is also referred to in *Black Swan Green*. 'Character Development' (2009) and 'An Inside Job' (2012) both feature Owen Yew, mentioned in 'Character Development' as the nephew of Tom Yew, who dies in the Falklands war in the novel. In both stories, Owen Yew is a traumatized young soldier who has returned from fighting in Iraq. In 'Character Development', he describes an army cover-up after he witnesses an unarmed, handcuffed doctor being shot in the head, while in 'An Inside Job' he describes the moments before breaking into his ex-wife's garden to see his son, revealing that he lost a hand in combat, and is now seeing a psychiatrist to help him cope with his anger. Published in 2009, 'The Massive Rat' features Nicholas Briar, one of the 'low-rank kids' from *Black Swan Green*, as a father and soon-to-be-divorced husband. This tale describes a moment of connection between Nicholas and his wife as they work together to remove a live rat – which turns out to be a trapped wren – from behind the fireplace, their fear of the unknown becoming shared relief at a simple truth revealed (156). In *Black Swan Green*, we also encounter Avril Bredon as a reliable, diligent student who hands out textbooks, gives a credible witness statement to the police, and is proficient in French (Jason remarks, 'I […] wished I was as good at French as Avril Bredon') (181); Avril Bredon later reappears as a professor in the short story 'The Siphoners' (2011).

In *Black Swan Green*, the reader is also introduced to Hugo Lamb, Jason's sociopathic cousin. Hugo's character is followed into adulthood in *The Bone Clocks*; in this novel, his social world is developed as a spin-off in which, as in *Black Swan Green*, its characters continue to develop across the macronovel. Dominic Fitzsimmons, the 'head honcho oarsman' from Hugo's canoeing team in *Black Swan Green*, appears in *The Bone Clocks* as one of Hugo Lamb's friends at Cambridge University (60). Also in Hugo and Dominic's university friendship group is Richard Cheeseman, whose foul review of Crispin Hershey's novel results in Crispin's revenge plot, in which he plants cocaine in Richard's suitcase before his aeroplane flight. By Crispin's own admission, his 'stupid prank' goes 'nightmarishly wrong' when Richard is caught and sent to prison (376). Mitchell's short story 'My Eye On You' continues Richard's narrative from the moment of its ending in *The Bone Clocks*, in which Richard, now released from prison, goes to take his revenge on Crispin in his university office. With Richard's gun pointed at him, Crispin closes his eyes and fears the worst – but when he opens them, Richard is gone. 'My Eye On You' begins from this moment, showing what happens to Richard following his decision to spare Crispin's life.

As this series of interconnected tales shows, Mitchell's short stories are situated in the continuous narrative world of his novels, strengthening their existing diegetic links, but also making unique contributions that remain undisclosed in any other part of his macronovel. However, when viewed as smaller island units within wider archipelagic groupings, these short stories cumulatively display their own patterning that hints at a larger design behind the world created. Approached as a body of works, they share fluid categories which merge genre with theme, in which Mitchell's adoption of genre conventions becomes tied to his use of subject matter, effectively joining the discrete narrative islands to create clusters with their own specific approaches to recurring Mitchellian textual preoccupations. The short story categories that will be discussed in this chapter are not exhaustive, or exclusive – a single work may fit into several of them – but viewed together they construct a narrative terrain which uses its expansive textual geographies to confront an ultimately unmappable force: the metaphysical, ethical world of belief itself.

The coming-of-age narrative as morality tale

As illustrated by Mitchell's many *Black Swan Green*-linked short stories, his narrative coming-of-age project is far more ambitious than a single novel. Of the twenty-six short stories discussed in this chapter, eleven directly develop characters from *Black Swan Green* (not including the implicit Silverwind connection between the novel and 'What You Do Not Know You Want'; the shared narrative worlds of Richard Cheeseman from

'My Eye On You' and *Black Swan Green*'s Hugo Lamb; 'Character Development' and 'An Inside Job', which both feature Owen Yew, the nephew of *Black Swan Green*'s Tom Yew; and 'A Forgettable Story', whose inclusion of *Ghostwritten*'s Satoru and Ai brings the short fiction into the same narrative universe as Neal Brose from *Ghostwritten* and *Black Swan Green*). *Black Swan Green*'s narrator Jason Taylor has not (yet) reappeared as an adult narrator in Mitchell's fictions. However, 'Earth Calling Taylor' (2010) is narrated by Ryan Taylor, Jason's alcoholic step-brother, as he visits their father in hospital, who notes that Jason is now 'a speech therapist in the Lake District' with children of his own. Of all of Mitchell's *Black Swan Green* short stories, 'Earth Calling Taylor' is the most directly connected to the novel's narrator, depicting the adult Jason visiting his father in hospital with his family, and ending with Jason's presence at his father's death. It also provides the most prominent link to its narrator at a specific moment in his wider coming-of-age tale: the moment that Jason's father dies, in which Jason's own primary familial role switches from son to father. In his 2006 interview with Robert Birnbaum, the author notes that he would like to write a piece in which Jason's world is narrated 'from the viewpoint of his 13-year-old son', stating that Jason 'will be reprised once in about 10 years' ('David Mitchell'). This comeback has not yet occurred. However, the cluster of *Black Swan Green* micro-narratives effectively creates a macro-narrative in which the novel's coming-of-age project is continued on a larger scale, becoming a stand-alone Mitchellian grouping which, chronologically, begins with thirteen-year-old Jason Taylor's struggles at school and continues into his own parenthood and loss of his father.

'In the Bike Sheds' (2012), a further interlinked short story, illustrates the wider thematic preoccupation of Mitchell's coming-of-age narrative project. This tale does not feature any of *Black Swan Green*'s characters – although sisters Maria and Grace Brubeck may be related to Ed Brubeck from *The Bone Clocks* – but its schoolyard setting and exploration of playground brutality make it a typical Mitchellian coming-of-age narrative. In the tale, the young narrator Heather O'Dowd accidentally witnesses a group of school bullies hanging a swastika-daubed effigy of their German teacher Mrs Weinstock. Having been sworn to secrecy, the final lines position its narrator at a moment of choice, in which she faces an ethical decision: to expose the perpetrators, or remain silent. By agreeing to say nothing, Heather realizes that '[t]he battle has already been lost'. However, after the bullies depart, the final two lines of the tale suggest that a larger war continues in the narrator's conscience:

> Coward, hums the warm and soupy dusk, coward, coward.
> Somewhere not far, Mrs Weinstock's having a quiet night in.
>
> ('In the Bike Sheds')

The tale's ambiguous ending allows for several different interpretations, framing the calm before the storm for Mrs Weinstock, and the unsettling proximity between Heather's and Mrs Weinstock's interconnected experiences as they unfold simultaneously at different locations. However, by emphasizing Heather's awareness of her own cowardice and the proximity of the victim at the end of the tale – rather than her relief at escaping Grace Brubeck's threats to break her fingers and blame her for the effigy – Mitchell effectively makes this coming-of-age story a form of contemporary morality tale, in which both narrator and reader are faced with the ethical consequences of personal inaction.[5]

Mitchell's other coming-of-age narratives also function as contemporary morality tales, emphasizing the importance of personal choices in shaping both individual and collective futures, and the far-reaching social consequences of ethical – or unethical – actions and inactions. This is visible in the myriad of thorny moral decisions that Jason faces in *Black Swan Green*. For example, his decision to expose his bullies is directly followed by his teacher's lesson on 'ETHICS', written in block capitals on the blackboard (337). As Jason recognizes, the word 'means morality', his observation followed by a lesson in which the teacher stresses the importance of personal actions to his classmates. However, each of Mitchell's individual coming-of-age narratives also replays the importance of personal choices on a cross-textual scale, a strategy visible within Mitchell's short stories and novels. By following *Black Swan Green*'s characters into adulthood, these narratives depict the long-term consequences of their individual ethical perspectives and actions. As Jason Taylor realizes at the end of *Black Swan Green*, '[t]he world's a headmaster who works on your faults [...]. Either you suffer the consequences of not noticing your fault for ever, or one day, you *do* notice it, and fix it', reflecting a process of ongoing ethical self-evaluation in which '[t]here are always more' shortcomings to improve on (368–9). Jason becomes a speech therapist, as discussed earlier, while Neal Brose, who relentlessly bullies Jason in *Black Swan Green*, becomes a soon-to-be-divorced money-laundering lawyer who suffers a breakdown (and dies) in *Ghostwritten*. Hugo Lamb's reckless sociopathic behaviour in *The Bone Clocks* is incipient in his childhood in *Black Swan Green*, as the young Hugo tries to trick Jason out of his pocket money, forces him to shoplift and coerces him into smoking stolen cigarettes (71, 78, 80).

This narrative strategy continues beyond *Black Swan Green*, also featuring in Mitchell's other novels. For example, *The Thousand Autumns* is also a coming-of-age novel, albeit a historical one; the tale follows Jacob de Zoet's struggles as he leaves home to forge a career in Dejima, and ends with his return as he leaves his own son in Japan. As Mitchell notes in a 2010 interview with Edward Champion, '[t]he book's just about these little, little compromises. [...] It's all fine step by step, but when they're compounded, that's how we cross a borderline into morality, or amorality' ('David Mitchell III'). Like the coming-of-age narratives in Mitchell's other works – including Eiji's struggle to take responsibility for his own future in *number9dream*, as will be discussed in Chapter 4 – *The Thousand Autumns* also simultaneously functions as an extended morality tale.

---

[5] The morality play and morality tale were popular entertainment forms in Europe from the fourteenth to sixteenth centuries, using allegorical characters to illustrate moral lessons. Rather than adhering to the original genre's conventions, including the use of personified virtues and vices, the term is applied more broadly here, without the older genre's conception of religious good and evil, but still using narrative to pose moral questions for the reader in a contemporary secular context, following each character's choices and actions, and their outcomes.

These ethical connections also continue across Mitchell's wider coming-of-age project. Several of his short stories function as stand-alone morality tales irrespective of their cross-textual implications, each depicting a specific moment in which the narrator – and subsequently the reader – faces an ethical dilemma. For example, in 'Character Development', *Black Swan Green*'s Owen Yew describes witnessing an unarmed doctor's unlawful killing during his time in the army. Originally published in the Amnesty International anthology *Freedom: Short Stories Celebrating the Universal Declaration of Human Rights* (2009), the end of the tale sees its narrator struggling with the decision to 'speak up' about what he has witnessed, asking his implied listener – and the reader – '[w]hat would you do?' (135). Similarly, at the end of 'An Inside Job', Owen finally tells his nine-year-old son Jimbo that he's decided to return to Afghanistan, relaying his difficult ethical decision to his son, who he refers to as 'my judge' (37). 'Muggins Here' also ends with its narrator facing a life-altering decision, ending with an unresolved personal choice: whether Pearl should return to her dead-end but secure supermarket job on time or disobey her boss and pursue her gift for helping others by taking an unexpected job offer as a carer. 'Earth Calling Taylor' ends with Ryan Taylor facing a similarly career-defining decision following his father's death: whether to accept a high-flying promotion as a financial portfolio manager or to turn down the offer and rejoin his recently bereaved family. A common theme emerges: the importance of personal responsibility and the collective consequences of individual ethical decisions, the 'right' choice often requiring an act of resistance against a real – or assumed – authority figure.

This exploration of a continuous world via an 'infinity of paths', as *Ghostwritten* puts it, in which characters are faced with a range of personal choices which each have their own ethical consequences, shares similarities with the multi-narrative strategy of the *Choose Your Own Adventure* book series (337). In the series, each tale places the reader as its protagonist, using second-person narration to create multiple narratives and endings, each of which depends on the reader's choices as the book progresses. In a 2015 interview by Loranne Nasir, Mitchell refers to one of these books as an influence for his own haunted house tale, *Slade House* ('David Mitchell'). Although Mitchell doesn't give the title or author in the interview, the narrative details that he provides ('set in a witch's house', one 'Sisyphean and dark' ending leaves the narrator picking up porcelain fragments forever) allow the book to be identified as *The Mystery of Chimney Rock* (1979) by Edward Packard. In the tale, the outcomes of its thirty-six endings are a mixture of chance – for example, taking a particular route through a mansion – and personal choice. One of the book's endings involves choosing whether to keep or give away a magical cat ('she is clearly not an ordinary cat; she seems like a creature in a dream') (62). The decision to look after it results in inheriting 'a quarter of a million dollars', while rehoming it sees the fortune pass to its new keepers (120–1). The tale's mysteriously recurring cat (which turns out to be lucky, like Mitchell's own resurfacing moon-grey cat), its structural fascination with the interplay between chance and choice (as in *Ghostwritten* and *Cloud Atlas*), and its role in shaping its readers' own engagement with moral decision-making (for example, in *Black Swan Green* and its many offshoots) suggest that the *Choose Your Own Adventure* novel's formative influence on Mitchell's writing extends beyond *Slade House* into his approach to these interconnected morality tales.

Mitchell's morality tales are not always cautionary; they also depict moments of possible redemption and efforts rewarded, providing a social commentary in which second chances and moments of hope can also spring from personal choices. 'The Massive Rat' ends with a redemptive moment between Nick and his soon-to-be ex-wife Lorna, in which their shared efforts to work together to free a trapped wren from behind the fireplace leave a glimmer of hope for a reconciliation, with Nick realizing in the final line: '[l]ooking at my wife's face, I wished that time would stop.' With this final realization as the tale's end, on a metafictional level, his wish comes true. 'Lots of Bits of Star' also ends with a redemptive moment for its narrator Leo, whose continued endeavours to communicate are rewarded as he successfully reveals the location of his mother's lost phone to his grandfather, his small-scale revelation greeted by surprise and praise from his family. Revealing the years of remorse that precede Clive's suicide attempt, 'All Souls Day' depicts his dream of a resolution with the late Mr Nixon while he is unconscious, in which he apologizes and is forgiven, the tale ending with another redemptive moment as this imagined reconciliation gives Clive a new-found will to 'fight' for his life (86).

'My Eye On You' also depicts a redemptive moment for its narrator, Richard Cheeseman, as he makes the ethical decision not to take revenge on *The Bone Clocks'* Crispin Hershey, instead opting to lead a life devoted to helping others. Having been framed by Crispin, Richard has been released from prison only to find that he has 'inoperable' cancer with 'eighteen months at most' to live (2). Continuing the fantastical atemporality of *The Bone Clocks*, as Richard begins a mental countdown to firing his gun at Crispin, time slows, and he is intercepted and given a second chance by an 'ancient woman' whose speed of time moves at a twelfth of standard time, rendering the world in slow motion (3). As time slows, he is given 'time to think again; to view from fresh perspectives' and realizes his 'collapse of judgement' (4). Choosing to accept the woman's invitation to follow her, he learns that she is a 'meanderer' whose slower pace of time means that she has lived for centuries, using her extended lifespan to help others: 'Do Unto Others. That's our code, she said, our key, our function. A cure-all for futility. Food for the hungry, drugs for the sick' (4–5). However, she is not immortal, and she tells Richard that she wants to pass her 'gift' to another who will continue in her place; with her slowed pace of time, Richard will effectively experience living for twelve times as long as his eighteen-month prognosis (5). He describes his subsequent journey to help others, which leads him 'to camps and favelas, hospitals and mosques; food-banks, slums' (6). As he travels, he realizes that 'ethics are grey and people build their private hells', drawing attention to the individual's capacity to help others, in spite of the absence of any concrete moral code (6, 2). Richard ultimately realizes that his 'conscience' is his 'constant companion', and learns to act on it to make positive interventions in the world around him: '[t]his world's in pain, there's too much fear and malice, murder, sorrow. Why add another gram?' (1).

Having demonstrated the narrator's ethical journey, 'My Eye On You' finally ends with a direct address to the reader. Richard reveals that his time as a meanderer is at its end, metafictionally breaking the frame of the narrative to address the reader. He prompts a continuation of his efforts outside of the text, having selected the reader to become the next civilian-turned-meanderer: 'I see compassion in your pain. Truth is, I've had my eye on you' (6). By showing the narrator's journey from would-be murderer to secular 'guardian angel', the reader is presented with a coming-of-age plot in condensed form, and is challenged to change their own actions (5). Richard's backstory from *The Bone Clocks* is rewritten as the precursor to a second chance, showing both the causality that leads to the character's decision to take another's life and the crucial moment of personal re-evaluation and ethical belief that leads to his compassionate actions. It is this experiential recognition of the individual's potential for change ('[n]one of us is born this way') that allows Richard to leave his own journey as an example to inspire others, in a Mitchellian morality tale that, again, ultimately urges real-world action (2).

In each case, the common approaches of these short stories highlight both an exploration of morality through the single moment of a potential turning-point, and a rewriting of genre as theme. Not all of Mitchell's wider morality tales are coming-of-age narratives, but his coming-of-age narratives function as morality tales, illustrating a moment of difficult ethical choices in which characters' decisions will have consequences that span far beyond the individual moment depicted. As Mitchell notes in a 2015 interview with Simon Mayo, 'teenage years are poignant times […] stuff that goes right – or stuff that goes wrong – in those years is nearly as formative on the rest of your life as your DNA' ('Radio 2 Book Club: David Mitchell'). This reflects an approach in which temporal development and ethical growth are deeply interlinked, just as the use of the coming-of-age genre signals an exploration of the ethical in the author's works – a process in which genre is rewritten as theme by embedding the subject matter within the narrative style itself.

Mortality and the supernatural

The themes of death and ageing – both composite themes of mortality – resurface throughout Mitchell's oeuvre, from the subject of suicide in *Sunken Garden* and the depiction of public and private grieving in *Wake*, to the exploration of the desire to escape death in *The Bone Clocks* and *Slade House*. Death and ageing are often interrelated in Mitchell's novels as part of a wider discussion of mortality; for example, in both *The Bone Clocks* and *Slade House*, the predatory atemporals steal souls in order to artificially prolong both their lifespans and their youth, while in *Cloud Atlas* Robert Frobisher describes his forthcoming suicide in terms of his reluctance to become a mass of 'dribblesome' tubes which 'no longer function' (489).

Death and ageing are also significant categories within Mitchell's short stories, with each of the tales in this thematic archipelago taking a different approach. In 'Dénouement', an ageing Graham Nixon is suffering from dementia, and describes being plagued by guilt years after the suicide of a former student. By contrast, personal guilt and self-doubt are strikingly absent in the short story 'Judith Castle', whose exploration of mortality opens with the death of its ageing narrator's lover, Olly. Throughout the tale, Olly's death is used to provide a comical portrayal of its 'busybody' narrator,

Judith, as she uses the news to garner sympathy (17). As she begins to believe the lies that she tells, her former one-time internet date soon becomes a late fiancé, and then a late husband, whose hit-and-run she embellishes as a 'long battle with leukaemia' and then as a death in Iraq (14). The initial news of the death at the narrative's start becomes a red herring twice over: first, as it becomes secondary to Judith's lies, and again as the story's end shows that the news was merely a decoy by Olly – who is alive and well – to escape from, as his brother Leo cruelly puts it, a 'tragic menopausal hag' who became obsessive after a first date (18). The tale's ending draws attention to Judith's loveless existence, her fantasies made more understandable in light of a traumatic childhood, and a father and daughter who continue to reject her affection (4). This short story takes several approaches to mortality simultaneously; while Judith's bizarre reaction to Olly's death drives the events of the tale, at the heart of the narrative is her own mother's death, which continues to haunt her family home. Revealed only in passing when Judith visits her father and his new wife Marion, the 'ghost' of Judith's mother and the implied years of depression, agoraphobia and verbal abuse from her husband haunt both Judith's childhood experiences and her adult family relationships: '[y]ou mustn't let Daddy intimidate you, or he'll turn you into Mummy' (13).

Whereas 'Judith Castle' takes a personal approach to the themes of death and ageing, 'The Siphoners' explores mortality from a wider societal perspective, depicting a scene from the speculative post-oil dystopia in *The Bone Clocks*. Set ten years earlier than the novel's events (although they both contain a bandit called Wyatt), 'The Siphoners' follows a retired academic couple, Avril Bredon and Bruno Toms, in 2033 as they struggle to survive in an isolated community in Ireland, during a near future in which – as Avril stops herself from saying to Bruno – '[e]conomics has eaten itself; dementia is eating you; climate change has crippled global agriculture' (132). Mortality is explored from physical, mental, ecological and economic perspectives as bandits roam the countryside, stealing the little fuel available and distributing 'suicide pills' to its elderly (137). In just a few pages, 'The Siphoners' imagines mortality from both individual and collective viewpoints, through a single elderly couple struggling to survive and the possible end of human civilization which they are witnessing. The story begins with a frame narrative in which Avril is reading a folk tale, which is interrupted and resumed at the end of the story. Both the folk tale and the 'real' events within the story warn against widespread social cruelty against the elderly, a message which has been lost in the speculative near future in which Avril and Bruno are encouraged to end their own lives.

'Variations on a Theme by Mister Donut' (2014) also depicts the end of life from several perspectives simultaneously, exploring a chance encounter that leads to an individual character's last moments; again, the topics of ageing and dementia are central. This short story presents a single incident from the interlinked viewpoints of six different narrators in a Japanese fast-food chain. Each of the tale's micro-narratives combine to describe the moment that Kaneda, an elderly man living with dementia, becomes violent, tripping over another customer and falling heavily to his death. As its second narrator, a kindly nurse who tries to help, remarks, it is the '[l]ittle things that speak of the big things', a Mitchellian micro-macro approach visible in this connected sequence of narrative vignettes (44). This compact story uses its polyphony of individual perspectives to raise the difficulties faced by survivors of the Fukushima nuclear disaster, the phenomenon of declining Japanese birth rates, and the problems facing its ageing population. Kaneda, misunderstood by those around him, is a living embodiment of his neighbour's observation that '[i]f you want to become the Invisible Man, just live to be eighty' (42). As in 'The Siphoners', mortality is examined from both individual and collective perspectives, linking the viewpoints of its characters to provide a social commentary on the shared difficulties of ageing. Just as the *Black Swan Green* cluster of micro-narratives shows the consequences of personal ethical decisions within a continuous narrative world, the linked narratives in 'Variations on a Theme by Mister Donut' also foreground the '[l]ittle things that speak of the big things', highlighting the shared causality between global events and the individual beliefs and actions that create them.

While not all of the short stories that discuss mortality use the supernatural genre, all of the author's works that feature the supernatural use the genre to provide a sustained exploration of mortality, again, conflating genre and theme. Mitchell's untitled short story from 'Six Shorts' (2015) forms part of an edited collection of fiction and non-fiction in *Freeman's: The Best New Writing on Arrival*; this tale is the fifth in a sequence of six shorts. Again, it is the '[l]ittle things that speak of the big things' in this condensed narrative, which uses an individual supernatural encounter to confront the aftermath of the atomic bomb dropped on Hiroshima during the Second World War, in order to discuss mortality from both individual and collective perspectives simultaneously. In the story, the first-person narrator – presumably Mitchell himself, from the autobiographical events mentioned – remembers an encounter with a ghost in 1996, while he 'was living alone on the ground floor of a musty old house at the edge of a Japanese town called Kabe in Hiroshima Prefecture' (19). This three-page ghost story begins with the description of the immediate aftermath of the 1945 atomic bomb, in which '[u]ncounted hundreds or thousands of people not incinerated in the blast made their way north along the Ōtagawa [river] in the vain hope of finding help' – the same river that runs behind the narrator's house fifty years later. His descriptions of its victims' burns, radiation poisoning and the 'hellish quantity of sudden death' are jarringly set against memories of the same area as a now 'peaceful spot', in which his youthful 'unlimited bank account of hours and days' spent gazing at the river is undercut by the inescapable haunting of the location by its history of mass fatality ('when I lived in or near Hiroshima, I couldn't not think about the A-bomb, daily').

The supernatural encounter at the crux of the tale, in which the narrator describes speaking to an apparition at the end of his bed, triggers a particular type of fear: not the 'fight-or-flight' fear of being attacked, or the 'helpless terror' of feeling an aeroplane 'lose power', but an 'ongoing, low-level electrical shock, and if it resided in any organ it was my skin' (20). The moment may be brief, but it creates an 'ongoing' connection with the invisible past of their shared locality, the tale depicting the intimately haptic 'shock' of the moment of domestic coexistence between the dead and living. At the end of the story, the reversal of their roles ('I half-hoped that I'd get another nocturnal visit […] but it seems that for him, one encounter with the transient was ample') recasts the living narrator as the displaced 'transient', while the ghost has no desire to repeat his 'encounter' with the living (21). By reversing their roles in this tale of human mortality, the ghost and its history become re-established as the permanent inhabitants of its setting. Conversely, the narrator becomes the intruder as this individual supernatural encounter is used to confront Hiroshima's atomic bombing, re-situating its victims at the centre of an ongoing cultural narrative that remains defined by such unresolvable fatalities (21).

The supernatural events in 'What You Do Not Know You Want' are far more sinister than the encounter in 'Six Shorts'; here, the supernatural is again used to discuss mortality, interlinking genre and theme. As the story progresses, the tale depicts the moral path by which its narrator's supernatural possession and forced suicide is precipitated by his own materialistic desires: his desire to possess women through casual sexual encounters ('I haven't wanted a woman as much as I wanted Grace'); his desire to possess the knife and the 'quick cash' that he can make from it; his loveless desire to marry a model who is only marrying him for his money ('Nightingale is attracted to my assets [...] and I am aroused by hers'); and the desire to possess his own death by controlling it ('[o]nly suicides can truly say, *Yes*, here *is my reason for dying, crafted by* my *hand according to* my *logic*') (26, 13, 19–22, 15). His 'livelihood' is built on exploiting the deaths of others for material gain: the objects of his trade are '[t]he sunglasses shading Oppenheimer's eyes' and the 'bullet that liberated Ernest Hemingway' (28), while the knife he seeks is 'worth as much as Princess Diana's damaged diamond Rolex [...]. More than the telegraph pole James Dean drove into', in a macabre currency of violent death and material fetishization (24). At the tale's end, the narrator's excessive material desires prove fatal, revealing this as another Mitchellian morality tale, as well as one of mortality. Having finally tracked down the valuable knife, his yearning to possess the source of his death is destroyed by his involuntary *seppuku* as both objects of his desire (supernatural femme fatale Wei and the knife) turn against him, his morbid desire to control his death overturned by its gory reality.

As a tale about materialism and mortality, when read through a Buddhist framework, 'What You Do Not Know You Want' ultimately evokes the second of Buddhism's Four Noble Truths (which will be discussed further in Chapter 2), an ethical sequence of causality whose second truth states that suffering stems from desire. In this case, the narrator's agonizing death is self-inflicted. Just as the narrator is 'jubilant with the promise of wealth' brought by material possession of the knife, his body is ripped apart by it (30). Wei watches him die, 'feeding' on his suffering, and delivers the tale's deathly punchline to the narrator: '[t]his is what you did not know you want' (31). As its title suggests – and its final line reinforces – 'What You Do Not Know You Want' is a tale about wanting: a contemporary secular parable which uses the theme of mortality and the supernatural genre to highlight the negative consequences of excessive materialistic desire. As in the supernatural plots in *Slade House* and *The Bone Clocks*, the overwhelming desire to control – or escape – the moment of death becomes an obsession, a theme shared by Mitchell's Twitter fictions 'The Right Sort' and 'I_Bombadil'. In each of these supernatural short stories, the narrators unwittingly become pawns in a larger war as the supernatural is used to discuss mortality as the ultimate materialistic desire – the desire to possess one's own body beyond its natural expiration – highlighting the human cost of materialism at its most excessive.

'Acknowledgements' takes a similarly supernatural approach to the desire to escape death, its narrator Clive Pike's pursuit of 'psychomigration' described as 'transferring a mind trapped in a dying body into the brain of a younger, healthier, host'. Clive's explanation, when read in light of Mitchell's wider macronovel, provides a crucial link between the wandering soul of the noncorpum in *Ghostwritten*, Enomoto's soul consumption in *The Thousand Autumns*, and the wars over the right to immortality in *The Bone Clocks* and *Slade House*. Another short story, 'The Gardener', again uses the supernatural to discuss mortality, albeit from a very different approach. Reflecting on 'half a lifetime of memories' in his back garden, the narrator only mentions that he was buried under the magnolia tree at the tale's end, a revelation that prompts the reader to reconsider the everyday domestic scene that he describes not merely as a moment of peace at sunset, but, when understood through the viewpoint of this friendly spirit, as the rewards of a life well spent.

As this cluster of short stories demonstrates, Mitchell's use of the supernatural genre is consistently linked with his exploration of mortality; again, genre is rewritten as theme. As evidenced in 'What You Do Not Know You Want', published in 2004, and 'Acknowledgements', published in 2005, this rewriting of genre as theme which uses the supernatural as a vehicle to discuss mortality has featured in the macronovel for far longer than the first sustained appearance of supernatural content in *The Bone Clocks*. This early usage is visible in his first novel with *Ghostwritten*'s noncorpum, and also with the early publication of 'Mongolia' (1999) as a stand-alone short story, featuring this disembodied spirit in its quest to understand its origins, a journey that brings it back to the moment of its own bodily death.[6] Viewed only from the perspective of his novels, Mitchell's textual universe appears to become more invested with the

---

[6] This separate publication of *Ghostwritten*'s Mongolia chapter is included here as a stand-alone short story for several reasons. In its publication as 'Mongolia' in the anthology *New Writing 8* (1999, ed. Tibor Fischer and Lawrence Norfolk), it is categorized with 'Short Stories', rather than 'Extracts from novels in progress' (vii–viii). The latter initially seems more fitting; however, its inclusion as a self-contained short story – and the publication of *Ghostwritten*'s most supernatural chapter, rather than one of its more realist sections – emphasizes the significance of the supernatural and reincarnation in the author's writing. Each version contains key differences; the short story appears to be more heavily edited and condensed, with some details and poetic phrasing omitted. For example, 'Sometimes language can't even read the music of meaning' in *Ghostwritten* becomes the far-less-nuanced 'Impossible', in 'Mongolia' (165; 523). However, the most significant differences affect its narrator, whose name is given as merely singular and plural in *Ghostwritten* ('what I am: *noncorpum*, and *noncorpa*'), but is renamed and gendered in 'Mongolia' ('my kind: *noncorpi. Noncorpo*, for male, *noncorpa*, for female'), followed by the final adoption of the masculine '*noncorpo*' in the short story, in contrast with *Ghostwritten*'s gender-neutral version (172; 531, 560). Its multilingualism and recognition of language's limits ('I know eleven languages, but there are some tunes that language cannot play') are also omitted from *Ghostwritten* (165). The noncorpum is also portrayed less sympathetically in 'Mongolia'; *Ghostwritten*'s tentative 'I have my gifts: I am apparently immune to age' becomes a more egocentric assertion in 'Mongolia': 'I am gifted: I am immune to age' (172; 530). Similarly, the noncorpum's admission in *Ghostwritten* that '[t]he only thing I can say for myself is that after my first host I never killed again. I cannot say I did this out of love for humanity' becomes more abrupt and sinister in the short story: 'I stopped short of killing, though not from a love of humanity' (170; 528). The differences create two simultaneous *noncorpa* in the macronovel: the more humanistic version in *Ghostwritten* and its subtly insidious twin in 'Mongolia'.

supernatural as it progresses. However, to include the author's short stories in a discussion of his macronovel is to reveal the use of the supernatural genre to explore the theme of mortality as a recurring technique – both in his later novels, but also throughout his short fictions.

Mitchell's metafictions

A further cluster of Mitchell's short stories extends the metafictional narrative games that run throughout the author's oeuvre. Patricia Waugh offers a useful definition of the genre in *Metafiction: The Theory and Practice of Self-Conscious Fiction* (1984): '[m]etafiction is a term given to fictional writing which self-consciously and systematically draws attention to its status as an artefact in order to pose questions about the relationship between fiction and reality' (2). Mitchell's novels deliberately expose 'the relationship between fiction and reality' with self-reflexive comments and metafictional devices. For example, as mentioned earlier, in *Cloud Atlas* Timothy Cavendish asserts that he 'disapprove[s] of flashbacks, foreshadowings, and tricksy devices' – all of which feature in the novel – while *number9dream*'s repeated narrative false starts in its first chapter repeatedly undermine the reader's trust in the narrator and in the act of storytelling itself, as will be discussed in Chapter 4 (152). In *The Bone Clocks*, literary agent Hal Grundy argues that a 'book can't be a half fantasy any more than a woman can be half pregnant', a remark that takes on greater significance when disproven by the book's next chapter – its unexpectedly fantastical fifth section (348). By inserting these acknowledgements of each book's inner workings, these metafictional intrusions repeatedly draw attention to the fictional nature of each narrative and the authorial decisions behind its construction, foregrounding the act of storytelling alongside the story itself. Each of these experimental narrative insertions deliberately disrupts readerly expectations in order to draw attention to the assumptions inherent in the reader's own process of narrative interpretation, effectively forcing the reader to confront their own interpretive role in their wider reality as constructed by narrative – a reality which is subject to the same assumptions and biases as the process of readerly interpretation.

As Mitchell's short fictions demonstrate, this approach is by no means confined to his novels, as the author again uses experimental and metafictional techniques to blur the boundaries between the fictional and the world outside the tale. 'The Right Sort' and 'I_Bombadil' use Twitter as an experimental medium that combines high artifice – an Oulipian 140-character writing constraint that truncates each narrative into micro-episodes – with the immediacy of a format typically used for instant media communication.[7] 'I_Bombadil', the longer and more recent of the two Twitter fictions,

---

[7] A further Mitchellian Twitter character can be found in the @CrispinHershey Twitter feed, published in twenty instalments during May and June 2015, several months after the September 2014 release of *The Bone Clocks*. However, due to its lack of significant new content and narrative progression, and its diegetic inconsistencies, it is not included as a stand-alone short story in this study. The fictional purpose of Crispin's Twitter feed is ostentatiously to promote his new book, 'Echo Must Die'. After incorrectly reproducing its name in four separate tweets as 'Echo and Shouter' –

goes further in its integration into the multimedia narrative strategies available to the platform. Its self-confessed 'tech-head' narrator posts interactive links to other web pages, music videos, hashtags and photos, tweeting other fictional characters, and referring to contemporary politics. He also has his own share of metafictional asides; as he tells his love rival Carl, 'have u never heard of an "UNRELIABLE NARRATOR"? JustFGoogleIt'. Further experimentation with micro-storytelling formats continues in 'Acknowledgements', in which the opening acknowledgements section of Clive Pike's book turns into a sprawling stand-alone short story, while 'Preface' uses a prose-poem format to tell a story set entirely on its narrator's drive home, its congested pathways, traffic jams and roundabouts running parallel to the narrator's complicated home life (15).

'A Forgettable Story', a short piece published in airline Cathay Dragon's in-flight magazine *Silkroad*, also uses a fictional journey to explore the intersected pathways of lived experience, using metafictional techniques to tailor the tale for its intended audience. Written from the point of view of a mysteriously forgettable passenger on the very next seat, it begins with a direct address to the reader: 'Hi. I see you're reading *Silkroad*. […] if you're thinking, Oh no, I'm stuck next one of those nut-job passengers who'll jabber non-stop until we land, don't worry'. The narrator gradually reveals his past, explaining that while being chased by the yakuza, his desperate wish to be forgotten backfires, meaning that he becomes instantly forgotten by all who meet him. The self-reflexive ending leaves the reader with an eerie forecast: 'Even a natural-born listener like you is going to forget me. […] I'm off to the bathroom now, and when I get back to this seat, I'll just be a stranger sitting next to you on a plane'. Also using the motif of travel, the genre-straddling 'Imaginary City' (2011) is a creative essay whose extensive fictional content merits its inclusion alongside Mitchell's short stories. The tale functions as an exploration of Jean Baudrillard's assertion in 'Radical Exoticism' (2002) that '[t]ravel […] is the only way we have of feeling that we are somewhere', and that 'in a new city' our 'body rediscovers how to look' (151). In 'Imaginary City', Mitchell reworks the concept by imagining this 'new city' before he experiences it, using the tale to capture his 'imaginary Vancouver' before his plane lands and the city's 'reality' destroys this 'mashed simulacrum of a not-yet-visited city'.

'The Earthgod and the Fox' (2012) is Mitchell's translation of a short story by Kenji Miyazawa, part of an experimental collection that sees Mitchell's original translation from Japanese to English again translated into Spanish. The resulting translation is then translated back into English, and then into Urdu, each stage of rewriting undertaken by a different author. The story is a fable about the rivalry between an 'insincere' fox and an 'honest', if tempestuous, earthgod for the affections of their mutual friend, 'a beautiful female birch tree' (59). Published a year before Mitchell's translation of Naoki Higashida's *The Reason I Jump* (2013), Mitchell remarks in his translator's note to 'The Earthgod and the Fox' that this text was his 'first foray into translation', and that he chose this tale 'because of the story's beauty, brevity, sadness, and its allegorical elasticity'

---

presumably the original name of Crispin's novel, left uncorrected – the Twitter feed fizzles out with an acknowledgement of the 'deliberate mistake', but no explanation. While the error may not be Mitchell's, it unfortunately destroys the suspension of disbelief required for a fictional Twitter feed; after just six further tweets, the feed remains inactive at the time of writing.

(76). Mitchell's participation in such a project is a testament to his writerly fascination with the theme of translation, and the perils and rewards of communication across language barriers.[8] Although the author's translation of 'The Earthgod and the Fox' does not itself employ metafictional techniques, its role as the first story in a sequence of interlinked translations unsettles the notion of a single authoritative version of a text, emphasizing the multiplicity of different ways of reading and rewriting the same narrative, and exposing the act of storytelling as an unreliable act of translation.

'The Siphoners' also uses metafictional techniques to introduce several nested narratives set within the larger frame of an ancient folktale, which is itself presented as part of an academic collection of translated cultural narratives. The short story begins and ends with this academic 'magnum opus', which introduces a translated 'wisdom-narrative' (129–31), before jumping from this text to the 'real' world as its reader is interrupted, and we enter the world of the monograph's authors (131). Their translation – which begins the short story – is prefaced with:

> the following modification of the Thoms-Bredon Cluster 14b (*On the Inadvisability of Geronticide*) [Narr. Ukbar Kishkiev /male /c.75 yrs /farmer /Guurjev Valley /1999 /trans. Avril Bredon and Bruno Thoms from Kurdish] illustrates best how an archetypal wisdom-narrative [...] can be mutated by the host-culture's folkways, topography and belief-hierarchies. (129)

This densely academic paratext, complete with citations and translators' notes, is the preface to a far simpler '[o]nce upon a time' folktale, which is in turn interrupted as the narrator breaks off from rereading her anthropological study to begin the central narrative of her own lived experience. It is this experiential narrative which in turn forms the innermost diegetic layer of the tale, before Avril – and the reader – returns to the second half of the translated folktale at the end of the story, its profusion of metafictional layers drawing attention to the inherent fictionality of each narrative register, whether folktale or academic monograph.

David Mitchell's fascination with frame narratives is also visible in his novels, for example, in the nested layers that form *Cloud Atlas*, and in the multiple narrative intrusions, diversions and stories-within-stories in *number9dream*. However, 'The Siphoners' offers the author's most condensed use of metafictional framing, its exploration of geronticide paralleled in each narrative layer. By foregrounding the folktale as part of a text translated by the narrator and her husband, 'The Siphoners' emphasizes their roles in the construction of each narrative, and also the individual's role in interpreting the series of events in which they find themselves. Here, Mitchell uses metafictional techniques to emphasize the problematic nature of authorship in both textual and real-world events. The moral of Avril and Bruno's 'archetypal wisdom-narrative' is that the elderly should be valued, but this academic 'magnum opus' is useless in a future in which its ethical message has been lost in practice.

---

[8] These also feature in Jacob de Zoet's comical struggles to work with translators in *The Thousand Autumns*, and in Mitchell's joint translations of *The Reason I Jump* and *Fall Down 7 Times Get Up 8*, their source texts themselves a form of translation that describes the experiences of an individual with autism for an unfamiliar readership.

Throughout this cluster of experimental short stories, metafictional techniques encourage a readerly questioning of the act of storytelling and the relationship between narrative and reality. Self-reflexive insertions continually unsettle the macronovel's 'real' diegetic events with reminders of its fictionality and, in doing so, present a textual universe which, like our own, is being continually constructed through narrative. In doing so, Mitchell's experimental narratives become metafictional parables, encouraging the reader to draw their own parallels between the process of narrative creation in both fictional and real worlds. These experimental stories fulfil a didactic function, deliberately exposing the reader to the components of narrative creation – whether an unreliable narrator, frame narratives or storytelling as translation – each intrusion undermining diegetic belief in order to effectively encourage greater narrative distrust and interpretive agency in the world outside the text.

David Mitchell's short stories and the building blocks of belief

To approach Mitchell's short stories as archipelagic clusters is to enter a fictional world in which genre is rewritten as theme: the realist coming-of-age narrative as morality tale, the supernatural narrative as mortality tale and the experimental metafiction as narratological parable. Linking each of these short story categories together reveals a metaphysical terrain that, cumulatively, depicts the normative Western components of faith from a secular perspective. The coming-of-age narrative used to demonstrate the path towards ethical maturity is an approach traditionally found in Judeo-Christian religious parables to chart the formative years of a prophet, for example in the New Testament's accounts of Jesus' experiences before crucifixion and ascension. The use of the supernatural as a means of understanding individual and collective mortality is presented in many religious belief systems as the foundational faith in the continuity of life after death, for example in the cross-denominational Christian belief in heaven and hell and Islamic belief in the afterlife or *akhirah*. The metafictional focus on narrative complicity in creating and sustaining our understanding of reality foregrounds the importance of individual belief itself in maintaining religious practice; after all, a religious narrative can only be instrumental as far as it sustains the belief that it refers to a sacred and unshakeable truth.

Each of these short story categories foregrounds a topic traditionally dealt with by religion; yet these approaches feature in secular tales that are otherwise removed from traditional Judeo-Christian contexts. By bringing each of these narrative preoccupations to the fore in his short stories, the macronovel cumulatively interrogates each of the secular components of belief, creating a world whose metaphysical exploration is as important as the physical movements of its characters across its narrative topographies. Like Avril's folktale in 'The Siphoners', Mitchell's world creates its own 'folkways, topography and belief-hierarchies' in order to dissect the components of the 'archetypal wisdom narrative' that sustains and justifies religious belief – which, viewed within a secular context, forms one of the failed grand narratives that Jean-François Lyotard suggests are widely mistrusted in *The Postmodern Condition: A Report on Knowledge* (1984). Moving forward from this postmodern dismissal of religious belief as part of a Lyotardian 'incredulity towards metanarratives', Mitchell's exploration of the individual components of faith examines their secular function when divorced from their traditionally religious associations (xxiv).

This pattern emerges from viewing Mitchell's islandic short stories as thematic and genre-based archipelagic groupings, which together create an ethical map of belief. However, the importance of personal belief as the precursor to collective action is also demonstrated in his novels. For example, Adam Ewing's final realization at the end of *Cloud Atlas* is that

[i]f we *believe* that humanity may transcend tooth & claw, if we *believe* divers races & creeds can share this world [...], if we *believe* leaders must be just, violence muzzled, power accountable & riches of the Earth and its oceans shared equitably, such a world will come to pass. I am not deceived. It is the hardest of worlds to make real. (528)

This statement of belief in the act of belief itself effectively forms the novel's ethical conclusion. In this passage, 'belief' and '*believe*' occur seven times over eighteen sentences; its repetition and italic emphases stress the importance of such belief in an ethical future to the reader. However, as Adam recognizes – and the chronological end of the novel illustrates – such a future 'is the hardest of worlds to make real', as shown by the dystopic futures in the novel's innermost sections. The noun 'belief' has both theological and non-theological definitions in the *Oxford English Dictionary*, as a 'mental conviction' that can refer to 'trust that the believer places in God', as well as a secular 'trust, dependence, reliance, confidence, faith'.[9] Although Adam's narrative is set within a Christian historical background, the novel exposes the oppressive practices of the Christian missionaries, presenting Adam's final declaration of belief as part of a secular, humanist conception of shared reliance ('races & creeds can share this world'), co-dependence ('the Earth and its oceans shared equitably') and confidence ('such a world will come to pass'), rather than an expression of religious piety. As Adam argues, such belief is the precursor to ethical action ('[w]hat precipitates acts? Belief.'), his affirmation presented as the first step towards turning theory into practice. While the novel doesn't offer a simple solution, this secular conception of belief is presented as an essential component for change within a personal and collective ethical framework that seeks to create meaningful action on a global scale.

While the novel's chronological trajectory is dystopic, its narrative ending offers hope for change amid the seemingly insurmountable difficulties that humanity faces in the novel. As Mitchell notes in a 2004 interview by Eleanor Wachtel, '[h]umans do destruction remarkably well, but we also do give grounds for hope [...] it is a matter of survival that we nurture this hope' ('Cloud Atlas'). Such momentary 'grounds for hope' as the belief in the possibility of change and human 'survival' are scattered throughout Mitchell's works as small-scale acts of resistance, often carried out with little hope of success, but undertaken nonetheless. These small-scale acts of resistance echo the philosophical approach of Albert Camus' concept of revolt, developed in his 1942 essay 'The Myth of Sisyphus'. Examining existentialism, Camus

[9] 'belief, n'. *OED Online*. Oxford University Press, December 2015. Web. 5 January 2016.

discusses the legend of Sisyphus, condemned to endlessly push a rock up a mountain only to see it fall again. Camus finds freedom in the inherent absurdity of existential action, stating the 'only truth […] is defiance', by which the act of 'revolt gives life its value' (55). However, what distinguishes the Mitchellian small-scale act of resistance from Camus' revolt is that whereas 'revolt is the certainty of a crushing fate, without the resignation that ought to accompany it', Mitchell's acts of resistance maintain hope for change within an unknowable future (54). The Mitchellian act of resistance shares Camus' rejection of 'resignation', but not its 'certainty'; where Camus' revolt is always futile ('[i]t is not aspiration, for it is devoid of hope'), Mitchell's remain hopeful, if only for the reason that what is almost certain to happen has not yet occurred, and, as such, is still at stake.

For example, in *Cloud Atlas*, Sonmi notes that her *Declarations* are based on 'ethics, denounced at my trial'; as in Adam Ewing's narrative, Sonmi shares his ethical desire to confront social oppression (363). While she recognizes that her uprising is part of a staged resistance used to manufacture corpocratic control, and therefore offers little hope for change, it is her personal belief in change that sustains her, realizing that her so-called 'blasphemies' will enable future resistance by being 'reproduced a billionfold' (365). Similarly, in *number9dream*, Eiji makes the ethical decision to use an email virus in an attempt to expose yakuza injustices, despite realizing that his involvement is 'suicidally dangerous' (339). When he receives a letter from one of the yakuza's victims telling him about 'men who abduct women and children to harvest their organs', its sender tells him to '[a]ct with your eyes open, as your conscience dictates […] for countless others, past, present and future, I implore you to act' (338). Eiji later receives the email virus software from his friend Suga, but is initially concerned about the moral implications of using it, telling Suga: '[s]preading junk mail to tens of thousands of people doesn't strike me as especially ethical' (347). However, Suga reminds him that as a method of resistance, it can be ethically repurposed: 'Miyake can spread whatever message of joy and peace he wants.' Later, Eiji sees 'an ad for an Internet advertising company', whose image motivates him into action:

> [a]n apple tree grows from a computer chip, and from its computer chips fruit grow more apple trees […]. The forest grows out of the frame and invades the advertising spaces either side. […] an enormous idea occurs to me. (363)

This rhizomatic image models the spread of Eiji's email virus, which he eventually uses to expose the yakuza's criminal operation. However, it also offers a model for the process by which theory becomes practice, showing the replicated knowledge – commonly symbolized by the apple in biblical artistic representations – breaking out of its expected area into new territories in the outside world.

The image of the advert escaping its expected remit replicates the process by which Eiji's knowledge becomes an act of resistance, depicting the moment in which theory breaks the boundaries of its cognitive remit to become practice. Eiji's subsequent ethical action in deploying the email virus to spread the information, carried out with the hope that it will bring change in a distant future, is another example of a Mitchellian act of resistance against a far larger organization, as will be discussed further in Chapter 4. Mitchell's structural decision to prioritize smaller narrative units, as discussed earlier, aligns with this prioritizing of small-scale, belief-driven actions over larger oppressive authorities in his works. Approached ethically, in each case it is the '[l]ittle things that speak of the big things', each individual action multiplied by its far-reaching consequences. By making this causality visible, this rewriting of genre as theme offers a narrative parallel of the process by which the metaphysical can take form and belief can become infrastructure.

Beyond the 'World-Machine'

To give a real-world example, these small-scale, belief-driven acts of resistance, conducted against a larger organization against overwhelming odds, can be seen in recent acts of protest by disempowered Tibetans against the Chinese occupation of Tibet. Perhaps the most extreme examples are visible in the numerous acts of Tibetan self-immolation that continue to occur, with the deaths of 153 monks, nuns and laypeople recorded since February 2009, according to the International Campaign for Tibet.[10] Self-immolation is an act of resistance that Janet Gyatso identifies in 'Discipline and Resistance on the Tibetan Plateau' (2012) as 'a forced witnessing of a spectacle that aspires to delegitimize the state' in its public visibility, in which 'some monks and nuns are using their discipline [...] to signal instead the devastation of their world'. Each individual act forms part of a collective struggle; as Gillian G. Tan notes in 'The Place of Hope in Acts of Protest and Offering' (2012), '[m]odern self-immolation is thus characterized by the fact that one acts on behalf of a collective cause'. In the face of Chinese state control, such individual acts are unlikely to bring about meaningful change, and are quite literally suicidal – as such, the grounds for hope for the individual protestor are virtually non-existent, to be found only in a future that they will never see. As Tsering Shakya argues in 'Transforming the Language of Protest' (2012), self-immolation 'is an act that is meant to coerce concessions. But in China, as in all authoritarian regimes, it is unlikely to lead to such an outcome', referring to 'a sense amongst the Tibetans of the impossibility of change under the current regime'. However, in spite of this recognition of the 'impossibility of change', the spectre of the Tibetan Buddhist nuns, monks and laypeople who have burned themselves to death in protest continues to haunt the Chinese government's attempts to bring the Tibetan people under state control. If humanitarian intervention is to be brought about, it will be due to the collective and continued efforts of the Tibetan people to regain agency – and, without condoning the loss of life involved, the real-life influence that such individual, small-scale acts of resistance have to play is by no means negligible in attracting the international scrutiny necessary for meaningful change.

This chapter has entered the 'World-Machine' of Mitchell's short stories, approaching these as archipelagically linked narratives to reveal the essential contributions of these

---

[10] Statistics taken from International Campaign for Tibet website *SaveTibet.org*, accessed 13 April 2018. See http://www.savetibet.org/resources/fact-sheets/self-immolations-by-tibetans/.

works to the author's continuous narrative world view. By reading the mandala as itself a form of metaphysical map of a belief-driven world that aims to create personal change in its participant, and taking a comparative approach to its methods of world-building, the individual's role in creating meaningful change becomes central to an understanding of Mitchell's narrative world as an ethically engaged social system. Unlike traditional cartographic representations, neither the macronovel's nor the mandala's world views create a 'faithful' picture of the world as it is. But neither aims to. Instead, each prioritizes the narrative pathways, experiential interconnections and belief-driven actions that form perhaps the only grounds upon which we can approach our labyrinthine, unfathomably complex world as a shared entity.

What differentiates the Tibetan Buddhist mandala from a work of religious art – again, a concept which remains shaped by the paradigms of Western Christianity – is its experiential and participatory nature, a structure created to help the individual simulate the experience of a metaphysical journey through an ethically informed world, in a process that is entirely dependent on individual belief and personal action. It is these elements of belief and ethical action that this chapter's 'reading' of the mandala brings to an understanding of Mitchell's fictional works. Reading a conventional map requires cognitive interpretation, but not belief or action; however, for its participant, the mandala generates such belief-driven action, as individuals visualize navigating its labyrinthine structure in order to internalize and act on the principles symbolized within it. This process uses belief to create action, both in the internal visualization of the journey, and in its intended real-world impact on the participant's behaviour on applying the Buddhist teachings of wisdom, compassion and knowledge represented therein. As a symbol of Tibetan diaspora, it continues to inspire further secular action, its ongoing creation overseas a visible reminder of the tens of thousands of displaced Tibetans in exile, as the next chapter will discuss.

As speculative fiction that imagines its own global past and future, David Mitchell's macro-scale narrative world depicts the global consequences that can grow from small-scale belief-driven actions, exploring the secular components of such belief as the precursor to change. The effects of such actions often remain immediately invisible, as in the real world – for example, as with Tibetan self-immolations, individual acts of resistance that stem from horrifying desperation. But whether a schoolchild reading Sonmi's heretical catechisms in a distant future, or international academic discussion of suppressed Tibetan protest, the collective multiplication of such responses can lead to real-world actions which contain the potential for change, no matter how remote or removed they appear. By depicting individual strategies of resistance in which it is the '[l]ittle things that speak of the big things', the macronovel's micro-narratives collectively amplify otherwise marginalized perspectives, revaluing even the smallest-scale belief-driven acts as potential agents of global change within an interconnected world-system.

2

'Right Yourself as Best You May': Voicing Tragedy in David Mitchell's Libretti

Having devoted the first chapter of this book to Mitchell's critically neglected short stories, this chapter turns its attention to the author's libretti.[1] Any study that seeks to understand the entirety of David Mitchell's macronovel cannot afford to critically overlook his writing for the stage. His libretti for the operas *Wake* (2010), composed by Klaas de Vries and with an electronic score by René Uijlenhoet, and *Sunken Garden* (2013), composed by Michel van der Aa, remain almost entirely overlooked in criticism of his works, with no published criticism devoted to discussing both of these works as integral parts of his fictional world at the time of writing. This chapter aims to redress this, discussing both of Mitchell's libretti as integral components of the macronovel. While each libretto requires no previous knowledge of the author's works, they feature several interconnections with Mitchell's wider fiction, offering visualizations of the reincarnated character of Marinus and the blurring of realism and fantasy explored in several of his novels. The inclusion of the author's writing for the stage within a wider discussion of his fiction also prompts a deeper understanding of his approaches to mortality, and his reworking of Buddhist philosophies of samsara or the cycle of life, death and rebirth. As the author notes in an interview with Jasper Rees, all his works are 'chapters in one bigger über-novel', and 'the libretti are also chapters in the über-novel'; as such, to ignore Mitchell's libretti is to leave part of this 'über-novel' unread ('10 Questions').

At the heart of each opera lies a shared focus on mortality and grieving; *Sunken Garden* explores the theme of suicide, while *Wake* was commissioned to commemorate the Enschede fireworks disaster in the Netherlands, which occurred on 13 May 2000, killing 23 people and injuring nearly 1,000. Drawing on interviews with the original cast of *Sunken Garden* and *Wake*'s composer alongside their performances, this chapter demonstrates the methods used by each opera to engage with personal and collective tragedy, each libretto using a secular reworking of Buddhist approaches to death and

---

[1] An earlier version of part of this chapter appears in the edited collection *David Mitchell: Contemporary Critical Perspectives*, eds. Wendy Knepper and Courtney Hopf (London: Bloomsbury, forthcoming), reprinted courtesy of Bloomsbury.

rebirth in order to prioritize shared hope, collective remembering and the potential for healing over grief.[2]

Having taken a comparative approach to the macronovel and the mandala as forms of ethical world-system, identifying the vital role of Mitchell's short stories in building his post-secular world, this study now shifts its focus from text to performance in order to examine these ethical worlds in action. To do this, this chapter discusses the libretti in performance alongside a specific type of mandala: the Tibetan Buddhist sand mandala. When constructed for international public displays, each sand mandala effectively becomes an act of performance, a form of cross-cultural translation in which a local tradition becomes transformed from private religious custom to cultural export for secular consumption. However, it also becomes a form of performative act, its ritual dismantling an enactment of the Buddhist philosophy of impermanence. Viewed as a form of drama, created by a highly skilled cast-of-sorts performing a carefully rehearsed craft and, in doing so, evoking a wider cultural awareness of Tibetan diaspora, the sand mandala becomes a fitting vehicle by which to discuss the secular reworking of Buddhist philosophies in each of Mitchell's libretti, each opera using public performance to confront and accept human impermanence.

The reincarnated character of Marinus reappears in *Sunken Garden* as Dr Iris Marinus, where she suggests that an understanding of Tibetan Buddhist mythologies is particularly relevant to the opera's mythology. Describing its garden setting as a metaphysical space connecting life, death and rebirth, she explains, '[i]f Life be Day and Death be Night, then [...] the Soul must cross the Dusk that lies between. Where we stand was built inside the Dusk', clarifying her cryptic description with: 'I'd make more sense in Sanskrit; or better yet, Tibetan' (5). As will be explored further in this chapter, Marinus' comments evoke the twilight stage of samsara, or the cycle of life, death and rebirth, as described in the Tibetan Buddhist text *The Tibetan Book of the Dead* and depicted in the Bhavachakra or Wheel of Life mandala (see Appendix F). Interpreted in light of her assertion that the languages of Tibetan and Sanskrit would make her description of this realm 'make more sense', this chapter elucidates how these operas redeploy Buddhist philosophies of samsara and impermanence – each vital concepts within the Bhavachakra and sand mandala's worldviews – to find secular regenerative approaches to tragedy, situating each of these works as integral facets of Mitchell's post-secular fictional world.

---

[2] Tragedy is defined here as '[a]n event, series of events, or situation causing great suffering, destruction, or distress, and typically involving death (esp. on a large scale or when premature)' (see 'tragedy, n'. *OED Online*. Oxford University Press, June 2016. Web. 15 June 2016). As such, this chapter discusses each libretto's representation of and response to human tragedy, rather than the formal classical conventions of theatrical tragedy as developed in ancient Greece, in order to investigate the role of Buddhist influences within these works. As George Steiner notes in '"Tragedy," Reconsidered' (2004), '[a]s our literatures evolve, the concept of tragedy extends far beyond the dramatic genre', and it is this fluid and evolving cross-cultural approach to tragic events that this chapter engages with (1).

Building the sand mandala

Before progressing further into the resonances between the mandala's world view and the approaches of Mitchell's libretti, it is important to contextualize the sand mandala's remediation when created in diaspora for public audiences, where it undergoes a form of translation from its traditional Tibetan origins. The Tibetan sand mandala is generally formed by applying coloured sand or powder to a flat surface using hollow, funnel-like hand-held tools called *chak-purs*, in a process that can take many days to complete. The *chak-pur* holding the sand is long and thin, with tiny vertebrae-like ridges, and acts as a form of 'pen' with which to apply the sand. Having been filled with sand or powder, it is held with one hand and a thin metal rod, or another *chak-pur*, is rubbed along its ridges with the other hand, the vibration causing grains of sand to flow from its narrow 'nib', allowing its holder to 'draw' lines of sand onto the surface to create the mandala's intricate patterns (see Appendix D).

Sand mandala creation is traditionally accompanied by complex symbolic rituals that take years to learn. As Barry Bryant details in *The Wheel of Time Sand Mandala* (1992), the Kalachakra sand mandala initiation rites include mudras or symbolic gestures, sacred items, costumes, blindfolds, meditation and visualizations (133–76). It is a form that creates its own ending; as noted by Jung A. Huh in 'Mandala as telematic design' (2010), its completion is marked not by the final grains of sand laid, but by its dismantling: 'only when the mandala is swept apart is it complete' (29). Once completed, the mandala is ritually swept up and its sands scattered into a nearby river or ocean as a blessing, a symbolic display of the fundamental Buddhist concepts of compassion and impermanence. As Susan M. Walcott observes in 'Mapping from a Different Direction' (2006), '[p]ublic constructions of mandalas are seen as bestowing benefits upon observers, at whatever level they are able to understand the process', a sacred act intended to engage both its makers and onlookers, whether or not they are familiar with its symbolism (81).

Although mandalas may be painted, or constructed from other materials such as rice, stones or jewels, their formation from coloured sand is widely recognized as 'the most common form of the mandala', as Walcott also notes (83). However, the Tibetan Buddhist sand mandala remained largely unknown to the Western public until the final decades of the twentieth century, as part of the secret teachings of Tibetan Vajrayana, or Tantric Buddhism. Tenzin Gyatso, the fourteenth Dalai Lama, notes in his foreword to *The Wheel of Time Sand Mandala* that while 'most are related to tantric doctrines that are normally supposed to be kept secret', he has 'encouraged a greater openness in the display and accurate description of mandalas' to counter incorrect speculations 'among people who viewed them simply as works of art' (xii). Following the Tibetan spiritual leader's exile from Tibet during the uprising of 1959, in which the Dalai Lama fled to India under fear of arrest by the Chinese government, the Tibetan Buddhist sand mandala has become part of a broader cultural diaspora by which the Tibetan heritage and political situation have been brought to the attention of the Western public.[3] The

---

[3]   The struggles of the Tibetan people under the Communist Party of China's regime have been widely documented. Robert Goss' 1997 essay, 'Tibetan Buddhism and the Resolution of Grief', reports that over 100,000 Tibetan Buddhist monks have been killed and 6,000 monasteries destroyed, while Barry

Dalai Lama's first visit to the United States took place in 1979; Bryant notes that the first Tibetan sand mandala to be publically created outside its traditional context was 'presented as a cultural offering' on a later visit in June 1988, an event that 'attracted hundreds of New York artists' and 'the simply curious' public, and would become the first of many sand mandalas created internationally for secular audiences (31).

Both its non-religious viewers and the language used here to describe the sand mandala are significant. In embarking on a journey into the Western gaze, the sand mandala shifted from esoteric local practice to international 'cultural offering', in a subtle transformation from private religious custom to cultural export for secular consumption. An otherwise hidden Tibetan tradition entered the global stage; public mandala-making was to become part of what Meg McLagan identifies in 'Spectacles of Difference: Cultural Activism and the Mass Mediation of Tibet' (2002) as a wider 'vigorous campaign for international support' as a result of a decision from the exiled Tibetan government to seek wider publicity for their cause, a move that would transform 'a tiny handful of exiles' into 'a transnational political movement' (93).

Subject to diverse interpretations from its non-native audiences, the sand mandala continues to be constructed internationally as a public offering, both for non-religious onlookers and in Buddhist ceremonies, at times becoming an act of political intervention within its context. For example, this can be seen in its 2002 construction in Washington DC's National Museum of Asian Art by the Drepung Loseling Monastery in response to the previous year's 9/11 attacks, following the Dalai Lama's call 'on Tibetan Buddhists throughout the world to offer healing through [...] the sacred healing arts', as well as in the creation of the sand mandala by the Tashi Lhunpo Monastery at the House of Commons in the UK in 2008, before the Dalai Lama's address ('Tibetan Healing Mandala'). With the Dalai Lama having spoken on secular matters at Western parliaments, including visits to the European, Swiss and Melbourne parliaments in 2008, 2009 and 2013 respectively, and again to the European parliament in September 2016, the creation of the sand mandala within political settings is a form of silent intervention and cultural remembering in a political space, a secular reminder of a displaced community bringing local action to a global stage. The recognition of this 'cultural offering' as more akin to a dramatic performance than a work of art is a distinction that acknowledges the crucial role of the actions of its creators. For example, in the 2014 protests against the shooting of an unarmed black teenager in Ferguson, Missouri, the participation of Tibetan Buddhist monks in exile from the Drepung Gomang Monastery in India, originally visiting to create sand mandalas as part of their Sacred Tibetan Arts Tour, itself became a high-profile political act as media coverage of the mandala-creating monks at the protest spread, as noted in Leah Thorsen's 2014 article ('Buddhist monks').

Bryant notes in *The Wheel of Time Sand Mandala*, '[t]he Chinese occupation of Tibet resulted in the deaths of a reported 1.2 million Tibetans from military activities, starvation, torture, and the hard labor inflicted during long-term prison sentences' (377–8; 110). In *The Buddhist Religion* (1996), Richard Robinson and Willard Johnson emphasize the 'unusually cruel, insulting and thorough' suppression of Tibetan Buddhism in the 1950s and 1960s, in which '[n]uns were raped, monks were tortured [...]. Prayer books were used as shoe linings, mattress stuffing, and toilet paper; printing blocks for religious books were used to pave roads' (296).

The complex cultural, political and social context behind the sand mandala raises many issues for its interpretation outside of its traditional setting. The endorsement of mandala creation and discussion in the Western world by the Tibetan spiritual leader and government raises problems of critical approach for an unfamiliar public encountering the sand mandala for the first time. Part religious artwork, part visual scripture and – when its accompanying rituals are conducted outside of its traditionally closed sacred setting – part public performance, the sand mandala encounters issues of definition. As Kay Larson wrote in 'Sands of Time' (1988) for *New York Magazine*, one of the media outlets covering the emerging creation of the sand mandala for the American public:

> [t]o the New York art world, which is used to measuring the spiritual value of a Van Gogh in millions of dollars, a sand mandala is an extraordinary thing: collaborative, ephemeral, unsigned, ahistorical – contrary in every way to 'art' as we mean the word. (64)

The sand mandala's sacred functions and impermanent form continue to problematize its categorization for unfamiliar international audiences; its inseparable rituals and integral process of assembly and dismantling complicate any attempt to approach this structure as a conventional artwork.

Created for secular Western audiences, the sand mandala's construction suggests the spectacle of dramatic performance, its unfolding sequences and circular form effectively echoing the performance space of theatre in the round. Discussing the seven-foot-wide Kalachakra sand mandala created at the American Museum of Natural History in July 1988, Bryant remarks that '[m]ore than 50,000 people came to see the exhibition', the sand mandala becoming a crowd-pulling dramatic spectacle constructed by four monks from Namgyal Monastery from the Tibetan community in exile in Dharamsala, India (33). As Bryant also notes, 'at least three years of technical artistic training and memorization' are required in Namgyal Monastery before its monks are allowed to construct a sand mandala; on the international stage, its makers become a highly skilled cast-of-sorts performing a long-perfected, meticulously rehearsed craft (196).

Filming the action, the gallery's 'overhead robotic camera [was] both comfortingly familiar and educational' for its American audience; Bryant also highlights that '[f]our large TV monitors placed throughout the gallery' provided live footage of the mandala at a 400 per cent magnification (33). Constructed from non-conventional materials for its US viewers, its traditional components – chalk, thread, coloured sand or powder, paper, *chak-purs* and a flat board – became props to be expertly manoeuvred by the now-televised 'performers'. Bryant describes how the process, traditionally taking six days, 'was slowed down so that the visitors could experience the entire process in detail over a period of six weeks'. Shown both live and in an artificially enhanced and slowed version, the camera directing the viewer's gaze to selected details on screen, the sand mandala's assembly became a form of mixed-media drama for audience consumption. In the eyes of the unfamiliar viewers, the monks assembling it effectively became actors in a carefully choreographed and tightly rehearsed performance. In its sacred context, the sand mandala is not inherently a work of performance art. But outside of its traditional setting, staged, translated and received as cultural export for international audiences, it arguably becomes one.

David Mitchell's libretti in performance

What critical avenues does a comparative approach to the sand mandala's 'performance', then, open up for Mitchell's libretti? The initial critical uncertainty surrounding the sand mandala's multimedia form serves as a fitting point of comparison with Mitchell's writing for opera, whose multimedia performances have struggled to gain recognition as integral parts of the author's textual universe. Each libretto is also a form of dramatic translation from its textual origins when in performance, with its own problems of reception; within literary criticism, these works remain far more elusive than his novels. Mitchell's libretti have also encountered their own issues of classification and reception, their comparative physical inaccessibility in performance contributing to their lack of critical recognition as a valuable part of his oeuvre (along with the fact that they are relatively recent productions – *Wake* was originally performed in 2010, and *Sunken Garden* was most recently performed in 2018 at the time of writing). To date, *Sunken Garden* and *Wake* have received very few mentions in literary criticism, perhaps the most significant being in Holly Rogers' 2016 essay discussing an aria from *Sunken Garden* ('The Public Will Only Believe the Truth If It Is Shot in 3D'), and Sarah Dillon's 'Introducing David Mitchell's Universe: A Twenty-First Century House of Fiction' (2011). Dillon's essay briefly compares the libretto for *Wake* with Mitchell's approach to his entire oeuvre, suggesting that the grid of nine rooms in its staging represents 'Mitchell's twenty-first-century house of fiction', complete with a 'cast of characters who move from room to room, unencumbered by divisions in time and space' (6). Dillon's essay productively suggests *Wake*'s relevance within a wider critical discussion of his works. This chapter investigates this further, examining both libretti alongside Mitchell's wider works and investigating their resonances with the Tibetan Buddhist sand mandala, using its structural, mythological and ethical perspectives to inform a reading of each opera's post-secular approaches to world creation.

As there is so little literary critical discussion on Mitchell's libretti, it is worth briefly contextualizing them here.[4] Both operas have Dutch composers and English-language libretti – *Wake* also has an opening Latin requiem – and each includes sung text and spoken dialogue. *Wake* was composed for a national commission to commemorate the Enschede fireworks disaster, and was first performed at the Nationale Reisopera in Enschede in May 2010, on its tenth anniversary. The opera begins with a requiem sung by a chorus on stage, with the opera's main characters in tableau in the foreground. The second act then depicts a cross-section view of the lives of nine characters and their

---

[4]   *Wake*'s libretto and score are available from Donemus, while *Sunken Garden* is published by Boosey & Hawkes. A documentary on *Sunken Garden* and excerpts from the opera can be found at https://vimeo.com/vanderaa/videos; see http://www.paulkeogan.com/wake-nationale-reisopera.html for photographs of Wake by Marco Borggreve, accessed 19 April 2018.

dramatic counterparts in a single apartment building, using a grid of nine video screens to show the action within each apartment unfolding simultaneously on screen and stage (see Appendix E). The building's occupants include the apartment's owner, Dot, and her housekeeper; Vita, a biology student; Otto, a guilt-ridden accidental hit-and-run driver; and Marinus, his mysterious friend 'cursed and blessed' with premonitions. *Wake*'s composer Klaas de Vries emphasizes how act 2 presents 'very condensed information' through the apartment rooms, shown on nine screens behind the live actors, depicting their everyday lived experiences with this 'small drama background' ('Interview by Rose Harris-Birtill'). Shared domesticity gives way to collective tragedy in act 3, an electronic soundscape interwoven with the characters' spoken experiences as they describe the night of an unnamed disaster. No single narrative is allowed to dominate, the cacophony of overlaid voices suggesting the many victims' experiences competing for recognition. The final act – a requiem with spoken interludes – uses a collective chorus on stage, as the voices of a shared memory, the living and the dead take part in what de Vries imagines as an 'impossible conversation' on the disaster's aftermath, ending the performance with a choral rendition of William Wordsworth's poem, 'A Slumber Did My Spirit Seal'.

Sunken Garden was first performed by the English National Opera at London's Barbican theatre in April 2013, with sold-out runs at the Holland Festival in Amsterdam in June 2013, and Lyon's Théâtre National Populaire in March 2015, and further performances at the Dallas Opera, Texas, in March 2018.[5] The opera begins as documentary-maker Toby secures funding from wealthy patroness Zenna Briggs to investigate the disappearance of Simon Vines. Filming interviews with Simon's landlady, Rita, and friend, Sadaqat, Toby tracks down another missing person, Amber Jacquemain, whose disappearance seems mysteriously connected. Toby's film project quickly becomes his obsession. As Courtney Hopf suggests in 'The Stories We Tell: Discursive Identity Through Narrative Form in *Cloud Atlas*' (2011), 'nearly all of Mitchell's characters are storytellers of some kind', and *Sunken Garden* is no exception (133). Toby is another Mitchellian storyteller, an 'artist' constructing a fragile identity through visual narrative (1). He finally finds the missing people – and himself – lured into the magical sunken garden of Zenna, a supernatural soul-stealer who extends her lifespan by feeding off grief-stricken victims inside her lair, its colourful setting depicted using 3D film. Helped by Dr Iris Marinus, a psychiatrist from Sadaqat's mental hospital, Toby escapes by jumping into Zenna's body in the real world, while Simon and Amber must decide whether to leave and live with their personal tragedies, or remain in the garden forever. While *Wake* depicts an unspecified disaster, creating a more universal approach to tragedy and regeneration, *Sunken Garden* explores a specific facet of human tragedy: why an individual becomes 'disengaged from life' – as Toby puts it – to the point of deciding to end it, and where alternative solutions may lie (1).

While each opera requires no previous knowledge of the author's works, the libretti feature several links to the macronovel, creating an uncanny sense of déjà

---

[5] For performance information, see 'Sunken Garden' on the Dallas Opera website at https://dallasopera.org/performance/sunken-garden/, accessed 9 August 2018.

vu. Alongside the reappearance of Marinus in each opera, other reincarnations from Mitchell's fiction include a lucky cat that always seems to survive. Although cut from the final performance, in *Wake*'s original libretto text, Willem's tomcat survives the 'explosion' and, as the stage directions note, is 'heard throughout most of the music of Act 3' (10). Other appearances of the fortuitous feline include the moon-grey cat that reveals Orito's escape route in *The Thousand Autumns*, appearing again in *The Bone Clocks* as the 'only reason' why Ed is saved from an explosion, shielded from the blast as he bends to stroke a mewing 'moon-grey cat' (228, 271; 259). Similarly, in *number9dream* Eiji's 'transdimensional' cat 'knows the secret of life and death' and seemingly 'came back from the dead' (44, 59, 370), while *Slade House* also features a moon-grey cat that comes back to life (7, 9, 194), and *Black Swan Green* also contains references to a mysterious moon-grey cat (46, 174, 291, 357).

Other references that strengthen the intertextual dialogue between Mitchell's libretti and the macronovel include the recurring motif of moths, used as a symbol of human fragility and shared vulnerability, providing a counterpart to the trope of predacity. Mitchell has spoken widely in interviews on the importance of predacity in his works; for example, in his 2010 interview with Adam Begley he notes, '[o]ne of my serial-repeating themes is predacity', while in a 2010 interview on *Cloud Atlas* with Harriet Gilbert he again remarks, 'this theme of predacity, of one thing eating another [...] appears in my other books a lot in other forms' ('David Mitchell, The Art of Fiction'; 'David Mitchell – Cloud Atlas'). The recurrent moth symbol in Mitchell's writing approaches predacity from one of these 'other forms' – that of victimhood, a theme explored in both *Wake* and *Sunken Garden*. In *Sunken Garden*, Zenna's victims are 'so easily torn, like moths', while Marinus describes Zenna's human prey as 'hundreds of moths. Ghosts without memories', evoking the ancient Greek mythological association of the *psyche*, or soul, with the moth or butterfly (6, 5). This recurring use of moths to represent a shared, anonymous victimhood is reinforced by the images of moths in the opera's video footage, which hint that Amber is to become one of these moth-like victims. Before she disappears, the audience sees 'I hear moths' spelled in magnetic letters on her fridge, while a sticker resembling a moth is visible in the background of the nightclub toilet cubicle she visits, and she traces the outline of a large moth tattoo across her lover's back, foreshadowing her eventual fate as Zenna's victim (2).

Number9dream also contains early references to moth-like fragility. The inclusion of '[a] moth drowns in the moonlight' emphasizes Eiji and Anju's vulnerability as they discuss their separation from their mother, while '[t]he last moths of autumn swirl around a stuttering light' appears later in the novel as Eiji's mother's abandonment is again discussed (59, 348). In another reference to moth-like fragility, *Cloud Atlas*'s Zachry watches lost holographic footage of Sonmi as a translucent 'ghost-girl', noting that '[p]apery moths blowed thru her shimm'rin' eyes'n'mouth too', reinforcing both the vulnerability of her holographic form and the fragility of her archived narrative (277). In *The Thousand Autumns*, '[a] moth careers into a candle flame' and is crushed by Ouwehand as he discusses the difficult prospects for Orito's future as an unmarried woman in eighteenth-century Japan (62). This association of moths with victimhood is also visible in Mitchell's 2004 short story, 'What You Do Not Know You Want', as Wei asks the narrator, '[d]id those black moths you [...] used to dismember ever complain, "Why me?" No, they blundered into the wrong room, at the wrong hour' (31). Here, the moths are associated with silent and arbitrary suffering, emphasizing the tale's supernatural power struggle as the narrator becomes manipulated into the role of victim.

A further shared motif – an otherworldly underpass – features in both *Sunken Garden* and *Wake*, as well as in *The Bone Clocks*, signifying a shift between real and imagined worlds in all three works. In *Sunken Garden*, a journey through a door in an underpass marks the beginning of a descent into the fantastic world of the sunken garden, as well as the start of the opera's 3D film footage, creating a visual shift into the hyperreal. In *The Bone Clocks*, Holly's journey 'down into the underpass' marks the beginning of the tale's descent into a realm between fantasy and realism, and the narrator's strange coming-of-age into the world of the supernatural (43). This motif resurfaces in *Wake* with 'grief' imagined as a three-dimensional space that interrupts reality, 'a hole that keeps the shape of what is lost', referred to as a transitional 'underpass' into another realm (2).

A similar reference to a twilight passage between two worlds is the use of the 'Dusk' in *Sunken Garden*. This deathly space is explained by Marinus as a passage between the living and the dead: '[i]f Life be Day and Death be Night, then that electricity you call the Soul must cross the Dusk' (5). This early concept from *Sunken Garden* would be developed in *The Bone Clocks* as 'a beautiful, fearsome' and tangible terrain 'between life and death', and also reappears in Mitchell's 2011 short story 'The Gardener' (430). This brief real-time narrative is set at the moment of dusk in which the narrator reflects on 'half a lifetime of memories', the tale beginning as '[t]hat shimmering gong of a sun has less than a minute to go' and ending just as 'the sun has gone'. It is only at the tale's end that the narrator reveals he is a deceased onlooker, the twilight similarly representing a place of transition between two worlds, as in Mitchell's use of the underpass as a passage between the real and the fantastic. Here, however, the 'dusk' signifies a more specific passage between two states of being: the moment of transition between life and death.

Another trope that connects Mitchell's libretti with his macronovel is the concept of life and death as a contractual bond. In *Sunken Garden*, Marinus notes, '[w]e are born already bound by a contract with life', its terms 'non-negotiable' (7). This metaphor is extended throughout the opera; its first clause is '*You Will Suffer*' and its second '*You May Hope*', while in the final scene Toby sings of 'Life's Third Clause: *It Must End And Shall*', the contract's final term envisaged as death itself (7, 9). This image of a legal contract that binds life and death also surfaces in *Wake*'s final act, in a conversation between the living, dead and memory, who remind the audience of life's universal 'small print': '[a]ll that is here shall cease to be' (4). This image of life and death as an inseparable part of a prearranged contract is also imagined extensively in *The Bone Clocks*, in which even immortality comes with 'terms and conditions' (407).

Rebirth in David Mitchell's libretti

By revisiting these images, Mitchell creates his own system of linked motifs that augment his works with their own symbolic intra-textual meanings. The macronovel is full of these shared echoes, yet it is significant that this particular cluster of images – the lucky cat, the moth as victim, the underpass as gateway between reality and the fantastic, the dusk as realm between living and dying, life and death as a contract, and the shared character of Marinus – are those that reappear in the libretti. Potential recurring tropes that could have been featured include, for example, an atlas of clouds, Russian dolls, bats, zoos or any number of narrative-hopping characters from the macronovel. Dealing with arbitrary survival and victimhood (cat and moth), the inseparability of life and death and the passage between them (contract and dusk), a journey between the known and unknown (underpass), and Marinus' reincarnations as a healing force in each opera, the resurfacing of these tropes in the libretti cumulatively evoke a specific Buddhist philosophy represented in the Tibetan mandala's visual scripture: samsara.

A concept that refers to the cycle of life, death and reincarnation, samsara is symbolized in the Bhavachakra mandala, also known as the wheel of life, whose images depict the causes of this endless cycle of rebirths (see Chapter 4). The teaching of samsara is an essential part of the Buddhist philosophies that the mandala depicts; as Rosita Dellios notes in 'Mandala: From Sacred Origins to Sovereign Affairs in Traditional Southeast Asia' (2003), the mandala 'seeks to impart the view of the illusoriness of the world (or 'samsara')' as a 'lesson' to be learnt (3). Once realized, as Dellios argues, '[s]uch a state, in Buddhist thought, permits a greater openness to life' and 'a compassionate disposition to others'; accepting the cycle of death and rebirth helps the individual to give up 'the delusion of a self' and develop 'a life-affirming practice of helping others to avoid suffering and to fulfil their potential'. Samsaric acceptance aims to transform perception of the self as a fixed, central and independent entity into a realization of the self as a transitory part of a collective identity in constant flux, viewing mortality as a single facet of a larger system – just as each opera depicts a world view that extends beyond individual tragedy to envisage collective strategies to adapt, recover and keep on living. The concept of samsara is also represented by the sand mandala's medium, its impermanent form a microcosm of the processes of birth and death embodied by its assembling and dismantling. As Rueyling Chuang notes in 'Tibetan Buddhism, Symbolism, and Communication Implications in the (Post) Modern World' (2006), the final scattering of its sands 'symbolizes the Tibetan Tantric Buddhist worldview that nothing in life is permanent' (20). In the impermanence of its form, and the Buddhist concepts represented within it, the Tibetan sand mandala provides a visual embodiment of samsara, its ritual assembly and limited lifespan becoming a symbolic performance of the human condition, the visible script to an ongoing metaphysical drama.

In drawing together this particular group of recurring samsaric motifs, *Wake* and *Sunken Garden* extend their approaches to human tragedy through a shared exploration of life and death as cyclical processes, reworking Buddhist philosophies of reincarnation within a secular format to offer humanistic approaches to healing after tragedy. In a 2013 interview by Emma Pomfret, Van der Aa describes the sunken garden as 'a new dimension between life and death' ('The Future of Opera'), while *Wake*'s composer, Klaas de Vries, comments on 'the whole frame of the piece being circular', noting of *Wake*'s cyclical 'carousel' structure: 'it was a kind of carousel which turned around three times, and all these little dramas in every room' ('Interview by Rose Harris-Birtill').

This depiction of life and death as part of an interlinked cycle – '[a] theme both ancient and modern', as Toby puts it in *Sunken Garden* – becomes a dramatic vehicle that allows each libretto to move towards acceptance, evoking the samsaric within a secular format to present a humanistic rather than overtly religious approach to tragedy (1). *Sunken Garden* also begins and ends cyclically. Toby's journey ends when, having shed his 'old life' and been reincarnated into Zenna's body, he accepts the inevitability of his own death, realizing '*It Must End And Shall*'; his samsaric journey comes full circle by the opera's end (9). Similar reminders of life and death as cyclically bonded also feature in *Wake*. For example, Ursula the midwife, a character for whom birth and death are a daily reality, realizes that her existence, both experientially and bodily – 'life' and 'organs' – is a mere 'loan', and 'what is loaned is repossessed' in a samsaric return (2). This concept resurfaces throughout the opera. Tom, playing a video game, sings, '[t]he dead don't want to stay that way', death's finality undermined by the possibility of rebirth, while McCroom remarks that 'a nebula is both the blasted open urn of a dead star' and 'the womb and the seeds of new stars', again, part of a larger system of beginning, ending and rebirth.

The Tibetan Buddhist mandala depicts its own 'circular world system', as described by Ken Taylor in 'Cultural Landscape as Open Air Museum' (2003); in the fragile and impermanent medium of the sand mandala, this 'circular world system' is effectively framed by its own creation and destruction (54). Using a similarly fleeting depiction of a microcosmic universe, each of Mitchell's libretti in performance briefly creates a self-contained world, its creation overshadowed by the threat of its destruction for the individuals that inhabit it – both metatheatrically by the performance's end and by the potentially fatal forces that threaten each character (54). While *Sunken Garden* uses a cyclical structure, beginning and ending the performance with Toby's individual tale, which frames the collective stories of Zenna's suicidal victims, *Wake*'s samsaric cyclicality begins and ends with a general chorus which frames the lives of individual characters in the central acts, moving from collective to personal tragedy and back again. As Klaas de Vries notes in interview, this dramatic cyclicality is reflected in the second act's 'carousel of different styles musically', leading to an ending in which 'the music of the fourth act is much more unified' ('Interview by Rose Harris-Birtill'). This musical unity echoes the plot's cyclical return with a sense of aural resolution, the mass chorus on stage at the opera's beginning and end contributing to a final visual collectivity in which all of the opera's inhabitants are depicted as part of this cyclical world-system.

Just as the sand mandala's final dismantling is expected from the first moments of its assembly, *Wake*'s basis in real-life events meant that its Dutch audiences came to each performance aware of its fatal ending. At its Enschede performance, many audience members would have been personally affected by the disaster it represented. In interview, de Vries highlights the importance of taking a more 'general' and 'universal' approach to a 'politically very tricky' and '*omstreden* [controversial]' commission, ending not with a specific depiction of the Enschede disaster, but a representation of the events immediately before and after an unspecified disaster ('Interview by Rose Harris-Birtill'). He emphasizes that beginning and ending with a commemorative chorus rather than individual characterization 'brought everything to kind of a reconciliation, as far as that is possible with such serious loss'.

As in *Sunken Garden*, this sense of 'reconciliation' is imagined through the opera's secular suggestion of death as part of universal, cyclical return to a pantheistic Wordsworthian 'slumber', rather than a single incomprehensible tragedy; as Vita and McCroom note in *Wake*'s final act, '[t]he universe uncrumples, indifferent and unfussed' (4). The final act's choral rendition of 'A Slumber Did My Spirit Seal' draws attention to the timelessness of these processes, ending its response to a twenty-first-century tragedy with an eighteenth-century narrative, in which the line '[r]olled round in earth's diurnal course' reinforces a humanistic sense of the end of life as part of a cyclical return to a larger force. Ending with this collective chorus, rather than individual characterization, death is presented as governed by forces only intelligible on a vast scale, a perspective shared by Buddhist philosophy and Wordsworth's Romantic pantheism alike – just as the sand mandala's individual grains only become part of a single ordered world view from a wider viewpoint.

'I'd make more sense in Sanskrit, or better yet, Tibetan'

In *Sunken Garden*, the reincarnated character of Marinus hints that an understanding of Tibetan Buddhist mythologies is relevant to her past. She explains the garden as 'the Dusk that lies between' life and death, noting, 'I'd make more sense in Sanskrit; or better yet, Tibetan' (5). This remark is never explained; the libretto script has her interrupted by Toby. However, this remark leaves the audience with the suggestion that there are greater forces at work within the opera's mythology. In a 2015 interview, Claron McFadden, who played the role of Dr Iris Marinus in *Sunken Garden*'s first three performance runs, and whose portrayal of Marinus was subsequently written into *The Bone Clocks*, explains that in performance she interprets this remark as symptomatic of Marinus' past as a 'reincarnated healer' ('Interview by Rose Harris-Birtill'). She notes:

> the references to Sanskrit, the Buddhistic references [...] the way I've interpreted it is that Sanskrit was in one of her lives, that's what she actually spoke, so she's quite an old soul, as it were. So it's not so much that she's studied these things, but that she's actually been them.

Although this line has been cut from the 2015 version of the opera to create a shorter performance – as Claron McFadden notes, from a director's perspective the enigmatic phrase 'raises more questions than it answers' – it forms an integral part of Mitchell's original libretto, drawing attention to the plot's resonances with Tibetan Buddhism, and suggesting that the opera's mythology is far more extensive than a two-hour performance can reveal.

Drawing on Tibetan Buddhist mythologies, *Sunken Garden* and *The Bone Clocks* both confront a Western cultural reluctance to discuss the inevitability of dying, a theme also explored in *Wake*. Mitchell remarks in a 2014 interview with James Kidd that he read *The Tibetan Book of the Dead* while writing *The Bone Clocks*, and that when it comes to a cultural contemplation of death, '[i]t's right that we think about it and do what we can to prepare for it. I don't like this aspect of our culture that sees death as the taboo' ('Time and again'). Popularly known in English as *The Tibetan Book of the Dead*, the *Bar-do Thos-grol Chen-mo* or 'Great Liberation by Hearing in the Intermediate States' provides guidance through death and rebirth. Its transmigration mythology is embedded in *The Bone Clocks* as Marinus explains that after death her kind 'wake up as children forty-nine days later', this period between death and rebirth spent in 'the Dusk' – illuminating Marinus' reference to 'the Dusk' in *Sunken Garden* (413, 461). The influence of *The Tibetan Book of the Dead* is clearly visible; in this text, the state between life and death is a dusk-like 'greyness, like autumn twilight, with neither day nor night', which lasts for 'up to forty-nine days in all' before rebirth (277). By reincarnating Marinus across *The Bone Clocks*, *Sunken Garden*, *Slade House*, *The Thousand Autumns*, *Wake*, 'I_Bombadil' and 'All Souls Day', this background retrospectively infuses each work with Tibetan Buddhist mythologies, reinforcing her suggestion in *Sunken Garden* that her world would 'make more sense' when approached through its philosophies.

As Marinus' remark demonstrates, the author's interest in Buddhism also resurfaces in his libretti. In a 2014 interview with Christopher Wallace, Mitchell reveals that while living in Japan he briefly stayed at a Buddhist temple, and confirms that '[t]he belief system which is most helpful to me is Buddhism' ('The Expansive David Mitchell'). *Wake*'s composer similarly remarks on the influence of Eastern spiritualities on his works, a shared interest visible in the opera's approach to tragedy. He explains: 'I regard myself as an atheist – but if I had to choose a religion, it would be Taoism', noting he is drawn to its cyclicality and lack of an iconic 'redeemer': '[t]he wheel finally returns around, and nothingness. There are of course resemblances with Buddhism, but I think that appeals' ('Interview by Rose Harris-Birtill'). While Taoism is a distinct set of philosophical principles, the importance it places on harmony, balance and compassion is shared with Tibetan Buddhist approaches. Klaas de Vries emphasizes that this 'harmony' and 'balance' in *Wake*'s performance was widely noted in its critical reception:

> the word 'harmony' was used a lot. And not only regarding my music, which is also very much about harmony [...] but also harmony between all these elements. The balance was there.

Significantly, both Mitchell and de Vries express the importance of these Eastern philosophies within secular world views. De Vries notes his atheism in tandem with his interest in Taoism, while Mitchell mentions to Christopher Wallace that while he isn't part of a group of Western Buddhists, 'the books and conversations, these are very important to me', its philosophies a notable interest to the author even from outside a formal religious practice. For each of these artists, there is a sense that their Taoist and Buddhist interests and their non-religious beliefs are not mutually exclusive, but create a post-secular hybridity of approach in which each world view enriches the other without being subscribed to any single perspective, moving beyond traditional Western Judeo-Christian approaches to human tragedy.

Elements of Buddhist perspectives are particularly evident in each libretto's approach to death. Discussing mortality, Mitchell notes in an interview with Wallace:

[y]ou need to find some kind of acceptance. Buddhist monks spend all of their lives preparing for death, accepting it, and seeing it as a facet of life. And this yearning, this longing for immortality is pernicious and dangerous. [...] you have to cure yourself of it. ('The Expansive David Mitchell')

Sunken Garden and *Wake* both show a finding of 'some kind of acceptance' of human impermanence, embedding a Buddhist-influenced contemplation of death within each libretto's secular framework. In this respect, *The Bone Clocks*, as an extended exploration of the struggle to accept human impermanence – and the dangers of 'longing for immortality' – perhaps shares the strongest thematic ties with Mitchell's libretti. Samsara is also discussed in *The Bone Clocks* as the venal 'sociopath' Hugo Lamb dismisses it as 'self-deception' ('our culture's coping strategy towards death is to bury it under consumerism and samsara') (149, 116). Hugo's cynicism reflects his heightened sense of self-preservation, displaying the anti-social attitudes that spur him to join the soul-stealing Anchorites. Yet his care for Holly finally makes him save her life instead of his own, choosing death in order to let her survive (518–20). Hugo's life may be finally saved by Marinus, but it is his concern for another's well-being that makes him voluntarily give up immortality; read within a Buddhist framework, the realization of his own compassionate capabilities allows him to accept his own death.

However, Hugo's remark also evokes the opposing perspective, that samsara – like any redemptive philosophy of death as part of life – can be seen as a 'coping strategy' to avoid death's finality. In typical Mitchellian fashion, both sides of the argument are presented, displaying what Timotheus Vermeulen and Robin van den Akker's 'Notes on Metamodernism' (2010) describes as the oscillatory metamodern 'double-bind' of encountering conflicting perspectives simultaneously (5). With Hugo's wry remark, the topic of reincarnation becomes caught in what Vermeulen and van den Akker recognize as a pendulous contemporary movement between 'modern enthusiasm and a postmodern irony, between hope and melancholy, between naïveté and knowingness', evoking samsaric sacrality alongside ontological secularity in order to create a text in which the real must be inescapably read within a framework of the mythological, and vice versa (5-6).

'Honour us, by living fully'

As part of this confrontation of the Western 'taboo' surrounding mortality, Mitchell's libretti draw from Buddhist ethical philosophies to offer their own form of secular guidance. In *Sunken Garden*, Marinus' explanation of the contractual rules that bind life and death – *'You Will Suffer'*, *'You May Hope'* and *'It Must End And Shall'* – can be read as a secular reworking of the Four Noble Truths, foundational principles within Buddhist teachings (7, 9). To briefly summarize these, the first clause corresponds with Buddhism's first Noble Truth, which refers to the universality of suffering; the second clause can be read against the second Noble Truth, which states that suffering stems from desire. Although the idea of an end to existence, as in the third clause (*'It Must End And Shall'*), at first appears incongruous with reincarnation's cyclicality, the third

Noble Truth suggests a productive alternative reading. This states that ending desire will end suffering, reworked in *Sunken Garden* as '*It Must End And Shall*', and also echoed in *Wake* as the dead sing '"All that is here shall cease to be" the not-so-very-small print reads' (4). Buddhist philosophies interpret death as a single facet of change within a vast system of impermanence, a single end in a *Cloud Atlas*-like multiplicity of endings; '*It Must End And Shall*' evokes the Buddhist striving for acceptance of life's impermanence, but also the third Noble Truth's reference to the end of suffering itself. At the end of the opera, Toby, now in Zenna's body, is struggling to accept the change. He mournfully notes, 'Youth is gone; my gender's switched; My old life's obsolete' (9). Yet this desire for his past life is followed with his invocation of 'Life's Third Clause: *It Must End And Shall*. Let these words prise open every January dawn, usher in my finite Springs', the promise of an end to his suffering becoming a mantra of sorts that allows him to accept the change and keep on living.

Sunken Garden only identifies three clauses of life's contract – yet there remains a fourth Noble Truth. This directs Buddhist practitioners towards further guidance, by recommending the everyday, practical steps of the Noble Eightfold Path as core actions to help alleviate suffering, including understanding how actions affect others, the practice of compassion, and aspiring not to do harm to others or oneself.[6] As Stephen Batchelor notes in *Buddhism without Beliefs* (1998), '[t]he four ennobling truths are not propositions to believe; they are challenges to act' (7). While *Sunken Garden*'s 'contract' stops at the first three steps, both *Wake* and *Sunken Garden* can be seen as a form of embodiment of this fourth Noble Truth, each offering practical guidance to help individuals find their way out of private suffering. In *Wake*, the narrative shifts from the mimesis of the central acts, which depict the characters' daily lives, to the diegesis of the final act, in which the voices of the living, dead and memory become stylized, the action now narrated to allow each group to comment on their situation to the audience. The dead impart practical steps of their own to the living, telling them to combat their suffering by embracing life: '[y]our prize must not be pain, but duty. Honour us, by living fully' (4).

This dramatic movement from naturalistic action to commentary blurs the division between actors and audience, evoking German playwright Bertolt Brecht's alienation effect, or *Verfremdungseffekt*. Brecht first refers to this concept in his 1936 essay '*Verfremdungseffekte in der chinesischen Schauspielkunst*', or 'Alienation effects in Chinese Acting', describing a theatrical technique that undermines the dramatic illusion of a 'fourth wall' between actors and audience. By directly addressing the disaster's survivors, *Wake*'s chorus of the dead also metatheatrically addresses the opera's original Enschede audience as survivors of an all-too-real tragedy. Their final role is therefore not to leave grief, but to offer guidance to the living, imagined as navigating a perilous journey: 'So navigate by maps or stars; Meet trouble and capsize, And right yourself as best you may; And improvise; and improvise' (4).

---

[6] As described in *The Buddhist Religion* (1996) by Richard Robinson and Willard Johnson, the Noble Eightfold Path is a series of practical actions that lead to greater knowledge and insight in the practitioner, including '(1) right view, (2) right resolve, (3) right speech, (4) right action, (5) right livelihood, (6) right effort, (7) right mindfulness, and (8) right concentration' (32).

Wake's depiction of human existence as a journey to be actively navigated forms a secular echo of the Eightfold Path. This nautical metaphor conceals a humanist imperative, to 'right yourself as best you may' and take self-directed practical steps to continue 'living fully' after tragedy, a conclusion that lies at the heart of each libretto's reconciliation. The repetition of 'and improvise' emphasizes the human condition's theatricality, with the living cast as unscripted actors and directed to find solace in personal resourcefulness. In *Sunken Garden*, a similar message is given to those contemplating suicide, envisaged as a premature terminus along life's journey: '[w]hy soldier on, then […]? Because Clause Two reads, *You May Hope*' (7). The knowledge that death is the unavoidable destination is presented as solace to those seeking it, with: '[t]he most painless way to die is to live'.

In this scene, the word 'hope' is repeated five times in as many lines, used each time as a verb to be actively pursued rather than an abstract noun. This sense of hope as an imperative, a positive action to be chosen, also underpins the Tibetan Buddhist approach to life and death as part of a larger cycle. As Robert Goss notes in 'Tibetan Buddhism and the Resolution of Grief' (1997), 'Tibetans recognize death all around them: The deaths of those they know and love cause them to search for the meaning of life with a sense of hope' (388). While it is important to acknowledge this statement's cultural generalization, it usefully recognizes the coexistence of hope within a narratological acceptance of death. Acknowledging that 'rebirth does not remove the pain of loss', as Goss explains, the Tibetan Buddhist framework of samsara provides a non-Judeo-Christian source of secular inspiration for a constructive approach to tragedy that can still find the 'sense of hope' and reconciliation that remains a hallmark of each libretto, and also of Mitchell's wider writing. As Diana notes in *Wake*, 'hope may be displaced, disappointed, but hope cannot be wrong' (2). A reading of the Buddhist influences within Mitchell's libretti therefore prompts a broader recognition of their multimedia formats to include non-Western influences, as the next section will discuss, offering an ethical approach whose secular content is enriched by Buddhist philosophies, the combination of Eastern and Western influences suggesting the value of cross-cultural approaches to tragedy and healing.

The sand mandala as *Gesamtkunstwerk*

The term '*Gesamtkunstwerk*' was coined by German composer and writer Richard Wagner in his 1849 essay *Das Kunstwerk der Zukunft*, or *The Art-Work of the Future*, signifying a total work of art, in which many forms – for example, music, dance and poetry – work together to express a continuous world view. Although the *Gesamtkunstwerk* has a complex sociopolitical history – Matthew Wilson Smith notes the form's multiplicitous legacy in *The Total Work of Art* (2007), citing its visibility in artworks of the Third Reich, Disney, Warhol and *World of Warcraft* alike – the term is used here in its 'most widely understood' definition as a form which synthesizes mixed media to create an immersive world (9). Approaching *Wake* and *Sunken Garden* as contemporary *Gesamtkunstwerks* emphasizes the importance of the contrasting elements that create each of these shifting forms, each depicting a

Mitchellian 'World-Machine' built on juxtapositions, simultaneously 'massive, unjust, beautiful, cruel, miraculous', as Simon puts it in *Sunken Garden*. Interpreting these operas as *Gesamtkunstwerks* draws attention to their revaluing of diversity by which heterogeneous elements become integral units of difference, forming a mosaic of interconnected approaches. This typically Mitchellian perspective surfaces throughout the macronovel, for example, in the narrative interconnections of *Ghostwritten*, and the simultaneous perspectives in 'Variations on a Theme by Mister Donut'.

As a self-contained depiction of a world that synthesizes many different elements, the mandala's multimedia format offers its own take on the *Gesamtkunstwerk*. A term that simultaneously signifies a metaphysical blueprint, a two-dimensional cosmogram and a three-dimensional temple, the mandala is itself 'multi-media', as Maggie Grey notes in 'Encountering the Mandala: The Mental and Political Architectures of Dependency' (2001):

> [m]andalas are multi-media: as murals in temples, monasteries and religious buildings; as portable cloth paintings […] coloured sands, semi-precious gems, wood, clay, butter or threads […] as dramatic tableaux of music and dance. (7–8)

With so many varied forms, the mandala is itself plural, its 'multi-media' format an embodiment of the diversity of its many manifestations. Involving its creators in an elaborate ritual of synthesis and dispersal, the sand mandala as 'cultural offering' in the Western world becomes akin to a form of *Gesamtkunstwerk* or total work of art, a multifaceted dramatic 'performance' that brings together a range of contrasting elements to create an integrated whole, incorporating rehearsal, action, direction, timing and its own sense of narrative drama, its ritualistic assembly, completion and dismantling forming a distinct beginning, middle and end to its composition.

As *Gesamtkunstwerks*, Mitchell's libretti in performance become embodiments of Grey's multimedia 'dramatic tableaux of music and dance' that integrate diverse components to form an artistic whole, each creating its own fictional world. As Klaas de Vries notes of *Wake*'s combined 'electronics, and film, and stage': '[i]t's a question if it's a real opera […] it has aspects of opera, but it also has a requiem, it has poetry, it has all these aspects' ('Interview by Rose Harris-Birtill'). Mitchell's libretto provides just one part of the opera's compositional ingenuity as a collaborative synthesis of film, electronic soundscape, orchestral score, choral and solo operatic voices; its ambitious approach combines Latin requiem with sung libretto and spoken dialogue, newly commissioned operatic lyrics with Romantic poetry. *Sunken Garden* takes this ambitious mixed-media collaboration even further, integrating electronic music into operatic score, and augmenting live action with 3D film. This stylistic breadth creates an immersive, dream-like world of contrasting forms, its bold juxtapositions an embodiment of Mitchell's artistic hybridity in his genre-crossing novels. The opera combines the realism of Toby's film documentary with abstract representation; the set's darkly lit minimalism contrasts with the 3D visuals of the ultra-colourful garden, the fusion creating an opera which challenges the boundaries and expectations of its genre. The use of 3D film begins midway through the opera as Toby enters the sunken garden, creating a visual hyperreality in which it becomes difficult to differentiate between live and filmed action, blurring the boundaries between the real and the fantastic – a narrative technique which is also visible in *The Bone Clocks* and *Slade House*.

Each opera uses the genre-crossing hybridity of Mitchell's narratives to create performances whose multimedia approaches reflect the author's fascination with the intersection between music and text, and the narrative possibilities of sound. Speaking in a 2014 Goodreads interview, Mitchell notes that in writing these libretti he 'wanted to learn about the opera world':

> [i]t's a peculiar form – a total art form. You have narrative, visual arts, costume, choreography, orchestral, and vocal music. All glued together with the logic of dreams. It's a strange, beautiful art form, and I am intrigued by it. ('Interview with David Mitchell')

David Mitchell's libretti in performance reflect an author intrigued by boundary crossings, both within narrative and between art forms, exploring the ability of language and music to augment each other to create a 'total art form'. While his libretti provide the words and storyline for each opera, these form the basis for vivid collaborative performances which use music, orchestral scores, film and live actors to bring his texts to life.

Although he describes his time as a librettist as 'a foray', his work as a librettist is also enhanced by the musicality of his wider writing. In *Cloud Atlas*, its narrative structure is imagined in musical terms as Robert Frobisher's description of his composition offers a metaphor for the novel ('a 'sextet for overlapping soloists': piano, clarinet, 'cello, flute, oboe and violin, each in its own language of key, scale and colour', 463). This envisaging of narrative as musical score, and novelist as composer, forms a background in which, as Frobisher puts it, 'the artist lives in two worlds', writing with an awareness of both the individuality of each component and their collective symphonic 'overlapping'. Mitchell's writing demonstrates a compositional foregrounding of this concept, in an approach to his fiction that lays bare the elements of composition available to it – temporal, structural, fantastic and realistic, 'high' and 'low' genres and registers – and also features in the musical references throughout his novels. Klaas de Vries remarks in interview that *Cloud Atlas*' polyphonous musicality led him to 'convince' David Mitchell to write the libretto for *Wake*: 'the book had so much to do with musical composition – the way it was constructed, but also the language was very musical' ('Interview by Rose Harris-Birtill'). Although the author has said in an interview with Jasper Rees that he has 'no musical training at all', the numerous intersections between music and fiction in his works reveals a writer highly sensitive to the nuances of musicality in language, and the narrative possibilities of sound ('10 Questions'). As well as *Cloud Atlas*'s extensive fictionalized rewriting of the musical relationship between English composer Frederick Delius and his amanuensis Eric Fenby, Mitchell has also co-written dialogue and monologues for English singer-songwriter Kate Bush's stage show *Before the Dawn* (2014), performed at the Hammersmith Apollo in London, as noted in the author's 2014 interview with James Kidd ('Time and again').

This fascination with the overlap between musical and textual narratives recurs throughout the macronovel. *The Bone Clocks* is perhaps his most overtly musically influenced work of fiction to date, from its embedded references to the American rock group Talking Heads to the eerily foreseen breaking of the bust of the composer Jean Sibelius that begins a chain of supernatural events (392). The novel's catalogue of musical references acts as a barometer of changing popular culture, and also enhances each section's changes in tone (52). For example, in the novel's fifth section, Dr Iris Marinus-Fenby is listening to Japanese composer Toru Takemitsu's symphony *From me flows what you call Time* (1997), an orchestral soundscape which acts as a cinematic mood-heightener for the supernatural events that follow (387). Yet the piece also forms an apt prelude to Marinus' narrative, playing on her car radio as she questions the meaning of her existence, asking: '[h]ave we evolved this way? Or are we designed? Designed by whom?' (387). As Briana Lehman discusses, Takemitsu's piece was designed to evoke Tibetan Buddhist 'ritual' and 'spirituality' – a particularly apt choice for a reincarnated healer on her thirty-ninth lifetime. Lehman notes that the piece was composed 'as a musical and theatrical representation of the concept of the "Wind Horse" [...] commonly used in the visual program of Tibetan Buddhist prayer flags'; this Tibetan Buddhist influence is

> mirrored visually in performance [...] by the composer's directions to use five differently colored ribbons that reach from the performers to the ceiling [...]. Chimes attached to these ribbons are intoned sporadically throughout the piece, representing the transmission of man's prayers to the deities. ('The Colburn Orchestra Play Takemitsu', 2012)

The polyphony of musical references in Mitchell's works infuses the mood of his writing with a form of compositional shorthand, using one art form to evoke another. Here, knowledge of Takemitsu's work resonates with the Buddhist influences that Mitchell draws on in the novel, the composer's use of 'coloured ribbons' to evoke 'Tibetan Buddhist prayer flags' adding, by proxy, a sense of spiritual contemplation to Marinus' opening 'scene'. As she listens to the piece, Marinus reflects on her day dealing with a psychiatric patient's 'Messiah Syndrome' that has evolved into something 'even stranger' (387–8). Simultaneously raising the theological and undermining it with the presence of religious delusion, evoking a post-secular musical allusion to Tibetan Buddhism alongside a fractured Christianity-based psychosis, Mitchell sets the tone for a character whose mythological and spiritual contemplations will prove far more complex than any single belief system can encompass.

Further extending the novel's musical ecosystem, the author's interactive playlist selected to accompany *The Bone Clocks* brings this extra-textual musicality into the world outside the novel. Created by the author for the 2014 BBC Radio 4 *Book at Bedtime* readings, Mitchell notes that although the playlist is an 'odd mix [...] it reflects the novel', a twenty-first-century hybrid of artificially superimposed styles ('Music For A Lost Horologist'). Oscillating in tone between Scarlatti's sonatas, late 1980s acid house music, and American rock, the playlist draws attention to the influence of these musical styles on the novel, mirroring its shifts in time, style and subject matter, and foregrounds the intersection of music and narrative that spans the piece. In its superimposition of contrasting musical styles, *The Bone Clocks* echoes the

Gesamtkunstwerk format of each of Mitchell's libretti in performance. Music is also an integral part of the world view created in *The Bone Clocks*; the works of Scarlatti become 'an Ariadne's thread' that connects all of Marinus' reincarnations, pulling this character's many lives into a single coherent self (448).

While the use of mixed media in each of Mitchell's libretti creates an immersive world whose many elements work together as a continuous whole, the juxtaposition of stage and screen also emphasizes the self as fragmented, reflecting the conflicted lives and fractured identities that each opera explores. For example, in *Sunken Garden*, a moving virtual duet takes place between Toby and Amber, her image multiplied across five screens in a visual fragmentation that emphasizes her vulnerability (2). The repeated lyric 'backstreets of waking and sleeping', at first sung tenderly between live actor and filmed actress, moves from harmonious duet to a swarming crescendo of looping image glitches and vocal repetition, the fragmented images and overlayered sounds emphasizing their deepening instability, using the abstract to confront the real. Operatic baritone Roderick Williams, who has performed the role of Toby in all of *Sunken Garden*'s productions to date, emphasizes Michel van der Aa's 'investigation of the blurred lines between live and filmed action in his operas', observing that the juxtapositions 're-orientate (rather than disorientate!) his audience into believing the screen and live performance are one', using film and live action to blur reality and fantasy ('Interview by Rose Harris-Birtill' 2015). Toby's connection with Amber may be purely virtual, but her filmed narrative becomes part of his lived reality, his fascination with her story leading him to the sunken garden.

In *Wake*, visual and auditory fragmentation are also used in the second act's juxtaposition of its characters' situations, presenting individuals who, while linked by shared tragedy, are every bit as different as the situations they inhabit. As Mitchell notes in his essay 'David Mitchell: Adventures in Opera' (2010), '[n]ine stories would unfold simultaneously: eventful stories, quiet ones, sad ones, comic ones, thoughtful ones, brash ones'. Yet behind this casual domesticity – the armchair football fanatic, the midwife discussing '[t]he secret of ironing shirts', the video game-playing teenager – intermittent discordant sounds and the sad, minor piano refrain that resurfaces throughout the action emphasize that the disaster behind the opera is never far away. The abstract and the real intermingle in the orchestral score as a clamour of background voices resurfaces intermittently throughout the domestic scenes, a metatheatrical counterpoint that prevents the audience from forgetting the tragic shared victimhood behind its commonplace events. Similar to *Sunken Garden*'s use of overlayered sounds, although these are musical rather than textual expressions, they become inseparable facets of the libretti in performance; as Nina Penner states in 'Opera Singing and Fictional Truth' (2013), within opera 'the orchestra music is also part of the ontology of the fictional world', an inextricable feature of each narrative realm (84).

Staging David Mitchell's libretti

For the trained participant, the mental journey through the mandala's imagined pathways is itself a dramatic experience. Just as entering the theatrical deception of performance requires an audience's willing suspension of disbelief, the mandala's participant must suspend their own connection to the physical reality around them in order to visualize a path through its world. Tibetan Buddhist practice stipulates that the practitioner begins this journey at the mandala's outermost east gateway, the teaching forming a visual 'script' that directs the individual's path through the imagined space. As Bryant notes of the mandala, when imagined as a three-dimensional space, 'students always circumambulate it beginning in the east, then continue walking around it in a clockwise direction', mentally spiralling inwards through its outer 'terraces' (180–1). Following this 'scripted' path, complete with a cast of deities, animals and even its own 'sunken garden' (see Appendix C), the practitioner progresses through the mandala's gateways, each a dramatic proscenium arch of sorts that leads the participant deeper into its imagined world view. As Giuseppe Tucci observes in *The Theory and Practice of the Mandala* (1961), these gateways are marked by T-shaped openings, or *toranas*, visible on each of the four sides of the mandala's internal structure (43); for the participant, upon entering the mandala 'the very drama of his soul' is 'spread out before his eyes' in a 'symbolic representation' of the human condition (132).

This fixed journey to the mandala's centre evokes both the centre-facing focus of theatre in the round and the participatory movement of promenade theatre. Within the conventions of Western theatre, each audience member is similarly socially 'taught' to become a complicit participant in a culturally learnt imaginative practice. Each theatrical genre comes with a preformed expectation of what the performance will offer, alongside the pleasure of entertainment; in the traditionally 'highbrow' dramatic form of opera, this is often an expectation of some form of greater emotional understanding of the human condition through the passionate conflicts depicted on stage, an echo of the mandala participant's witnessing, as Tucci puts it, 'the very drama of his soul'. As Richard Robinson and Willard Johnson describe in *The Buddhist Religion* (1996), there is also an 'easy familiarity [...] between human and spirit worlds' in the Tibetan Vajrayana Buddhist tradition, which has its own ancestral shamanic roots (22, 290). This 'easy familiarity' between the real and the fantastic surfaces in the fluidity of visible and invisible realms in each opera's envisaging of the twilight spaces of human existence. This concept is also found in the mandala, itself a form of 'magic realism' in which the metaphysical palaces of deities co-exist with minute functional details of its microcosmic world, for example, visible in the minute detail of each gateway's 'white lines forming triangles, which represent downspouts that release rainwater from the palace roof', as noted by Barry Bryant (*The Wheel of Time Sand Mandala* 205; see Appendix C).

An understanding of the dramatic nature of the Tibetan Buddhist mandala, as a complex visual 'script' that merges real and imagined realms, can be used to critically approach to the representation of metaphysical spaces in Mitchell's libretti. Just as the mandala uses abstract visual representations for its imagined setting – such as the dots used to symbolize its deities – the sets of Mitchell's libretti in performance create abstract spaces which require an audience to enter, complicit, into formally ambiguous settings. Roderick Williams remarks on Toby's minimalistic set in *Sunken Garden*:

we are never quite sure whether Toby is rearranging his flat or a cinema, some sort of abstract warehouse space or even rooms in his 'mind-palace'. Because the set is so abstract, it can suit any reading. ('Interview by Rose Harris-Birtill')

The design of the set, a shifting steel cube comprised of frames and veils, provides an 'abstract' structure whose sharp vertical and horizontal lines evoke the stainless steel setting of a morgue, or the bars of a prison. The set changes, initially carried out by Toby himself, suggest a Brechtian fluidity between the worlds of the real and imagined. The sight of Toby rearranging his own set is an act of theatrical alienation that both reminds the audience of the character's fictionality and serves as a visible reminder of his traumatic past, depicting a single character struggling alone against the confining forces that shape his world.

With the change of setting to Zenna's garden, Toby's mundane domestic reality is replaced by a three-dimensional fantasy, filmed inside the artificial biodomes of the Eden Project in Cornwall, England. The muted greys of Toby's set are superseded by the colourful hyperreal of the garden and the gravity-defying special effects of its vertical pond. The allure of the sunken garden as a manifestation of suicidal impulse – and an escape from Toby's visibly muted reality – becomes instantly recognizable, drawing the audience into a magical and dangerous fantasy world. *Wake* shares *Sunken Garden*'s initial use of minimalist set design, with stark geometrical frames, monochromatic lighting effects and dark, receding perspective lines creating a surreal performance space. Mitchell has indicated in interview that his involvement with set design took the form of a 'presidential veto principle', and that the sets were designed by others ('Interview by Rose Harris-Birtill', 2015). However, the minimalistic sets form a fitting backdrop for the 'abstract' scenario of the final 'impossible conversation' between the living and the dead, as noted by Klaas de Vries ('Interview by Rose Harris-Birtill').[7] By using abstract forms of visualization, each opera demonstrates a mandalic valuing of imaginary and symbolic space over realist representation, shifting the focus to each character's inner journey within each libretto's fictional world.

'When remembered, we exist'

Like any dramatic work, the Tibetan Buddhist sand mandala in diaspora and Mitchell's libretti in performance both depend on the reactions of their viewers to continue to reach new audiences. While *Wake*'s performances met with 'very positive' critical acclaim – Klaas de Vries notes that '[t]here were five four-star reviews and three five-star reviews' – *Sunken Garden*'s initial reviews were mixed, its ambitious format dividing critics ('Interview by Rose Harris-Birtill'). As Roderick Williams remarks, '[w]hether everyone in an opera audience is happy to mix a touch of science fiction with opera [remains] to be seen' ('Interview by Rose Harris-Birtill'). Yet each opera challenges its audiences by engaging with wider sociopolitical issues, as in *Wake*'s

---

[7] See the photographs of *Wake*'s original set design by Marco Borggreve, 'Wake Nationale Reisopera' (2010).

remembering of a national disaster, and in *Sunken Garden*'s engagement with suicide, a topical issue for the native audiences of both its English librettist and Dutch composer. The Office for National Statistics notes that in 2012, the year before *Sunken Garden*'s first performance by the English National Opera at London's Barbican theatre, UK suicide rates were 'significantly higher than five years before' ('Suicides in the United Kingdom' 2).[8] Showing a similar increase, the Dutch *Statistics Netherlands* (CBS), a government organization that collects statistics on the Dutch population, reported 'an increase by 30 percent' in the number of suicides between 2008 and 2012, as noted in a 2013 article by Jan Hoogenboezem et al. ('More suicides since 2008').

Both *Sunken Garden* and *Wake* present communities threatened with destruction, demonstrating the importance of shared approaches to collective tragedy, each offering its own form of guidance to 'right yourself as best you may' (*Wake* 4) and again dare to hope for renewal: '[h]ope the hydras run out of heads; hope endurance triumphs; hope for friendlier cards; hope that suffering is fractured by change' (*Sunken Garden* 7). Each opera's constructive approach evokes a revaluing of hope; *Sunken Garden* ends not with Amber's suicide, but with Simon's choice to live, while *Wake*'s reminder that '[t]o re-remember, recreates' presents memory as transformative, a force able to make something from nothing, in a regenerative approach that uses this collective act of bearing witness to find acceptance (4).

Like poetry – or opera – the sand mandala makes nothing happen. Its fragile structure and brief lifespan make it an unlikely tool, existing only in the brief moment of its assembly before being deliberately unmade by the hands that create it. Yet as the memory chorus sing in *Wake*'s final act, 'when remembered, we exist' (4). It is as an act of remembrance that the world views offered by these performances survive, finding a voice for the silenced victims that they represent – whether the displaced Tibetan Buddhist community in exile, the thousands of suicides registered in the UK and the Netherlands every year, or the 947 people injured and 23 killed in the Enschede fireworks disaster. Each opera's samsaric act of remembrance portrays memory as multifaceted; at the heart of each opera lies the recognition that 'each grain of memory is – look close – of smaller grains composed', the pain of remembered grief inseparable from the sustaining shared memories that it contains (*Wake* 4).

Discussing Mitchell's libretti in performance alongside the sand mandala in diaspora, this chapter has identified their shared methods of compassionate world creation, discussing the samsaric philosophies that contribute to their regenerative approaches to tragedy. While Mitchell's libretti in performance become collaborative translations from their textual origins, the cross-cultural 'performance' of the sand mandala in secular spaces effectively translates a private religious custom into a public cultural spectacle. Its multimedia staging in diaspora allows it to reach a wider audience, just as Mitchell's libretti in performance reach new audiences from outside the author's assumed readership, their innovative formats allowing them to break the

---

[8]   Source: Office for National Statistics, licensed under the Open Government Licence v.1.0. See https://www.ons.gov.uk/peoplepopulationandcommunity/birthsdeathsandmarriages/deaths/bulletins/suicidesintheunitedkingdom/2014-02-18, accessed 20 April 2018.

conventionally esoteric boundaries of the opera genre and reach a wider public. As Susan M. Walcott notes, by

> venturing into visual portrayals of places not on the face of the earth [...] [w]e sharpen our vision by seeking worlds other than those we are accustomed to viewing, and seeking to understand them as seen through the eyes of their creators. ('Mapping from a Different Direction' 75)

It is by 'venturing into visual portrayals of places not on the face of the earth' – whether the sand mandala's metaphysical realm or the libretti's visualization of Mitchell's fictional world – that these works demonstrate the value of viewing through different eyes, whether the minority perspectives that each work represents, or the critical insights revealed by comparing these art forms. Each opera's mandalic enactment of the human condition demonstrates the value of collective approaches to rebuilding after tragedy, their samsaric influences forming an important part of the macronovel's wider post-secular reworking of reincarnation – as the next chapter will discuss.

3

'Looking Down Time's Telescope at Myself': Reincarnation and Global Futures in David Mitchell's Fictional Worlds

In the second section of *The Bone Clocks*, Cambridge student Hugo Lamb visits his headmaster's old friend, Brigadier Philby, in a nursing home. The brigadier, a former 'linguist and raconteur', is now suffering from dementia, and is largely 'non-verbal' (118). After he leaves, Hugo realizes, '[w]hen I look at Brigadier Reginald Philby, I'm looking down time's telescope at myself' (120). For Hugo, the metaphor of time's telescope reflects his anxiety about his own unavoidably finite lifespan (he notes, 'the elderly *are* guilty: guilty of proving to us that our wilful myopia about death is exactly that'), a preoccupation that leads him to join the soul-stealing Anchorites (116). However, as this chapter will demonstrate, the notion of 'looking down time's telescope at myself' as a form of future-facing temporality has far greater significance: both for Mitchell's literary approach to time across his oeuvre and for the exploration of alternative cyclical temporalities that it prompts outside of his fictional world.[1]

While the concept of 'looking down time's telescope at myself' emphasizes Hugo's self-centred attitude to his own mortality, it also provides an apt model for discussing David Mitchell's treatment of time in his wider narrative universe. As an imaginary model, 'time's telescope' makes visible the gaze of the present self at its own future and, by implication, the causal relationship between them. The telescope holder becomes both immediate viewer and future subject, a simultaneously cross-temporal spectator and actor, allowing the individual to see their future self as a separately observable entity. It is an image that evokes the macronovel's fascination with cyclical temporality, transmigration and reincarnation. The sight line created is both linear and cyclical – a linear device that provides a means of cyclical self-observation. However, such self-observation does not form a perfect circle but a spiralling gaze which continues to move forward in time, creating a feedback loop: having seen their future self, the present self can choose to modify their actions in response, in a relationship that fosters a heightened awareness of personal responsibility and agency. After all, it is only by choosing to gaze down this metaphorical instrument that the actions of the future

---

[1] An earlier version of part of this chapter appears as '"Looking down time's telescope at myself": reincarnation and global futures in David Mitchell's fictional worlds' in *KronoScope: Journal for the Study of Time* 17.2 (2017), reprinted courtesy of Brill.

self become visible, magnifying a temporally distant self which is *other* to the self, but 'othered' only by time, creating a relationship in which the actions of each self – present and future – can become mutually influential.

Mitchell expands on this concept of 'time's telescope' in a 2016 interview, noting:

> if you had a powerful enough telescope and pointed it in any direction, you would eventually see the back of your own head [...] because the universe is spherical. [...] Isn't that beautiful? Isn't it an antidote to the pollution, and the spilled mercury sulphate, and the albatrosses dead in oil slicks, and the Russian president's bombing citizens in Syria [...]? ('Interview by Rose Harris-Birtill', see Appendix H)

Mitchell's comment adds important detail to the idea of 'time's telescope': that such a telescope can operate not merely on a personal level, but across a 'spherical' self-contained 'universe' and all of its inhabitants, its line of sight forming a circular path that spans a single interconnected entity, taking in the action of a universe before finally returning to the individual viewer. This comment also raises the issue of collective sociopolitical and ecological responsibility, a telescope somehow able to see beyond a seemingly endless list of twenty-first-century global ecological and humanitarian crises to some form of 'antidote', a countermeasure whose cyclical mechanism of cross-temporal self-observation and future insight suggest a way forward.

Interrogating this idea of 'looking down time's telescope at myself', this chapter builds on the previous chapter's focus on samsaric cyclicality and rebirth in the author's libretti to explore the treatment of reincarnation across the wider macronovel. Drawing on the visualization of the Buddhist model of reincarnation in the Bhavachakra mandala, it argues that Mitchell uses a reworked form of reincarnation to build an alternative approach to linear temporality, an approach whose spiralling cyclicality warns of the dangers of seeing past actions as separate from future consequences, and whose focus on cross-temporal interconnection demonstrates the importance of collective, future-facing ethical action in the face of ecological and humanitarian crises.

'Time's telescope' and reincarnation

In the same interview, Mitchell adds:

> linguistically time is singular, but actually it's plural – there are so many different kinds of time. There's a lifespan [...] there's geological time, there's planetary time [...]. There's Marinus time, there's reincarnation time [...] these tiny, tiny moments where vast things can happen. ('Interview by Rose Harris-Birtill', 2016)

Mitchell's works reflect this fascination with 'many different kinds of time', often using the micro-temporal to depict the heightened significance of immediate present-time decisions as 'these tiny, tiny moments where vast things can happen'. For example, the short story 'My Eye On You' introduces a simultaneous dimension in which time is experienced at a twelfth of the speed of 'normal' time. This slowed timescale lengthens the lived present to introduce an alternative temporality embedded within our own, a form of reflective time in which its narrator is able to make life-changing ethical interventions to help others, as discussed in Chapter 1.

As several critics have noted, this concept of temporal plurality runs throughout Mitchell's works. In 'David Mitchell's Fractal Imagination: *The Bone Clocks*' (2015), Paul A. Harris rightly notes the 'labyrinthine nature of time' portrayed with the novel's temporal shifts (149), while in 'The Historical Novel Today, Or, Is It Still Possible?' (2013), Fredric Jameson explores *Cloud Atlas*'s layered temporalities using the model of an elevator lurching through 'disparate floors on its way to the far future' (303). Similarly, Patrick O'Donnell notes in *A Temporary Future: The Fiction of David Mitchell* (2015) that Mitchell's depiction of temporality occupies 'multiple domains' (16).

Alongside this recognition of temporal plurality, several critics also note the author's portrayal of cyclical timescales, often presented in conjunction with a disrupted linear temporality. For example, Jay Clayton suggests *Cloud Atlas* displays a 'paradoxical combination of linear and cyclical perspectives on time' ('Genome Time' 2013, 58), while in '"On the Fringe of Becoming" – David Mitchell's *Ghostwritten*' (2004), Philip Griffiths discusses the novel's 'disparate, discontinuous and cyclical view of history' whose 'linear chronology [...] is broken down' (80–4). Similarly, in *The Cosmopolitan Novel*, Berthold Schoene describes *Ghostwritten* as an 'oddly timeless and dislocated' work whose ending 'dissolves the novel's linearity' altogether (111). Peter Childs and James Green note in 'David Mitchell' (2013) that *Cloud Atlas*'s structure is 'at once linear and cyclical' (149). In 'Cannibalism, Colonialism and Apocalypse in Mitchell's Global Future' (2015), Lynda Ng describes *Cloud Atlas* in terms of an ouroboric timescale which disrupts Western conventions of linear temporality (107, 118), while Marco de Waard, writing in 'Dutch Decline Redux: Remembering New Amsterdam in the Global and Cosmopolitan Novel' (2012), argues that *The Thousand Autumns* 'articulates a cyclical conception of history' (115). In each case, a cyclical temporality is identified in Mitchell's works which disrupts readerly expectations of temporal linearity, but doesn't necessarily overturn it altogether, suggesting that a model which combines the linear and the cyclical – the spiral – may be more appropriate.

In the same interview, Mitchell names 'reincarnation time' as a specific form of temporality ('Interview by Rose Harris-Birtill', 2016), while in his essay 'The view from Japan' (2007), Mitchell also refers to the artistic process of 'bending [...] time's false straight line into its truer shape, the spiral'. Read as a temporal model, 'reincarnation time' shares the spiralling cyclicality and future-facing self-awareness evoked by 'looking down time's telescope at myself'. Defined in the *Oxford English Dictionary* (OED) as '[r]enewed incarnation; the rebirth of a soul in a new body or form', reincarnation or rebirth forms part of many global belief systems, including Buddhist, Hindu, Jain, Native American, Inuit and Tibetan Bon traditions.[2] However, it is also defined as 'revival, rebirth, or reinvention', providing the basis for a secular interpretation focused on causality, change and rebirth. The concept of 'reincarnation time' offers a flexible and specifically human temporal model, measured not by the mathematically calculated

---

[2] 'reincarnation, n'. *OED Online*. Oxford University Press, March 2016. Web. 3 May 2016.

second – a base unit calculated from a fixed rate of radioactive decay – but by the individual lifespan. The duration of a single human life provides a flexible temporal unit that is different for every individual, its finite length based not on assumed similarity, but on constant change. Read within a secular framework, 'reincarnation time' provides a means of approaching the overlapping linearity of intergenerational interconnection, seeing each generation of species reproduction as not merely the beginning of another life, but as a form of rebirth in which past actions are unavoidably connected to – and visible in – the future lives of others.

The author has spoken on his interest in reincarnation in several interviews. In an interview with Richard Beard (2005), he notes that '[t]he history of our species is made of endings and beginnings [...]. The Buddhist model of reincarnation is particularly elegant' ('David Mitchell Interview'). In a 2004 interview with Eleanor Wachtel, although he states that he doesn't believe in literal reincarnation, he again notes that 'it's an elegant, beautiful idea', adding that 'there are more humans alive who believe there is such a thing as a soul [...] than humans alive who believe there isn't such a thing as a soul. So may I be wrong' [*sic*] ('Cloud Atlas'). In a 2010 interview by Adam Begley, he emphasizes the redemptive value of the concept in a secular, ecological sense: '[t]here is solace, however, in the carbon cycle, in the nitrogen cycle. Biochemically, at least, reincarnation is a fact' ('David Mitchell, The Art of Fiction'). Similarly, in a 2014 interview by Laurie Grassi he notes that there is 'solace in the notion we can have another go and try and fix things [...]. Reincarnation is a useful idea' ('Best-selling author David Mitchell'). Throughout, the author discusses his interest in reincarnation in secular terms as a 'useful' cross-transferrable model, a metaphysical concept which also has value for interpreting the physical world.

Reincarnated and transmigrated characters span the full length of Mitchell's writing, from the disembodied spirit in Mitchell's first novel *Ghostwritten*, to *Cloud Atlas*' reincarnated characters, to the 2005 short story 'Acknowledgements', whose narrator discovers 'psychomigration', and the vast plot of reincarnations and transmigrated souls in his latest novels, *The Bone Clocks* and *Slade House*.[3] However, as Caroline Edwards notes, 'Mitchell's use of transmigration' is 'not a common trope in twentieth- and twenty-first-century literature' ('Strange Transactions' 191). While several critics have mentioned Mitchell's unusual use of reincarnation, there is little sustained analysis of its role across the macronovel. For example, in '"Gravid with the Ancient Future": *Cloud Atlas* and the Politics of Big History' (2015), Casey Shoop and Dermot Ryan briefly note that 'the promise of reincarnation rises above the novel's bleak record of predacity' (105), while in '"This Time Round": David Mitchell's *Cloud Atlas* and the Apocalyptic Problem of Historicism' (2010), Heather J. Hicks goes further towards a discussion of reincarnation in the novel, suggesting Sonmi's ascension is 'the fabricant equivalent of the Buddhist state of Enlightenment', but concludes that 'the complexities of Buddhist spirituality are beyond the scope of this essay'. Caroline Edwards also comments on the 'symbolic figure of transmigration' in these novels, discussing the use

---

[3] Mitchell confirms the shared comet-shaped birthmark that links *Cloud Atlas*' narrators as evidence of their reincarnation in several interviews. For example, in a 2010 interview by Harriet Gilbert, Mitchell notes, 'they're the same person [...] it's the same soul, being reincarnated in different stages' ('David Mitchell – Cloud Atlas').

of this trope as part of a construction of 'a trans-historical community' that fosters 'a forceful, oppositional agency' in the face of 'colonial power' (190). Berthold Schoene's *The Cosmopolitan Novel* (2009) identifies the 'eternal cycle of reincarnation' depicted in *Cloud Atlas* as a 'general rather than specific symbol of humanity's potential for communal affiliation' (115–16). In 'Food Chain: Predatory Links in the Novels of David Mitchell' (2015), Peter Childs also rightly notes the 'transcultural' influence of 'Eastern philosophies' across Mitchell's works, observing '[t]he soul thus seems to represent the site and agency of reanimation for Mitchell', but again, the discussion is tantalizingly brief (190).

Existing criticism has tended to limit its mentions of reincarnation in the author's work to *Cloud Atlas* and *Ghostwritten*, with no sustained discussion of this trope across his fictional universe. Drawing on the Buddhist philosophy of samsara, or the cycle of life, death and rebirth, this chapter investigates the reworked use of reincarnation across Mitchell's fictional world as a transferrable temporal model, whose secular application provides a productive means of 'looking down time's telescope at myself'. As a human-centred exploration of a spiralling cyclical temporality, 'reincarnation time' suggests that a greater focus on generational interdependence and ethical causality are urgently needed in order to challenge the seemingly inescapable linearity of the 'end of history' narrative of global capitalism. As Fredric Jameson observes in *The Cultural Turn* (1998), '[i]t seems easier for us today to imagine the thoroughgoing deterioration of the earth and of nature than the breakdown of late capitalism'; such imagined 'deterioration' seems all the more worrying in light of the proposed geological epoch of the Anthropocene, marking a new era defined by global human impact (50). Under the current geological system, the formal categorization of this epoch will form a permanent addition within an irreversibly linear geological timescale. The challenge within such an era, then, will be to imagine other temporal counter-strategies which may help our species not merely to survive, but to regenerate. As the macronovel demonstrates, 'reincarnation time' offers one such strategy.

'Reincarnation time' and transmigration

Disembodied souls first appear in Mitchell's fictional world in his first novel. In *Ghostwritten*'s Mongolia chapter – also published as the short story 'Mongolia' in 1999 – the spirit of the noncorpum is revealed as the soul of an eight-year-old boy imprisoned during the implementation of brutal communist 'social engineering policies' in 1937. During this time, thousands of Mongolians – many of them Buddhist – were persecuted and killed in the violent 'dismantling of the monasteries' referred to in the novel (199). Left starving 'in a prison cell, smaller than a wardrobe', the noncorpum, then a young monk in training, is held captive with his 'master', a kindly 'monk in a saffron robe' who 'wears a yellow hat that arcs forward' (199, 189). Having 'promised' the boy's father that his son wouldn't die, the monk intones a 'mantra' moments before their execution, and begins to 'transmigrate' the boy's soul into the body of a nearby girl, beginning by transferring the boy's memories (200–1). However, he is killed before being able to fully transmigrate the boy's soul, leaving his disembodied consciousness searching for its identity. The monk is described as being from 'the Sect of the Yellow Hat', his clothing and headwear identifying him as a member of the Gelug school of Tibetan Buddhism, of which the fourteenth Dalai Lama is its most internationally recognized figure, and which has been practised in Mongolia for many centuries (201).

Significantly, reincarnation and transmigration are introduced within a specifically Tibetan Buddhist framework, suggesting that its philosophies have wider relevance for interpreting these tropes throughout the macronovel. Transmigration is an important part of Tibetan Buddhist belief which exists alongside the wider Buddhist concept of reincarnation. While reincarnation is defined in the OED as 'the rebirth of a soul in a new body or form', transmigration is defined as the '[p]assage of the soul at death into another body'.[4] In secular usage, the terms are often used interchangeably. However, in Buddhist belief systems, reincarnation or rebirth at the end of life broadly refers to the process by which past actions influence future rebirths in an ethical model of cause and effect based on karma, defined as '[t]he sum of a person's actions [...] regarded as determining his fate in the next [life]; hence, necessary fate or destiny, following as effect from cause'.[5] Compassionate actions are believed to result in being reborn as a 'higher' lifeform, a process which repeats until the individual breaks the seemingly endless cycle of life, death and rebirth, or samsara, to reach a state of Enlightenment, or nirvana – complexities which are largely absent from its secular English-language usage.[6]

Whereas Buddhist understandings of reincarnation refer to the cycle of samsara and the shared goal of reaching its exit, by contrast, the term 'transmigration' is also used in this chapter to refer more specifically to the passing of the individual's consciousness into another body. As their etymologies reveal, both English-language terms are more strongly associated with the physical and permanent, rather than the metaphysical and transitory, an important distinction whose neglect risks skewing any meaningful understanding of the Tibetan Buddhist concepts of reincarnation and transmigration altogether. The etymology of 'transmigration' reveals its Latinate roots, which refer to a change of country, or an action, and its primary definition in the OED still refers to '[t]he removal of the Jews into captivity at Babylon'; within common usage, its focus on the physical, and its specifically biblical heritage make this broadly inadequate for conveying the metaphysical use of the concept in Tibetan Buddhism. Similarly, 'reincarnation', from the Latin *incarnāre*, meaning 'to make flesh', misses the complexities of the Buddhist understanding of reincarnation, which is based on the philosophy of *anātman* or *anatta*.[7] This is a concept of 'no-self', a foundational belief that there is no permanent soul or fixed, unchanging identity; the Buddhist philosophy of *anātman* therefore disrupts the OED definitions of transmigration as the '[p]assage of the soul' and reincarnation as 'the rebirth of a soul'. While the term

---

[4] 'transmigration, n'. *OED Online*. Oxford University Press, March 2016. Web. 5 May 2016.
[5] 'karma, n'. *OED Online*. Oxford University Press, March 2016. Web. 5 May 2016.
[6] The Buddhist goal of Enlightenment or nirvana is variously described as a state of understanding, peace and total release from the cycle of rebirth, rather than a fixed place (see 'Nirvāṇa' (322) in *The Buddhist Religion* (1996) by Richard Robinson and Willard Johnson), and by John Snelling as 'a Way Out of the system, one that did not lead to a temporary resting place' (see 'The Buddhist World View' (1987) in *The Buddhist Handbook*, 48).
[7] 'incarnate, v'. *OED Online*. Oxford University Press, March 2016. Web. 22 May 2016.

'soul' is used within this study, it must also be borne in mind that whereas the English-language concept of the soul generally refers to a singular and unchanging entity (the 'Soul'), Buddhist understandings of the 'soul' would generally refer to a more fluid consciousness without a fixed identity – if the term 'soul' is to be used, it would certainly be with a small 's', so to speak. Within this framework, the disembodied noncorpum aligns more with the Tibetan Buddhist understanding of a roaming consciousness without a fixed identity than with Christianity-centric understandings of a permanent and unchanging Soul-self that remain embedded within the English language.

To address the problems inherent in imposing any single religious interpretation, it is also worth noting here that Tibetan Buddhism is influenced by several different schools of Buddhism, each with its own focus and complexities. Tibetan Buddhist approaches towards transmigration traditionally include belief in the abilities of individuals to affect their destination after death, a belief developed in Tibetan Vajrayana practice to include the use of esoteric techniques – such as the mantras intoned by Mitchell's monk – to influence the soul's passage from the body. For example, as John K. Manos notes in 'Tibetan Buddhism' (2016), '[t]he concept of *incarnate lamas* is unique to Tibetan Buddhism. This concept is the belief that the mind of a dead lama can reappear in a newborn child', referring to the 'unique' beliefs which determine the succession of the Dalai Lama, the spiritual head of Tibetan Buddhism. The Tibetan Buddhist phenomenon of transmigration is discussed further in *The Tibetan Book of the Dead*, a text believed to be written in the eighth century, to guide the individual through – and help them to influence the outcomes of – death and rebirth. In a 2014 interview with James Kidd, Mitchell notes that he was reading this text while writing *The Bone Clocks*; as discussed in Chapter 2, the influence of its mythologies can be seen in the transmigrations and rebirths of the novel's characters, including their forty-nine-day period spent in a twilight realm before rebirth. This Tibetan Vajrayana concept of esoteric transmigration is suggested from the earliest introduction of reincarnation in Mitchell's works, its inclusion allowing a more detailed exploration of the model of reincarnation and its associated philosophies from outside the boundaries of realist constraint and the dominant Christianity-centric understandings embedded in their conventional English-language usage.

Tibetan Buddhism contains elements of three major Buddhist systems: Hinayana, also known as Theravada Buddhism; Mahayana; and Vajrayana, also known as Tantric Buddhism.[8] As discussed in Chapter 2, it is the Vajrayana system that traditionally makes extended use of sand mandalas to aid meditation, each mandala's ultimate aim being to further the individual on their quest to break free from the cycle of rebirth by developing the fundamental Buddhist principles of wisdom and compassion, the practice of which cumulatively leads the individual towards Enlightenment. A specific type of Tibetan Buddhist mandala offers a visualization of 'reincarnation time', whose depiction is particularly useful in understanding how such a temporal concept may be applied: the Bhavachakra or Wheel of Life mandala, which will also be discussed

---

[8] For example, see *Buddhist Civilization in Tibet* (1987) by Tulku Thondup Rinpoche, which notes, 'Tibetans are followers of *Mahayana*, and there is no traditional Tibetan who has not also been initiated into *Vajrayana* training. Tibetans also study and practice *Hinayana* teachings' (3).

in Chapter 4 (see Appendix F). The Bhavachakra makes visible the patterns of cause and effect that drive the endless cyclicality of suffering and rebirth; it is a structural model of reincarnation's causal stages which represents a Buddhist doctrine variously known as *Pratityasamutpada*, Codependent Origination, Dependent Origination or Dependent Co-Arising.[9] In doing so, the Bhavachakra mandala offers a visual model of reincarnation whose time scale is fluid, a model based not on a fixed conception of days, years or geological aeons, but on behavioural causality and human action. As Richard Robinson and Willard Johnson note in *The Buddhist Religion*, 'samsara is said to have no discernible point of origin in time', the Bhavachakra's depiction of reincarnation forming 'not simply a map of the cosmos, but also an analysis of karma and an evaluation of its results'; breaking free from the cycle requires the cumulative effects of positive action over many lifetimes, reflecting its 'ethical basis' (22, 23).

As a model of temporality, the Bhavachakra mandala offers a depiction of 'reincarnation time' that is fundamentally human, the linearity of its causal stages undercut by its focus on the cyclicality of lived experience across many human lifespans, this forward movement again suggesting a spiral, rather than a perfect circle. As John Snelling notes in 'The Buddhist World View' (1987), breaking the cycle 'is only possible from one of the destinations in a world-system: that of human beings [...] from the Buddhist point of view, the human realm is the centre of the action' (48). Similarly, Robinson and Johnson also note the importance of human agency within this model: '[h]uman volition lies at the centre of the wheel and powers its every turn' (23). In 'The Bhavachakra or Wheel of Life Mandala as a Buddhist Paradigm for International Relations' (2006), Maggie Grey rightly suggests the transferable value of the Bhavachakra mandala for international relations in providing an alternative temporal model whose longer timescale counteracts the 'short-term state and corporate perspectives that are dangerously insufficient' for addressing 'the global community of the 21st century' (2). Grey argues that the Bhavachakra mandala's focus on causality 'actively posits an interdependent and environmentally sustainable' global system, its recognition of the collective consequences of negative as well as positive actions simultaneously providing 'an explicit warning for this new 21st century "global" community' (3, 6).

Read as a temporal model, its causality can flow in both directions, towards regeneration or degeneration, its variable scale allowing for the effects of cumulative actions over innumerable lifetimes. As Giuseppe Tucci notes in *The Theory and Practice of the Mandala* (1961), the temporal focus of samsara is one of 'incessant movement', demonstrating that 'although I suffer from my past, I remain always the free author of my future', a shared future in which '[l]ives repeatedly develop, linked together like

---

[9]   The causal stages of reincarnation are visible in the twelve images in the outer ring of the Bhavachakra, which represent the interlinked causality that leads to the cycle of rebirth. While the complexities of Codependent Origination are beyond the scope of this study, to provide a brief overview, each stage causes the next: (1) ignorance leads to karmic action; (2) action leads to consciousness; (3) consciousness leads to the creation of bodily form and identity; (4) form leads to the formation of the six senses; (5) the senses lead to contact; (6) contact leads to feeling; (7) feeling leads to craving; (8) craving leads to attachment; (9) attachment leads to worldly existence; (10) existence leads to birth; (11) birth leads to (12) ageing and death. See 'The Bhavachakra or Wheel of Life Mandala as a Buddhist Paradigm for International Relations' (2005) by Maggie Grey (1).

the rings of a chain' (3). At the centre of the Bhavachakra mandala are the root causes of the cycle of collective suffering and reincarnation depicted in the model: symbolic representations of ignorance (represented by a pig), greed (a bird) and aggression (a snake) – all transferrable within the paradigms of corporate irresponsibility, self-interest and free-market competition that continue to define global capitalism.

'Treading on spirals': Reincarnation in the macronovel

Read within a secular framework, the Bhavachakra mandala provides a useful visualization of 'reincarnation time', an alternative to linear temporalities whose long timescale, focus on human causality and potential for progression or regression all suggest an ethical means of approaching a new geological epoch defined by the shared consequences of compounded human actions over many lifetimes. 'Reincarnation time' maintains the dual possibilities of positive change or dystopic decline, its emphases on causality prompting a greater focus on individual ethical action and shared consequences. Applied to Mitchell's macronovel, 'reincarnation time' provides a model through which to approach its expansive temporal dimensions, its timescale 'stretching back approximately seven millennia' from Moombaki's distant past in *The Bone Clocks* (415), to several hundred years into the future in *Cloud Atlas*. The concept of 'reincarnation time' also addresses the author's fascination with temporal cyclicality; as Mitchell notes in a 2015 interview with Paul A. Harris, 'metaphorically time can seem mighty circular or phase-like for something allegedly linear' ('David Mitchell in the Laboratory of Time' 9).

Mitchell further explores the concept of temporal cyclicality in *Cloud Atlas*, referring to the Nietzschean concept of the eternal return. The eternal return or eternal recurrence, described in Friedrich Nietzsche's 1882 text *The Gay Science* (2001) as the identical repetition of lived experience 'innumerable times' as if the 'eternal hourglass of existence [...] turned over again and again', suggests a potential alternative cyclical model for understanding Mitchell's treatment of temporality in the macronovel (194). The eternal return refers to a temporal cycle in which life is destined to endlessly repeat itself, as described in Robert Frobisher's suicide note in *Cloud Atlas*:

> Nietzsche's gramophone record. When it ends, the Old One plays it again, for an eternity of eternities. [...] my birth, next time around, will be upon me in a heartbeat. [...] Such elegant certainties comfort me. (490)

Frobisher's Nietzschean conception of time as an endlessly repeating set of events provides a particularly 'elegant' possible temporal model within a book whose tribal warfare in its distant future disturbingly resembles that of its distant past. However, the eternal return is ultimately an ethical thought experiment which interrogates the possibility of acceptance of life as it is, and whose non-linear cyclicality refuses meaningful change. As such, it suggests a paradoxically anti-temporal model of temporality, whose focus is not on the course of lived events, but on the certainty of their endless recurrence. While Frobisher's imagining of an endlessly cyclical temporality may serve to 'comfort' him at the moment of his death, this temporal model is not able to account for the vital moments of change that are at work across the macronovel. If such a future is unalterably destined to be repeated – as suggested by Frobisher's reference – then the long-term efforts of the reincarnated Horologists in *The Bone Clocks* are ultimately fruitless, while the narrator's urging of the reader to take up his compassionate lifelong course of helping others in 'My Eye On You' is little more than an endlessly repeated plea. As *Cloud Atlas* demonstrates with Frobisher's suicide, the lived outcome of such temporal fatalism may be ideologically comforting, but practically futile. By contrast, the inclusion of reincarnation in the macronovel suggests an alternative cyclicality that allows for ongoing change and progression, for better or worse, spiralling across unimaginably long timescales and individual moments alike. The depiction of 'reincarnation time' in the macronovel reinforces that what is at stake isn't whether change is possible, but whether such changes will result in ethical progression or regression.

Unlike the cyclical model of the eternal return, the spiralling model of 'reincarnation time' is visible across the macronovel's narrative structures, as well as in its content; a progressive narrative cyclicality is frequently embedded into Mitchell's works. For example, this is visible in *Ghostwritten*'s interlinked beginning and ending (its narrative begins and ends with '[w]ho was blowing on the nape of my neck?' and '[w]ho is blowing on the nape of my neck?' respectively) (3, 436), in *Black Swan Green*'s depiction of a single January to January year in its narrator's life, in *Cloud Atlas*'s journey from the distant past into the distant future and back again, and in *Slade House*'s repeated depictions of victimhood and soul-stealing, each successive generation of entrapment carried out in the same way, by the same people, in the same setting, for each of its characters. Yet even within these cyclical structures, a sense of ethical progression is maintained which prevents each narrative loop from being fully closed, allowing for change and movement within each text. For example, *Ghostwritten* returns the reader to the start of the novel, but it is with a new awareness of the fragility of human existence gained from witnessing its near-destruction by the sentient global security system in its final chapter. *Black Swan Green* returns to the beginning of another year for its narrator, Jason, but his life has been irrevocably altered by his parents' divorce as he leaves his childhood home at the end of the novel. The author's endings are often beginnings, rebirths in disguise: for example, the last words of *Black Swan Green* are Jason's sister Julia telling him 'it's not the end' (371), while *The Bone Clocks*' final line is '[f]or one voyage to begin, another voyage must come to an end, sort of' (595). Similarly, *number9dream*'s final words, 'I begin running', indicate a new beginning for its narrator (418), while *Slade House* ends with the rebirth of Norah Grayer as her soul leaves her dying body and transmigrates into 'a foetal boy' (233). In each case, the narrative's structural cyclicality is accompanied by definitive narrative progression in its content, providing a spiralling temporal frame of reinvention and rebirth.

Nietzsche's *Thus Spoke Zarathustra* (2006), first published in four parts between 1883 and 1885, also discusses eternal recurrence, containing the assertion that '[a]ll that is straight lies […] All truth is crooked, time itself is a circle' (125). However, the macronovel's cyclical narrative structures refuse to provide such perfect closure, maintaining the possibility of change; this Nietzschean circularity is overturned in favour of a temporal model based on a simultaneously cyclical and linear 'reincarnation time'. As opposed to a perfect circular temporality, 'reincarnation time' maintains a spiralling possibility of forward and backward progression in a revaluing of the linear within the cyclical, even while conventional linearity itself is disrupted. In *The Bone Clocks*, we meet a benevolent race of compassionate reincarnated beings, called Horologists, who 'live in this spiral of resurrections' (431). Significantly, their reincarnations are described as a 'spiral', rather than the simpler circle that such rebirths would suggest. It would seem fitting, therefore, that when Crispin hears a mysterious premonition that mentions spirals, it is only at the moment of his death that he finally realizes the spirals were there all along, stitched into the carpet under his feet: 'Not dots. *Spirals*. All these weeks. Treading on spirals. Look' (382).

'Being born's a hell of a lottery': Marinus and the role of the bodhisattva

While the concept of 'reincarnation time' can be seen across the macronovel's narrative structures and content, it is also visible in its characterization, in its inclusion of transmigrated and reincarnated characters, and also in the shared characters who return across this fictional world (see Chapter 1 for examples). However, the introduction of one particular reincarnated character – Dr Marinus – from the 2010 publication of *The Thousand Autumns* and first performance of *Wake* onwards has particular significance when read alongside the concept of 'reincarnation time'.

In *The Thousand Autumns*, Dr Lucas Marinus is introduced as a Dutch 'physician, scholar and traveller' who teaches medical students on the island of Dejima in Japan, and – after a few mischievous pranks on Marinus' part – becomes friends with Jacob (156). However, the novel contains several hints that there is more to Marinus than he is revealing; it isn't until his reappearance as the female Dr Iris Marinus-Fenby in *The Bone Clocks* that his comments are retrospectively revealed as hints that he has been reincarnated. For example, Lucas Marinus tells Jacob that he is 'indestructible', and that after his death he'll 'wake up tomorrow – after a few months – and start all over again' (502). The day before his death, Marinus jokes that he is 'a grass-snake, shedding one skin' – a fittingly ouroboric image – and when he dies, his funeral procession is 'led by two Buddhist priests' (533, 531). It is only when reread against the knowledge of his reincarnation, as discussed in *The Bone Clocks*, that his mysterious comments become identifiable as facets of his past lives. His later incarnation, Iris Marinus-Fenby, reveals in *The Bone Clocks* that she is reborn into the body of a dying child each time she dies; reread in light of this, Lucas Marinus' figurative assertion in *The Thousand Autumns* that 'sentience in this life began' when he 'was a six-year-old boy who had been taken to death's door' becomes part of the lived history of his rebirths (136).

In *The Bone Clocks*, its teenage narrator Holly remarks that '[b]eing born's a hell of a lottery', a statement that has far greater resonance in light of Marinus' centuries of lived experience (54). In the novel, Iris Marinus-Fenby – like her previous selves, including Yu Leon Marinus, Pablo Antay Marinus and Lucas Marinus – is again a medical doctor, now an African-Canadian 'clinical psychiatrist based in Toronto' (418). Within the book's mythology, Marinus is one of several Atemporal Horologists who are reincarnated across many lifetimes, a 'Returnee' who 'live[s] in this spiral of resurrections involuntarily' (413, 431). Each time she dies, she is reborn alternately male and female into the body of a dying child, after a forty-nine-day period spent in 'the Dusk', a twilight space 'between life and death' (430). Having originally been born in 640 AD as the Sammarinese 'son of a falconer', Iris Marinus-Fenby has lived in forty previous bodies, over a 'metalife of one thousand four hundred years' (462, 440). While Marinus and the other atemporals are benevolent individuals who are involuntarily reborn, they are engaged in an ongoing secret war with the Anchorites, a group of soul-eaters who prey on 'engifted' humans with rare psychic abilities, consuming their souls in order to artificially increase their own lifespans (436).

Predating the 'revealing' of Marinus' reincarnations in *The Bone Clocks*, further hints can be found in Mitchell's libretti, both of which were first performed before the publication of *The Bone Clocks*. As discussed earlier, *Wake*, first performed in 2010, contains a male character called Marinus who is 'cursed and blessed' with premonitions (3); *Sunken Garden*, first performed in 2013, offers an earlier depiction of Iris Marinus-Fenby from *The Bone Clocks*. In the novel, Marinus mentions a previous 'freelance Carnivore' that she 'disposed of [...] after quite a strenuous duel in her sunken garden'; *Sunken Garden* tells the story of this battle, and so stands as a prequel to the novel (485). As Mitchell has confirmed in a 2016 interview, Claron McFadden's portrayal of Marinus was subsequently written into in *The Bone Clocks*; the author notes, 'in my imagination, when I was writing the book, she was Claron for all intents and purposes in my head', his writing for stage directly influencing the future trajectory of this reincarnated character ('Interview by Rose Harris-Birtill').

In both operas, Marinus is marked as visibly different to the other characters from the outset, emphasizing this character's unique role in the macronovel. In *Wake*, his long pale coat, which reaches almost down to his feet, provides an instant contrast with the more everyday clothing of the other characters, and in the tableau of all the characters presented in the opening requiem, he enters separately, walking slowly across the front of the stage to take the last seat among them (1). Similarly, in *Sunken Garden*, Marinus' bright red suit sets her apart from those she encounters, whose more realistic, everyday costumes are more muted and casual, with the exception of Zenna's bright green dress. *Slade House* and 'I_Bombadil' both also feature Iris Marinus, adding further details to her character. *Slade House* reveals that she was born in Baltimore in 1980 (221), while 'I_Bombadil' acts as a prequel to *Slade House*, revealing the etymology of her name, as discussed in Chapter 1, and even detailing its correct pronunciation. A further incarnation of Dr Marinus ('a rugged Indian, removing his surgical mask') pumps Clive's stomach after his overdose in 'All Souls Day' (84). Read together, *The Thousand Autumns*, *Wake*, *Sunken Garden*, *The Bone Clocks*, *Slade House*, 'I_Bombadil' and 'All Souls Day' form a seven-part subset of David Mitchell's writing in which the reincarnated character of Marinus features more prominently, and is more fully realized, than any other character in the macronovel.

Throughout each of these reincarnations, Marinus is consistently depicted as a compassionate 'healer', drawn to help alleviate the suffering of others (*The Bone Clocks*

63, *Sunken Garden* 6). As Iris Marinus-Fenby, she notes that she 'gravitate[s] towards medicine' and has been a doctor in several lifetimes; her past lives include roles as a psychiatrist, a surgeon and a 'herbalist' (*The Bone Clocks* 463–4). Even where Marinus isn't explicitly described as a healer, she continues devoting her lives to helping others; in *Wake*, Marinus befriends the elderly Otto, who lives alone, tortured by his guilt at accidentally killing a child in a hit-and-run years before. Realizing that Otto 'punishes himself more than any judge could', Marinus continues to visit Otto in his apartment as a non-judgemental source of support (3). When Marinus experiences a premonition that a disaster is imminent, he tries to 'persuade Otto to come night-fishing' three times in an effort to save his life, concerned that telling the police only risks adding to the forthcoming 'carnage'. Marinus' compassionate role also extends to the audience, which, at the opera's first performance in Enschede in 2010, would have included survivors of the real-life disaster that it narrates. It is Marinus who quietly announces the off-stage disaster and fatalities without harrowing detail, simply telling the audience: 'the waiting was unbearable [...] and the waiting was over.' Similarly, in *Sunken Garden*, Marinus helps Toby to come to terms with his grief over helping his terminally ill mother to die, and risks her own life to save those trapped in Zenna's supernatural garden. From Lucas Marinus' unwavering determination to stay with Jacob as he faces almost-certain death in *The Thousand Autumns*, to Iris Marinus-Fenby's war against the soul-eaters in *Slade House* to protect future victims, to Harry Marinus Veracruz's efforts to save Holly's grandchildren from the impending ecological disaster depicted in *The Bone Clocks*, Marinus' numerous compassionate and selfless acts to help others run throughout the macronovel.

However, Marinus isn't portrayed as a God-like or Messiah-type figure in any of her lives. Instead, this character remains fallible; in *Wake*, he notes, 'I can't play God, and I can't second-guess causality' (3); while facing down the warship in *The Thousand Autumns*, he confesses to Jacob: 'I pissed my thigh from fear' (503). As Iris Marinus notes in *The Bone Clocks*, a 'metalife of one thousand four hundred years is no guarantee that you always know the right thing to do' (440). Marinus may be reincarnated, with powers of transmigration, but she is certainly not omniscient. While the concept of reincarnation is introduced into the macronovel from within a wider framework of Tibetan Buddhist mythology in *Ghostwritten* and 'Mongolia', as mentioned earlier, further references also suggest that a Buddhist-influenced reading may prove illuminating for understanding the function of the reincarnated characters in the macronovel. For example, referring to the forty-nine-day period which Marinus spends in 'the Dusk' before being reborn, David Mitchell confirms in a 2015 interview that '[t]he 49-days thing is Buddhist, as you probably know. When you die [...] the soul is around for 49 days before it actually leaves'; this forty-nine-day period is also discussed in *The Tibetan Book of the Dead* ('Interview by Rose Harris-Birtill').[10] Marinus also notes in *Sunken Garden*, 'I'd make more sense in Sanskrit; or better yet, Tibetan' – explicitly referring to the languages of Tibetan Buddhism, and suggesting

---

[10] It is worth noting here that the number forty-nine is also significant in some Judeo-Christian traditions in which Pentecost or Shavuot is observed forty-nine days after Passover, with Pentecost or Shavuot as the fiftieth day. My thanks to Professor Martin Paul Eve for this observation.

that her role would 'make more sense' when interpreted through these belief systems (5). Read within a Tibetan Buddhist-influenced framework of 'reincarnation time', Marinus' compassionate role within the macronovel can be read as a secular version of a particular Buddhist figure: the bodhisattva.

A term from the Sanskrit '*bodhi*', meaning perfect knowledge, and '*sattvá*', meaning being or reality, within Buddhist philosophy, the bodhisattva is a being 'of infinite wisdom and compassion' who devotes their lives to helping those around them to escape the endless cycle of suffering and rebirth, a would-be Buddha who delays reaching Enlightenment, choosing instead to continue being reborn in order to help others.[11] The concept is particularly significant in Mahayana Buddhism as a principle by which individuals should aspire to become bodhisattvas themselves. Significantly, the bodhisattva is not a god, but a human who has chosen to help all others reach the Buddhist goal of Enlightenment before themselves breaking free from samsara. Rosita Dellios notes in 'Mandala: From Sacred Origins to Sovereign Affairs in Traditional Southeast Asia' (2003) that '[a]ccording to the Mahayana ('Greater Vehicle') school of Buddhism – practiced predominantly in Tibet [...], China, Korea and Japan – the path to liberation is to liberate others from suffering', a school which emphasizes the individual's ability to themselves become a bodhisattva, in contrast to the older Theravada school of Buddhism, in which the focus is on the individual's responsibility to reach Enlightenment for themselves (11).[12] The bodhisattva of compassion, known as Avalokitesvara, or Chenrezig in Tibetan, is one of the most widely recognized bodhisattvas in Mahayana Buddhism, whose role is particularly significant in Tibetan Buddhism.[13] The importance of the compassionate qualities and actions of the bodhisattva are symbolized in the visual scripture of the Chenrezig mandala, or mandala of compassion, a mandala devoted to these ethical principles (see Appendix C).[14] Vessantara observes that Avalokitesvara, as the 'bodhisattva of compassion', is the embodiment of a fundamental principle: 'compassion is the distinguishing mark of the Bodhisattva', the defining attribute 'which makes a Bodhisattva a Bodhisattva' (*Meeting the Buddhas* 2003, 137).

With her multiple rebirths, her compassionate actions to help others and her specifically human – rather than divine – nature, Marinus' role across the macronovel becomes that of a secular bodhisattva, whose actions display a post-secular realization

---

[11] 'Bodhisattva, n'. *OED Online*. Oxford University Press, March 2016. Web. 10 May 2016.
[12] As Richard Robinson and Willard Johnson note in *The Buddhist Religion* (1996), 'Mahayana innovation was to advocate the bodhisattva course for all Buddhists' and 'lay out a detailed Path for aspiring bodhisattvas' (84). Vessantara also notes in *Meeting the Buddhas: A Guide to Buddhas, Bodhisattvas, and Tantric Deities* (2003) that 'Mahayana vision sees the Bodhisattva working for aeons, in endless rebirths, at the service of living beings, helping towards Enlightenment' (130).
[13] Robinson and Johnson also note: 'In Tibet, Avalokitesvara was revered as the country's patron, protector, and founder of the Tibetan race. Tibetans everywhere worshiped him for his compassionate response to the sufferings and trials of life' (108).
[14] As well as providing a sacred representation of an imagined space, Tibetan Buddhist mandalas also feature representations of both bodhisattvas and Buddhas, which may be represented with symbols, characters or dots of sand. As Jung A. Huh notes in 'Mandala as telematic design', '[t]he mandala arranges Buddhas and Bodhisattvas in a harmonious and orderly pattern in sacred space', a reminder for the participant not merely to learn from the ideal behaviours of these individuals, but also to themselves embody their lived principles of wisdom and compassion (21).

of this role's principles, while being influenced by – but ultimately detached from – an explicitly religious framework. In a 2014 interview for *Herald Scotland*, Mitchell adds a further post-secular dimension to Marinus' character while discussing *The Bone Clocks*, describing her as 'A Time Lord without a Tardis or sonic screwdriver. A Buddhist version of the Wandering Jew personality', in a role that combines influences from science fiction, Buddhist and Christian mythologies alike ('Sex, drugs and Talking Heads in writer's latest incarnation').

In a 2016 interview, Mitchell discusses the role of the bodhisattva; he is 'familiar with the concept' and has been since his 'late teens', finding 'a beauty in it'. He goes on to note that the principles behind the reincarnated characters were

> first identified in *bodhisattvas*, but co-opted for my own, in a way, more secular purposes. In the Buddhism that I've read about, they don't really feel that religious, and that's why I'm attracted to them. ('Interview by Rose Harris-Birtill')

It is important to note here that one of the main factors which differentiates Marinus as a secular, rather than strictly religious bodhisattva, is this notion of religious purpose. While Buddhist bodhisattvas consciously choose to continue being reborn, with the concrete aim of deferring Enlightenment in order to help others, Marinus does not know why she exists and continues to be reborn. In *The Bone Clocks*, she asks, '[h]ave we evolved this way? Or are we designed? [...] To what end?' (387). She is not otherwise depicted as a religious practitioner, and her attempts to help others are not overtly focused on reaching religious forms of Enlightenment for herself or others. However, her commitment to upholding her own sustained practice of compassionate acts through multiple reincarnations can be seen throughout the macronovel, in a post-secular echo of the bodhisattva's many 'aeons' of compassionate service as described by Vessantara: '[r]ather than escaping from the wheel of suffering as fast as possible, he or she is prepared to work within it, for aeons if necessary' (131). Marinus is also born alternately male and female, an embodiment of the Buddhist belief that becoming a bodhisattva is a practice that 'transcend[s] the boundaries of gender', as Vessantara also notes (144). Robinson and Johnson observe that the Buddhist principle of compassion must be based on action, and crucially must not just include 'sympathy for the suffering of others, but also an effort to alleviate it', as exemplified by Marinus' extensive efforts to help others (*The Buddhist Religion* 43). Robinson and Johnson also note that one of the foundations of the bodhisattva career is striving to practice this behaviour 'without self-consciousness, ulterior motives, or self-congratulation' (43, 101). Marinus' actions to help others are consistently motivated by compassion, without seeking any recognition or payment in kind. As she tells Toby when she risks her life to save his in *Sunken Garden*: '[i]f I die, perhaps it's time – if not, not' (8).

Marinus' role as a doctor is a symptom of her cross-temporal vocation as a healer who provides both physical and mental support to those around her, a role which also aligns with the concept of the bodhisattva. For example, in *The Thousand Autumns*, Lucas Marinus serves his community as a physician, but also provides psychological support, refusing to let Jacob face his almost-certain death alone. As Robinson and Johnson note, in Mahayana Buddhism, 'Bodhisattvas, as physicians, were instructed to treat both corporeal and spiritual aspects of disease as part of the perfection of giving', the bodhisattva traditionally envisaged as a healer of both physical and metaphysical ills (116). Rosita Dellios also notes that in Buddhist ethics, '[g]iving up the delusion of a self permits a life-affirming practice of helping others to avoid suffering and to fulfil their potential' ('Mandala: From Sacred Origins' 3). Marinus' compassionate actions, stemming from her many rebirths, show this ethical principle in action; having lived many lifetimes, she has effectively given up the egocentric behaviour of living as a single self, an experience which has enabled her to experience the long-term consequences of individual actions over many centuries. As Mitchell notes of the reincarnated atemporals, 'that spiritual development just comes from bitter, hard-earned experience [...]. It's just that they've had more of it' ('Interview with Rose Harris-Birtill' 2016).

While Mitchell demonstrates the transferrable secular value of bodhisattva philosophies, the dangerous potential of such figures within an explicitly religious setting is also depicted. In *Ghostwritten*, the terrorist Quasar describes his indoctrination into the cult of 'His Serendipity [...] A boddhisatva [*sic*] who can make himself invisible at will, a yogic flier, a divine being', justifying his actions in accordance to a higher power (11). In a 2010 interview by Adam Begley, Mitchell notes that the real 1995 subway attack that *Ghostwritten* responds to was carried out in part due to 'the desire to *be* brainwashed – and abdicate personal responsibility to a guru, a higher authority, a god' ('David Mitchell'). Applied within an exclusively religious framework, and divorced from the essential principle of human compassion, the belief in such figures as 'divine' is depicted as dangerously open to exploitation, ultimately valuing personal responsibility within a secular reinterpretation of the bodhisattva's role, and employing a metamodern strategy in which religious belief is both potentially constructive and destructive. Mitchell's macronovel reflects a world in which, as Timotheus Vermeulen puts it in a 2012 interview by Cher Potter, '[g]rand narratives are as necessary as they are problematic'; while Marinus' secular realization of the bodhisattva's role acts as a reminder of their necessity, *Ghostwritten*'s bodhisattva cult provides an important warning of its potential for harm within an overtly religious setting ('Timotheus Vermeulen Talks').

The macronovel's inclusion of reincarnation ultimately presents the reader with a long view of the shared historical consequences of human action – or inaction. As Robinson and Johnson note, while reincarnation isn't unique to Buddhism, its focus on karma offers a quintessentially Buddhist 'moral causality' which is 'intended to be experiential and concrete' (*The Buddhist Religion* 18–19). Mitchell's reincarnated characters make visible these generations of human cause and effect, a narrative strategy that is particularly representative of Buddhist approaches to reincarnation, using a post-secular version of its experiential moral causality which depicts the far-reaching positive or negative consequences of individual actions, and portraying the macronovel's dystopic future as caused by compounded human activity. As Holly realizes in *The Bone Clocks*, we are 'leaving our grandchildren a tab that can never be paid', the ecological disaster in the novel caused by generations of damaging behaviour in a secular depiction of the karmic model; she laments, 'the regions we deadlanded, the ice caps we melted [...] the species we drove to extinction, the pollinators we wiped out, the oil we squandered [...] all so we didn't have to change' (533).

Cumulatively, Mitchell's secular depiction of 'reincarnation time' and the repeated reincarnations of Marinus as a form of secular bodhisattva suggest a form of collective experiential time with its own ethical foundations and consequences, based not on mathematical formulae or radioactive decay, but on the revisited consequences of human actions over many lifetimes, and the importance of individual action as the essential precursor to collective change. The measure of such a temporal system is what may be achieved – or destroyed – for current and future generations at any stage in the cycle, each individual human lifespan providing a critical opportunity to help others. As Fredric Jameson notes in 'The Historical Novel Today, or, Is It Still Possible?' (2013), 'for better or for worse, our history, our historical past and our historical novels, must now also include our historical futures as well' (312). The macronovel's depiction of 'reincarnation time' allows for such an incorporation of past and future temporalities. What is important in such a system isn't a literal belief in reincarnation, but living *as if* the individual will be reborn to see their own behavioural consequences and, in doing so, 'looking down time's telescope' not at an abstract future, but at future versions of 'myself' – the lives of other finite yet interconnected beings who will inherit the future that we create, just as we inherit the consequences of others' past lives. Crucially, such a model uses Buddhist ethical influences to build a post-secular, humanist approach that isn't dependent on a final redemptive heaven or nirvana, but also avoids the ethical stagnation of a self-centred postmodern nihilism. Such a model overturns the Western European Enlightenment model of 'self and other', just as the Buddhist philosophy of *anātman* disrupts the Western concept of the self with its insistence that there is no fixed 'I', and therefore no true separation between one individual and another. As Mitchell notes in a 2016 interview, in the absence of an overarching 'meaning of life' presented by a system of endless rebirth, 'this is why I come back to compassion – that's it. That's your meaning [...] Marinus and their ilk, this is where they get their meaning [...] from helping people anonymously' ('Interview by Rose Harris-Birtill'). The essential principle of compassion ensures that such a temporal system is rooted in humanist action, rather than the potentially damaging ideologies of utilitarian sacrifice or religious doctrine, by which the individual is marginalized for the greater good.

Mitchell's short story 'My Eye On You' demonstrates the principle of the secular bodhisattva in action as a 'cure-all for futility' in the face of the breakdown of religious grand narratives, depicting the far-reaching consequences of Richard Cheeseman's choice to follow his 'conscience', abandon his murderous plans and embark on a lifetime of compassionate action (1). Devoting the rest of his life to enacting the principle 'Do Unto Others' – a cross-cultural, pan-religious statement of altruism also known as the Golden Rule – Richard similarly encourages the reader to act on their own 'compassion' at the end of the tale (5, 6). By doing so, Richard effectively demonstrates the principle of 'reincarnation time' in action, experiencing a metaphorical rebirth in which he chooses to live by his own ethical code, his decision driven by a recognition of human interconnection in the present, and a future-facing concern that such actions will continue to benefit others – even though his terminal cancer means that it is a future that he will never see. In a 2014 interview by Erica Wagner, Mitchell notes that such compassion and kindness are 'massively underrated': 'the good things that happen in the world only happen because of it. [...] This is how the world keeps spinning [...]

it's the utterly obscure, kind people' ('David Mitchell, the master builder'). Richard may not have the benefits of literal rebirth that Marinus has, but his decision to use his finite lifespan to help others again shows the compassionate actions of the bodhisattva realized in a secular form. As Vessantara notes, 'Bodhisattvas are self-aware, and work on their own development [...] they feel a kinship with the whole evolutionary process' (*Meeting the Buddhas* 130–1). This is a role which requires the individual – like Marinus, or Richard – to become 'self-aware' of their behaviour and its consequences, taking responsibility for their actions beyond the immediate present of their own lived experience and acting accordingly, a practical strategy whose shared adoption of compassionate action could eventually affect the course of human evolution itself.

'Reincarnation time' and the Anthropocene

David Mitchell's use of 'reincarnation time' suggests the value of alternative temporalities in the face of the Anthropocene, a new geological epoch proposed to succeed the Holocene. As Simon L. Lewis and Mark A. Maslin note in 'Defining the Anthropocene' (2015), '[r]ecent global environmental changes suggest that Earth may have entered a new human-dominated geological epoch' in which the 'impacts of human activity will probably be observable [...] for millions of years into the future', and that consequently, 'human actions may well constitute Earth's most important evolutionary pressure' (171). At the time of writing, no date for the beginning of such an epoch has yet been agreed on. However, these geological changes created by global human activity are already visible in the macronovel, a project that effectively traces the evolution of this human-centred epoch, from the early depiction of imperial conquest in *The Thousand Autumns*, to the near-future oil crises in *The Bone Clocks*, to the far-future civilization breakdown in *Cloud Atlas*. For Mitchell's fictional world, the categorization of this human-engineered global era isn't under debate: it's already here.

The author's engagement with these concerns is by no means limited to the macronovel; Mitchell also notes the worrying ecological trajectory of globalization in several interviews. In a 2004 interview by Wayne Burrows he notes that '[t]he logical extension of neo-capitalism is that it eats itself [...] corporate interests really will pollute the land that supports them, because they can make money by doing so' ('An Interview with David Mitchell'); in a 2010 interview by Adam Begley he observes that '[w]hat made us successful in Darwinian terms – our skill at manipulating our environment – now threatens to wipe us out as a species' ('David Mitchell'); and in a 2014 interview by Zahra Saeed he notes that 'the increases in the standards of our living are being bankrolled by the standards of living of our children and our grandchildren' ('Cork-based Cloud Atlas author').

In a 2015 essay, Paul A. Harris usefully recognizes that Mitchell is a 'novelist of the Anthropocene'; this is an author whose interconnected fictions, with their shared past and future, illustrate the shared causality – and consequences – of the Anthropocene in action ('David Mitchell in the Labyrinth of Time' 5). The macronovel forms a huge project that effectively depicts the evolution of this human-centred epoch, its earliest novel to date set in 1779 (*The Thousand Autumns*) during the age of imperial global navigation and trade. Read cumulatively, the macronovel shows the human actions and predatory attitudes that contributed to the creation of such an epoch of anthropocentric global impact, and warns of the potential futures created by such actions. However, while the categorization of a new epoch exists within an irreversibly linear geological temporality, the use of a spiralling 'reincarnation time' in the macronovel complicates this with the possibility of a multiplicity of beginnings and endings at any stage, suggesting the value of the cyclical within the linear for envisaging productive strategies for change.

Mitchell notes in a 2005 interview with Richard Beard that '[t]he history of our species is made of endings and beginnings', as mentioned earlier; the macronovel's use of 'reincarnation time' depicts this concept in action ('David Mitchell Interview'). For example, its oldest reincarnated character to date is Moombaki from *The Bone Clocks*, revealed not in terms of her age or birth date, but through the combined names of her previous selves which together form her 'long, long, true name' (416). Listing rebirth after rebirth, Moombaki gradually reveals to Marinus that she has lived in 207 'previous hosts', and is 'not thought of as a god [...] but as a guardian, a collective memory'; it is Marinus who calculates that her lived history dates back 'approximately seven millennia' (414–15). Moombaki's long name reimagines geological time's linearity in specifically human terms, each interconnected life becoming a unit of measurement, a literal depiction of Mitchell's envisaging of the 'history of our species' through individual human 'endings and beginnings'. As Mitchell also notes in a 2016 interview, '[t]he atemporals are perhaps core samples [...] that record the human experience' ('Interview by Rose Harris-Birtill'). Moombaki's long name offers a particularly human form of core sample, whose compacted layers aren't comprised of geological strata, but the grit of individual human lives.

Read through a purely linear sequence of events, the macronovel is heading towards widespread dystopic decline. However, Mitchell's macronovel disrupts such linear temporalities with its shifts backwards and forwards in time, as in *Cloud Atlas*, but also in the publication of its narratives along a chronologically discontinuous timescale – for example, a 1980s period-piece (*Black Swan Green*) is followed by a late-eighteenth-century historical novel (*The Thousand Autumns*), which in turn is followed by a novel which envisages the near future (*The Bone Clocks*). Such strategies deliberately complicate any attempt to read this body of works through a strictly linear chronology. Throughout, the possibility of meaningful change for each generation becomes a form of rebirth as another chance to alter the future, made possible through the ethical actions of individuals engaging anew with their responsibility to protect future generations within a global framework of impending ecological destruction. Such efforts can be in the form of big-scale interventions, such as Mo Muntevary's efforts to safeguard potentially devastating military technology in *Ghostwritten*, or in small-scale ethical decisions, such as Marinus' efforts to protect Holly's grandchildren in *The Bone Clocks* – regardless of their positions in the macronovel's chronological sequence of events. This is a narrative world infused with the possibility that 'reincarnation time' brings, a human-centred model of a spiralling cyclical temporality which isn't doomed to repeat the past, but finds the agency and determination to begin again in each successive generation.

If, as Berthold Schoene accurately notes, 'no one person or group of persons is ultimately in charge' of global events now unfolding, we must ask how humanity 'can still hope to make a difference and shape such a world' in which 'political agency is dilapidating into crisis management' (2). Mitchell's use of 'reincarnation time' places intergenerational human action at the centre of this global 'crisis'. As he notes in a 2015 interview with Paul A. Harris, the reincarnated Horologists 'are role models for me [...] I value the notion of reincarnation as a kind of metaphor for a single life' ('David Mitchell in the Laboratory of Time' 13). He adds:

> Horologists, then, are metaphors of mortals. They have repeated lives to slouch towards Enlightenment, and we have just the one to scramble there as best we may, but the methods and the destination are the same.

The author's reference to supernatural beings that 'slouch towards Enlightenment' evokes William Butler Yeats' poem 'The Second Coming', first published in 1920. Although in Yeats' poem it is a 'rough beast' – and not a reincarnated Horologist – which 'Slouches' towards birth, the poem's opening line, 'Turning and turning in the widening gyre', offers a structure for the imminent rebirth that it describes, again evoking the spiralling cyclicality of 'reincarnation time' (189–90). However, as 'role models', the Horologists provide a collective example of the ethical actions that must be achieved in a 'single life' if we are to avoid the same debilitating ecological and social meltdowns that they face. Although the Buddhist terminology of 'Enlightenment' is used, its dual meaning makes it particularly relevant to the macronovel, here referred to as the secular 'action of bringing someone to a state of greater knowledge, understanding, or insight'.[15] However, the difficult 'scramble' towards such insight must be undertaken without the benefit of the Horologists' many lifetimes of lived experience. As such, the macronovel provides a shorthand depiction of the cooperative, compassionate actions that could be learnt through living in 'reincarnation time'. As in the macronovel, it is by no means certain whether such changes will be sufficient to avert global crises, but such collective action forms our only chance at redemption. The concept of reincarnation may be thousands of years old – but as Mitchell's macronovel demonstrates, it suggests a new temporal strategy whose interconnected past, present and future reinforce the vital importance of intergenerational ethical action in imagining meaningful change.

---

[15] 'enlightenment, n'. *OED Online.* Oxford University Press, March 2016. Web. 14 May 2016.

4

'What a Sick Zoo': Escaping the Panopticon in David Mitchell's Macronovel

This chapter moves its focus from the temporal to the spatial, using the mandala's distinctive structural design to suggest new critical approaches to the structures that underpin the macronovel. The use of any structural model within literary criticism – even one based on a symbol with as diverse a heritage and as many different manifestations as the mandala – risks imposing a single framework whose limits may ultimately prove exclusionary to opposing perspectives. While this study aims to use the Tibetan Buddhist mandala to generate productive openings into a discussion of Mitchell's macronovel, as a critical framework the mandala is by no means innocent. From a Jungian perspective, the mandala's central point and concentric outer boundaries are interpreted as symbols of an innate human potential for self-healing. C. G. Jung observes in *The Archetypes and the Collective Unconscious* (1969) that 'the protective circle, the mandala, is the traditional antidote for chaotic states of mind', noting its cross-cultural creation at times of 'disorientation or panic' (10, 360). However, this holistic interpretation runs counter to its darker structural hierarchies; any inclusionary boundary is also an exclusionary one, and any central point of power a potential point of dominance over its surrounds. This chapter seeks to gain deeper insight into the mandala as a critical framework by envisaging its Derridean deconstruction, exploring the potential opposites suggested from within Mitchell's own works in order to interrogate this complex symbol from its inverse perspective and, in doing so, address the controlling structures, boundaries and hierarchies that feature in the macronovel.

The mandala as political paradigm

Before deconstructing the mandala, then, what – of its many features – are its essential structural components at their most simplified? The Tibetan Buddhist mandala's structural design is visually dominated by order and precision, from its outermost concentric circles to the exact proportions of its inner palace. As Rosita Dellios notes in 'Mandala: From Sacred Origins to Sovereign Affairs in Traditional Southeast Asia' (2003), the three fundamental principles of the mandala's construction are its 'centre, symmetry and cardinal points' (2). At its most basic, this spatial arrangement provides a hierarchical diagram in which the mandala's features are organized around its visually dominant centre, providing a simplified blueprint for a net of power relations structured around a single entity.[1] At its apex resides 'a deity, symbol, or letter' which, rather than being an object of worship in itself, represents specific qualities for the practitioner to aspire to, as Susan M. Walcott notes in 'Mapping from a Different Direction: Mandala as Sacred Spatial Visualization' (2006) (78). During meditation, participants visualize the mandala's centre as physically set above its surroundings, as Barry Bryant describes in *The Wheel of Time Sand Mandala* (1995), further establishing the hierarchical prominence of the mandala's central concept; as Bryant notes, '[i]n the three-dimensional mandala, this is the uppermost or "penthouse" level of the palace' (179–80).

Containing this raised inner palace structure, the mandala's outer circular rings form a simultaneously inclusionary and exclusionary boundary. In the Tibetan Buddhist mandala, its outermost ring depicts a border of fire which, as Walcott notes, 'represents the wisdom of complete emptiness', preparing the participant for the intense focus required to enter its metaphysical world (77). Inside this sits a ring of *vajra*, symbolic weapons that represent a great power 'cutting the ropes of attachment [...] to this worldly samsara state', severing the ties to the shared materiality of lived experience.[2] In *The Wheel of Time Sand Mandala*, Bryant emphasizes that this *vajra* circle is symbolically 'protecting the mandala', and that within the Tibetan Kalachakra mandala, six concentric circles form a multilayered boundary that separates the mandala's inner palace from the outside world (153–4). As Walcott notes, '[t]he innermost mandala is thus set off and protected from all outside elements', surrounded by a reinforced circular 'fence' which contains and protects the metaphysical world within (77).

This fundamental mandalic structural arrangement provides a useful template for mapping power relations between a controlling force and its sphere of influence, whether between individuals or entire nations. From this perspective, the Tibetan Buddhist mandala, an intricate world map built on the Buddhist philosophies of wisdom, compassion, knowledge and *ahimsa*, or non-violence, also contains the seeds of its opposite: the blueprint for a network of power, structured around a dominant centre and protected by multiple containing and exclusionary boundaries. The use of this mandalic map in political structures is almost as old as Buddhism itself. As noted by Maggie Grey in 'The Bhavachakra or Wheel of Life Mandala as a Buddhist Paradigm for International Relations' (2006), the mandala's 'political application' can be seen as early as the third century BCE, by Indian statesman Kautilya in the *Arthashastra* (7). This treatise on government, economy and relations between states, also known as

---

[1] This simplified mandalic structure can be found in several cultures and historical periods. As Maggie Grey notes in 'Encountering the Mandala: The Mental and Political Architectures of Dependency' (2001), '[t]he basic concept of the mandala, a circle and its centre, is also culturally abundant: though most notable within the Tibetan Mahayana tradition, mandalas are significant for the religious and secular lives of many peoples', for example, in Native American art and Islamic architecture (1–2).

[2] The *vajra* has a complex symbolic function within Tibetan ritual practice and visual scripture. As Giuseppe Tucci notes in *The Theory and Practice of the Mandala* (2001), the '*vajra* (in Tibetan rdorje – pronounced dorje) is a bronze or brass instrument employed in various initiatory ceremonies', a symbol of power that 'signifies both 'thunderbolt' and 'diamond'' (33).

'The Science of Means' or 'The Science of Material Gain', uses the mandala as a political concept to explain the realm's workings in terms of its balance of power, explicitly employing its structure for political ends.

In the twenty-first century, the mandala is still being used to conceptualize global political power balances. As Rosita Dellios notes in 'Missing Mandalas: Development and Theoretical Gaps' (2004), 'the mandala as metaphor acts as a way of thinking about the massive and often emotionally-charged issues of the day – global development strategies and political relations' (8). Of course, there are other 'massive and often emotionally-charged issues' in contemporary society, but Dellios rightly argues for the transferability of the mandala's framework and its relevance to global geopolitical relationships as illustrating a co-dependent 'system' of nations, its structure forming a 'platform upon which relationships are enacted' between a source of power and its tributaries. As Dellios also highlights, the mandala structure remains relevant for understanding contemporary global power relations, having been 'adopted by 20th century Western historians' and 'employed to denote traditional Southeast Asian political formations', providing an alternative framework for understanding international relations where existing Euro-centric structures simply don't fit ('Mandala: From Sacred Origins' 1). From its basic arrangement of centre, circle and cardinal points, the structural principles of this religious artwork have evolved into a powerful antitype of their own: from its internal organized hierarchies to its application in international relations, the mandala is inescapably political.

Deconstructing the mandala

David Mitchell notes in his 2005 essay 'Asia in English Literature': '[i]n my notebook I keep a Sei Shonagon-type page headed *Unobvious Opposites*. For example, an opposite of the Pacific Ocean might be [not the Atlantic but] a pint of sand' (13). Following Mitchell's own search for 'unobvious opposites', then, what might a critical 'opposite' to the mandala look like, and what would its function be? An 'obvious' place to search would be within the mandala's own spatial arrangement, seeing this structure not as a visual scripture built from the peaceful Buddhist principles of wisdom, compassion and non-violence, but as a map of power relations based on hierarchical dominance, containment and control. However, more complex 'unobvious opposites' emerge from this initial oppositional structure; having begun to approach the controlling structures and centres of power whose origins can be found within the mandala itself, it becomes vital to investigate the mandala's 'unobvious opposites' to help address its potential limitations as a critical tool.

Without addressing its critically problematic internal contradictions, any interpretive framework based on the mandala risks becoming dogmatic, reading the texts against a single world view whose philosophical standpoint is in danger of imposing a reductive reading on the text. Mitchell's works are characterized by their multiple and simultaneously oppositional perspectives, combining hope and despair, optimism and dystopia, just as they feature a post-secular juxtaposition of the religious and the secular. While his continuous narrative universe allows for the possibility of healing after almost unbearable psychological suffering, as in his libretti (see Chapter 2), this same universe also contains the seeds of its own destruction. For example, in *Ghostwritten*, delusional cult member Quasar laments, '[w]hat a sick zoo the world has become' (22). His words evoke the troubled personal beliefs behind his 'gas attack' on a subway train, and also take on a double significance in which this instantly recognizable figure of the global terrorist demonstrates the truth of his own assertion with his actions, as part of a 'sick', self-destructive and animalistic society that the novel critiques (14). As this episode demonstrates, any comparative tool used to critique Mitchell's body of works must be capable of addressing their unsettling dualities and oppositions. Another potential approach is to search for critical alternatives to the mandala, rather than opposites, but the concept of an 'alternative' mandala has a remit so broad that virtually any structure could be an alternative framework (see the introduction for structural frameworks that have already been put forward for Mitchell's works), rendering the approach ineffectual.

A critical exploration of the mandala's opposites, then, suggests the relevance of Derridean deconstruction, a concept notoriously resistant to definition. As Jacques Derrida puts it in 'Letter to a Japanese Friend' (1985), 'deconstruction is neither an *analysis* nor a *critique* [...] Deconstruction is not a method and cannot be transformed into one [...] deconstruction is not even an *act*' (3). While acknowledging that any single definition is problematic, broadly speaking, a deconstructivist reading seeks to identify and challenge the structural assumptions and hierarchies underpinning a concept's dominant meaning and usage, in order to expose its inherent instability and the irreconcilability of its multiple contradictions and oppositions, thereby strengthening the critical understanding of the original concept.

While Derrida's deconstructive approach stems from questioning the binary oppositions that structure Western linguistics, and thereby its philosophical assumptions, its usefulness as a critical approach is by no means limited to individual terms. As Gayatri Chakravorty Spivak notes in her 1997 translator's preface to Jacques Derrida's *Of Grammatology*:

> deconstructive criticism must take the 'metaphoric' structure of a text very seriously. Since metaphors are not reducible to truth, their own structures 'as such' are part of the textuality (or message) of the text [...] both literature *and* its criticism must open itself to a deconstructive reading.[3] (lxxiv–lxxv)

Employed as a literary critical tool, the mandala serves as a '"metaphoric" structure' for the texts that it is being used to examine; the applied framework effectively becomes part of the wider 'textuality', or textual meaning, of the writing that it critiques. Spivak rightly emphasizes that criticism should therefore be subject to the same careful scrutiny expected of the text itself. Taking a deconstructive approach, this chapter therefore interrogates the mandala's ideological assumptions as a critical framework by critiquing the forms that its structural and philosophical opposite could take, and

---

[3] See Derrida's essay 'White Mythology: Metaphor in the Text of Philosophy' in *Margins of Philosophy* (1984) for further discussion of the role of metaphor in philosophical criticism (207–71).

discovering what the application of such an oppositional structure brings to the literary criticism of Mitchell's body of work.

While deconstruction follows an established critical methodology that risks introducing binarism, its insistence on ultimately destabilizing a given term makes it valuable for approaching a structure that has not previously been fully explored within literary criticism, and particularly one whose holistic associations risk generating a one-sided reading. This chapter's deconstructive approach seeks to engage in the deliberate reversal and disruption of the mandala-based critical framework developed within this study, identifying its potential opposites, and investigating the issues that surface if its antitheses are allowed to assume hierarchical prominence. The investigation into a potential anti-mandala aims to address the unavoidable multiplicity inherent in any search for a 'single' opposite, exploring the concept of an anti-mandala within several different frameworks. While accepting that such a search can never be complete, this chapter identifies an anti-mandala that best addresses the dystopian power structures found within Mitchell's writing. However, as Spivak also argues, '[n]o text is ever fully deconstructing or deconstructed. Yet the critic [...] performs what declares itself to be one (unitary) act of deconstruction' (lxxviii). In its eventual prioritization of a single oppositional framework, this chapter's deconstruction of the mandala is one such act.

To engage in a deconstructive reading of the mandala is already to suggest an oppositional approach to this traditionally sacred symbol, venturing into inverse readings of its structure and world view not necessarily intended by its creators. At this point, it should be stressed that the aim of such an approach is not to engage in a cultural 'ransacking' of this ancient religious symbol, but to conduct a deeper analysis from a post-secular critical standpoint in order to learn more about its theoretical foundations outside of its sacred settings. Rosita Dellios makes a case for such an analysis in 'Missing Mandalas: Development and Theoretical Gaps' (2004), arguing that '[t]he mandala model [...] needs to be more fully theorized if it is to make a conceptual contribution to the pressing tasks of the day' (1). It is therefore hoped that future studies will extend these critical enquiries, treating this exploration of mandalic opposites as an opening from which to move into further theoretical analyses.

This chapter's deconstructive approach identifies several possible anti-mandalas which deploy the relationship between its circle, centre and cardinal points to very different ends. As such, it builds on Derrida's assertion in his 1967 work, *Of Grammatology*, that

> movements of deconstruction do not destroy structures from the outside. They are not possible and effective, nor can they take accurate aim, except by inhabiting those structures. [...] Operating necessarily from the inside, borrowing all the strategic and economic resources of subversion from the old structure. (24)

Using the mandala's spatial arrangement as the starting point, then, this chapter's search for an anti-mandala therefore begins on familiar ground, 'by inhabiting' the mandala's own structure, using its hierarchical assumptions as its 'resources of subversion'. The search then extends beyond the mandala in order to uncover less conventional oppositional structures which can be found in Mitchell's own works, embodying, as far as possible, an inversion of the mandala's holistic world view while maintaining its distinctive structural traits.

There are many types of mandala, each with different purposes and teachings, from many temporal, geographical and cultural backgrounds. For example, while the Chakrasamvara mandala, also known as the wheel of great bliss, is recognized as a distinct single type of mandala, it exists in 'hundreds of forms', as noted by Denise Patry Leidy and Robert A. F. Thurman in *Mandala: The Architecture of Enlightenment* (1997) (72). As Leidy and Thurman demonstrate, it can be found in early Nepalese cloth paintings from the eleventh century, in hammered bronze from seventeenth- to eighteenth-century Tibet, and continues to be created in the twenty-first century for Western audiences in the form of the sand mandala. As such, to refer generally to 'a' mandala – a necessary shorthand for the Tibetan Buddhist mandala in this study – is itself a reduction, with so many variations in existence. 'The mandala', by definition, encompasses over two millennia of multiplicity. Yet one particular type of Buddhist mandala stands out as a form of frightening anti-mandala: the Bhavachakra, or wheel of life mandala (see Appendix F).

While several types of Tibetan Buddhist mandala, including the Kalachakra, Chakrasamvara, Chenrezig and Yamantaka, feature more visually harmonious portrayals of an ordered realm, each a blueprint for a raised palace structure with four gateways, offering gardens, and a border of fire and *vajra* protecting the world within (see Appendix C), the Bhavachakra mandala presents a very different approach. Translated from the Sanskrit, the name of this early form of mandala means 'wheel of becoming'; thought to have been created for a king in the sixth century BCE, as noted by Maggie Grey, its regal origins suggest its important political function within the monarch's realm ('The Bhavachakra or Wheel of Life Mandala' 1–2). It presents a range of scenes depicting different realms of rebirth, rather than a single central nested palace structure, and crucially, the world shown in the Bhavachakra mandala is that of the pathway to torment. As Grey suggests, the Bhavachakra shows 'a violent global spectacle: monstrous Death tyrannizing life, causing pain, conditioning terror'; the fearful images depict representations of '*ignorance, desire* and *aggression*' at its centre, causing lifetimes of cyclical suffering (1). As Grey also identifies in her 2001 paper, 'Encountering the Mandala: The Mental and Political Architectures of Dependency', this type of mandala serves as 'a warning' to its viewers, an illustration of a 'road map to Hell' that depicts the horror of samsaric torment alongside its causality (12).

While the creation of the Tibetan sand mandala for secular Western audiences effectively becomes a display of skill rather than an overtly religious teaching – many international audiences will have little understanding of its complex symbolism – the Bhavachakra is overtly didactic, its bold images deliberately difficult to misunderstand. It appears on the walls of religious buildings as a visual reminder of eternal samsaric suffering (or *dukkha*), with the Buddha depicted on the outside of the mandalic wheel at the top right of the image, showing that escape from this frightening cycle is possible via the sacred knowledge within the temple that it adorns. However, while the Bhavachakra moves some way towards suggesting the conflicts to be found underneath the mandala's ordered appearance, it is still a Tibetan Buddhist mandala, and, as such, will ultimately be tethered to the Buddhist philosophies that it represents; an 'unobvious' Mitchellian opposite must ultimately be found from outside the mandala's own realm.

Zooming out further still, then, a potential oppositional structure from outside the mandala's own framework is Gilles Deleuze and Félix Guattari's rhizome, as discussed in *A Thousand Plateaus: Capitalism and Schizophrenia* (1987). The rhizome structure has already been used by Peter Childs and James Green to describe Mitchell's writing; discussing *Ghostwritten* in 'The Novels in Nine Parts' (2011), they note that '[t]he Deleuzian figure of the rhizome seems apposite here, as the novel spreads through a kind of textual diffusion' (31). Yet the rhizome structure also suggests a potential anti-mandalic approach of its own. As Deleuze and Guattari describe, the rhizome is a boundless structure-without-structure that 'spreads like a patch of oil', based on centreless 'multiplicity', and forming a continuous plane without hierarchy in which '[t]here are no points or positions' (8). Without any form of centre, outer limits or points of focus, the rhizome 'is not amenable to any structural or generative model', as Deleuze and Guattari emphasize (12). Set against the implied powerful centre of the bifurcating tree-branch model, its 'acentred systems' make it a fitting potential opposite, an example of a limitless system without containment or hierarchy (17). However, such a radical anti-structure, while an impressive thought experiment in itself, remains necessarily ungraspable. Its deliberate abstraction and viral nature – '[a] rhizome has no beginning or end' (25) so that even 'Buddha's tree itself becomes a rhizome' (20) – make it more useful as a point of critical inspiration, rather than a theoretical anti-mandala. While Mitchell's narratives have been described as rhizomatic, it is a model that suggests form without ordered content, negating the global structures, hierarchies and ethical approaches that underpin this narrative universe.

If the rhizome lacks the rigid principles suggested by the basic anti-mandala framework of multiple confining boundaries and a single controlling centre, a more relevant theoretical model would incorporate not merely the structure of an anti-mandala, but also an inversion of the mandala's philosophies. Thomas Pynchon's 1973 experimental war novel *Gravity's Rainbow* envisages its own mandalic opposite which goes further in imagining an anti-mandala's more sinister forms. This text uses the typographic symbol of a Jungian mandala as a parallel for a rocket's control switch, the cardinal positions of its dial described as '[t]he Schwarzkommando mandala', echoing of the rocket's aerial view: '[t]he four fins of the Rocket made a cross, another mandala' (570–3).[4] The superimposition of a weapon of mass destruction with the Jungian mandala emphasizes the novel's hyper-apocalyptic world, in which humanity's hastening of its own extinction is pursued with such fervour that its roots are depicted

---

[4] The introduction to *A Gravity's Rainbow Companion* (2006) by Steven C. Weisenburger also briefly suggests that *Gravity's Rainbow* is itself structured like a mandala (9–11). Weisenburger's study also lists Jung's *Mandala Symbolism* (1968) as one of its source texts; like Pynchon, Weisenburger's reading of the mandala is also predominantly Jungian, referring to a simplified mandala symbol defined by 'four quadrants' in a 'circular mandala, a symbol of opposites held in delicate equipoise' (10). John M. Muste's article 'The Mandala in *Gravity's Rainbow*' (1981) gives further discussion of the mandala's role in the novel, also implicitly following the Jungian structural model that Pynchon uses. See the Introduction for a discussion of the dominance of the Jungian mandala within literary criticism.

as extending beyond organized religion into pre-Christian archetypes. While Pynchon's mandalic antitype wields an impressive shock factor, the model of the bomb as anti-mandala lacks a more subtle approach that can also address the mandala's ethical and philosophical principles.

A still-more insidious 'unobvious opposite' presents itself, a symbol embedded not in the switch of a nuclear weapon but in the everyday mass-market consumerism critiqued in *Cloud Atlas*: the Coca-Cola logo. An instantly recognizable red circular icon with a single image at its centre, its horizontal white font and vertical bottle outline form a cross of visual information distinctive enough to be easily recognized on the cap of a bottle or the side of a building.[5] While the mandala has evolved over millennia, only recently gaining wider recognition in diaspora following the fourteenth Dalai Lama's encouragement,[6] in just over a century the Coca-Cola logo has grown from a nostalgic image of Americana to become one of the most recognized symbols in the world. Like the mandala, it represents a cross-cultural phenomenon; its marketing website, *Coca-Cola Journey*, asserts that '94% of the world's population recognize our red & white logo' ('Who We Are'). Michael Konik's article, 'On Not Getting Away From It All' (1991), summarizes the ubiquity of this global product, from 'the foothills of the Himalayas' to 'fishing islands off the coast of Nicaragua': 'Coke is inescapable. [...] no matter how far you think you've ventured from the comforts and conveniences of the modern world, Coke will find you.' This isn't merely an illusion generated by the company's global marketing strategies; as Mark Pendergrast notes in *For God, Country and Coca-Cola* (2013), as of 2012, Coca-Cola officially operates in all but two of the world's countries: Cuba and North Korea (450). Whatever globality may be, Coca-Cola has it.

Its simple mantra, 'Enjoy Coca-Cola', contains an imperative – the instruction to take pleasure in the intensely present moment of the sip of a drink – and the promise of enjoyment, the universally longed-for counterpoint to Buddhism's universal truth of *dukkha*, or suffering. Yet the seemingly meditative quality of enjoying each moment is undercut by this simple circular logo's most fundamental purpose: to sell more Coke. Eric Schlosser claims in *Fast Food Nation* (2002) that 'McDonald's sells more Coca-Cola than anyone else in the world' (54). Alongside the McDonald's Golden Arches, the Coca-Cola logo has taken on the almost mystical quality of a *yantra*, an emblematic diagram in a world where, as Schlosser asserts, more people recognize the logo of a fast-food chain than the image of the cross, reflecting the 'hollow faith' of free-market capitalism which facilitates the 'excessive corporate power' behind it (4, 261). As Pendergrast notes, 'Coke has achieved the status of a substitute modern religion', its 'all-inclusive worldview' and 'perennial values' carefully constructed to maintain the

---

[5] The image of the Enjoy Coca-Cola logo in red disc bottle-top format is publically accessible at https://juliegilhuly.files.wordpress.com/2014/03/enjoy-coca-cola.jpg, accessed 14 August 2017.

[6] In his foreword to *The Wheel of Time Sand Mandala* by Barry Bryant, the fourteenth Dalai Lama Tenzin Gyatso notes of the Tibetan Buddhist mandala, '[a]lthough some can be openly explained, most are related to tantric doctrines that are normally supposed to be kept secret. [...] Because the severe misunderstandings that can arise are more harmful than a partial lifting of secrecy, I have encouraged a greater openness in the display and accurate description of mandalas' (xii).

broadest possible global customer base, create maximum brand-loyalty and maximize company profits (472).

As a potential anti-mandala, the Coca-Cola logo certainly displays an inversion of mandalic purpose.[7] As Matthieu Ricard notes in 'Introduction to the purpose and symbolism of the mandala in Tibetan Buddhism' (1997), the Tibetan Buddhist mandala's

> purpose is not to escape reality but to see it as it is. It is not to [...] fabricate unneeded entities, but to realize the unity of appearances and emptiness [...] to generate boundless compassion for beings who have lost awareness of the buddha nature within themselves. (157)

While the notion of a single, fixed version of reality remains problematic, for Ricard, the mandala's role is to generate greater awareness of the everyday processes of meaning-making that constitute such a reality. Where the mandala's purpose is to foster a greater contemplation of reality, then, it may be argued that the Coca-Cola logo's is to escape it. A scientific report by Michael F. Jacobson, 'Liquid Candy: how soft drinks are harming Americans' health' (2005), concludes that 'Americans consume gargantuan quantities of carbonated soft drinks and suffer untoward health consequences' as a result, including obesity, diabetes and osteoporosis (iv). As an icon for the largest beverage company in the world, Coca-Cola's simple circular logo has a fundamentally escapist function: to sustain a brand image powerful enough to escape the reality of its own effects, facilitating soft drink sales to consumers already suffering health problems from their consumption. As Pendergrast notes, '[t]he Coca-Cola religion has no real morality, no commandment other than increased consumption of its drinks' (481). Where the mandala's purpose is to highlight emptiness in appearance, the Coca-Cola logo generates meaning from emptiness: sugary liquid equals perfect happiness.[8]

---

[7] The dichotomy between Eastern spiritualities and the Coca-Cola brand are also wryly suggested in the final episode of American television series *Mad Men* (season 7, episode 14; first broadcast on 17 May 2015). This 1960s period drama, created by Matthew Wiener, sees its advertising-mogul protagonist Don Draper have his greatest advertising epiphany while meditating cross-legged in a hilltop retreat, a moment that leads not to this troubled character's personal fulfilment but to an iconic milestone in the history of Coca-Cola's branding. The moment of meditation is portrayed as the inspiration behind the real-life 'I'd Like to Buy the World a Coke' television commercial that aired in 1971, using the same meditative space of the hilltop to market Coca-Cola as an international, multiracial and compassionate brand, a significant advertising campaign in shifting the company's public image from a quintessentially American household name to a global phenomenon.

[8] At the time of writing, the World of Coca-Cola tourist attraction at the company's hometown in Atlanta, Georgia, includes the 'Coca-Cola Theatre', its full-size cinema looping a six-minute promotional film – 'Moments of Happiness' – which, as *WorldOfCoca-Cola.com* explains, 'celebrates some of life's most memorable moments experienced by people of different ages and cultures around the world' ('Coca-Cola Theatre', accessed 26 October 2016). Its sequences of uplifting experiences shared by families across the world associate a montage of global lived experience and everyday celebration with the Coca-Cola logo. During a research visit in May 2015, several members of the audience were visibly and audibly in tears during the moving and highly emotional sequences, arguably a moment of brand nirvana for a company whose primary output is brown liquid. The phenomenon of high-budget, high-emotion, low-relevance film advertorials might perhaps be termed 'propabranda', the advertising triumph of triggering an involuntary bodily response to validate a corporate non-sequitur ('Coke = happiness').

Where the mandala aims to foster compassion for others, the Coca-Cola logo is the symbol of a global corporation whose net revenues totalled $35.4 billion in 2017 alone, according to its February 2018 press release.[9] The validity of such a corporate, consumer-facing anti-mandala is suggested within Mitchell's own writing, which addresses the human cost of multinational corporations, for example, with Sonmi's experiences of corpocracy as a fast-food worker in *Cloud Atlas*. The grotesque world of fictional fast-food chain 'Papa Song's' evokes the familiar global environment of its possible ancestor McDonald's, a 'dinery [...] starred and striped in reds, yellows and the rising sun' (187). Papa Song, a clown-like marketing figure that '[c]hildren love', entertains customers by 'juggling fiery burgers' in a parody of Ronald McDonald's fast-food-themed antics (188). While Coca-Cola's corporate partnership with McDonald's allows its sugary drinks to be manufactured, sold and consumed in ever-increasing quantities, Papa Song's beverages have their own insidious function. The 'sacs of Soap' fed to its servers act as physical and mental sedatives ('Soap deadens curiosity'), made from the 'reclaimed proteins' produced from servers' own bodies, which are dismantled in a hidden 'slaughterhouse production line' (189, 359). The process of slaughter and protein recycling depicted is frighteningly similar to the inhumane animal killing and dangerous waste meat reuse reported in the American meatpacking industry, as described by Schlosser in *Fast Food Nation* (169–90).

David Mitchell's engagement with multinational consumerism isn't limited to *Cloud Atlas*; problematic encounters between individuals and corporations intrude throughout his works. For example, in *Ghostwritten*, as Satoru is at work discussing '[w]hat is it that stops the world simply ... seizing up?' with a customer, his thoughts are interrupted by the memory of witnessing a worker's suicide with eerie proximity: 'I tried to think, but I kept seeing pictures [...] I was walking out of McDonald's and a businessman slammed down onto the pavement from a ninth floor window of the same building. He lay three meters away from where I stood' (61). The businessman may have been from a different office above the restaurant, but the abrupt intrusion of his dead body outside McDonald's suggests a twofold answer to Satoru's question – what stops the world seizing up is the flow of capital generated from consumerism, a flow that demands extensive (and here, almost literal) human sacrifices.

Similarly, in 'Variations on a Theme by Mister Donut', six lives interconnect in a fast-food chain encounter, the store built to serve the twenty-first-century 'tribes' of 'salarymen, students, Office Ladies' that 'flow' past the store (52). Like the workers in Mister Donut, the businessman who falls to his death from the McDonald's building, and Sonmi's forced allegiance to Papa Song's food chain, their tribal connections are defined not by geography or ethnicity, but by their roles within the larger organizations that they serve. As an iconic symbol for a powerful global corporation, the Coca-Cola logo offers an anti-mandalic framework that resonates with Mitchell's own commentaries on the sinister corporate machinations that underpin the everyday trivialities of popular consumer culture.

---

[9] See https://www.coca-colacompany.com/press-center/press-releases/the-coca-cola-company-reports-strong-operating-results-for-fourth-quarter-2017, accessed 29 April 2018.

If the rhizome represents an inversion of the mandala's structure, the circular Coca-Cola logo certainly offers an inversion of its philosophies. Yet neither of these potential anti-mandalas can address both the principles and the structure suggested by the mandala's own internal oppositions. However, a further anti-mandalic model is suggested within one of Mitchell's own works, in his 2001 novel *number9dream*, providing an alternative framework which encompasses both the form and structure of a deconstructed mandala: the panopticon. An eighteenth-century prison design based around a centre-circle spatial arrangement, with inmates arranged in individual cells around a central inspection tower, its hyper-utilitarian principles, psychological methods of control, and self-replicating structure make it a fitting anti-mandala. As the following sections will demonstrate, the panopticon is similarly defined by its own controlling centre, circular boundary and surrounding points, effectively employing the mandala's basic structure to present a darkly political opposite.

The mandala as panopticon[10]

In 1786, Jeremy Bentham began a series of letters detailing a controversial prison structure. Printed in 1791, the preface opened with a hefty promise: *'Morals reformed – health preserved – industry invigorated – instruction diffused – public burthens lightened* [...] *all by a simple idea in Architecture!'* (*The Panopticon Writings* 31). Bentham's 'simple idea' was the panopticon, a new architectural concept aimed at reforming an outdated prison system. In his design, prisoners were separately housed in transparent cells around the outer ring of a circular prison, built around a central inspection tower. Allowing a perfect view of all inmates at all times, blinds at the windows of the tower made it impossible for prisoners to see when they were being watched. Run by a single inspector, it harnessed a powerful method of psychological control. Bentham's letters emphasize 'the most important point' of its design: inmates 'should always feel themselves as if under inspection', fostering constantly compliant behaviour (43).

Bentham's model penitentiary was never built. Yet its principles of surveillance, mental control and societal self-regulation continue to resurface as contemporary criticism explores their wider implications. In *Discipline and Punish* (1977), Michel Foucault's reading of Bentham's legacy moves the critical focus from the prison's architecture to a more widespread theory of panopticism, investigating a leaking of these principles into everyday life as a sinister and dehumanized method of control. Leading on from Bentham's later plans for other panoptic structures – in mental institutions, hospitals, and even schools – Foucault uses the term 'panopticism' to warn of its 'generalizable model of functioning', arguing that 'the Panopticon presents a cruel, ingenious cage' whose surveillance-based discipline and control 'spread throughout the whole social body' (205–9).

---

[10] An early version of part of this section appears as '"A row of screaming Russian dolls": Escaping the Panopticon in David Mitchell's *number9dream*' *SubStance* 44.1 (2015): 55.70. © 2015 by the Board of Regents of the University of Wisconsin System. Reprinted courtesy of the University of Wisconsin Press.

Read through Foucault's vision of the panopticon, Bentham's panoptic prison structure becomes a sinister anti-mandala, its disciplinary principles and use for incarceration in direct opposition to the mandala's holistic function as a vehicle to 'generate boundless compassion'. The panopticon's circular outer boundary presents a dark inversion of the mandala's outer ring of *vajra*, a 'fence' which both includes and excludes, containing its inmates within an inescapable circular structure as it simultaneously separates them from the world outside it. Within the mandala, its *bindu* or centre provides the structure's focal point, and the source from which its surrounding world is created, housing its most powerful deities and symbolic concepts. Similarly, the panopticon's raised central tower is the heart of its method of control, its all-seeing resident inspector making its entire world of self-regulated surveillance possible. The panopticon, like the mandala, has its own 'cardinal points' which radiate outwards in every direction: a circle of outer cells, each inmate a mere satellite within a framework whose structure and philosophies combine to form an inversion of the mandala's principles. Where the Tibetan Buddhist mandala is built on wisdom, compassion and knowledge, the panopticon is built on paranoia, surveillance and uncertainty. If the mandala's 'purpose is not to escape reality but to see it as it is', as quoted earlier from Matthieu Ricard (1997), the panopticon's purpose is to obscure reality: to create the illusion of total, unescapable surveillance. To truly enter the mandala, we must also enter the panopticon.

At this point, it's worth mentioning that by bringing Bentham's principles into contemporary social structures, Foucault's reading of the panopticon's darker associations has had such far-reaching impact – in literature, comics, computer games and even *Doctor Who* – that social historians are now at pains to defend Bentham's original panopticon.[11] In 'Deconstructing Panopticism into the Plural Panopticons' (2012), Anne Brunon-Ernst emphasizes the liberal, utilitarian aims of Bentham's project, arguing for the use of the term 'panoptic paradigm' to discuss its legacies beyond Foucault's panopticism (38). Brunon-Ernst also usefully argues that the panopticon is in fact plural, with 'at least four different versions of Bentham's surveillance machine' developed during his lifetime, of which his prison panopticon was merely the first (40). From the plurality of Bentham's vision, to the terms used to trace its legacy, to its absorption in popular culture, the panopticon has gone viral. Just as the Tibetan Buddhist mandala contains many different nested mandalas, each contained within another, the panopticon displays an inherent tendency towards replication, becoming greater and more complex with each iteration.[12] It is this sinister panoptic

---

[11] Appearances of the panoptic paradigm in literature include Jenni Fagan's *The Panopticon* (2012), Angela Carter's *Nights at the Circus* (1984), Gabriel Garcia Marquez's *Chronicle of a Death Foretold* (1981) and George Orwell's *Nineteen Eighty-Four* (1949). The panopticon also features in Season 14 of *Doctor Who* as a meeting chamber on planet Gallifrey. In comics, panopticon references can be found in DC Comics' *JLA: Earth 2* (2000) as the base for the Crime Syndicate of Amerika, and in Chris Onstad's *Achewood* online comic, dated 26 October 2005. Computer game references to the panopticon include in *Deus Ex: Human Revolution*'s (2011) multiple ending, and in the *Batman: Arkham Origins* (2013) panopticon prison fight scene.

[12] As Barry Bryant notes, in the Kalachakra mandala, the 'outermost square is the Mandala of Enlightened Body', inside which sits the 'Mandala of Enlightened Speech, the Mandala of Enlightened Mind, the Mandala of Enlightened Wisdom, and the innermost square, the Mandala of Enlightened Great Bliss' (*The Wheel of Time Sand Mandala* 154).

multiplicity that this chapter harnesses in order to embark on a deeper exploration of the controlling boundaries and hierarchies in Mitchell's work than would otherwise be possible through any simple comparison with the mandala.

This viral panoptic paradigm becomes an insidious presence in *number9dream*; the panopticon is directly referred to throughout the novel in several different forms as multiple overlapping panopticons are created and internalized by its protagonist Eiji. The panopticon's virality in Western cultures, echoed within the mandala itself, builds its own form of religious model: that of the Judeo-Christian God, the panoptic gaze providing an omniscient presence by which we are constantly being monitored, and, as such, should monitor ourselves, both externally and internally. Reading the panopticon as anti-mandala, this chapter departs from the mandala to discuss the external and self-created panopticons that contain Eiji in *number9dream*, exploring the ways in which the panoptic paradigms imagined by Bentham and Foucault surface and replicate as part of a wider panoptic virality within the novel. Eiji's obsession with his paternal origins is finally exposed as another panoptic model constructed around a powerful controlling centre, with Eiji's final rejection of his quest to find his father as one of his textual acts of resistance that provide a form of escape from the viral panoptic structures that surround him.

The panoptic paradigm in *number9dream*

Number9dream opens with a triple-tiered panopticon, establishing a preoccupation with power, imprisonment and escape that resurfaces throughout the text. This coming-of-age novel sees its nineteen-year-old narrator, Eiji, on a quest to discover his father's identity and make a life for himself in Tokyo, while coming to terms with his traumatic childhood. The first chapter, entitled 'Panopticon', introduces the 'zirconium gothic skyscraper' of the PanOpticon building, a corporate 'fortress' that guards the secret of Eiji's father's identity, and becomes a symbol of Tokyo itself (3, 4). A third panopticon emerges in Eiji's subsequent daydream, as both the title and subject of a film, providing a surreal frame to his imagined first meeting with his father. Yet each of these multilayered panopticons is illusory. Only one – the film screened in Eiji's third fantasy – refers directly to Bentham's original prison panopticon, and even this is refracted through Eiji's imagination in his daydream of a film, a reference twice removed from reality. There is no physical, concrete prison in this opening chapter; instead, a narrative is established which explores a virtual and internalized mental imprisonment, an aspect of the panoptic paradigm that Bentham describes in his letters as '[a] new mode of obtaining power of mind over mind' via architectural principles (31). The multilayered panopticons in the first chapter present a novel preoccupied with the interplay between such architectural principles and the mental structures that they create and reflect. Eiji may interpret the PanOpticon building as the cause of his repeated inability to act within the first chapter, but as this chapter will discuss, his almost obsessive reading of the panoptic paradigm within corporate Tokyo becomes a symptom of the confining mental architectures that he must overcome by the end of the novel.

Mitchell reveals in a 2007 interview with Tishani Doshi that his work is similarly fascinated with such psychological 'secret architectures', stating that the central questions behind *number9dream* are 'what is the mind [, …] where does it work and how does it function'? ('Secret Architectures'). In an undated interview with Ron Hogan he again notes, '[t]he book's about the mind, which is the home of fantasy and imagination, the origins of the surreal' ('David Mitchell'). This psychological exploration is positioned as a central preoccupation of the novel from the opening pages of its first chapter, as Eiji asks, '[h]ow do daydreams translate into reality?', before entering into a series of daydream-based narrative episodes which obscure the boundaries between reality and imagination (4). However, within both his 'daydreams' and 'reality', or his fantasies and his everyday lived experience, Eiji is subject to surveillance and control from a number of competing schemata – his workplaces, Tokyo's corporate and social worlds, and its organized crime – all of which come with competing rules, expectations and methods for control.

Setting the stage for this thematic exploration, the novel's virtual panopticons introduce and frame Eiji's multiple circles of mental imprisonment. Paralysed by his daydreams in the Jupiter Café, the triple-tiered panopticons that feature in the first chapter are echoed by the microcosmic structures of social containment that surround Eiji in the café. One waitress chastises another, saying, '[w]hen *you* marry be sure to select a husband whose dreams are exactly the same size as your own', a warning against transgressing an invisible preset perimeter of personal ambition, imagined here as a spatial boundary that must not be crossed (5). In a more direct echo of the language of panoptic incarceration, another waitress 'is serving a life sentence at the sink', in which this functional container becomes a metaphorically inescapable prison (4). When Eiji sees a group of laughing pregnant women, the experience becomes another vehicle for restriction as he imagines the 'nine pouched-up months' endured by their babies (21). Reinforced by these multilayered boundaries, the first chapter's panopticism becomes a metafictional device that establishes Eiji's overarching coming-of-age quest: to learn to escape the internalized panoptic constraints conjured by his own imagination, navigate the controlling structures around him, and wrestle a form of agency amid these forces of internal and external control.

In the opening chapter, we find Eiji in the Jupiter Café, contemplating entering the PanOpticon skyscraper to uncover his father's identity. As he notes, it should be 'a simple matter'; he knows which lawyer he must approach for his father's name and address, and is already outside her workplace (3). However, the tale's reality is undercut by three disorientating glitches from Eiji's imagination, disrupting narrative coherence and deliberately subverting any expectation of adherence to traditional plot linearity from the outset. Each of Eiji's imagined realities play out competing scenarios, revealing a protagonist torn by frequent, vivid fantasies that impinge on his capacity to take action. The third, and perhaps most elaborate fantasy, sees Eiji enter the Ganymede Cinema. Named after one of Jupiter's moons, the Ganymede Cinema's name contains a hint that this is yet another narrative false start dreamt up from Eiji's seat in the Jupiter Café. The cinema's 'psychedelic carpet' and 'tatty glitz' atmosphere provide a fitting backdrop for a surreal dreamscape of never-ending stairs and ushers with 'trotters' (26–7). Yet its most revealing visual motif is on an external advertisement that makes

Eiji 'hesitate' before going in (26). He notices: '[t]oday's presentation is a movie called *PanOpticon*. The poster – a row of screaming Russian dolls – tells me nothing about the movie'.

Eiji may decide that it tells him 'nothing' about the film, but this embedded image reveals several key facets of the novel. As well as representing the novel's structure, the image of these circular nested mannequins echoes Eiji's fragmented grip on reality within multiple panoptic circles of containment and control, and also prompts a revaluing of *number9dream*'s relationship to the author's wider narrative designs. This structural metaphor of Russian dolls would later be developed further, woven into *Cloud Atlas* to represent a narrative of six separate stories, each nested inside another (409). However, as this poster reveals, this structure was already a source of narrative fascination within *number9dream*. In a 2012 interview with James Rocchi, the author discusses this Russian doll structure, already a well-worn metaphor used to describe *Cloud Atlas* by critics and reviewers at the time of the interview. During the interview, Mitchell extends the Russian doll image further, to

> a woodworm eating its way through a nest of six wooden Russian dolls through the navels and getting to the middle of one and then coming out through the spinal columns … which is quite a grotesque image at this time of day. Sorry. ('Interview: Novelist David Mitchell')

This macabre image of a journey through a set of nested containers reflects the wider structure of *number9dream*, whose metafictional poster of 'a row of screaming Russian dolls' is dreamt up by Eiji's unconscious. The author's introduction of a worm eating through the structure's core seems particularly apt for a coming-of-age novel charting its young narrator's metaphorical pupation from adolescence to adulthood, and suggests a narrator struggling to escape the multiple containing panoptic boundaries that lead him to seek refuge in the fantastic.

A cross-section of these worm-eaten dolls provides the basic structure of both the mandala and panopticon: multiple containing circular boundaries structured around a dominant central point, cumulatively symbolizing the viral, self-perpetuating nature of the panoptic paradigm. Each chapter, by itself, functions as one of these nested boundaries; as Eiji escapes one form of imprisonment, he encounters another, the chapters becoming a 'row' of textual containers for his mental imprisonment. Reflecting this narrative movement, Mitchell reveals in his 2002 interview with Michael Silverblatt, '[e]ach of the sections is about an estate of the mind', listing each chapter's perception-based theme, including a first chapter about imagination, the second on memory and the third about image ('David Mitchell on Bookworm'). Shomit Dutta extends this list in 'Eiji, Anju, Ai and Goatwriter' (2001), noting that the author describes the linked themes of each chapter as 'imagination, memory, the moving image, nightmare, fiction, meaning and dreams (he confesses to not yet knowing the theme of the penultimate chapter)' (22). Together forming an extended exploration of the protagonist's inner world, these interconnected chapters stack like Russian dolls to create Eiji's adult self by the end of the novel, a self constructed in – and ultimately contained by – this textual progression through an interior landscape. The 'screaming' of these figurines also pre-empts the novel's exploration of Eiji's 'waking nightmare' in the book's fourth chapter, in which the yakuza force Eiji into a violent bowling game using human heads (153, 188). As Mitchell notes in 'What use are dreams in fiction?' (2008), 'where better to look for what petrifies the human mind than those horror movies we ourselves produce, direct and star in? [...] nightmare is undeniably a rich, rich, vein' (439–40). Their frozen terror a nightmarish inversion of matryoshka dolls' traditionally benign expressions, the 'screaming' dolls also emphasize the distressed subject's cry for self-expression – or the panopticon inmate's horror at the totality of their prison.

Bentham notes that circularity is crucial for his panopticon, describing its circular framework as 'the only one that affords a perfect view', its centre-circumference design creating perfect control through its observational totality (43). Analysing this circularity, Foucault draws attention to panopticism's radial 'centres of observation disseminated throughout society', noting the 'formation of knowledge and the increase of power regularly reinforce one another in a circular process', suggesting this structure's self-perpetuation (212, 224). This paradigm of a powerful confining circularity also runs across Mitchell's wider oeuvre. For example, the narrative circularity in *Ghostwritten* and *Cloud Atlas* sees each polyvocal novel end with the narrative voice of its first chapter, while the confining outer boundary of Dejima in *The Thousand Autumns* contains the claustrophobic artificial island used to isolate international traders, restricting Jacob's access to Japan to a space just 'two hundred paces along its outer curve' and 'eighty paces deep' (18).

While the multilayered image of the 'row of screaming Russian dolls' has several important connections within the novel's primary diegetic level, it also resonates with the novel's diegetic jumps. The profusion of superimposed panopticons in the first chapter shifts the novel from conventional realism towards hyperreality, while the opening chapter's panopticism becomes almost parodic in its viral reiterations. Alongside these hyper-panoptic layers, the narrative itself splits into multiple strata, cumulatively creating a text that, from its opening, appears in danger of becoming rhizomatically schismatic. Each of Eiji's narrative false starts forms a new layer of narrative artifice, creating repeated boundaries that the reader must break through in order to engage with the 'real' events within the novel.

While the inclusion of multiple narrative false starts emphasizes Eiji's fragmented psychological state, it also has significant implications for the novel's extra-diegetic realms in a subtle problematization of the author's panoptic authority. Even from the first narrative false start, Eiji's textual double bluffs hint that the opening chapter's first scenario of his meeting with the lawyer is purely a fantasy. It is only on rereading that Eiji's seemingly throwaway comment, '[t]he actual lair of Akiko Katō matches closely the version in my imagination', becomes a wry red herring; both the 'lair' and Eiji's experience of it will be revealed as products of his 'imagination' (9). However, these multiple narrative false starts also prompt a readerly questioning as to whose imagination has really conjured these incidents: the narrator (Eiji), the writer (Mitchell) or a more insidious panoptic conditioning (Bentham and Foucault). Again, the text's typographic symbols – an outline of a square for Eiji's fantasies, and a filled-in diamond for his narrative 'reality' – are only recognizable as paratextual hints on rereading, a code which requires careful readerly attention to decipher it. As conventional authorial control is repeatedly subverted with three narrative false starts in the first chapter alone, the reader receives an early lesson in distrusting the narrator, as in the labyrinthine plot in Italo Calvino's *If on a Winter's Night a Traveller* (1983) in which the reader's attempt to follow a conventional story is continually and deliberately frustrated.

By using metafictional techniques to disrupt readerly expectations, Mitchell creates a text in which Eiji's Calvino-esque narrative deviations threaten to subsume the plot entirely, setting the scene for a novel fascinated by structures of containment and control, while also itself contained and controlled by them. In its extended exploration of Eiji's mental worlds, *number9dream* becomes a metafictional exploration of the nature of fictional creation and the act of storytelling, from the seductive 'underworld' of video game narratives to the Goatwriter's embedded fiction on the 'study of tales' (98, 251). However, contained within an otherwise largely realistic genre, the coming-of-age novel, the inclusion of Eiji's narrative false starts subverts the constraints and expectations of the genre, creating a text whose erratic opening is an embodiment of imaginative digression itself, and allows an early breaking of any readerly expectation of a conventionally linear tale. On first reading, these narrative glitches mask the novel's genre to such an extent that it arguably changes the nature of the reading process, creating an experimental text in which the reader-turned detective must proceed with caution, each new narrative layer prompting a questioning as to whether the events are in fact 'real', or if the unfolding narration is part of yet another layer of diegetic instability. The novel's panoptic virality replicates even outside the text, pre-positioning the reader within an established theoretical paradigm that is likely to influence any critical approach to the novel, encouraging its reading through the contrasting poles of Benthamite or Foucauldian theories of panopticism, a reading which itself becomes a further meta-panoptic boundary that ensnares the reader. The first chapter's reference to Bentham by name – as the prison warden in Eiji's film 'PanOpticon' – further encourages a reading of the text in accordance with the principles of the panopticon's creator (29).

In a text fascinated by both the panopticon and the metafictional, reading the text through a combination of these two components – the former preoccupied with control, and the latter with escape – suggests a deeper game of 'cat and mouse' is occurring. Or, to include the panopticon itself, 'cat, mouse, and trap'. If the three basic physical components of a panoptic prison are inmate, prison and (presumed) inspector, a reader-response approach to a metafictional panoptic text might relate these to the basic components of narrator (or character), author and reader. Writing on the inspector at the centre of the panopticon, Guillaume Tusseau notes in 'From the Penitentiary to the Political Panoptic Paradigm' (2012), '[a]s the inspector is himself invisible, he reigns like a spirit. The inspector is omniscient, omnipresent and omnipotent, he is like God' (130). If Eiji is the narrator-turned-inmate attempting to escape the author's panoptic structures by retreating from the predestined narrative reality into fantasy, the reader is the 'omniscient' yet 'invisible' inspector, scrutinizing every textual move. Alongside the conventional diegetic reality of the events in his textual universe, Eiji's mental worlds – his imagination, dreams, nightmares and fantasies – may be laid bare, but the typographic hints hidden in the text indicate that the inspector-reader will have to work hard to follow them.

This panoptic meta-framework is itself plural, replete with paradoxical iterations that remain simultaneously true; on another level, Eiji's labyrinthine narrative forms an inescapable prison, in which the reader-inmate is controlled by the God-like inspector-author. Or to move still deeper into the viral panopticon, the author, narrator and reader meet in the unsettling role of the 'invisible' inspector, each driven by a voyeuristic desire that perpetuates the model's psychological entrapment. Read through this panoptic framework, after Eiji's repeated attempts at escaping the narrative from the first pages of the novel, Eiji's quest takes on an additional extra-textual dimension: whether, by the end of the text, he will eventually succeed in escaping the viral panoptic control of the narrative framework that contains him.

Eiji and the PanOpticon

Throughout *number9dream*'s opening chapter, the PanOpticon building is presented as the realization of both Bentham's utilitarianism and Foucault's reading of its methods of surveillance. Its imposing physical presence as a 'zirconium gothic skyscraper' marks it as a highly visible symbol of its own power that echoes Foucault's panopticism (3). Yet this stylized building is also a functional workplace, just as Bentham's panoptic designs ultimately sought to maximize the utilitarian potential of their inhabitants. Its method of control relies on a surveillance-based visibility that, as Foucault puts it in *Discipline and Punish*, 'reverses the principle of the dungeon', a building in which '[f]ull lighting and the eye of a supervisor capture better than darkness, which ultimately protected' (200). Eiji imagines the building's surveillance extending even outside the PanOpticon building, fantasizing that the 'old man' in the café is a 'spy' warning the PanOpticon of his presence; for Eiji, the PanOpticon building has become the all-pervasive eye of Foucault's panopticism (12).

This power of the gaze is central to the panoptic paradigm, reinforced by both the PanOpticon building's imposing exterior and the features of its imagined interior. Bentham's letters on the prison panopticon emphasize the power dynamic between seer and seen, noting: 'the more constantly the persons to be inspected are under the eyes of the persons who should inspect them, the more perfectly will the purpose X of the establishment have been attained' (34). Or, as Foucault puts it, '[v]isibility is a trap' (200). Looking up at the PanOpticon building, Eiji remarks, 'Tokyo is so close up you cannot always see it' – but, as we are to learn, it can see him (3). In one fantasy in which he enters the PanOpticon, Eiji becomes visible in the extreme. He is scanned from 'head to foot' by a 'tracer light', under the 'amber spotlight' of the CCTV reception, the building alerted by an exterior 'eye-cam linked to PanOpticon central computer' (6–12). It may later be revealed as a fantasy, but for both Eiji and the reader, at that moment, the interior of the PanOpticon is real; it is only in retrospect that the narrative episode reveals the protagonist's internalization of its principles of surveillance.

Writing on the inhabitants of his prison panopticon, Bentham refers to the prisoners of lowest utilitarian value as 'drones', a phrase that also reflects their identical treatment according to its principles (55). His use of the term to classify and rank inmates as workers in descending order, synecdochically labelling them 'the *good* hands, the *capable* hands, the *promising* hands, and the *drones*', evokes the rigid hierarchies of the beehive. The desired result is not the production of honey, or any other commodity, but pure labour itself, or as Bentham puts it, '*whatever that you can persuade them to turn their hands to*'. In an echo of Bentham's terminology, Eiji watches the PanOpticon's workers and sees purely '[p]in-striped drones', and 'drone clones'; 'drone' is repeated eleven times in the opening chapter alone, emphasizing his perception of a dehumanized corporate workforce (3, 39).

For the protagonist, the sight of identical 'drones' swarming into the city becomes a visual representation of the feelings of panoptic entrapment that he experiences in the opening chapter. The building's name triggers an internalization of the panoptic structure of its title, as Eiji becomes both the subject and creator of a new panoptic paradigm peopled by Bentham's 'drones'. Using Bentham's terminology to rewrite the panopticon, and echoing his situating of its principles within a physical structure in the PanOpticon building, this narrative episode demonstrates a panoptic paradigm created by both the imagination and the infusion of Bentham's panoptic schema into our understanding of the world. Eiji is too intimidated by the building's exterior and workers to enter, his sense of psychological exclusion stemming from his perceived social separation from its drones, and the larger panoptic framework that he imagines as a result of his reading of this social stimuli. This sense of exclusion is a key feature of Foucault's panopticism, which reads the social separation of inmates in Bentham's prison panopticon as 'a guarantee of order' (200). This imagined panoptic entrapment adds a further dimension to Eiji's quest, in which he will have to overcome the panoptic structures of his own creation and find his own method of escape without succumbing to a drone-like loss of identity.

In her defence of Bentham's original liberal aims, Brunon-Ernst argues that 'Panopticons are built so that no more Panopticons will be needed' (40). However, as panoptic structures grow and replicate within *number9dream*, the opposite becomes true for the novel. As Eiji imagines the viral structures of control conjured by the building's name, the panoptic paradigm spreads into Eiji's perception of its 'drones' and corporate façade. His experience of the PanOpticon building becomes a dark inversion of Brunon-Ernst's statement, spawning further internalized panoptic structures which mutate and infect Eiji's imagination. Its external schema so entirely convinces Eiji that he will be excluded that he becomes paralysed within his fantasies. He does not need to be told not to enter – contained within an internal replication of a viral panoptic system, he already has a fear of doing so. Intimidated by what he sees, he remains in the safety of the café, chain-smoking ahead of his 'stressful meeting', and cocooned from reality by elaborate daydreams until the final pages of the chapter (15). This portrayal of Eiji and the panopticon demonstrates and warns of its insidious means of functioning. What is being internalized is not merely the panoptic sense of being watched and self-policing accordingly, but the tendency to structure the self, the world and the mechanisms of self-control through the inmate-prison-supervisor model, the desire for escape restrained by the desire for oversight and control.

The yakuza and the panoptic paradigm

While the PanOpticon building becomes a symbol for the authorized structures of control in Eiji's society, he meets their illegitimate counterpart in the form of the yakuza, the 'ninety-thousand strong state' of organized crime that operates via extortion and bloodshed (338). They gain power over Eiji by promising to reveal his father's identity in return for his '*Loyalty, Duty* and *Obedience*' for one night (183). Having made a blood pact, he is coerced into a bowling game using live human heads as skittles. As one criminal brags, their system is one of unrestrained physical power: '[i]n most places the muscle is at the beck and call of the masters. In Japan, we, the muscle, *are* the masters' (194). In contrast to the PanOpticon building's depersonalized methods of control, the yakuza run a far older form of discipline. Foucault emphasizes that panopticism 'automatizes and disindividualizes power', and that in the panoptic system of control, '[p]ower has its principle not so much in a person as in a certain [...] distribution of bodies, surfaces, lights, gazes' (202). This diffused control of lights and gazes is reflected in the sterile, 'refrigerated' power of the PanOpticon building, imagined by Eiji as a world where 'computers humanize and humans computerize' (38, 6). By contrast, the yakuza's power over Eiji is based on immediate physical force and individual patronage, or as one criminal puts it, '[g]uns, and fairy godmothers' (192). Foucault notes that before panopticism, a far less 'diffused' power was exercised by the figure of the monarch, maintained through bodily visibility: '[t]he body of the king, with its strange material and physical presence [...] is at the opposite extreme of this new physics of power represented by panopticism' (208). Eiji sees this principle at work in the yakuza underworld, run on the authority of king-like bosses who dominate through the physical visibility of their actions. For Foucault, before the perfection of panoptic surveillance came the imperfect 'power of spectacle', at work in its passive form through a king's pageantry, but also actively enforced through bloody capital punishment – as practised by the criminal gangs in *number9dream* (217). This rule by spectacle is visible in an entire catalogue of violent criminal activity, targeted at small groups of individuals and designed to personally intimidate and control through terror and bodily violence. Aside from the yakuza's gory bowling match, this is also demonstrated as they take '[o]ne litre of blood' from Eiji's friend Yuzu, send back an ambassador 'minus his arms and legs' and conduct a card game in which '[t]he loser will donate organs' (172, 165, 357).

However, these older symbolic displays of physical power ultimately have a far more limited reach than panopticism; as Foucault notes, they have been 'extinguished one by one in the daily exercise of surveillance, in a panopticism in which the vigilance of intersecting gazes was soon to render useless both the eagle and the sun' (217). Just as panopticism renders these symbols of imperial power 'useless', yakuza boss Mr Tsuru – the king-like symbol of the gang's methods of control – meets his end in a grotesquely humorous spectacle, satirizing his violent reign. Dictating the card game's rules as the 'voice of god' behind a screen, Mr Tsuru suffers a stroke and dies, falling onto his barbecue (356). The blackly comedic announcement that 'Mr Tsuru has grilled his face to the hotplate' is met by the intermingled noises of vomiting and 'joyful' dog barking, a macabre juxtaposition that removes any remaining dignity or authority from the yakuza 'Father' (361, 184). Eiji describes the scene as a 'riot of improvised theatre', a spectacle that echoes both Tsuru's rule through terror, as well as the inevitability of its failure – and an end, for Eiji at least, to the yakuza's outmoded structures of control (361).

Eiji's encounter with the yakuza tests a potential escape route from the viral and internalized panoptic structures that he encounters in the first chapter. By contrast with the diffused psychological control that the PanOpticon building is imagined to wield through its panoptic methods of surveillance, the yakuza represent a non-intellectual, irrational form of escape through the physical immediacy of bodily sensation. If the panopticon is the self-policing Freudian superego, the yakuza forms its opposite, as the impulse-driven, pleasure-seeking id. In the extreme violence, anti-social consequences and ultimately self-destructive urges pursued by the yakuza in *number9dream*, the possibility of a bodily escape from the psychological model of the panopticon is ruled out. In order to escape the panoptic structures that surround him, Eiji must find a way to live that avoids both the drone-like loss of identity of Bentham's prison inmates and the damaging violence of the Foucauldian pre-panoptic 'power of spectacle' demonstrated by the yakuza.

Escaping the panopticon

By the end of the novel, Eiji has learnt how to resist the panopticon; as Brunon-Ernst and Tusseau note, 'resistance' is one of the ways of challenging the panopticon model ('Epilogue' 192). Eiji's gradual creation of distinct home and work lives and social groups, each with its own seemingly incongruous characters, becomes what Berthold Schoene identifies in *The Cosmopolitan Novel* (2009) as a 'strategy of resistance' to the isolating panoptic forces around him (5). Through the course of the novel, Eiji rejects both public and private frameworks of control, by the public act of sabotaging 'a Yakuza network which steals people, cuts them up and [...] sells the body parts', and by the private decision not to reveal his identity to his powerful father, even though they 'will never meet again' (378, 374). As he finds the courage to act, the frequency of his daydreams decreases; in combating panoptic paralysis with action, the psychological with the physical, these acts of resistance show Eiji breaking free of the public and private frameworks of mental control acting upon him.

This is also reflected in Eiji's shift in perception by the end of the novel. On his final visit to the PanOpticon building, he notices its more vulnerable human facets, rather than its machine-like qualities. Overturning its imagined robotic precision, the environment is strikingly drone-less: a 'one-legged man crutches across the polished floor', while the guard has a 'smear of shaving foam [...] under one ear' (371). In confronting the building's interior, rather than imagining it, the lack of 'drones' reveals a protagonist who has learnt to view the world outside the Benthamite language of the panopticon. Similarly, the high-tech gadgetry of the PanOpticon's imagined interior gives way to Eiji's realization that it is far less hostile than he feared; he notices, '[t]he carpet is worn, the air-con is old, the walls need repainting' (372). Compared to his anticlimactic discovery of his paternity through his father's 'unusual' pizza order, this change in perception is revealed as Eiji's larger quest, a change put in motion by his confrontation of reality through his own acts of resistance against the viral panoptic structures around him (373, 369).

Reinforcing this change in perception, the novel begins and ends with a natural disaster. While the first chapter's disaster is imagined, a flood that sees Eiji fantasize about 'the beauty' of his comically hyperbolic death-by-crocodile in the Pacific Ocean, the reality of the final chapter's 'massive earthquake' puts it into perspective (20, 417). Eiji imagines his girlfriend Ai in danger, 'a pane of glass exploding' next to her, a 'girder crashing through her piano' (418). However, with this second disaster, his imagination is no longer a confining force, but a liberating one. The image prompts Eiji to take action and 'begin running' to do what he can, now a possible hero of his fantasies rather than a victim of them, as the protagonist's paralysis within the first chapter gives way to his movement and action in the final chapter. Yet a humanist point is also being made; so many real global crises occur, in which help is desperately needed, that to become enamoured with personal fantasized traumas risks missing vital opportunities to help others.

Motivated by his concern for Ai, it is this vital connection to others that prompts Eiji's change in perception by the novel's end. Foucault notes that the 'separated cells' of the panopticon 'imply a lateral visibility', with this separation of its inmates ensuring that 'there is no danger of a plot, an attempt at collective escape'; its order relies on the suppression of any sense of collectivity (200). In *The Panopticon Writings*, Bentham also emphasizes that the panopticon's circular design is aimed at preventing any communal solidarity: 'to the keeper, a *multitude*, though not a *crowd*; to themselves, they are *solitary* and *sequestered* individuals' (50). By contrast with Eiji's perceived separation from Tokyo's 'drones' in the opening chapter, by the end of the novel his isolation has given way to a growing sense of community, as the novel has followed his transformation from 'semi-orphan' fantasist to rebuilding his own family of sorts (171). It may be dysfunctional – his father has no idea that they have met, his mother has 'dropped any "Mother" role' on their meeting, and Eiji only finds out after his grandfather's death that he met him in disguise as Admiral Raizo – but he has made contact with all of them and returned to the island on which he grew up to confront his past (399).

In combating the isolating panoptic boundaries that foster total psychological separation, *number9dream* highlights the importance of community in the face of predatory isolation. When the earthquake strikes, it is his newly found home and work communities that he calls: 'Ai's number is dead. So is Buntarō's. So is Nero's. No reply from Ueno', while real concern for another spurs him into action at the novel's end (418). If Eiji's flight at the end of the eighth chapter mirrors his escape from the novel's panoptic structures, it is the fragile but real community that he has built by the end of the novel that makes his escape a truly collective one, freeing him from the text's multiple forces of panoptic control and containment.

A tale of two endings

Yet this ending is another Mitchellian metafiction, an escape from one viral panopticon into another. The eighth chapter's false narrative ending stops before the 'real' final paratextual ending: a blank ninth chapter in which Eiji's world disappears entirely. In creating a text with two endings, operating on two levels, *number9dream* prompts a second conclusion. The blank pages of the final chapter, immediately following the description of Eiji beginning to run, employ a metafictional use of textual space to suggest a protagonist that has finally escaped not merely the confines of his prewritten plot, but also the panoptic gaze of the reader, imagining a break from authorial control to escape from the text. With this second ending, the novel suggests that Eiji has managed to accomplish what he has been attempting all along: to escape from the predetermined narrative reality in which he finds himself, whether through his imaginative false starts and fantasies in the first chapter, in the dream and nightmare sequences throughout the novel, the virtual worlds and 'video games' of the third chapter, or the fifth chapter's Goatwriter narrative in which Eiji's reality becomes sidelined as a tale in its 'margins' (95, 205). As Mitchell reveals in an interview with Silverblatt, *number9dream* is 'about a fragmented person becoming a more whole person in the tradition of the Romance (with a large R) of the eighteenth and nineteenth centuries' ('David Mitchell on Bookworm'). Just as Carlo Collodi's marionette protagonist must leave the confines of his wooden body in order to become a real boy in *The Adventures of Pinocchio* [1883], Eiji must ultimately escape the confines of the text in order to become a metafictionally 'whole' individual.

While *number9dream* explores Eiji's experiences of both Bentham's hyper-utilitarian prison panopticon through corporate Tokyo, and Foucault's imperfect pre-panoptic alternative through the yakuza, Mitchell moves the panoptic paradigm forward by exposing its fractal virality, building on each of these portrayals while suggesting the panoptic gaze replicates even beyond the confines of the tale into the complex relationships between reader, author and narrator. The core of Eiji's quest is to escape from the self-spawning panoptic fantasies that prevent him from engaging with reality, but also, extra-diegetically, from the text itself. The metafictional disruptions in the text – Eiji's narrative false starts and the novel's blank final pages – deliberately obstruct the gaze of the reader-as-inspector, bringing the panopticon out of its historic and theoretical permutations into a world in which the watcher's desire to observe is exposed. The novel's paratextual ending highlights that the dangers of the panopticon aren't merely external; just as the panopticon requires a prison and an inmate, it also needs a potential observer in order to wield psychological control. Using the model of text-as-panopticon, the reader's part in this surveillance machine is implicated as the ability to see Eiji's every movement through each panoptic chapter-turned-cell is suddenly withdrawn. The narrative hiatus exposes and frustrates our desire to see into the world of another, with Eiji's textual escape laying bare the universal compulsion that perpetuates the panoptic gaze.

Just as in *If on a Winter's Night a Traveller* – a self-reflexive tale in which the reader becomes the main character searching for the final part of a book – the reader's search for an ending remains suspended, permanently frustrated by the knowledge that the text's final words are being deliberately withheld and the plot metafictionally disrupted. While Eiji's escape is, on one level, another metafictional illusion – even the blank chapter is inescapably part of the author's panoptic design – in as far as the text is able to allow, Eiji has escaped the world of prewritten narrative, even if he is ultimately caught in the double bind of authorial control. In this way, the multiple endings of this multifaceted text engage with and problematize the concept of panoptic escape on several levels, both inside and outside its narrative. However, the blank final chapter remains an embodiment of Eiji's psychological freedom from internal panoptic paralysis, imagining an escape from the containment of the author's predestined narratives towards a real world of unforeseen and unobservable possibility and agency that, for the young protagonist, remains unwritten.

Panoptic control across the macronovel

Having critiqued the role of the panopticon in *number9dream*, it is also worth mentioning the influence of some of these psychological frameworks and controlling boundaries in the author's wider works. While *number9dream* depicts the self-made nature of the controlling frameworks that make its methods of control so pervasive, viewing Mitchell's other works in light of a panoptic model of power similarly emphasizes the individual complicity that is required to sustain such panoptic boundaries. While the panopticon is explicitly referred to in *number9dream*, panoptic structures can be found throughout his fictions, their methods of control often driven by internal, self-policing impulses as much as physical boundaries.

For example, the models of predation shown in *The Thousand Autumns* prove far more complex than one individual preying on another, and are often panoptic in their multiplicity and their reliance on the individual's psychological complicity. Orito's successful break away from the Mount Shiranui shrine becomes 'her escape and voluntary return' (320). Kept against her will as a midwife for the shrine's pregnant nuns, when she finally escapes and hears the distant sound of the bell warning that one of the women has gone into labour, she immediately realizes '[t]he Bell could be a trick […] to *lure you back*' – yet she still returns (308). After going back, she finds that returning has 'elevated her status in many, subtle ways', including her safety from the shrine's ongoing system of legitimized rape or 'Engiftment', all 'in return for Orito's silence' about the infant murders taking place. In spite of her good intentions, her return facilitates the system; as the cult leader Enomoto tells her, she is now its 'instrument', caught in a psychological double bind which draws her back within its frameworks of control (341). Repeating frameworks of panoptic control can also be seen in *Slade House*, in which the same form of entrapment continues to be carried out in the same house for several generations, each individual victim's inadvertent complicity and ghostly efforts to warn future victims becoming part of a trans-temporal collective struggle against the psychological control exerted by the soul-eaters.

Another example that draws attention to the individual's complicity in maintaining such insidious power structures is the short story 'In the Bike Sheds', in which the young narrator, Heather O'Dowd, accidentally witnesses a group of bullies hang an effigy of their German teacher Mrs Weinstock, adorned with swastikas, after school. The intimacy of the dialogue between the narrator and the perpetrators as they manipulate her into silence reveals the everyday processes of psychological control that render the witness powerless. The repeated use of 'coward' in the penultimate sentence is set against the story's final line, '[s]omewhere not far, Mrs Weinstock's having a quiet night in'. Leaving the tale's ending with the victim, her innocuous 'quiet night' at home a stark contrast with the malicious hanging that has taken place, the story's final line emphasizes not merely the human cost of Heather's silence but also its proximity. This final reminder that her teacher is 'not far' from her evokes the causality of Martin Niemöller's 1946 holocaust memorial poem, 'First They Came for the Jews', using a simple playground dynamic to illustrate the consequences of individual capitulation within a larger framework of control. By exposing the myriad forms of panoptic self-regulation, Mitchell's narratives make visible the uncomfortable complicity of the victim within larger self-reinforcing hierarchies, demonstrating both the positive outcomes of resistance within such frameworks, as in *number9dream*, but also the consequences of failing to act as a means of perpetuating these systems of control.

'I *should've been born*, hissed Unborn Twin, *not* you'

Having explored the model of the panopticon as anti-mandala, and investigated the effects of its principles within the author's works, a better grasp of their relationship is needed to understand how these two structures relate to one another within a larger critical framework. While the mandala's dark counterpart emerges from *number9dream* in the form of the panopticon, another of his novels – *Black Swan Green* – suggests the critical relationship between the frameworks of the panopticon and mandala: that of an unborn twin.

The panopticon's structural and political similarities with the mandala make it too closely aligned to be a straightforward opposite – defined here as from the Latin *oppositus*, meaning adversary or opponent, and the French *opposite*, meaning contrary or opposed to – definitions by which each of its features would need to be fundamentally opposed to the original structure's principles and form.[13] Yet their relationship is also too complex to be a case of mirroring, by which each of its features would be reversed but their appearance and properties maintained; these are, after all, two very distinct entities which have grown from similar structural and political roots. However, as this section will discuss, the concept of the unborn twin embodies the closeness of their critical relationship, the nature of the connection that it suggests itself prompting a deeper probing into the theoretical structures underpinning the author's works. As Paul de Man notes in *Blindness and Insight* (1983), '[h]owever negative it may sound, deconstruction implies the possibility of rebuilding', a critical approach which aligns with Mitchell's own reconstructive narratives, which allow

---

[13] 'opposite, n., adj., adv., and prep'. *OED Online.* Oxford University Press, September 2015. Web. 4 November 2015.

for hope in even their bleakest moments (140). The deconstructive destabilization of assumed hierarchies exposes this intimate and ultimately reconciliatory connection between the original structure and its deconstructed form – in this case, the mandala and the panopticon – their relationship more akin to a twin-like siblinghood than an irreconcilable opposition.

In the semi-autobiographical novel *Black Swan Green*, the narrator Jason Taylor is a form of textual representation – or unborn twin – of the author himself. Describing his own experiences of growing up with a stammer, Mitchell's essays 'On Becoming a Non-Stammering Stammerer' (2006) and 'Lost for Words' (2011) both discuss the personal struggles that shaped Jason's portrayal. One of the facets of this portrayal is Jason's alter ego, 'Unborn Twin', a more confident persona who goads the narrator to action. For example, when Jason's sister threatens him for touching her magazine, this inner monologue comes into play, interrupting Jason's narration with: 'I should've been born, hissed Unborn Twin, not you' (45). The recurring presence of Jason's imagined 'Unborn Twin' as it continues to intervene throughout the novel draws attention to its proximity to the narrator as a separate entity, albeit one that is never fully realized, remaining 'unborn' in a physical sense. Yet 'Unborn Twin' appears twenty-three times throughout the novel – enough to make it a character in its own right, and suggesting that the concept of the unborn twin has an important critical function within the text.

This concept of the unborn twin influences the narrative on several levels. As Mitchell notes in a 2011 interview with Geordie Williamson, 'me and the protagonist [of *Black Swan Green*] would have much DNA in common', the narrator himself a form of unborn twin to the author ('David Mitchell in conversation'). Mitchell notes his similarities with Jason in interview, including their shared ages and upbringing, while he also confirms in an interview with Adam Begley that '*Black Swan Green* is loosely drawn from a village called Hanley Swan in Worcestershire where my family lived', and that he saw a speech therapist at the same age ('David Mitchell, The Art of Fiction'). He also notes that, like Jason, he wrote poetry for the parish newsletter, and that while Jason's writerly pseudonym was Eliot Bolivar, Mitchell's was James Bolivar. If Jason's character hadn't been developed further, it would have remained merely an autobiographical echo of Mitchell's childhood. Yet from these genetically similar beginnings, Jason Taylor continues to grow and develop in Mitchell's alternative textual universe, as discussed in Chapter 1. In *Black Swan Green*, the reader is therefore presented with an unborn-twin-within-an-unborn-twin, in the form of the author's literally 'unborn' textual twin, Jason, and his metaphysical alter ego.

The narrative world of *Black Swan Green* also presents two additional unborn twins of its own. The author's short stories 'The January Man' (2003) and 'Hangman' (2005) provide two earlier versions of *Black Swan Green*'s first and second chapters, respectively, each depicting an 'unborn' version of the novel. For example, in 'Hangman', Jason's best friend Dean is instead named 'Stu', and the bus driver Norman Bates is 'Psycho Spike', while speech therapist Mrs de Roo is 'Mrs Warwick'; Mitchell's characteristic moon-grey cat would only make it into the novel's final cut (102, 90). To venture further into this extra-diegetic twinning, in Mitchell's foreword to *David Mitchell: Critical Essays* (2011, ed. Sarah Dillon), the author describes the uncanny sense of doubling caused by attending a conference on his own works, imagining his writing to be authored not by himself but by yet another unborn version of David Mitchell – which he describes as 'a sort of dodgy twin' (1).

The relationship between the mandala and the panopticon shares some essential characteristics with this repeated motif. These are not mere opponents or mirroring structures: as a critical model, the panopticon functions as the mandala's unborn twin. In his 2007 interview with Tishani Doshi, Mitchell reveals: '[t]he unborn twin is the evil alter-ego – the Mr. Hyde to the Dr. Jekyll. […] it's mythic isn't it? The ability to be two even though you are one' ('Secret Architectures'). The panopticon therefore presents an unborn alternative to the mandalic world view, a form of 'evil alter-ego' which depicts a dark doubling of the mandala's traditionally holistic principles in its mythical imagining of a confining, rather than a liberatory, space.

As Susan M. Walcott describes, '[m]andalas function as moral and mental maps', using the participant's 'interior space' to do so ('Mapping from a Different Direction' 86). However, so does the panopticon, providing a mental map of a metaphysical dimension that creates its own sinister morality. The panopticon replaces the mandala's mythology with a self-policing totality in which the spatial arrangement of its dominant centre, cardinal points and controlling circular boundary become part of a psychological model. Whereas the mandala aims to foster self-consciousness and mental engagement, the panopticon turns this self-consciousness into a weapon that encourages paranoia as a disturbing method of control. Offering a paradigm for the relationship between both structures, the concept of the unborn twin illustrates that the panopticon is the necessary counterpart to the mandala as a critical framework. It serves as a warning that the darkest of purposes can lurk beneath even the most well-intentioned of structures, and that any regulated framework can become a prison.

Barry Bryant observes in *The Wheel of Time Sand Mandala* (1995) that '[t]he sand mandala reminds us of something almost lost in our society […]. What we are reminded of most forcefully, as we come into this space, is the depth and capability of the human mind' (255). Bryant's words could just as easily apply to the panopticon. To take a deconstructive approach to the mandala is to uncover a duality to this holistic structure which, given the correct conditions of surveillance, paranoia and control, can become its unborn twin. *Number9dream* offers a vivid example of the ways in which Mitchell's narratives synthesize both mandalic and panoptic perspectives, warning that the human mind can succumb to either realm. Yet despite Eiji's initial fears, the novel ultimately demonstrates that he already possesses all that he needs to escape the confinement of this psychological superstructure: not the red herrings of violent physicality, but his ability to act, combating panoptic paralysis with his own powerful acts of resistance and community-building.

5

'Little Things that Speak of the Big Things': Towards a Mandalic Literature

The previous chapters of this study mapped David Mitchell's complete fictions as an interconnected ethical terrain, using the mandala as a comparative critical tool to help identify the Buddhist influences that draw his narratives into a continuous post-secular world. However, if the interconnections between Mitchell's fictions extend far beyond their shared themes and characters, and even beyond the limits of each discrete narrative publication, as this study has demonstrated, it's worth considering whether the interconnections in Mitchell's fictional terrain extend beyond the macronovel itself. How do the shared preoccupations within his post-secular world, then, relate to the literary world outside the author's works? This final chapter now shifts its engagement with the mandala in order to address this question. While each of the previous chapters used the mandala to help map Mitchell's fictional world view, this chapter moves its use of the mandala from an individual interpretive framework to the basis of an emerging literary category whose traits can also be found within other post-secular contemporary fictions. As such, the following sections take the combined features of his world view that have been revealed by using the mandala as an interpretive framework, using these features to identify other contemporary fictions that use shared narrative strategies to re-evaluate the concept of belief, building their own post-secular ethical worlds. Finally, this chapter also discusses the wider implications of the mandala's theorization – and the pressing need to resituate this 'holistic' Jungian symbol within the ongoing sociopolitical struggles that led to its increased international visibility outside of its Tibetan origins.

Identifying other mandalic narrative worlds

Before we progress into other narrative worlds, it's worth briefly summarizing the journey through Mitchell's macronovel so far. To recap this study's earlier findings, then: the first chapter analysed Mitchell's short stories as a vast narrative cartography, arguing that these together form an ethically structured world whose episodic narrative units, when combined, demonstrate the vital importance of belief in galvanizing compassionate action. The second chapter discussed Mitchell's libretti as a vital part of this post-secular world, investigating the Buddhist influences behind each opera's narrative prioritization of hope in the face of tragedy. The third chapter discussed the macronovel's cross-textual creation of 'reincarnation time' as a post-secular narrative strategy from outside the paradigms of Christianity, used across Mitchell's works to foreground the ethical importance of shared causality and collective action amid crises. The fourth chapter deconstructed the mandala's structure and principles, identifying the panopticon as the mandala's 'unborn twin', and using the framework of the panopticon as a form of 'anti-mandala' to examine the dystopian controlling forces that threaten these narrative worlds. These distinct narrative ingredients, each found by approaching Mitchell's works through the mandala's structures and philosophies, together suggest a set of traits that form a transferrable mandalic world view which is similarly visible in a cluster of other contemporary fictions from the same period. From the localized mandala-like patterning of Mitchell's world view, a wider set of shared narrative traits emerge.

As the following sections will demonstrate, a range of contemporary literary works published in English since the millennium redeploy these traits in different ways to create their own mandalic world views, a handful of which will be considered here: *Anil's Ghost* (2000) by Michael Ondaatje, *Hotel World* by Ali Smith (2001), *Life of Pi* by Yann Martel (2002), *The Book of Dave* by Will Self (2006) and the *MaddAddam* trilogy by Margaret Atwood (*Oryx and Crake* 2003, *The Year of the Flood* 2009, and *MaddAddam* 2013). Each of these fictions merits far greater discussion than space permits here, and like the list of mandalic traits that will be identified later in this chapter, this list of texts is by no means exhaustive. However, this study does not aim to create a rigid literary manifesto, but to identify these growing shared approaches in Anglophone post-secular literary fiction in order to question how, and why, these features are recurring at the current moment.

Building on the critical traits previously identified by embarking on a mandalic tour through Mitchell's macronovel, this chapter analyses these traits in order to suggest the emergence of a shared literary category, as noted above. As Kristian Shaw rightly asserts in his conclusion to *Cosmopolitanism in Twenty-First Century Fiction* (2017), '[l]iterary critics must acknowledge both the unavailability of terminology to encompass twenty-first century fiction, and the insufficiency of existing terms to describe its recent transformation', a call to which this chapter responds (182). However, the traits that will be identified in this chapter remain more important than the terminology employed. The term proposed here, 'mandalic literature', is simply easier to use as a shorthand within this chapter than 'contemporary post-secular literature which frequently: engages in self-consciously compassionate world-building, re-examines the ethical value of belief, suggests hopeful alternatives to the imagined dystopian futures created by late capitalism, and deliberately foregrounds the value of both small-scale communal endeavours and individual compassionate action, however Sisyphean'. Such works share a particular blend of traits previously discussed under the various critical umbrellas of the post-secular, metamodern, cosmopolitan, global, dystopian and New-Sincerity-style optimism within contemporary literature. However, these are works that don't fit neatly within any single one of these existing categories, but cut across them, signalling the emergence of an as-yet-unnamed 'something else' – and as such, the term 'mandalic literature' is adopted here in an attempt to move closer towards illuminating what this as-yet-unnamed 'something else' may be.

The mandala's established fluidity across art forms, as well as its individual variance, gives it a useful cross-transferability for this particular group of narrative traits. In 'Encountering the Mandala: The Mental and Political Architectures of Dependency' (2001), Maggie Grey observes that '[m]andalas are multi-media', existing in a huge variety of art forms including 'as murals in temples [...] as portable cloth paintings; as impermanent three dimensional images of coloured sands [...] as dramatic tableau of music and dance [...] and as the ground plan for religious architecture' (7). In its diversity, the mandala is a pluralized form which continues to evolve as it is redeployed across cultures; a further layer to this redeployment is added by this study. Perhaps, then – for the purposes of literary criticism – a text can also be a form of secular mandala in the shared traits of its world view, even while its outward forms resist uniformity. Brought into the realm of literary criticism, such an assertion must necessarily depart from the physicality and religiosity of the Tibetan Buddhist mandala, and its Jungian rewriting as a cross-cultural psychological symbol, in order to identify a group of contemporary narratives which share a particular set of common strategies. Each of the many different forms of mandala remains different according to its creators, recipients and cultural context, and ultimately exists in isolation with its own unique world view, while simultaneously contributing to the shared understanding of 'the mandala' as a discrete category. The study of mandalic literature shares such an approach. As such, it does not seek to minimize difference, but to approach and examine these shared features as part of an evolving framework.

It is also worth noting that the list of shared traits discussed below is not exhaustive, or exclusive; a 'mandalic' text will not necessarily include all of the following criteria, and will favour a more detailed depiction of some of these traits more than others. But taken together, the concept of mandalic literature is ventured here to refer to a subset of texts which build an interconnected world view whose patchwork of different narrative perspectives demonstrates the importance of collective causality, conducting a post-secular interrogation of ethics and belief, and foregrounding individual compassionate action while presenting such hopeful actions amid dystopic violence. This section will discuss each of these traits in turn, drawing on Mitchell's macronovel as a form of *urtext* for the purpose of their identification. Incorporating other examples from contemporary Anglophone literature, the common strategies that will be discussed below together address a literary engagement forged in the shared zeitgeist of the new millennium, suggesting that a specific form of post-secular dynamic is emerging in twenty-first-century literary fiction.

Compassionate cartography

These are narratives whose restless world exploration eschews the stasis, familiarity and insularity of settled domesticity, taking the reader on a journey through a narrative cartography – whether across a nation, an ocean or the ecosystem of a global hotel chain – in which the setting refuses to anchor in any single version of 'home'. Mitchell's macronovel moves relentlessly across such a fictional world-system, a trait which can also be seen in a cluster of other contemporary works, as will be discussed below. Each narrative's world view is often created using snapshots of contrasting perspectives that emphasize the difference between individual lived experiences and the interconnections that link them, creating a world which itself is built from its linked differences. This technique is visible both across David Mitchell's macronovel as a whole, and also in many of its individual narratives; for example, such an interconnected world view may be primarily formed from units of geographical difference, as in *Ghostwritten*, temporal difference, as in *Slade House*, or local difference, as in *Black Swan Green*'s focus on Worcestershire or *The Thousand Autumns* on Dejima. Such works may also use a combination of these to create their world map, such as *Cloud Atlas*'s juxtaposition of geographical and temporal shifts to form its interconnected narrative units.

More broadly, then, mandalic narratives construct a world in which such human interconnection is foregrounded across both local and global world views, with these chains of causality as the vital 'glue' that makes the fictional world into a world-*system*, cumulatively depicting separate yet interconnected narrative realms whose horizons have been irreversibly expanded by the ultimate world-system of globalization. As in Mitchell's fictional world, such works often use an intensely localized focus on the everyday lived experiences of their characters, each individual perspective contrasted with the machinations of the larger world in which they operate, with the narrative focus expanding and shifting as the text progresses to form a world view formed from experiential narrative episodes. In doing so, these works break away from narrative linearity to create an interconnected narrative realm in which multiple and often conflicting perspectives are shown simultaneously, foregrounding the chains of causality that connect – and divide – each world's inhabitants.

Like Mitchell's macronovel, such worlds create a distinctly *compassionate* cartography, building a localized atlas of human experience from a self-consciously representational – rather than strictly realist – narrative perspective, creating a world in which compassionate acts and perspectives take on particular significance (see Chapter 1). In 'Genesis, Retold: In Search of an Atlas of the Anthropocene' (2014), Wolfgang Struck rightly identifies that although 'within the last decades, the atlas has lost its dominance as a medium of spatial representation […] it has recently attracted a significant aesthetic interest' within the work of contemporary artists and writers (217). Struck also notes that the 'most important' feature of an atlas is that it aims to create a world view in its entirety, and that 'the atlas can only present this whole in partitions'; as such, '[t]he atlas is constituted by an interplay between part and whole', this interplay often emphasized in mandalic narratives (222). As part of his aesthetic exploration of the atlas, Struck uses the phrase 'compassionate cartography' (230) to describe the rewriting of the atlas form by Judith Schalansky in her publication *Atlas of Remote Islands: Fifty Islands I Have Not Visited and Never Will* (2010), an unconventional atlas whose hand-drawn versions of fifty remote islands with accompanying tales portrays the atlas form as one of self-conscious world creation rather than world reproduction. Building on Struck's terminology, the concept of compassionate cartography is used here to refer to texts whose narrative world, interspersing interconnected local and global world views, does so from an explicitly ethical perspective – just as, for example, Mitchell's libretti for *Wake* and *Sunken Garden* use their interconnected world views of individual experiences of grieving to finally urge their viewers to find ways to continue living in the face of inexplicable tragedy (see Chapter 2).

This technique of using individual narrative perspectives to build a distinctly 'compassionate cartography', taking the reader on an ethical journey through a world-system comprised of difference, can also be seen in several other contemporary post-secular narratives, each reworking the concept in different ways. Published in 2000, *Anil's Ghost* by Michael Ondaatje is set in Sri Lanka in the aftermath of the civil war that took place in the 1980s and 1990s, a bloody conflict between government and anti-government groups which left innumerable unidentified bodies in its wake. The novel tells the story of forensic pathologist Anil Tissera and archaeologist Sarath Diyasena as they work together to identify the skeleton of a recently killed man. When they discover that the government appears to have been involved in his death, their quest to uncover the victim's identity becomes increasingly politically dangerous; when the skeleton is confiscated by state officials, Sarath helps Anil to flee the country, before himself being killed due to his involvement.

Anil's Ghost joins together the disparate pasts of its characters to build an interconnected narrative terrain, situating the localized lived experiences of Anil and Sarath within a wider system of ongoing casual corruption and brutality whose effects extend across a nation. The story is told using an episodic structure, in which each section focuses on a different character or incident. These sections are interspersed with italicized anecdotes about the island's history, geography and people – one summarizes the National Atlas of Sri Lanka's seventy-three versions of the island (39–40) – creating a patchwork narrative of multiple perspectives to cumulatively build a self-contained, ethically engaged world view which foregrounds the tireless efforts to rebuild by small communities of individual families, doctors and forensics. Throughout the novel, the narrative focus shifts from the single skeleton to the countless other nameless victims of the war, and from the individual forensic search to the many grieving relatives themselves searching for the bodies of missing family members. The seemingly endless backdrop of human suffering presented foregrounds the caring actions of the doctors and forensics who work tirelessly amid an endless tide of bodies and victims, creating a compassionate cartography that uses the novel's shifts between localized ethical struggles for justice and the world-system of the island to depict the chains of causality that connect the victims and perpetrators.

Ali Smith's *Hotel World* (2001) uses a similarly episodic narrative technique to map its own compassionate cartography, exploring the localized experiences of a group of characters whose lives intersect in a single branch of a global hotel chain. The narrative, which is told through five interconnected female characters, uses the hotel as a microcosmic world-within-a-world which forms the setting for the novel. The tale begins with the story of a ghost of a girl, Sara Wilby, who tells the reader that she has a message to deliver ('I have a message for you. Listen') (29). As the first section progresses, the reader learns of Sara's accidental death in the hotel's lift shaft; the second section shifts the narrative focus to Else, a homeless woman stationed outside the hotel; the third section introduces the hotel receptionist, Lise, who offers Else a hotel room for the night. The fourth section features the journalist Penny, who is staying in the hotel; it is here that she meets Else, and Sara's grieving sister, Clare. The fifth section follows Clare's final memories of her sister as she struggles to come to terms with Sara's death. The novel's last section creates an omniscient ghost's-eye view that ties the novel's episodes together into an interconnected world-system, describing a panorama of human activity across 'turn-of-the-century England' in a nameless setting that could reflect '[a]nywhere up or down the country, any town' (229). Cumulatively, each of the localized sections of the novel presents the reader with one facet of an interconnected whole, creating a narrative cartography in which the title of the hotel chain ('*GLOBAL HOTELS*', 55–6), the journalist's newspaper ('*The World on Sunday*', 169), and the nearby showroom ('World of Carpets', 55) all emphasize this narrative 'worlding'. This emphasis on globality presents the tale's localized issues as part of a wider ethical commentary on social inequality, exposing the chains of causality that connect those living in poverty with those who fail to help, as is visible in the novel's portrayal of the interactions between the affluent journalist Penny and homeless Else.

Yann Martel's *Life of Pi*, published in 2002, also uses a range of different techniques to create its own version of a compassionate cartography. The tale follows the story of Piscine Molitor Patel, known as Pi, as he recounts his survival at sea for 227 days after his ship – which is full of zoo animals – is wrecked, leaving Pi stranded on a lifeboat with a tiger. This is a tale that is infused with global travel, from Pi's formative childhood experiences in Pondicherry, India, to his interrupted voyage to Canada, which leaves Pi adrift on the Pacific Ocean, before he eventually lands in Mexico. Although Pi's narrative forms the body of the novel, his tale is also told through episodes which contribute multiple narrative perspectives on a single story, creating an interconnected narrative world view from several simultaneous versions of the same event: from the 'author' who begins the novel, the mythical tale created by Pi of his survival at sea following a shipwreck, and the disturbing 'truth' in the transcript from the Japanese officials at the end of the novel. It is only when he has arrived on land, and is in discussion with officials from the Japanese Ministry of Transport, that Pi reveals a different version of events: a horrific tale of survival that tells of a dysfunctional community of survivors who turn against each other, with disastrous consequences. He describes to the official the horrifying truth of seeing his mother get killed and eaten, before himself murdering her killer and cannibalizing him to stay alive. Asked which story they prefer, the baffled officials finally agree that '[t]he story with animals is the better story' (317). Following the revelation of the human cruelty that Pi has survived, the officials accept that his invented tale of the tiger is '*an astounding story of courage and endurance*' [sic], regardless of its accuracy (319). In doing so, the novel emphasizes the practical value of belief – which as the multi-perspective world view demonstrates, is as indispensable for secular survival as it is in sacred contexts – and the need for the compassionate acceptance of such beliefs. Such a moral perspective doesn't overturn the horrific violent 'truth' revealed at the end of the book, but simultaneously uses multiple perspectives on the same story to demonstrate the ethical value of Pi's narrative self-preservation in its creation of hope from extreme trauma.

While *Life of Pi*'s episodic narrative is constructed through different versions of the same story, *The Book of Dave* (2006) by Will Self uses episodic storytelling to move the narrative focus between a dystopic future world and how such a world came to be. The novel tells the story of Dave Rudman, a racist, misogynistic taxi driver who suffers a psychotic breakdown following a break-up with his wife and loss of contact with his son. Lost in the grip of his illness, he pours his anger and resentment at the world into a tome and buries it – where it lies until it is found 500 years later and worshipped as the blueprint for human civilization, becoming known as 'the Book'. Dave's hate-filled rants become the 'doctrines and covenants' of the new world, his 'revelation' used to explain the post-apocalyptic island of Ham and make sense of 'its shape, its isolation, its peculiar character' (76). In this violent future world, there is no divide between sacred and secular; according to the Book, men and women are forcibly separated and share custody of their children, who are cared for by genetically engineered 'motos', grotesque beasts with the faces of giant babies, whose generations of caregiving become increasingly threatened as they are persecuted and killed throughout the novel.

The story of Dave's life is told in narrative episodes from the late 1980s and the first decade of the new millennium, interspersed with the stories of characters living in the dystopic future. These interconnected tales cumulatively build up a detailed exploration of a vast narrative cartography, detailing the history and evolved belief systems of this self-contained world through the eyes of its inhabitants, as well as its effective creator. As such, this cartographic narrative overlays the 'mapping' of this world view and its belief systems alongside detailed descriptions of the novel's physical locations. The novel's opening illustrations depict the remaining land masses in the south of England following an ecological disaster, which has flooded the land and turned it into a series of self-contained islands, encouraging the reader to approach the tale that follows as part of a self-contained and fully immersive narrative world-system, complete with an eighteen-page glossary to help decode the language of its inhabitants. This satirical dystopian novel builds its compassionate cartography by using this detailed fictional terrain to depict the brutal consequences of a world view whose defining belief system has been created entirely *without* compassion. The subsequent era of violence and persecution built by Dave's warped world view makes this story an important warning about the ethical uses and misuses of belief in the twenty-first century, while Dave's attempt to make amends with the compassionate doctrines of his second Book provide a glimmer of hope for ethical change in the future, as will be discussed later in this chapter.

To give a final example of another work that builds its own compassionate cartography, Margaret Atwood's *MaddAddam* trilogy is a series of three speculative fiction novels – *Oryx and Crake* (2003), *The Year of the Flood* (2009) and *MaddAddam* (2013) – which also cumulatively depict a dystopian near future. These novels together describe a dysfunctional world-system by which vast swathes of human population will ultimately be wiped out, leaving behind pockets of survivors and a group of bioengineered humanoids known as Crakers, a peace-loving species bred to replace humans after their near-extinction through a worldwide pandemic. The three-part tale is told through the localized viewpoints of interconnected survivors, whose experiences cumulatively fill in a wider narrative terrain with events across the fictional world before, during and after the fallout. The narrators include fast-food worker turned beekeeper Toby, cult leader and former scientist Adam, whose sermons punctuate the narratives of *The Year of the Flood*, and the young Craker Blackbeard, whose written words at the end of *MaddAddam* record the events of their survival for future generations. Again, each novel features different episodes in the timeline of the apocalypse, which join together to create a vast narrative cartography with a distinct ethical message, warning of the dangerous futures created by the failure of multinational companies to take responsibility for their actions, and the globally damaging consequences of excessive consumerism.

The post-secular interrogation of the ethics of belief

The creation of a specifically compassionate narrative world view in these works, as in David Mitchell's short story 'My Eye On You' – or a world view in which the importance of such compassion is amplified by its absence, as in the bleak dystopian realm created in *The Book of Dave* – allows for an exploration of the implicit ethical codes and belief systems that underpin these worlds. These are categories that have long been traditionally associated with Christianity in the Anglophone world. However, following increasing secularization in Western societies following the atrocities of the Second World War, the post-war climate of ideological distrust has arguably paved the way for the creeping rise of secular neo-liberal ideology. As Jürgen Habermas identifies in 'Notes on Post-Secular Society' (2008), the 'term "post-secular society" can only be applied to the affluent societies [...] where people's religious ties have steadily or rather quite dramatically lapsed in the post-World War II period' (17). The spread of secular neo-liberal values through globalization has been made possible by an implicit corresponding set of encouraged behavioural ideals for the consumer-as-worshipper ('thou shalt buy'), in a form of global secular crusade led not by the Latin Church, but by the hired branding strategists of multinational companies. Any normative assumptions of twentieth-century secularism have been replaced by a twenty-first-century post-secularism in which the rise of capitalist ideology and Western consumerism – as thoroughly internalized by its practitioners and defended by its leaders as any sacred belief system – are now the focus of increasingly prominent groups of neo-religious fundamentalists, from America's growing Evangelical far-right movements to the global acts of terrorism by Islamic State.

It is within such a climate that mandalic literature explores what it means to live and act in a post-secular world, moving beyond the assumed polarities of Christian and non-Christian to explore a greater diversity of belief systems from outside these pluralized and destabilized categories. The re-examination of the concept of belief in these narratives responds to the ethical problems created by Enlightenment rationality, and its use to legitimate neo-liberal exploitation, by seeking new forms of cross-cultural knowledge from outside dominant Western epistemes. As John A. McClure notes in 'Postmodern/Post-Secular: Contemporary Fiction and Spirituality' (1995), '[r]eligion returns [...] as it always has, when worldly life becomes intolerable [...] as secular modernity's promises of peace, prosperity, and progress fail to materialize' (10). However, this is not a simple return to religion; such texts interrogate the concept of faith with a postmodern understanding of its destructive capabilities. As Manav Ratti notes in *The Postsecular Imagination: Postcolonialism, Religion, and Literature* (2013): 'the postsecular does not represent a return to religion [...]. The postsecular can be a critique of secularism and religion, but it cannot lead us back to the religious, and certainly not to the violence undertaken in the name of religion and secularism' (21). Working within a secular framework, mandalic fiction deliberately problematizes that framework by drawing on, pluralizing and inventing non-dominant belief systems adapted from a variety of different sources in order to provide an ethical revaluation of a shared humanity, in which the concept of belief provides a vital key to understanding – and redeploying – human action in the face of contemporary humanitarian and ecological decline.

How, then, does this manifest itself in the texts discussed earlier? *Anil's Ghost* takes its post-secular approach to the ethics of belief from outside Western paradigms of Christianity. Mentions of local Buddhist practices and icons are interwoven throughout the tale alongside painful descriptions of the violence from the civil war, in a narrative that resists any simple sense of religious consolation. The depictions of Buddhist icons are set within a post-secular framework in which their destruction evokes the fragility of the ethical principles that such icons were intended to symbolize; in the novel's first section, an anecdote describes the destruction of a Buddhist cave temple in which statues have been decapitated and hands '*broken off*', the remainder of the figures removed and '*the Bodhisattvas quickly bought up by museums in the West*' (12). The archaeologist later reflects that 'the removal of a wise sixth-century head, the dropping off of arms and hands of rock as a result of the fatigue of centuries, existed alongside human fate' (278–9). Within a novel similarly filled with shattered human bodies, the text prompts the reader to compare the religious destruction with the widespread loss of life, and question whether such destructive impulses are indeed part of an unavoidable 'fate' in which an ancient wisdom which recognizes the sanctity of human life has been lost. However, no answers are given, the post-secular inclusion of religious practice providing a respectful acknowledgement of individual religious practice and personal faith even as any overarching sense of religious consolation is disrupted. For example, in the doctor Gamini's hospital, there is 'a small Buddha lit with a low-watt bulb in nearly every ward' and 'one in surgery as well' (242). The peaceful scene is interrupted by the horrific brutality of the description immediately following it: Gamini's memory of the 'nine-month-old-twins' brought to the hospital, 'each shot in the palms and one bullet each in their right legs', their injuries 'no accident'.

Such juxtapositions of human brutality and religious iconography raise questions of the breakdown of wider ethical responsibility for the sanctity of human life depicted throughout the novel, in which the best efforts to rebuild by the few are painfully inadequate. However, while the penultimate chapter depicts the horrific aftermath of a suicide bombing, the novel's final chapter features a broken 120-foot-tall Buddha statue being repaired by a local artisan, Ananda. Several months are spent rebuilding its head and face in a painstaking reconstruction which ends with the Nētra Mangala ceremony, in which the eyes are painted on by a skilled artist. This act of giving sight is believed to be the moment that the statue becomes sacred; as Anil learns, '[w]ithout the eyes there is not just blindness, there is nothing. […] The artificer brings to life sight and truth' (99). By ending the novel with the reconstruction of 'the great scarred face' made 'from damaged stone', which is 'no longer a god' but an image with a 'pure sad glance', the text's final imagining of the act is not one of pure secularity or religious belief, but a post-secularity which re-examines the ethical functions of religion, and the role of the individual in creating or destroying such belief (307).

While *Hotel World* doesn't draw on a named religious framework, it offers a post-secular exploration of death and grieving through its engagement with the supernatural, depicting imagined ghosts that continue to haunt the living, beginning with Sara's ghost in the first chapter and continued with the anonymous ghosts that swarm over the town in the novel's final section. However, in the penultimate chapter, in which Clare comes to terms with her sister's death, a reworked invocation of the religious is introduced: 'God' is repeated seventeen times in her stream of consciousness, interwoven with her memories of Sara and the aftermath of her death. Although each repetition of 'God' is given as a vernacular exclamation, its sustained repetition and the repeated use of typographical spacing for emphasis ('Sara you are lucky oh God what am God no I don't mean it Sara', 214) make this chapter into a form of secular Kaddish. In this final invocation, Clare's use of '& since' to start each unpunctuated phrase is repeated thirty-two times throughout the chapter. Becoming a mantra of sorts, '& since' also starts each of the final twenty line-broken phrases, giving Clare's mourning the ritual repetition of a secular liturgy, whose repetition is not to affirm a divine world view, but to chart the narrator's gradual rebuilding of her own fragmented world view, in which each '& since' is followed by a different memory, finally ending in the reconciliation of her memory of her sister's virtuoso ability to dive with her final fall to her death.

It is Clare's final post-secular invocation of the numinous ('& since maybe now you can walk on air too // & since wherever you are now I know you will be keeping us [...] safe', 220) which ends the chapter. However, her mourning gives way to the 'Morning' that begins the final chapter, a promise of new beginnings which punctuates the panoramic description of morning breaking across an anonymous town (225). One final compassionate act remains as the section ends with a simple kindness in which 'the girl who works in the watch shop' that Sara fell in love with from a distance – and who knows nothing of Sara's love, or death – keeps her unclaimed watch on her own wrist, vowing to return it to her family without charge (235). It is this hopeful affirmation that shifts the narrative focus from the afterlife to the living, a post-secular gesture that uses the novel's supernatural evocation of the numinous to reaffirm the possibilities and ethical responsibilities of living within a globally interconnected world.

Life of Pi by Yann Martel similarly conducts its own post-secular interrogation of the ethics of belief. The novel begins with an author's note in which the narrator describes meeting an elderly man while travelling in India, who tells him, '*I have a story that will make you believe in God*' – having heard his story, the narrator affirms this message to the reader: '*this was, indeed, a story to make you believe in God*' (x). Before his tale begins, this author-narrator also delivers a warning: if artists aren't supported, '*we end up believing in nothing and having worthless dreams*' (xii). From the outset, then, this is a post-secular tale about belief itself, a tale of religious pantheism told for an audience that, like the contemporary Western readership, is assumed to be secular. Pi's tale constructs a world of his own telling, a self-contained fantasy world which proves not the existence of God, but the essential role of belief in human survival, in a post-secular ethical re-evaluation of the practical value of religion. As Pi notes, '[d]oubt is useful for a while [...]. But we must move on. To choose doubt as a philosophy of life is akin to choosing immobility as a means of transportation' (36). However, the belief system that he adopts is not conventionally religious, but a post-secular revaluation of the freedom to choose such belief. It is the 'strange religious practices' that Pi adopts in childhood – when he becomes a practicing Hindu, Muslim and Christian simultaneously – that give him the essential fluidity of belief that allows him to choose to retell his own narrative and in doing so, create a new truth that allows him to survive his ordeal (3).

With its own distinct take on the post-secular, *The Book of Dave* is a novel in which everything – and nothing – is sacred. By inventing its own religion, this tale critiques the damaging social effects of religious doctrine, estranging the reader from established religions to shift the focus onto their doctrines and ethical consequences for the worlds in which they are adopted. Although Dave eventually recovers from his illness, rebuilds his life and finds love for his family and new partner, the damage of his selfish and hate-filled world view has been done. His subsequent remorse over his rant does not undo its future damage, and the Book remains buried in his ex-wife's garden, his words later used to build a violent and oppressive world whose anger-fuelled doctrine normalizes religious persecution and censorship. The final chapter of the novel ends with the burial of a second Book at Dave's funeral, which his family places in the ground in his memory – a 'new Book' that he wrote to make amends, which tells his son to 'RESPECT MEN AND WOMEN BOTH, to strive always for RESPONSIBILITY' with 'no CONFLICT, no tug of HATE' [*sic*] (420). Whether such compassionate action will ever be enough to shape the dystopian future remains undisclosed, but as the omniscient narrator notes of the forthcoming ecological breakdown, 'ice caps may melt, the jungles shrivel [...] the family of humankind may have, at best, three or four more generations before the BREAKUP [...] yet there can be no EXCUSE for not trying to DO YOUR BEST and live right' (420–1). The novel's hope for change lies in these words, whose message is spread heretically in the future as 'Dave's second testament' which contains 'an everyday faith for everyone' (195). Such a simple ethical code based on compassionate action may prove painfully inadequate in a future in which inequality and social oppression are so widespread, but their inclusion provides a fragile hope for ethical change within such a world-system, demonstrating the far-reaching consequences of individual beliefs.

Explorations of alternative belief systems are depicted throughout all three books in Margaret Atwood's *MaddAddam* trilogy, including the group of post-apocalyptic survivors known as God's Gardeners in *The Year of the Flood*. The narrative doesn't depict an unquestioning return to religion; Toby notes that 'the prayers were tedious, the theology scrambled' (46). However, this makeshift belief system becomes a vital part of their survival. In *MaddAddam*, the Crakers, who have evolved their own belief systems and rituals, are helped by Toby to learn to read and write. The tale ends with their writing of their own scripture-of-sorts in 'the Book', as Toby puts her time in God's Gardeners to good use, using the group's humanist teachings to create a practical record of the story of their survival for future generations (385). Its festivals and feast days create a pantheistic, post-secular ecological calendar that combines several religious influences, including the '*Feast of Kannon*', the Japanese bodhisattva of compassion, whose feast day is linked to the celebration of roots, the '*Feast of Saint Fiacre of*

Gardens', from the Irish patron saint, and the '*Festival of Saint Geyikli Baba of Deer*', referring to the Sufi dervish (378-380). By building its new civilization's mythology on this interlinking of nature and the numinous, Atwood shows the practical aspects of such post-secular belief in transmitting essential experiential knowledge to future generations, demonstrating the value of belief narratives for human survival (390).

As is visible in the above texts, there are many different types of creative engagement with the post-secular in twenty-first-century literature, effectively creating many different potential 'post-seculars', as discussed in the Introduction. However, these texts are grouped together here for their particular shared use of the post-secular to re-examine the role of belief systems in creating ethical frameworks. Crucially, these works destabilize dominant Western paradigms of Christianity by drawing on other faiths – and even inventing them – while allowing for the simultaneous criticism of such beliefs. These are works that deliberately refuse the assumed binary of religious/ non-religious *as* purely Christian/non-Christian in order to discuss the wider concept of belief itself. This is not to say that such texts necessarily ignore Christianity altogether, but that where Christian paradigms are included, these are refused dominance, pluralized, questioned or satirized.

The contemporary fictions discussed in this chapter are also texts whose particular incorporation of the post-secular doesn't primarily focus on a single character's journey into – or out of – a specific belief system, but on the creation of a wider post-secular narrative world, in which the post-secular becomes a recurring ethical preoccupation that infuses the overarching narrative worldview. Even where individuals do encounter their own spiritual journeys, as in *Life of Pi* – or Richard Cheeseman's secular ethical revelation in 'My Eye On You' – the individual's personal journey is given less prominence than its effects on the wider world view that it contributes to. So: Pi's religious pantheism is contained within a wider post-secular frame narrative that presents the overarching tale as one that revalues the act of belief in and of itself, while Crispin Hershey's secular epiphany contributes to the macronovel's larger post-secular revaluing of the role of belief itself in forging ethical action.

Such texts recognize that, as Erin K. Wilson and Manfred B. Steger put it in 'Religious Globalisms in the Post-Secular Age' (2013), 'the post-secular is still fluid', and as such 'religion can also be an important source of meaning and identity, one that can open up alternative ways of being in and responding to the world' which can, in turn, 'positively contribute to emancipatory forms of resistance […] while remaining critical of religion's own tendencies to domination and exclusion' (482–3). These texts do not revel in the religious, but tentatively re-examine a broader understanding of faith 'as a lost or at least hidden dimension in a largely materialistic world', as Ursula King puts it in *Faith and Praxis in a Postmodern Age* (1998), revaluing the seeming irrationality of sacred belief as a form of resistance to the ruthless logic of late capitalism, even while acknowledging the problematics of such belief.

Collective causality: Shared responsibility, shared consequences

A further shared trait that this study identifies for mandalic literature is its narrative foregrounding of collective causality, and the small communities – rather than lone 'hero' figures – that forge meaningful ethical change within such a system. At the heart of each text's ambitious compassionate cartography are the lives of a global multitude, living and dead, whose actions are often depicted as permeating far beyond their localized present. As mentioned earlier, Berthold Schoene identifies in *The Cosmopolitan Novel* (2009) that if 'no one person or group of persons is ultimately in charge' of 'the general course of events' in the contemporary world, such texts respond to a pressing problem: '[h]ow can humanity still hope to make a difference and shape such a world' (2). The response by mandalic texts is the tentative suggestion that individual actions, no matter how small, have consequences far beyond their author's intentions, and that the worlds in which such actions take place are not built by individual lone actors, but by communities working together, in a process by which the local and the global are inextricably linked. As Peter Boxall notes in 'Sovereignty, Democracy, Globalisation' (2013), Mitchell's 'sweeping world fictions' are examples of 'a new kind of global literature, that responds to the failure of existing networks to produce a world community' (189). Mandalic literature's world-building narratives respond to this real-world 'failure' not with a utopian portrayal of a world community in perfect harmony, but with a focus on the shared strivings – and struggles – of small communities, illustrating their vital ethical role in forging social and ecological change in the world around them.

To give examples from the above texts, *Anil's Ghost* offsets the overwhelming violence of the conflict with its depictions of small communities of characters working together to help rebuild: the compassionate actions of the doctors and nurses who work together to help wave after wave of injured and dying victims at local hospitals, and the combined efforts of the forensic pathologist and archaeologist as they put their lives at risk in an attempt to expose the government's cover-up of its involvement in the killings, working together to help local families find justice. *Hotel World* builds its own small community from five interconnected women, each of whom plays an indirect part in Clare's grieving and healing process, from the journalist who inadvertently helps her to access the lift shaft where her sister died, to the homeless woman who donates most of her collected change ('[t]hirty-two pounds fifty') to the distraught stranger that she helps in the hotel corridor (152). In its main plot, *Life of Pi* shows the disastrous consequences when a dysfunctional small community of survivors turn against each other, quite literally tearing each other apart. However, this is set against another small community of sorts whose global interconnections only become clear from the frame narratives at the tale's beginning and end, a group of strangers brought together by their shared belief in the value of Pi's story. Within the ontological fictional world, each plays an essential role in the sharing of this remarkable tale: from the 'author' that writes Pi's story, the '*bright-eyed elderly man*' [*sic*] who helps him discover it, and the Japanese ministers, all of whom legitimate Pi's exceptional tale with their own belief in it, recognizing that this is a story about the triumph of belief itself (x). In *The Book of Dave*, it is the continued efforts of the small communities to forge change in both temporal settings that remain the only hope for renewal, however small, within each world-system – whether Dave's adopted family of Phyllis and her son, and the compassion that it inspires in him, or the small-scale future communities of heretics that break away from the oppressive teachings to spread and live by their own ethical interpretations of the Book. In the *MaddAddam* trilogy, the practical agricultural knowledge of the nature-worshipping survivors allows them to build their own small community in which their skill sharing, from beekeeping to scavenging, collectively helps to keep them safe from the worst effects of the 'massive die-off of the human race' (47). In each text, the emphasis is on collective causality and the individual's role not as a lone operator, but as part of vital local communities and global networks in which shared actions have shared consequences.

These depictions of the importance of small communities for collectively bringing about meaningful change aligns with Stephen Batchelor's observation on the Buddhist concept of *sangha*, or community, in 'The other Enlightenment project: Buddhism, agnosticism and postmodernity' (1998). Batchelor notes that the concept of *sangha* refers to a tradition in which such a way of life 'is maintained for those who will come later only by what we do now'; to practice such values 'entails participation in a communal endeavour' in which 'we are simultaneously indebted to and responsible for a community of which we are a part' (115). With this shift in perspective from individual to community, the focus on the individual protagonist as lone agent at the centre of their world, as developed in the Western tradition of the novel and perpetuated in the Hollywood film industry – arguably a further symptom of the penetration of the Messiah-model into Western secular culture – is destabilized. By contrast, the narrative world view presented by mandalic texts often confronts, as Schoene puts it, 'the challenge of imaging pan-global community' through an examination of the shared pitfalls, rewards and responsibilities of small-scale communal endeavours (185).

Hope in the face of dystopian futures

While mandalic texts often foreground collective causality and shared attempts at hopeful reconstruction, this is often accompanied by the threat – and, frequently, the realization – of dystopic violence and human suffering, as is visible in the cumulative narrative trajectory of Mitchell's interlinked body of fiction towards the dystopian futures of *Cloud Atlas* and *The Bone Clocks*. Overturning any simple chance of resolution or utopian ending, it is this interwoven depiction of dystopian possibilities – which may be social, ecological, political or humanitarian – that frames ethical action as desperately needed within the world views presented. From amid this threat of dystopian outcomes, these texts depict their characters' precarious ethical struggles towards uncertain futures, in an attempt at rebuilding narrative meaning that dares to imagine the possibility of change in the face of disaster, and a refusal to abandon hope for the future, no matter how bleak the present. Such a perspective aligns with Václav Havel's assertion that hope 'is a state of mind, not a state of the world', 'an orientation of the spirit' whose 'deepest roots are in the transcendental, just as the roots of human responsibility are' (*Disturbing the Peace* 1990, 181). This sense of hope as part of 'human responsibility' is also discussed by Mitchell in a 2015 interview, in which the author notes the value of hope as a real-world survival strategy, an attitude that could equally apply to many of the other works discussed in this chapter ('Interview by Rose Harris-Birtill'). Having observed that averting ecological destruction 'depends on what we do now', Mitchell adds: 'Hope's good. If you're lucky enough to have a sufficiently undamaged life for you to be able to nurture hope, then do it. We need it.'

Such hopeful attitudes respond to a twenty-first-century Anglophone literary readership whose growing experiences of global interconnection and cultural difference have outgrown postmodern literature's dominant secularity, moral ambiguity and political disenchantment. The turn-of-the-century texts discussed earlier, like Mitchell's macronovel to date, span the millennial moment and the first decade and a half of the twenty-first century. Written from this historical shift from one era to another, these mandalic works acknowledge the painful failure of grand narratives in the previous century while tentatively moving forward from such a position, reimagining ethically engaged narrative worlds whose self-conscious recognition of the seeming impossibility of change does not stop the pursuit of such change. Discussing this cultural moment by drawing on various works of architecture, art installations, collages, paintings and films, Vermeulen and van den Akker identify that 'new generations of artists increasingly abandon the aesthetic precepts of deconstruction, parataxis, and pastiche in favor of *aesth-ethical* notions of reconstruction, myth, and metaxis', in which their works self-consciously 'pursue a horizon that is forever receding' ('Notes on Metamodernism' 2, 12). This study responds to this striving for reconstruction within contemporary literature, looking more specifically at the role of post-secular world-building in creating such reconstructive perspectives. Like the works discussed by Vermeulen and van den Akker, mandalic literature replaces an outdated postmodern irony and detachment with hope and the desire for change – even while they acknowledge that the possibility of such change is 'forever receding'.

To return to the texts discussed earlier, it is significant that *Anil's Ghost* ends not with the violence of the civil war, or with the aftermath of the suicide bombing described in the penultimate chapter, but with a compassionate attempt at reconstruction, however fragile. In the final paragraph of the text, Ananda sees along the rebuilt Buddha's sight line; however, it is a post-secular rather than a sacred world view that Ananda takes in, aligned not with a divine revelation, but with the beauty of the natural world ('with human sight he was seeing all the fibres of natural history around him', 307). The narrative focus effectively 'zooms out' to encompass an entire world view through Ananda's vantage point, which encompasses both human violence and the timeless power of natural forces ('the smell of petrol and grenade' and '[t]he great churning of weather above the earth'). The statue's face may be 'scarred', and rebuilt 'from damaged stone', but it is a facet of the destruction that one individual 'had helped knit together', in a hopeful ending that focuses not on the seemingly irreconcilable conflict, but on the Sisyphean act of rebuilding.

While *Hotel World* is a story of death and grieving, its final section moves the narrative focus from Sara's death to regeneration in the natural world, and the promise of 'spring' amid the depths of winter ('Winter, with more winter to come [...]. But the cranesbill is still flowering. The marigolds are flowering. The daisies and the campanula are finally flowering' 225). This regenerative ending is again emphasized at the very end of the novel; in the first section, Sara's ghost repeats 'I have a message for you' three times (27, 29, 30). Her 'message' effectively becomes the novel's final moral, where it is typeset on the centre of the penultimate page for emphasis. It is a three-part message to the reader, delivered in the ghost's dissolving language: 'remember you must live // remember you most love // remainder you mist leaf' (a reworking of 'remember you must live, remember you must love, remember you must leave') (237). This hopeful conclusion, which uses death's certainty as a reminder to embrace life and love others, is first introduced early in the novel with a direct address to the reader ('You. Yes, you. It's you I'm talking to', 30). Its direct repetition at the novel's end emphasizes that this is a tale with a specific extra-diegetic moral, creating a compassionate ethical message in which a violent sudden death and its effects on the interconnected characters depicted in the novel become recycled into a hopeful affirmation to keep on living (30).

Life of Pi also features a regenerative ending; the horrific truth of the violence that Pi has endured is refused prominence, the tale instead concluding with a hopeful affirmation of his resilience in *'an astounding story of courage and endurance in the face of extraordinarily difficult and tragic circumstances'* (319). Even the bleak future described in *The Book of Dave* ends with a seemingly impossible glimmer of hope, the final chapter leaving the reader at the burial of Dave's second Book, whose compassionate doctrines hint at the potential for ethical change in the dystopian world that lies ahead, however remote. The final book in Atwood's trilogy, *MaddAddam*, ends with its small community of survivors working together to build a new civilization amid a violent dystopia, creating their own optimistic celebrations from the natural world. Following the shared struggles of the remaining humans and bioengineered Crakers to work together to build a new community, the trilogy ends with the promise of a new interspecies birth, described as 'a thing of hope', leaving the reader with a depiction of the sustaining power of such hope in even the bleakest of circumstances (390).

These works deliberately withhold the conciliation of any simple 'happy ending' with their ambiguous and often precarious outcomes; inescapable undercurrents of past, present or future violence, dystopia, and human suffering overshadow any attempt to read these as purely optimistic narratives. However, what each of these texts shares is a refusal to abandon hope, no matter how impossible. Whether such hope is ultimately futile remains up to the reader. However, perhaps what these narratives demonstrate, then, is that the seeds of regeneration can still emerge from the most adverse of circumstances. As David Mitchell notes in a 2010 interview by Caroline Edwards, quoted in '"Strange Transactions": Utopia, Transmigration and Time in *Ghostwritten* and *Cloud* Atlas', 'You only need a small amount of hope – it works as a trace element. Of course, it's best if you've got loads […]. But in the mean time, trace elements will do' (195).

The urgency of individual compassionate action

Like Mitchell's macronovel, each of these literary works offers its own response to a wider zeitgeist of 'compassion fatigue', a concept that took on particular significance in the late twentieth century. The term's first noted usage is in 1968, in the Lutheran World Federation's Minutes of the Committee of World Service, becoming officially recognized in the OED in 2002 as 'apathy or indifference towards the suffering of others […] typically attributed to numbingly frequent appeals for assistance […] (hence) a diminishing public response'.[1] Written from within this late twentieth-century cultural climate of Western 'compassion fatigue' following the multiplication of global media images of international humanitarian crises, and their increasing incorporation into corporate fundraising and consumer marketing strategies, these twenty-first-century texts use their post-secular world-building to re-emphasize the urgency of individual compassionate action.[2]

Each of the texts discussed in this chapter draws attention to the role of personal agency and ethical action within the world views depicted in order to engage anew with the vital importance of compassionate action amid crises. This approach makes Buddhist philosophy particularly relevant to both the content and criticism of these works, as is particularly visible in Mitchell's narrative universe. As Tulku Thondup Rinpoche notes in *Buddhist Civilization in Tibet* (1987), 'Buddhism is characterized by compassion, which is the foundation of its training' (1), while Rosita Dellios similarly notes in 'Mandala-Building in International Relations as a Paradigm for Peace' (1996), '[t]he aim of Buddhism is to develop compassion for all living beings' (2). With their foregrounding of the value of individual compassionate actions, the fictions discussed in this chapter resonate with Buddhist attitudes to compassion as a central component of its worldview. As Marjorie Garber also discusses in 'Compassion' (2004), '[a]lthough numerous religious groups – Catholic, Jewish, Unitarian-Universalist, and Christian nondenominational – also continue to reiterate their commitment to compassion, it may be symptomatic that most current books in print on the topic are voiced from the perspective of Tibetan Buddhism' (25). However, while these literary works aren't necessarily directly influenced by Buddhist philosophies of compassion, each prompts a secular revaluing of hopeful compassionate acts whose presence – or absence – will have far-reaching consequences for future generations. It is also important to note that Buddhist perspectives are by no means the only belief systems explored within such compassionate cartographies, as discussed earlier. These texts often draw on a variety of alternative religious influences as part of a post-secular exploration of the role of belief in fostering – or sabotaging – such ethical action. Each text's construction of a compassionate cartography does not mean utopian optimism, however; such worlds often portray the practice of compassionate actions within their world views as precarious or in decline, depicting the dystopic consequences of their removal.

In mandalic narrative worlds, individual actions are often portrayed as crucial opportunities to perpetuate or resist the larger systems that the characters find themselves in – just as *number9dream*'s Eiji is given the chance to help bring down a human trafficking network, should he decide to risk his own safety by getting involved, and *Hotel World*'s affluent journalist Penny has the chance to help the homeless Else by sharing her own wealth. However, even when these characters do choose to take positive

---

[1] 'compassion, n'. *OED Online*. Oxford University Press, September 2016. Web. 26 September 2016.

[2] For more on the political uses of the term 'compassion', see Lauren Berlant's 'Compassion (and Withholding)' (2004), which notes that 'compassion [...] implies a social relation between spectators and sufferers, with the emphasis on the spectator's experience of feeling compassion and its subsequent relation to material practice', and that 'there is nothing simple about compassion apart from the desire for it to be taken as simple, as a true expression of human attachment and recognition' (1, 7).

ethical action, this is not to say that these individual actions are always successful; characters within such narratives often face seemingly impossible situations, in which the actions of a single individual will not be enough to change the social, political and economic structures around them. However, these are worlds in which the practice of compassionate action remains more important – and ultimately more urgently needed – than the ideology that motivates it. While this study has already discussed this concept within Mitchell's macronovel, the author has also spoken on the importance of compassionate action in his works in several interviews. For example, in a 2016 interview, he speaks of the value of compassionate acts as providing a secular reason for living in the absence of any form of redemptive afterlife ('Interview by Rose Harris-Birtill'). Using his immortal characters as an example, Mitchell notes, '[t]he expiry date: if we don't have one, then where do we get a meaning of life from? [...] this is why I come back to compassion – that's it. That's your meaning [...]. This is fulfilment: fixing something that's broken, even if it's just someone who hasn't eaten that day'. In a 2015 interview by Paul A. Harris, he also notes that '[t]o pass on compassionate knowledge is nourishing [...]. This act makes our lives count for more, whoever and whatever and wherever we are' ('David Mitchell in the Laboratory of Time').

While such compassionate attitudes are visible in the future-facing ethical decisions made by the macronovel's characters, mandalic works of literature also demonstrate the importance of compassionate action by showing the far-reaching consequences of its removal, taking tentative steps towards a reprioritization of the ethical within these otherwise secular narratives. Just as Penny's actions towards Else in *Hotel World* – writing her a cheque, and then promptly cancelling it – show the all-too-real consequences of compassion fatigue in action, *The Book of Dave* takes the concept even further. While the novel ends with Dave's attempt to make amends for his actions with a compassionate statement of his new-found ethical principles in his second Book, the almost total absence of compassion in the dystopian future inversely serves to stress its importance, reinforcing the consequences of a world without it. *Anil's Ghost* ends not with Ananda's contemplation of the forces that shape his world, but with an action: the single human 'touch' from his 'concerned' helper ('[h]e felt the boy's concerned hand on his. This sweet touch from the world.'), ending the novel not with the promise of religious salvation, or the violence of the suicide bomb, but with a simple gesture of human compassion as one character reaches out to offer support to another (307). It may only be a single moment of contact, but this symbolic action at the end of a novel bearing witness to the human rights violations that occurred during the civil war contains within it the seeds of hope for a future built not on conflict, but on the recognition of the value of peaceful human interconnection and active concern for another. *Life of Pi* ends with the official report on the shipwreck, in which Mr Okamoto includes the recognition that Pi's story is not merely '*an astounding story of courage and endurance*', but that '[*v*]*ery few castaways can claim to have survived so long at sea* [...] *and none in the company of an adult Bengal tiger*' [*sic*], in a compassionate suspension of disbelief that recognizes Pi's right to retell his own story (319). *MaddAddam* ends with Toby's last compassionate actions to help the next generation survive: teaching the young Craker Blackbeard how to write in order to store and share knowledge, showing him 'what to do when there should be no more pens', and how to teach the following generations how to document their own knowledge and actions in order to help their descendants (386).

This foregrounding of compassionate action aligns with the metamodern sense of hope, described by Timotheus Vermeulen in a 2012 interview by Cher Potter as 'hope in spite of one's better judgement'; such hopeful undertaking of compassionate action also forms a vital component of contemporary activism ('Timotheus Vermeulen Talks to Cher Potter'). As Vermeulen notes, such 'hope in spite of one's better judgement' is visible in activist movements such as Occupy Wall Street: 'they realise that what they are doing might be futile; that doesn't mean that they cannot at least give it a try.' In using their narrative worlds to foreground practical ethical interventions, mandalic works share the political conviction and humanitarian commitment also seen in politicized works of activist art, such as street artist Banksy's *Dismaland* installation that took place from 21 August to 27 September 2015 in Weston-super-Mare, England. This anti-capitalist parody of a Disneyland-esque theme park featured multimedia artworks that emphasized corporate culpability and consumer complicity in perpetuating humanitarian and ecological crises, using the event to protest against economic and social inequality. After the show's closure, its political impact continued; the materials used to build it were dismantled and used to build a temporary shelter for refugees in Calais, providing practical aid and drawing further media attention to the issues depicted in the art installation.[3] Such destabilizing of the boundaries between art and activism can also be seen in the work of Assemble, a London-based collective of designers and architects whose Granby Four Streets renovation project won the Turner Prize for contemporary art in 2015 for the sustainable and community-led renovation of four Victorian terraced streets in Liverpool. Mandalic works similarly construct narratives that demonstrate the ethical importance of compassionate action within social, political and humanitarian crises. As Manav Ratti notes in *The Postsecular Imagination*, such a revaluing of the power of literature 'to inspire reaction and action' is 'not a manifesto for a new beginning; it is a courageous and modest imagining of how to make a difference', daring to engage anew with the problem of how to transform words into tangible – and urgently needed – ethical action amid contemporary crises (210).

While Mitchell's macronovel, and the narrative works described above, have been used here to identify the emerging category of mandalic literature, several other works from the same period also share many of these traits. For example, *A Tale for the Time Being* (2013) by Ruth Ozeki similarly creates a compassionate cartography of human interconnection through an ethical post-secular framework, whose globally linked chain of events blends Zen Buddhism with quantum theory. The novel charts the parallel worlds of a suicidal Japanese American girl in Tokyo, a Japanese American writer living on an island off the west coast of Canada, and the tale of the Zen Buddhist nun whose philosophies enable them to help each other, even while 5,000 miles and many years apart. Similarly, *The Tesseract* (1998) by Alex Garland and

---

[3] See 'Banksy's Dismaland Arrives In Calais "Jungle" To Shelter Refugees, Becomes Dismal Aid' (2015) by Jack Sommers in *The Huffington Post* at http://www.huffingtonpost.co.uk/2015/10/16/banksys-dismaland-arrives_n_8311696.html, accessed 24 August 2016.

Saturday (2006) by Ian McEwan also use localized experiential narratives to create compassionate narrative cartographies, each of which promote ethical action and a revaluation of hope in the face of violence, focusing on small-scale communities to highlight the value of human interconnection and shared causality. The writings of David Foster Wallace also merit far more discussion for their own post-secular perspectives on compassionate action, hope and belief – and far more is to be said on these than space permits here. Such narrative storytelling techniques also needn't be limited to literature. Further studies could examine the shared preoccupations that also resurface in film and television from the same period, including *The Matrix* trilogy (*The Matrix* 1999, *The Matrix Reloaded* 2003, *The Matrix Revolutions* 2003), *Avatar* (2009), *Samsara* (2011) and *Sense8* (2015), whose similarly compassionate cartographies and post-secular ethical approaches to belief suggest that the shared tropes of a mandalic literature may well extend to other narrative storytelling forms in the early twenty-first century.

Towards a mandalic literature

By adapting and tracing elements of the Tibetan Buddhist mandala's structural framework, non-linear world view and Buddhist philosophies across Mitchell's macronovel, this study has identified a set of shared post-secular literary traits that extend far beyond one author's fictional world. Elements of mandalic literature can also be traced through its twentieth-century precedents; for example, Anglophone literature that revisits religious influences within secular frameworks is by no means a purely contemporary phenomenon. Such exploration can be seen in the works of earlier postmodern writers, including Philip K. Dick, Russell Hoban and Thomas Pynchon, and the Beat Generation writers, who rediscovered and reworked religious themes in their works while maintaining a commitment to twentieth-century secularism. Existing criticism has also usefully identified several literary traits which share common ground with mandalic literature. For example, Irmtraud Huber's *Literature after Postmodernism: Reconstructive Fantasies* (2014) rightly identifies a reconstructive turn that includes 'a careful, self-critical optimism about the possibilities of fiction' (216). John A. McClure also notes an 'untidy resurgence of magical, sacred, pre-modern and non-western constructions of reality' within postmodern literary fiction ('Postmodern/Post-Secular' 148). The category of mandalic literature builds on these perspectives, adding an updated focus on these traits not merely as stand-alone aesthetic considerations, but as essential components of a wider contemporary narrative movement which confronts the ongoing problem of how to forge compassionate ethical action, and identifies the importance of post-secular modes of belief for doing so.

Huber also notes that since the 1990s, 'a widely emerging consensus suggests that we are currently in the process of leaving postmodernism behind us' (2). The identification of mandalic literature as an emerging category within the broader cultural phenomenon of the post-secular does not seek to definitively answer what comes next for 'post-postmodernism' – like any literary period, its texts will be far more diverse than can be encompassed by any single set of traits. However, this book engages with this question by identifying a growing body of texts whose shared approaches suggest a new engagement with the ethics of belief and the possibility of compassionate action, in spite of the dystopic violence present within such world views. At the turn of the millennium, Western societies were experiencing a communication revolution, with the advent of mobile phones and worldwide internet fuelling the technological dream of a globally interconnected world. It was only in the first decades of the twenty-first century that the real face of such globalization was revealed in a new succession of catastrophic global 'posts', whose long-term effects are far from over: post-9/11, post-global financial crisis, post-ISIS, post-Anthropocene, post-refugee crisis, 'post-truth' – and, for the European Union, post-Brexit. After decades of the questioning of grand narratives following the atrocities of the Second World War, Mitchell's fiction heralds a new generation of writers raised on such postmodern caution in literature and theory, and determined to explore new modes of writing that break away from the aesthetic pessimism and existential paralyses that failed to prevent their own twenty-first-century humanitarian and ecological crises from occurring.

To such a bleak global outlook, mandalic literature brings the paradox of impossible hope: a desire to look beyond theoretical stalemates to the faiths, myths, folktales and individual experiential truths that Enlightenment reason left behind, seeing potential for change in the small communities passed over by global capitalism, and the simple truth of individual compassionate action. Mandalic literature responds to the inhuman mechanics of global capitalism and multinational politics with alternative belief systems that can't yet be replaced by the flow of profit and the sheen of mass consumerism, in a Sisyphean attempt to assert that ethical intervention may still be possible. These texts maintain the impossible hope that, in spite of previous generations' deconstructive assurances to the contrary, something remains real: our interconnected human fates, the physicality of global lived experience, the power of individual belief in shaping our ability to act – and the urgent necessity of compassionate action. Whether such action will be sufficient is by no means certain. But by identifying these emerging narrative voices, this study contributes to vital debates on the ethical role of contemporary literature – which, in light of recent events, is set to become increasingly important in the decades to come.

This research also raises several wider implications, both for future criticism of David Mitchell's works and for the theorization of contemporary literature. Further research is particularly needed into other areas that fall outside the remit of this study, including the reworking of Buddhist influences in other contemporary fictions, and the wider post-secular narrative strategies currently being employed to engage with the Anthropocene in the works of other contemporary authors. Aspects of Vermeulen and van den Akker's theory of metamodernism have also been referred to in this study as useful concepts by which to understand the reconstructive and hopeful perspectives that are deployed in tandem with the dystopic in Mitchell's macronovel. While Vermeulen and van den Akker's 'Notes on Metamodernism' identifies metamodern tendencies in architecture, art and film, this essay does not expand on the concept for contemporary literature, an area that recent studies of literary metamodernism have begun to address.[4] Further research is now needed on the ways in which Mitchell's oeuvre contributes to – or even reshapes – other aspects of this emerging literary paradigm, and its wider implications for the theorization of contemporary fiction's ethical engagement.

A particularly striking feature of the macronovel's use of metamodern traits is its simultaneous employment of a relentlessly transnational, trans-temporal decentring of the individual subject, cumulatively shifting the narrative focus on to *Homo sapiens* as a species and its precarious potential futures in light of the Anthropocene, as discussed in Chapter 3. While this chapter conducts a preliminary exploration of an emerging category of works whose traits suggest that shared preoccupations are emerging within the field of contemporary post-secular literature, further research is needed into the connections between such works and the Anthropocene. What may be emerging is an ethical counter-approach to the postmodern representation of dystopian environmental and humanitarian crises which imagine the human race succumbing to a grizzly and inevitable end (for example, Thomas Pynchon's *Gravity's Rainbow*, Russell Hoban's *Riddley Walker* (2006 [1980]), and Cormac McCarthy's *The Road* (2006)). Such works rightly warn that the inevitable end point of social Darwinism's 'survival of the fittest' behaviour is the death of the species. However, the emerging approaches discussed in this study counter such postmodern disillusionment with re-enchantment, undercutting their portrayals of dystopic self-annihilation with a Sisyphean insistence on the essential role of hope, belief and human compassion in imagining meaningful change. Refusing postmodern nihilism and ironic detachment, such works suggest that imagining the near-inevitable final death rattle of our species is now all too easy. A much harder task is to dare to imagine how a broken civilization might, over many generations, begin to adapt and rebuild against improbable odds – a task that will require a post-secular leap of faith and a revaluing of the essential function of compassion in human survival. It is this ethical engagement with the role of hope, belief and compassion that contemporary literary theory must now investigate in light of the Anthropocene and its transnational, trans-temporal implications.

Conclusion: The mandala beyond Mitchell

This study has sought to demonstrate the importance of critiquing David Mitchell's works as a continuous fictional world which encompasses his novels, short stories and libretti alike, revealing the Buddhist influences that play a vital role in drawing these discrete fictions into a post-secular ethical world. However, while approaching

---

[4] For examples, see 'On Literary Metamodernism' (2013) by Seth Abramson, which discusses the poetics of metamodernism; 'Metamodernism: Narratives of Continuity and Revolution' (2014) by David James and Urmila Seshagiri, which discusses the legacy of modernism in contemporary fiction; and 'Thomas Pynchon, David Foster Wallace and the Problems of 'Metamodernism' (2012) by Martin Paul Eve, which critiques Vermeulen and van den Akker's model, rightly arguing that metamodern traits can also be found within postmodern literature. It is also worth noting here that this study draws only on aspects of Metamodernism that prove useful for this study; while a full exploration of this paradigm is outside the remit of this discussion, it is worth noting that its overarching framework has been the subject of further critical debate (see Eve 2012).

Mitchell as a post-secular author highlights the wider importance of the recurring Buddhist philosophies that underpin his compassionate ethical approaches to fictional world-building, critical investigations into other areas of his post-secular fictions are certainly needed. Further research could productively explore the role of other religious influences within his works, including Christian, Hindu and Zen philosophies; after all, this is an author whose work interrogates the concept of belief itself, often simultaneously providing a post-secular critique of its many organized forms. Situating his interconnected macronovel as part of a growing body of post-secular contemporary storytelling exposes a wider desire to re-examine and rework the domain of religious morality, a shared narrative strategy that confronts and resists the ethical quagmire presented by late capitalism.

However, this study does not seek to ultimately 'label' Mitchell as a post-secular writer above all else; there are many other connecting threads which run throughout his body of fictions, and many literary dissonances, as well as congruities, which need further critical investigation. To mention just one area of needed further study, such a macro-scale project may well be usefully illuminated by using computational techniques, such as those productively begun by Martin Paul Eve in 'Close Reading with Computers: Genre Signals, Parts of Speech, and David Mitchell's *Cloud Atlas*' (2017), in order to explore the entire macronovel via a process of 'distant reading'.[5] The previous chapters of this study have also demonstrated the value of taking a large-scale approach to Mitchell's macronovel as a multifaceted yet continuous world; whether such work is undertaken computationally or thematically (or both), more detailed research is undoubtedly needed on this author's entire fictional project as a whole.

This book has ventured a post-secular critical approach to the task of critiquing a post-secular world, seeking to broaden the boundaries of traditional methods of mapping literary worlds with a critical theorization of the mandala, rereading its sacred features for secular purposes. As Rosita Dellios rightly argues in 'Missing Mandalas: Development and Theoretical Gaps' (2004), '[t]he mandala model of development in a globalizing world is both missing and missed. It needs to be more fully theorized if it is to make a conceptual contribution to the pressing tasks of the day' (1–2). This study has therefore sought to produce a more fully theorized model of the mandala and, in doing so, contribute to a wider conversation on the techniques and influences found in contemporary post-secular storytelling. However, where the mandala is discussed in existing literary criticism, it is primarily with reference to the Jungian interpretation of the mandala, a perspective which this study ultimately seeks to move beyond for several reasons – and it is to this Jungian conception of the mandala that this final chapter now turns.

The traditional Jungian interpretation of the mandala detailed in C. G. Jung's *The Archetypes and the Collective Unconscious*, published in 1959, notes that its basic form arises 'spontaneously' in artworks across cultures during 'certain states of conflict', a universal process which 'occurs in conditions of psychic dissociation or

---

[5]   See *Graphs, Maps, Trees: Abstract Models for a Literary History* (2005) and *Distant Reading* (2013) by Franco Moretti; a survey of a decade of research in digital humanities and an overview of distant reading techniques can also be found in 'On Close and Distant Reading in Digital Humanities: A Survey and Future Challenges' (2015) by S. Jänicke et al.

disorientation' (387). Jung argues that mandalas 'often represent very bold attempts to see and put together apparently irreconcilable opposites and bridge over apparently hopeless splits', created for their psychologically 'healing effect' (389–90). To apply this theory to a body of literature which interrogates the concept of post-secular belief to create its own ethically ordered world view, this approach suggests that these works are responding to a wider cultural 'disorientation': the post-war distrust of grand narratives in increasingly secularized Western societies, which occurred simultaneously with the unchecked rise of global capitalist ideology at the end of the twentieth century. Indeed, the argument that the creation of such an ordered literary world is part of an attempt to connect these 'apparently hopeless splits' and 'irreconcilable opposites' aligns with a metamodern literary criticism. The creation of such mandalic literary worlds can be seen as an artistic recognition of the double bind confronted by post-secular contemporary literature coming to terms with the recognition that '[g]rand narratives are as necessary as they are problematic', as Timotheus Vermeulen notes, resulting in a literary text whose world view relentlessly oscillates 'between hope and melancholy', as Vermeulen and Robin van den Akker put it ('Timotheus Vermeulen Talks'; 'Notes on Metamodernism' 2). While Mitchell's macronovel demonstrates this mandalic response to metamodernity in action, the socio-historical conditions in which his works were written are not his alone. As such, this study has ventured 'mandalic literature' as a category of post-secular fiction whose texts use shared narrative strategies as a response to a specific historical moment.

So far, so Jung. However, while the argument may be made that such literary works seek a conciliatory narrative path in the wake of ecological and capitalistic destruction, this raises a further issue: is the creation of such worlds indicative of an avoidance that contributes to the problem? An example of this issue in practice can be seen in the contemporary incorporation of meditation into corporate mindfulness workshops ultimately geared towards minimizing worker dissatisfaction and maximizing profits. While Western mindfulness and meditation are frequently removed from Buddhist dharma, these are often discussed as a debased version of Buddhist practice. For example, Slavoj Žižek critiques a '"Western Buddhist" meditative stance' in 'From Western Marxism to Western Buddhism' (2001), asserting that 'although "Western Buddhism" presents itself as the remedy against the stressful tension of capitalist dynamics [...] it actually functions as its perfect ideological supplement'. While such an issue is beyond the scope of this study, the foundation of many types of Buddhist teaching is the active practice of compassion, as discussed earlier. Unlike the Christian concept of pity, which has been read as a form of othering which reinforces the privilege of the 'pitier' as critiqued by Nietzsche in *Daybreak: Thoughts on the Prejudices of Morality* (1997 [1881]) (85), the Buddhist concept of compassion necessitates personal action under the karmic model (see Chapter 3).[6] This is also reinforced in its etymology; from the Latin *com*, meaning together with, and *pati*, to suffer, its OED definition reflects compassion as not merely the shared experience of another's suffering, but crucially,

---

[6] As David E. Cartwright notes in 'Schopenhauer's compassion and Nietzsche's pity' (1988), whereas '[p]ity is ultimately self-regarding' because of its 'enhancement of the pitier's own feelings of superiority', by contrast, '[c]ompassion [...] has as its ultimate end another's well-being' (560).

'the desire to relieve it'. While Buddhist philosophy foregrounds the practice of compassionate ethical action, secular corporate mindfulness training appears geared towards minimizing it – a fundamental difference between Buddhist teaching and its corporate reworking.

This principle can be seen in an incident that took place at the 2014 San Francisco 'Wisdom 2.0' technology conference, discussed by Glenn Wallis in 'Mineful Response and the Rise of Corporatist Spirituality' [sic] (2014). At the conference, a talk by Google ('3 Steps to Build Corporate Mindfulness the Google Way') was interrupted by protestors from Heart of the City Collective, who took the stage calling on the multinational companies present to stop the evictions of local community members to create living spaces for affluent tech workers. After the non-violent protestors were removed, one of the corporate mindfulness speakers immediately incorporated the incident into a training exercise, telling the audience to 'practice' silently and passively experiencing 'what it's like to be around conflict and people with heartfelt ideas that may be different than what we're thinking'.[7] Mindfulness undoubtedly continues to be useful as a form of therapy and relaxation across the globe. However, within a wider framework of globalization, and removed from the foundational Buddhist concept of compassionate action, the corporate adoption of mindfulness to cultivate an atmosphere of passive acceptance in the workplace presents an important challenge to the future of anti-corporate protest and trade unions alike.

The clash of activist demands for change and the practised passivity of corporate mindfulness also presents an ongoing challenge to Western Buddhist theory and practice as it becomes increasingly incorporated within global capitalism, as Žižek asserts. However, to return to the creation of hopeful narratives in contemporary literature, as discussed earlier, when such post-secular narrative worlds as Mitchell's simultaneously embed a guarded optimism within a wider framework of dystopic violence, their hopeful perspectives are deliberately overshadowed by the impending destruction of the world view created, by which any simple Jungian notion of 'healing' or reconciliation is destabilized. The creation of such texts may well arise due to a desire for order and completion – but, as they self-reflexively note by including the threat or realized destruction of their sociopolitical, ecological or humanitarian world-systems, such desires are often painfully inadequate in the world at large. As the above clash of activist demand and passive acquiescence to corporate will suggests, it is compassionate action – rather than encouraged quietism – which remains the urgently needed agent of change in such secular worlds. While this study identifies a group of contemporary narratives as 'mandalic', whose hopeful perspectives show a revaluation of post-secular belief and compassionate action in the face of dystopian violence, to read this body of mandalic literature through a Jungian framework would suggest that such literature does not merely arise through disorientation, but that it is, in itself, somehow fundamentally 'healing'. However, mandalic literature does not provide the Jungian consolation of implicit self-healing within the world views that it depicts. Instead, it suggests that the only fragile hope for change in the face of humanitarian

---

[7] Footage of the event, 'Interrupting Google's Wisdom 2.0 on "Mindfulness"' by Heart of the City, can be seen on YouTube at https://www.youtube.com/watch?v=xMmlSpk0skI, accessed 12 April 2018.

and ecological crises lies outside its own framework – with real-world human action, as Eiji's panoptic escape demonstrates (see Chapter 4). This, then, is where a traditional Jungian reading of the mandala quickly becomes unstable ground.

So, too, does a Jungian reading of the Tibetan Buddhist mandala which neglects to critique or investigate: Jung's own bias that '[t]he best and most significant mandalas are found in the sphere of Tibetan Buddhism' (*The Archetypes and the Collective Unconscious* 356); why this particular type of mandala subsequently became so widely known in Western popular culture; the portrayal of mandala installations by the media; and the wider sociopolitical circumstances behind its diasporic deployment in the late twentieth and early twenty-first centuries. As Andrew Samuels – who originally introduced the term 'post-Jungian' in his 1985 study *Jung and the Post-Jungians* – notes in his foreword to *Post-Jungian Criticism: Theory and Practice* (2004), '[i]t is said (rightly) that there is a massive Eurocentrism in Jungian explorations of non-Western cultures, including the demeaning idealization of traditional cultures' (xi). This study therefore takes a post-Jungian approach, in its broadest sense, by critiquing Jungian mandala theory within a twenty-first-century sociopolitical context. As Samuels notes, a post-Jungian approach allows for 'both a connection to and a critical distance from Jungian thought and practice' (vii). In the 1999 study, *C. G. Jung and Literary Theory: The Challenge from Fiction*, Susan Rowland also rightly argues for 'the need to take a post-Jungian and not a Jungian position, where post-Jungian implies a critical distance from, a challenging and rewriting of Jung' (38). For the mandala, this greater 'critical distance' from Jung's theorization is vital; post-Jungian theory must include a recognition of this symbol not as an unchanging psychological object, but part of a constantly developing living heritage, whose present-day creation – and creators – link traditionally esoteric aspects of Tibetan sacred heritage with contemporary cultural diaspora, while under ongoing global scrutiny by the media.

However, there are certainly grounds for further careful post-Jungian readings of Mitchell's fictions; the author has already indicated in several interviews that Jung's work informs his writing. For example, in a 2006 interview with Tom Cox he refers to Jungian individuation to discuss identity formation in *Black Swan Green* ('Black Swan Green'), while in a 2006 interview with Michael Silverblatt he again discusses Jungian individuation ('David Mitchell'). In a 2014 interview with Zack Ruskin, he notes that Jung's works contributed to the etymology of the language created to describe the atemporals' psychic powers in *The Bone Clocks* ('The Blank Screen Is the Enemy'). Jung is also the instinctual guide of his longest-standing reincarnated character; in *Slade House*, Marinus notes, '[w]hen I'm in doubt […] I ask myself, "What would Carl Jung do?" – and act accordingly. Call it a gut instinct' (207). Future studies could productively trace the author's reworking of Jungian theory, for example, investigating the Jungian concept of the *unus mundus* or unitary world for the author's interconnected macronovel, an approach that continues to be retheorized, as in *The Syndetic Paradigm: The Untrodden Path Beyond Freud and Jung* (2007) by Robert Aziz, and which is further explored for literary criticism in Matthew A. Fike's study *The One Mind: C. G. Jung and the Future of Literary Criticism* (2014). These references within the author's works and interviews indicate the critical need for post-Jungian literary studies to ask how – and why – Jungian influences are being reworked in this author's body of writing, whether such concepts as the *unus mundus* and collective unconscious are also being revisited in the works of other contemporary writers of speculative fiction, and how such psychological perspectives on the self are being rewritten in response to the homogenizing superstructures of globalization.

Beyond Jungian and post-Jungian mandala studies, some foundational critical work has productively opened up the discussion of the circumstances of the Tibetan mandala's international presence, but much more needs to be done. These studies usefully emphasize this process as culturally translated through the Western media, an area in which further research is needed to chart the mandala's portrayal and subsequent absorption into Western popular culture. Such work forms an integral component for understanding its ongoing sociopolitical heritage in which, as Susan M. Walcott recognizes in 'Mapping from a Different Direction: Mandala as Sacred Spatial Visualization' (2006), overseas mandala creation has served 'to place Tibet back on the mental map of global consciousness' (85). Questions remain as to how, why and to what end.

Dibyesh Anand's study, *Geopolitical Exotica: Tibet in Western Imagination* (2007) undertakes much important theoretical groundwork on the Western exoticization of Tibet, highlighting that '[i]n the process of strategically deploying their culture to the Western audience for mobilizing political support, Tibetans have redefined and reconstructed Tibetan culture and identity', a process in which 'the entire category of culture has to be understood as political' (100; 121). While Anand's study usefully suggests that 'we must consider not only the way in which politics affects the works of art but in what sense an artwork may itself constitute a political act', it does not follow this argument further for the Tibetan Buddhist mandala. Similarly, while Clare E. Harris' study *The Museum on the Roof of the World* (2012) does important work to expose the far-reaching political implications for the display of Tibetan art in museums across the globe, mandala displays are mentioned only briefly in passing; further research is needed into the political implications of its public display and the international impact of its increased visibility in diaspora. Meg McLagan's short study, 'Spectacles of Difference: Cultural Activism and the Mass Mediation of Tibet' (2002) begins vital research in looking beyond the mandala to its effective marketing in the West, its creation contributing to a popular 'narrative of Tibetanness' which 'has tended to reinforce and perpetuate Western stereotypes and fantasies […] rather than provide representations of them as historical actors with serious and legitimate political claims' (96). However, McLagan's study concentrates primarily on the 'Year of Tibet' events in New York City in 1991; as such, updates are needed to track the impact of international mandala displays on changing narratives of 'Tibetanness' by analysing their public reception, media portrayal and absorption into popular culture in the late twentieth and early twenty-first century.

Further critical work on the mandala's cultural and historical context must therefore investigate both the current sociopolitical circumstances of the mandala's production and its popular reception as it appears in literature, television and film, as well as its shifting portrayal in recent decades. The Jungian understanding of the mandala was soon adopted and developed by Anglophone writers, with mandala references across literary fiction, poetry and science fiction (for example, Patrick White's *The Solid*

Mandala, 1966; Thomas Pynchon's *Gravity's Rainbow*, 1973; David Bischoff's *Mandala*, 1983). However, following the creation of the first Tibetan sand mandalas for American audiences in the 1980s, the previously dominant Western Jungian narrative was disrupted with the mandala's visibility as a cultural artefact. This new proximity inspired a revival of popular culture mandala references, including horror and mystery genre fiction, travel writing, science fiction and graphic novels (e.g. Jamyang Norbu's *The Mandala of Sherlock Holmes*, 1999; Andrew X. Pham's *Catfish and Mandala*, 1999; M. John Harrison's *Nova Swing*, 2006), and American television and film (e.g. *Seven Years in Tibet*, 1997; *The Last Mimzy*, 2007; *Breaking Bad*, 2008; *Samsara*, 2011; *Orange is the New Black*, 2013; *House of Cards*, 2013; *Doctor Strange*, 2016). The mandala in popular culture is now so widely associated with stereotypes of Tibetan mysticism that its prominence risks directing attention away from the precarious political situation that originally led the Tibetan government-in-exile to seek international support through its creation. As McLagan notes, Tibet's political struggles entered the global media following 'a decision by the Tibetan government-in-exile [...] to wage a vigorous campaign for international support' (93). Future studies must ascertain whether such a campaign is still in Western public consciousness and what part the international creation of the Tibetan Buddhist mandala plays in this.

To return to the discussion of the mandala, then, for the final time within this study, this structure has been employed as a useful critical tool for envisaging some of the seemingly disparate facets of Mitchell's macronovel as part of a meticulously structured, post-secular ethical world. However, this book's application of the mandala as an interpretive model is not necessarily a neatly transferrable one; what works for one textual universe is by no means a universal tool across the field. In its traditional Tibetan Buddhist usage, a mandala is ultimately a form of tool, and as such, is a functional structure that may be put aside once its work is done. It is for these reasons that this study finally shifts its engagement with the mandala, necessarily parting ways from its individual application to focus more broadly on shared traits emerging in contemporary literature. However, the mandala will be employed once more, in order to make one final pressing assertion.

Although Jung's theories on the mandala were developed before the subsequent mass migration of tens of thousands of Tibetan refugees to India, the decades of political struggles for international help to restore Tibetan self-governance that continue to this day mean that the Tibetan Buddhist mandala can no longer be discussed with such ahistorical and apolitical innocence. A more detailed political and historical contextualization of the mandala within post-Jungian literary criticism is now essential. In spite of the continued prominence of the mandala in Western popular culture and media, the ongoing struggles for Tibetan self-determination within Chinese borders continue to go largely unreported, in part due to political and practical difficulties in gaining unrestricted access to the Tibet Autonomous Region. As Carole McGranahan and Ralph Litzinger note in 'Self-Immolation as Protest in Tibet' (2012), at the time that their article was published no anthropologists or journalists were allowed within Tibet's 'self-immolation zone': '[t]he global media could not get to Tibet, and the Chinese media was noticeably silent; Time magazine declared the Tibetan self-immolations the #1 most under-reported story of 2011'.

Limited media reporting indicates that the self-immolations continue. The International Campaign for Tibet reports that '153 Tibetans have self-immolated in Tibet and China since February 27, 2009', the most recent of the known cases at the time of writing – reported as a Tibetan man in his forties, Tsekho Tugchak – taking place in Ngaba, eastern Tibet, on 7 March 2018.[8] As Janet Gyatso notes in 'Discipline and Resistance on the Tibetan Plateau' (2012), 'a deeply distressed and disenfranchised monastic population has decided that extreme acts are the only way to bring attention to a remote part of the world'. However, as the International Campaign for Tibet reports, such extreme acts now extend beyond the Tibetan monastic population, with self-immolations also recorded in Tibetan laity and exile communities. With the mandala as one of the most visible aspects of Tibetan culture in the West, academic scrutiny has its part to play in ensuring that the prominence of such a well-ordered and tightly patterned world view does not mask the least visible but most pressing aspects of ongoing sociopolitical tensions that would otherwise remain hidden. It is for this reason that this study concludes here: not with the theorization of the mandala, or of Mitchell's post-secular fictions, but with the humanitarian crises that led to the increased visibility of the Tibetan mandala in the West, a real-world post-secular narrative which post-Jungian mandala theory must now recognize, revisit and repoliticize.

---

[8] Statistics taken from International Campaign for Tibet website *SaveTibet.org*, accessed 13 April 2018. See http://www.savetibet.org/resources/fact-sheets/self-immolations-by-tibetans/.

Appendix A:
David Mitchell's UK Book Sales

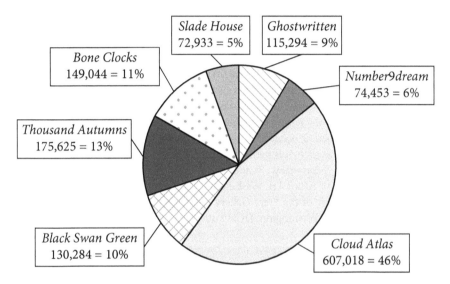

Figure 1 Graph showing UK book sales for David Mitchell's seven novels to date as a percentage of the author's total UK sales, including paperback and hardback, and excluding eBook and audiobook data. Graph generated by Rose Harris-Birtill from sales report data provided by Nielsen on 23 March 2018, for sales data accurate to 17 March 2018.

Appendix B: Tibetan Buddhist Mandala Sand Painting

This seven-foot-square mandala was created in 2002 by twenty Buddhist monks from the Drepung Loseling Monastery at the Sackler Gallery, Washington, DC. The *Tibetan Healing Mandala* website that this image is featured on, hosted by the Smithsonian's Museums of Asian Art, notes that this mandala was created in response to the tragedies of 11 September 2001 (see https://archive.asia.si.edu/exhibitions/online/mandala/default.htm, accessed 12 February 2018). As the website notes, the mandala depicts a plan of a palace as seen from above, and is visualized as a three-dimensional structure. Used as a tool to foster wisdom and compassion, it is traditionally believed to bestow 'positive energies' on all those who encounter it, at whatever level that they are able to understand its symbolism. It is said that no subscription to its doctrines is required to benefit from seeing it; as such, it is perhaps a fittingly post-secular symbol in itself.

Drepung Loseling Monastery. *Buddhist Sand Mandala*. 11–22 January 2002. Smithsonian Museum of Asian Art, Washington, DC *Tibetan Healing Mandala*. Web. 7 January 2013. Courtesy of the Freer Gallery of Art and Arthur M. Sackler Gallery, Smithsonian Institution, Washington, DC. Photograph by John Tsantes.

Figure 2 Example of a Tibetan Buddhist Mandala sand painting. Courtesy of the Freer Gallery of Art and Arthur M. Sackler Gallery, Smithsonian Institution, Washington, DC. Photograph by John Tsantes.

Appendix C: Enlarged Mandala

This type of mandala features Avalokitesvara, the bodhisattva of compassion, represented by the lotus flower depicted in the middle of the mandala.

The enlarged and rotated diagram shows a sand mandala gateway, in which a representation of clouds can be seen within an outer border of multicoloured lotus petals (a large coloured version of this image can also be found at https://commons. wikimedia.org/wiki/File:Chenrezig_Sand_Mandala.jpg, accessed 12 February 2018). The garden outside the inner mandala structure is visible as the green background within the outer circular borders. Inside the top of the gateway, white triangular downspouts for the release of rainwater are visible against the blue of the roof. The outer ring of fire can be seen around the edge, with a row of interconnected *vajra* symbols between the outer ring of fire and the lotus petals.

Tashi Lhunpo Monastery. *Chenrezig Sand Mandala*. 22 May 2008. House of Commons, London, UK. Web. 25 April 2017. https://commons.wikimedia.org/wiki/File:Chenrezig_ Sand_Mandala.jpg. Reproduced under Creative Commons Attribution-Share Alike 3.0. Photo credit: Colonel Warden.

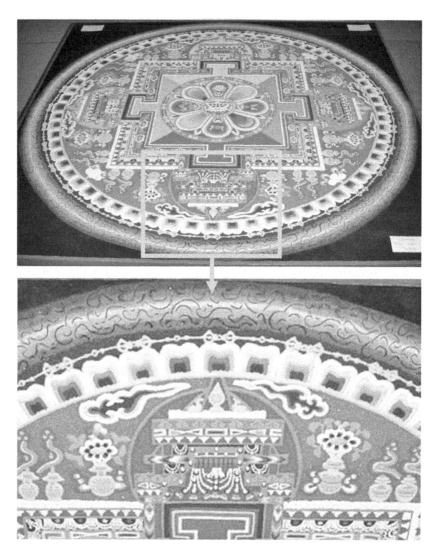

Figure 3 Photograph of a Chenrezig sand mandala, also known as the Avalokitesvara mandala, or mandala of compassion, created and exhibited at the House of Commons for the visit of the Dalai Lama on 21 May 2008. Reproduced under Creative Commons Attribution-Share Alike 3.0. Photo credit: Colonel Warden. A section of the image has been enlarged and rotated below the original for clarity.

Appendix D:
Sand Mandala Construction

This sand mandala was created by Buddhist monks from Drepung Loseling Monastery, India, at the Sackler Gallery in the Smithsonian Museum of Asian Art, Washington, DC, in 2002, using hand-held *chak-purs* to apply grains of coloured sand to a raised, flat board.

Drepung Loseling Monastery. *Buddhist Sand Mandala.* 11–27 January 2002. Smithsonian Museum of Asian Art, Washington, DC *Tibetan Healing Mandala.* Web. 26 April 2017. Courtesy of the Freer Gallery of Art and Arthur M. Sackler Gallery, Smithsonian Institution, Washington, DC. Photograph by John Tsantes.

Figure 4 Photograph showing the construction of a sand mandala. Courtesy of the Freer Gallery of Art and Arthur M. Sackler Gallery, Smithsonian Institution, Washington, DC. Photograph by John Tsantes.

Appendix E:
Wake Act 2 Photograph

'Wake Nationale Reisopera.' Photograph of Act 2. *Paul Keogan Lighting Design.* 2010. Web. 22 April 2018. http://www.paulkeogan.com/wake-nationale-reisopera .html. Photograph by Marco Borggreve.

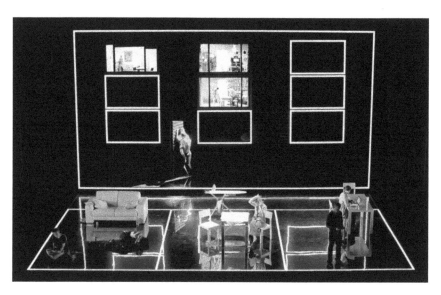

Figure 5 Photograph of Act 2 of *Wake.* Reproduced courtesy of Marco Borggreve.

Appendix F:
Wheel of Life Mandala

This mandala shows death surrounding a central mandalic wheel that depicts the causes of samsaric suffering, with the Buddha depicted at the top right of the image.

Bhavachakra Mandala. Namdroling Monastery, Bylakuppe, India. 18 October 2015. Photo credit: Rose Harris-Birtill.

Figure 6 Photograph of a Wheel of Life mandala, also known as the Bhavachakra (or 'Bhavacakra'), taken at Namdroling Monastery in Bylakuppe, India, in 2015. Photo credit: Rose Harris-Birtill.

Appendix G: An Interview with David Mitchell, 2015

Interview with David Mitchell by Rose Harris-Birtill, 14.08.15.

[DM = David Mitchell; RHB = Rose Harris-Birtill.]

RHB: Thank you so much for your time today and for coming here …

DM: You're very welcome …

RHB: To start off, I'd like to ask you a few questions that pertain to my research at the moment. I'm interested in the mandala, which is an ancient Hindu and Buddhist meditation aid and intricately geometrical cosmogram, as a mode of Buddhist thinking that you haven't mentioned before, but I believe ties in with your work.

In particular, I think the Tibetan Buddhist approach to the mandala resonates with your narrative structures, your engagement with political issues and the resilience of hope and compassion across your textual universe. You've mentioned that you were reading *The Tibetan Book of the Dead* while writing *The Bone Clocks*, and the influence of Eastern spirituality also resurfaces in its inclusion of reincarnations, mystical powers, chakras and so on.

So what I wanted to ask is, have you come across the Buddhist mandala before, and can you say a little more on your thoughts on this, and the influence of Eastern or Buddhist spiritualities more generally on your work?

DM: The latter probably more, and the former probably less. Mandalas … so probably first I would have encountered them in Ladakh, in the north of India. You can't get to it these days, unfortunately, but I was there just in a brief window when Kashmir was open, and you could. I was a kid, a backpacker walking around, not really knowing what I was seeing – I got altitude sickness, that was fun. I went to temples, just as a tourist, and got fleeced by the toothless old men charging me money to get in. I had no knowledge of the philosophy behind the symbols, but I would have seen them, and probably thought about them, and they would have imprinted themselves, obviously on my retina, but perhaps on my mind. Then, around the same time I read Jung's *Memories, Dreams, Reflections* – he talks about mandalas a lot in that. He used to draw them all the time, didn't he …

RHB: Yes …

DM: Did I draw them? Probably not if I'm honest. But I've always had a soft spot for both Jung and that book. I was interested way back as an undergraduate in his theory of archetypes and the idea that our minds are un-individuated propositions with different parts that represent different impulses, and that these figures, such as the other, such as the wise old man I think – or is it the wise old woman? I'm being vague, it's been years! – but that they actually appear in literature, as well as our dreams, as well as exercising influence on our actions. To what degree they are merely metaphors – to what degree a metaphor is 'mere' – and to what degree either Jung or I think they are in some way literal or real, I don't know. But the idea that a limited number of archetypes roam world literature, and have always roamed the human mind, that change form … The other if you're an eighteenth-century Yoruba may well look rather like me. If you're an eighteenth-century me, then the other may look rather like a Yoruba tribesperson. So they change form, but they fulfil the same psychosocial roles. That's a juicy idea! That's nourishing. There's a lot in that. So I was interested in that idea, and for a while I was reading looking out for archetypes. And I got that through Jung. And I love that book – there's something haunting about it.

So, more generally: Buddhism … While I was in Japan I read some of the early Japanese Buddhists who went to North America in the early twentieth century. The names escape me – there's one called *The Zen Eye* by Sokei-An, was the monk's name. They were bearers of an exotic philosophy; then as now, their audiences were mixtures of seekers of novelty, and maybe more sincere, more genuine explorers of world thought, and presumably they also found more genuine converts who thought that they had an answer that was of deep significance, and had a beguiling potential for them. There are genuine Western Buddhists, loads of them. It was new for me, and it resonated more for me as a philosophy than a religion.

My mum had too much religion in her childhood diet, but she had an idea as a somewhat uneducated working-class Wolverhampton girl that Sunday School would keep my brother and I on the straight and narrow, and that it was insurance against delinquency. Bless her, she meant well – it wasn't anything wacky, it was Methodism.

So we went to Sunday School probably between the ages of five and … she finally gave up with me when I was about fourteen, fifteen, around then. It bored me. It gave me a foundation in Bible Studies that's handy, that I'm grateful for. I know who Abraham is, I know the difference between Elishah and Elijah – just – and I'm glad. And the New Testament's even more important. But I don't believe it. I feel that Christianity and its – I know very little about Islam but I think it's the same story – its sort of insistence that you unquestioningly accept the whole dogma of whichever sect you are buying into, demands that I anaesthetize or even amputate parts of my rational mind that I'm just not happy doing, and I'd rather not. I'm quite happy as an agnostic in that sense.

I feel that Buddhism never asks you to make the same deal. Buddhism is more pick 'n' mix, in large part because it itself is more a cluster of sects, a cluster of beliefs. Pure Land Buddhism believes in heaven, and you go there; Zen Buddhism, as I'm sure you know, it's imported karma from India and is more an endless cycle of birth and rebirth; there's earlier, nastier forms where it's almost like Greek paganism – 'I'm afraid it's hell, and that's where you go, sorry'. The Namo Amitabha sect, you can obtain Enlightenment simply by repeating this mantra many thousands of times. Yet they're all Buddhists, but they believe in complete opposites.

[9m 10s]

I've encountered this – I worked at a technical university for my second batch of four years while I was living in Japan, and the Dean was a Buddhist Priest. And I thought, oh great, this is a real chance to find out about what Buddhists really believe. So early in my tenure, I said, 'so what do Buddhists believe happens to you after you die?' And he was all, 'well [huffs] … you know … that's a tricky question. Who knows?' Ask an Anglican Vicar, or a Catholic Priest, and no, there's no doubt – the whole point is, you pay and this is the answer, and it's clear! And here I had this Buddhist Priest … I was shocked! It was all through my ignorance, but I was shocked. But okay!

So that was my first … Buddhism is this very nebulous zone of possible beliefs. But it's habits of mind, it's ideas that a lot of our unhappiness comes from insatiable appetites, that the world is geared to feed, and stimulate, and provoke, and advertise to, and generate demands that can never be fulfilled. And this lack of fulfilment is a big part of human suffering, which incidentally is inevitable anyway, so don't be too outraged or shocked because you're suffering: hey, join the club! But the thing about the insatiable appetites, that's helpful to me, in a way that the Parable of the Sower is of less help to me.

And you feel really good after meditating for a little bit – just three or four minutes. I just use a number method which I learnt in a brief stay in a monastery in Okinawa. A lot of English teachers did this when we couldn't afford the fare home for Christmas. You'd stay at a monastery – it was an international fare! – and the Western monk who looked after us was aware of it, but you wouldn't have gone if you weren't interested as well. And the method of mediation that was taught there was really simple: you count to eight, and then count back. Each inhalation and exhalation, you breathe in light and breathe out murk, like cigarette smoke, and try to think of nothing but the number.

Very soon though, your mind monkey starts barging in. But okay, it's just, 'here comes the mind monkey – hello mind monkey, goodbye mind monkey'. Even now I can do this and it's like I've had an hour's sleep. Prayer never did that. That was sort of a shopping list, or a litany of complaints – and I don't believe it anyway, I didn't think anyone was listening, so it was a dead loss. Whereas this isn't about praying to anyone, I don't want anything. It's just about calming my mind down. You feel great after it. And so I thank Buddhism for that. That's my exposure to Buddhism.

Obviously I've read a lot of Japanese novelists, Natsume Sōseki was very interested in Zen Buddhism, and influences there, and books like *Kokoro*, which means 'heart' but is translated as *The Three-Cornered World*, a lovely thing. It's got one of the great opening lines in English translation – I can't remember the Japanese, and it would take me weeks to try to read in Japanese – but: 'Climbing up the mountain path I fell to thinking'. 'Climbing up, I fell to thinking': isn't that brilliant? It's *kangae ni ochita* I suppose, in Japanese. We say 'end up', but to get the same idea, they use the verb 'fall'. It's clever – '*Climbing* up the mountain path, I *fell* to thinking' – isn't that great?

RHB: It's beautiful …

DM: Mishima – well, we're a short hop and a skip away from reincarnation, which yes, is a theme … I did go through a phase in my twenties when I was half believing it. Now I'm a lot less sure. I don't know, and am happy not knowing at this point. I'm a happy agnostic. It is, to me, the only … that makes sense to me, in the way that hardcore belief has no proof at all. Possibly even hardcore atheism …

RHB: … it almost becomes a religion in itself, doesn't it, hardcore atheism …

DM: It can do. Both sides in a sense might say they have their hearts in the right place. If faith helps, is faith such a bad thing? When it tends to ISIS, yes. But when there's an abused Liverpudlian Catholic woman who can keep the show on the road because she's going to church and has a decent human being in the form of a priest to confide to, is that such a bad thing? But the atheists can also say all these people are drugged, and they're God-intoxicated, and they want to make the world aware that if maybe the abused Catholic Liverpudlian woman didn't rely on this to help but actually attacked the problem itself, she might be better off. So there's arguments for both sides. I'm not a hardcore agnostic mocking the others, but it works for me – with Buddhism in the background. Is that okay so far?

[15m 40s]

RHB: Yes, absolutely. I was just going to ask about *The Tibetan Book of the Dead*, because that's a really interesting and unusual source, and I don't think that anybody that I can see has really picked up on that or asked about it further. But I think it's a fascinating source …

DM: … It's a mile deep, and it's not that I've given up, but I'm still in it. In a way, it points out that it makes no sense at all to postpone thinking about death until we're on our deathbeds – it's too late there. As I understand it, that author's form of somewhat more esoteric Buddhism … how you are when you die, whether you are filled with panic and terror, or calm, has a direct impact on your next incarnation. In the same way, actually, hardcore vegetarians will say that if you want another reason not to eat meat, it's because the cow is terrified when it knows it's about to have a bolt put through its head in an abattoir, and its blood is … its adrenal glands are just pumping out what they pump out when you know you're about to die, and you're eating those chemicals. It's in the meat, and they aren't very good for you.

In a sort of spiritual way, if you get ready to die now, hopefully years before you will – I'm slipping into *Bone Clocks* roadshow spiel – but we need a better working accommodation with this thing called mortality, with this thing called death, than our culture generally gives us. Our culture venerates youth and beauty at the expense of age and mortality. We worship it – that's what celebrity is. There are very few older women on TV, and even fewer that haven't been made over to be 'presentable'. It's as if there's something profoundly wrong with Ursula Le Guin as she looks now: a white-haired, deeply wrinkled, wise, wonderful and – if I may say so – beautiful woman, but she's eighty, and there's very few of them on the telly, compared to the number of eighteen-year-old females. I think we need no more proof … ageing is a form of disease that beauty clinics exist to cure of us, and advertising overwhelmingly presents images of youth, and health, and beauty. This has a long-term pernicious effect on us. We don't think about death properly. The only strategy we're given is to deny it, and to not think about it, which is kind of okay up to a point, but not when you get a diagnosis of cancer. That experience is made worse because of this drug of denial that I feel our culture drip-feeds us.

Perhaps East Asian cultures have something of an advantage here. It's a culture with more Confucian DNA in it, where I think older people are less routinely rubbished. There is elder abuse there, of course there is, but there's more embarrassment about it, I suppose. 'Old bag' … it's an insult, 'old git' … it's a two-part insult. One is the 'bag' and 'git', and the other is 'old'. So *The Tibetan Book of the Dead* is something that might be healthy for Westerners to read, even if you don't get that far into it, to just make you think about it. It's too late when you're dying. Do it now.

This is embarrassing, but to quote Jean-Luc Picard, in the film where he reads William Shatner's obit. – you find profundity in odd places, but why not! – he says something like, 'we must think of death as a companion, who walks with us through life' – do you know the bit I mean? – 'and who is with us at our shoulder the whole way, and who reminds us, don't waste this day, don't waste time, because they're not infinite'. And that relationship with death, that's no longer a grim spooky reaper, it's a trusted advisor. And that's healthier, isn't it?

RHB: Yes, certainly. I really like one thing from that, from *The Tibetan Book of the Dead*, which concentrates on different states of death – life, death and rebirth – and that was one thing that I noticed when I read *The Bone Clocks*, that you've imagined that lovely space of the dusk, that twilight space between death and rebirth ...

DM: Thank you, thank you! Yes ... thank you ...

RHB: ... and why shouldn't narrative, shouldn't fiction enjoy and think about those states in the same way that that book does. I think it's lovely ...

[22m]

DM: Yes, Alain de Botton's recent one, *Religion for Atheists* ... it's all too good to leave to the religious. We've got art, we make metaphor for a living. Why do we have to leave that to clubs that charge you to join and issue passports to the afterlife that are probably fraudulent passports? We can do that. And it helps ... I'm glad you liked it! The forty-nine-days thing is Buddhist, as you probably know. When you die, at least in Japanese Buddhism – all forms, I think – the soul is around for forty-nine days before it actually leaves, and there's a ceremony that's performed at various points. But the forty-ninth day is the big one, that's when the healthy soul would go. My wife would know more about this than me. But that's where I got the forty-nine from, plus it's a beautiful number.

The sand dunes, I realized afterwards, it's a bit embarrassing, I haven't told her, but it's from Ursula Le Guin's *The Farthest Shore*. There's a bit where Ged and Estarriol, I think ... no, that's the wrong name ... there's a prince he's with, who's going around with him as a kind of apprentice, who will emerge as the ruler of all of Earthsea. But they go into the afterlife. It's very dusty, very very dry, and there's a town they go through. There's a beautiful line that I'm going to quote in the next thing I do, where the dead are just walking around, and those who died for love pass each other in the street without recognizing their faces. It's beautiful ... so there's a bit of that, and yes, I'd forgotten that bit ... this sort of undulating thing going down to the blank ocean at the end. Thank you, thank you very much!

RHB: ... it's really fascinating to hear more about it ...

DM: We should work out a way to do this more!

RHB: ... the other thing I was going to say was that you've mentioned Jung in previous interviews as well, which I think resonates with the use of mythology in your work, and the idea of a shared or collective unconscious in some way. That comes to the fore, I think, in your writing in *The Bone Clocks*, and it's suggested by the shared characters and what I've called the Mitchellian archetypes which link your works together. So for example there's the recurring moon-grey cat, and the recurring images of moths as associated with victimhood, I think, in your work. Jung's ideas are discussed in a book called *The Syndetic Paradigm* by Robert Aziz – have you read that book?

DM: No … I am thinking of moths though, you'll like *Slade House* … there's a group of moths in *Slade House* …

RHB: … that's excellent – I was just going to ask if there were any other Jungian texts or similar writers that influenced your attitudes to myth and spirituality, beyond the Jungian one that you mentioned earlier?

DM: He was huge in the seventies … is it Toronto … he was an interpreter of Jung for literature and an academic at Kent got me to read him, and it was good – a big, thick thing. I'm sorry, I can't believe I've forgotten … it'll come back to me and I'll email you! It's fiction, in a way, more than philosophical or theological texts, that does it for me. Art's a Trojan Horse that the Greek soldiers of ideas hide in, to get into my head and get to work.

Myths, yes – just as a kid, I had those Roger Lancelyn Green books, the Greek myths, and played Dungeons and Dragons. And there was a book of deities in there that were culled from the world's literatures … I read those with great interest and pleasure. I'm trying to think if there was anything else … but the answer is, I learnt about the Green Man through *Gawain and the Green Knight* more than through Robert Bly, or books about the Green Man, say. So it was sort of in the original settings, I suppose. But I'm aware of, and interested in utilizing, the muscularity of symbols, and of mythological figures. They bring heft, and weight, and gravitas. They are more than what they appear to be. I only have a murky understanding of these forces, but when I write, I'm sort of aware, I guess, of the hero figure, say, and I like to think about these things. But I don't have an impressive bibliography.

RHB: Okay, that's fair enough. Moving on to the Mitchellian macronovel as a whole, your fictional world seems like a parallel reality to our own, with a strange metaphysical dimension in which characters can be reincarnated and seem to follow a predestined 'script' of some kind, as in *The Bone Clocks*. What is the 'script', and what does it bring to your macronovel?

DM: Within my universe, it's my word for fate or destiny. Looking at my universe through my authorial eyeballs, it's a facilitator of plot lines that I want to take in a certain direction. It's an ultimate *deus ex machina* maybe – 'no actually, the story has to go this way for it to do what I want' – for it to have the ripeness that I sense it needs. It's almost my take on the Victorian novel coincidence of monumental proportions, where what's-his-name's nephew from *Bleak House* happens to be working there, and it's the Gilbert and Sullivan operetta coincidence where the old sailor and the young sailor realize that they're father and son. It's the necessary facilitator of the narrative. I'll have my cake and eat it! It has the metaphysical function, but also the craftsmanship level function.

[30m 40s]

RHB: When creating this fictional universe, what are the rules that make the Mitchellian world different to our own, and why did you choose those differences?

DM: Is it different?

RHB: In terms of, for example, the fantasy content that comes in, the reincarnation – does it have different laws of physics, or different rules?

DM: Physics and fantasy, that's matter and anti-matter … Yes, you need a constitution of special powers for people who are violating the laws of physics. Once

I'd got it right, I'd kind of lost interest in it or preserving it really – what the Anchorites can do, or what Marinus' lot can do. It sounds a bit highfalutin … this might sound odd, I've acceded in its description as fantasy, but it's science fiction for me. I have no truck with magic. Sometimes it can look like magic, sometimes – what's the difference between telekinesis moving a bottle of Lucozade across the table and Harry Potter waving a wand and saying something that makes it move? For me it's actually the former which sometimes looks like the latter, and these are the laws of physics that have been successfully reproduced in a laboratory. A lot of people would think that they could be. There are true believers in psychic phenomena, and I borrow their beliefs for *The Bone Clocks*, and I guess, therefore for the universe at large. But in my head at least, it's never magic, it's never the Harry Potter answer – 'it's magic, stop arguing, shut up'. It's kind of a mind power that might be interpreted as magic, and the sneaky advantage of happy agnosticism is, 'I'm sorry but you tell me there isn't a dusk – go on, prove it, you prove to me that that's fiction'. I mean, you can't, right?

RHB: … Absolutely …

DM: … and so I write it from the point of view that it is non-fiction. It's possible. It's a possible reality. You do this lot with your proofreading – all the contentious stuff I subject to a court of plausibility. You often get this, where proofreaders say, 'well, he does this on Tuesday, could he actually be there by Wednesday?' Now, if the answer in the court of plausibility is, 'possibly, yes', then it's not guilty, and it stays in. It doesn't have to be likely, it has to be possible. And that's how I adjudicate these calls. I've used a similar principle with the world-building. 'Well, prove to me it isn't …' If you can, I probably wouldn't put it in. This is obviously a conversation I have in my head as I write; at a structural and a world-building level I subject my decisions to this test. Magic, fantasy … it sort of makes something dismissible in a way that isn't dismissible when it's science fiction, so I try to keep it on the science fiction side of the 'laws of physics' line. Fantasy will blithely … I mean, it is a violation of the laws of physics, as it's magic.

Science fiction is more about possible laws of physics that haven't been discovered, understood or quantified yet, which is of course what intergalactic or interstellar travel is, or faster-than-light travel. The Star Ship Enterprise is not powered by magic – it's powered by a type of engine that we haven't discovered yet, but as far as it's concerned, it's science. The Tardis is even closer to the border, which might be more about British culture, and American culture perhaps, than fantasy and science fiction. So that's a valid and true thing to say – there's no magic in my universe. It's just laws of physics that haven't been discovered yet.

RHB: That's a nice way of putting it …

DM: … and the dusk is a liminal zone between life and death … it is the country from whose bourn no traveller returns. No travellers come back to say it's not like this, so it could be …

RHB: So if you stopped writing tomorrow, and there were no more Mitchell publications of any kind, what would be missing from the macronovel?

DM: All the books that were still to come to deepen it, and broaden it, and heighten it … I don't know yet, because I haven't written them. That's not supposed to be a smart-ass answer!

[38m 35s]

RHB: The Horologist's Labyrinth section of *The Bone Clocks* is really fascinating …

DM: Thank you …

RHB: What is it all about? Is it a metaphor for anything?

DM: Reincarnation's already a metaphor for the phases we move through, through life. When you first get your heart properly broken, that's a kind of death. When you realize that you can no longer blame your parents, that's a kind of rebirth! When you get divorced, when these unspeakable tragedies happen, if your kid dies, that's a kind of death too.

Marinus' life is kind of a metaphor for our own lives; therefore, his or her metalife is a metaphor for life. One day, maybe the end of the third book – *The Bone Clocks* is kind of part two in a very loose Marinus trilogy. The last one I want to have the structure of *Gulliver's Travels*, the last four lives of Marinus, about a hundred and twenty, a hundred and thirty pages each, in weird post-2070s civilizational life-rafts/dystopian hellholes, Ebola-ridden, McCarthy's *The Road* kind of scenarios. At the end of that she'll kind of – he? She? Maybe she – will discover what these involuntary atemporals are for. So a bit of myth-building there. And they're organic soul-based libraries of human experience. That's what they're for.

Is that a metaphor for anything? I suppose, the limitless potential of human existence. Because our lives are finite, so is every given individual's ability to gather experience. But if you come back again and again and again and keep what you've already had, then obviously your bank account of experience will get considerably greater. So, again, I'm not sure that means that she's a metaphor for anything – it's maybe more what she is. And that's something that wouldn't get done if I stopped writing tomorrow.

RHB: That would be sad. Please keep writing!

DM: As long as I'm alive, I will, Rose. There isn't anything else I love doing remotely – remotely – as much as this. I love my job! It's the stuff that goes with it that can be a bit of a … unfortunately also I always have to be in company, and I also have to promote the thing. But if this is as hard as it gets [waves chocolate macaroon and laughs], how sorry do you really feel for me! While I bite your biscuits!

RHB: Well from there I was going to say, I think your work seems to oscillate between hope and despair, particularly in the near-future ecological catastrophe in *The Bone Clocks*, and in the futuristic sections of *Cloud Atlas* as well. Yet hope and compassion persist in even the bleakest futures in your work, I think. Is such hope gratuitous in the face of almost-certain ecological destruction? Is change possible – can we avert the endarkenment?

DM: Two things there. One you're asking me as a human being living towards the end of the Holocene era, and the other as a writer. The human being: we're in for some kind of a crash landing. Whether that crash is hard and fatal, or relatively soft, depends on what we do now, whether we can convert our civilization, for example, to a non-carbon burning one … We have to devise, we have to bring about an unprecedented level of international cooperation, and then sell it to our electorates – good luck – before it becomes transparently the right thing to do, by which point it'll be too late, and the window of opportunity for global cooperation will be shut, because we'll all be having to look after our own loved ones. What we hear about Bangladesh: four more degrees centigrade – I'm making up these figures, but they could well be conservative ones – and that's another meter and a half. All of a sudden come these tropical storms and you've got no viable Bangladesh. What do you do with that?

There's still time for international cooperation of an unprecedented degree, but the window is closing. I don't know, no-one knows – that's the point – whether an inevitable, very hard crash landing … well, whether a hard crash landing is inevitable. We'll find out.

As an author, the compassion is there because I can't be doing with these miserable, godawful books. They might be well written, but you just feel like slitting your wrists when you've finished them. I don't want to read them. And I'm not going to write things I don't want to read. If you want misery, just open a paper – there's all you can eat there. Someone's given me their money and their time. I'm not going to repay them by making them feel like shit, and that it's all hopeless, and why bother, why go on. I can't do that to people! That is also a self-fulfilling prophecy of course. Hope's good. If you're lucky enough to have a sufficiently undamaged life for you to be able to nurture hope, then do it. We need it. You don't have to be a lost-cause, self-help book-reader to believe that hope brings about good stuff. Trying to see the glass as half full, it's just good for you. It's more likely to bring about full glasses in the future than Eeyore-ish despair.

[48m 25s]

RHB: Absolutely … in interview I know you've mentioned the need to worship as one of a set of fundamental human traits. Do you see this as something to be nurtured, or something to be overcome?

DM: Overcome … but we'll only get there when we achieve a kind of society closer to utopia than the one we're living in. And whether or not that's even possible is also an open question. We need to work out how we distribute resources, for example. Prayer is an anaesthetic because of misfortune. Science, at least in some richer countries, has done a great job of alleviating a lot of that misfortune. Unfortunately there's an economic aspect as well, which we seem to be going backwards with – I can't even remember the statistics now, what percentage of American wealth do the fifty richest Americans have?

RHB: It's absolutely crazy … [America's richest 3% have over double the wealth of America's poorest 90% of families at the time of interview. Source: http://inequality.org/wealth-inequality/, accessed 4 September 2015]

DM: … It is pharaonic. I think even the pharaohs did this better actually, and this brings about misfortune. This is just wrong. It engenders misery, needless misery. You can't even spend that money. You can't even spend that money in ten lifetimes. While there is injustice and misery, there will be an impulse to pray. While there is suffering, perhaps there will be an impulse to pray. This is deep stuff, Rose. Middle-class Muslim kids running off to ISIS – what's going on there? That would appear to invalidate my theory just now by the way, I'm aware. Maybe it's the adventure they're after, maybe it's not actually the religion …

RHB: … Perhaps they're looking for a story in a world in which stories have fallen by the wayside in the face of Capitalism. I won't put words into your mouth, but maybe it's the idea of a culture that has a narrative, and has a meaning, and can offer maybe some form of consolation, in a world where the consolation is products being marketed …

DM: … and status. Yes … this is a symposium's worth of questions to explore, isn't it!

RHB: Moving on to the libretti, if that's ok – I'd like to talk a bit more about how you approached writing them. How did the writing and redrafting process differ from your approach to writing novels, for both *Sunken Garden* and *Wake*? Was it a very different experience for you?

DM: Not quite, not really. I thought about the characters, I wrote their autobiographies, and thought about the plot … For *Wake*, I think I worked more with Klaas [de Vries] in the beginning. We built that together. Klaas' English is less fluent than Michel's [van der Aa], and he's a generation or two older as well, so he's a bit less confident regarding contemporary English, so he had less to say about things on a word-by-word level. In both cases I wrote the words, gave them, and didn't have to fit the music to the words, because the composers did that for me. Michel, we had more variants and ideas – it gave me a very early version of what's turned into *Slade House*, actually. And this was just from a 'what we're working on at the moment' kind of conversation. He had an idea about doing something about a sort of a Jason Bourne thing, where a guy wakes up and doesn't know who he is – that's a bit of a classic first novel at a creative writing workshop kind of thing, and it's very … why are you going to care about a character who doesn't know who he or she is? It's so hard to do that.

So without realizing what I was doing, I kind of put him off that idea, and just discussed what I was working on. And he said, 'I'd like that, please' – 'Really?' [laughs] Yes, we decided to work together and have a go. Plot: this will happen, this will happen, this will happen, and the characters are these people, and this is how they interact – that's what I always do.

Then I just needed to write it in such a way that it scanned, and there was a rhythm to the words – a 'da-di-da-di-da-di-da-di-da' kind of rhythm, that I felt could slot into musical phrasings. Mostly they did. Occasionally Michel would say 'I just can't make this fit, can you find another way to say it'. And he's a very gifted man, he's got a storytelling instinct of his own that was valid and helpful. So textually, that was more collaborative. It won't happen, but if *Sunken Garden* were ever to be filmed, he would certainly need a credit as a story consultant. We should go halves on the money really, because he did make a contribution to the language that improved it. It wouldn't be what it is now without his textual input as well.

[55m 35s]

RHB: Absolutely. You said that the libretti were also part of your macronovel, and I think that their approaches and their mythologies, as well as Marinus' presence in each of them, make them very valuable in your larger textual universe. Why did you decide to include the libretti in the same fictional world as the rest of your novels and short stories?

DM: It makes sure that my side projects are not side projects. It allows me to justify time away from my impatient list of novels that want to get written. It justifies my decision to say, 'yes, I'll do it'. It's that. I hit a problem with Marinus – I couldn't have the *Wake* Marinus; it didn't fit the chronology of *The Bone Clocks*. Something had to give. So that's in the oubliette. I might still go back and take characters from them one day. I may, they were pretty well realized. Artistically, well, I discovered the reason why you can't have nine simultaneous narratives going on at once. You can't follow them all. Nice idea, top marks for following your vision, but there's just too much to look at. You can only look at one. And all of them work … maybe it is valid. No surprise *Wake* hasn't been a commercial hit that hasn't been reproduced all over the world – you just couldn't, and it would be too much of a hard sell.

I do feel I fell foul of the genre police with some of the UK opera critics with *Sunken Garden*. There's a bit of momentum building up for future performances, but getting kicked in the teeth by the four people who pretty much have a monopoly on opera in the UK. The Americans liked it, the Dutch liked it, but it premiered in the UK, and the mixed reviews make it a really hard sell for future directors of opera houses to do. I didn't realize how crucial those four reviews were. It's really hard work to kill a book – you basically can't. You can try, but if your mum likes it – if people's mums like it and give it as birthing presents, then a book can come out of nowhere. A soundly rubbished book at a critical level can still do really well, and make fools of the critics. It happens quite often. Opera doesn't work like that. They are the gatekeepers, and if they feel … have you seen *Birdman*, the film with Michael Keaton? He plays an actor doing a review – there's a great drama critic in that, every artist who's ever been rubbished by a critic is like, 'yeah, that's what they're like!' It's got this great scene, where she just says, 'you don't get to come and play here' – she's profoundly proprietorial, territorial.

This is all a roundabout way of saying I'm proud of both – *Sunken Garden*'s a neat piece of work. It's not perfect, but at least it's trying to be different. It's got a weird twisty story, and it's followable. It's not an artistic experiment, not as far as me and Michel are concerned. I mean, the 3D stuff, great, and to a degree it hadn't been done before, and using digital media perhaps wasn't done before. But it's kind of a traditional story. It's an Orpheus kind of story. And that slots in. … And that's my Marinus. That's my Marinus from *The Bone Clocks*. I couldn't have that Marinus and the *Wake* Marinus, so that's in with one or two other things in the oubliette, of things I just can't make fit. I'm proud of them, I want them to be in there but … Timon of Athens doesn't really work, Pericles is all over the bloody shop, Cymbeline's ropey here and there – it's got some good scenes in, but it doesn't really hang together. Troilus and Cressida is kind of oubliettish – talking about Shakespeare, I'm not saying I'm like him, I'm just saying if he can do it, then I can. He can't make everything quite fit. He has a Shakespearean universe and there's a few things that aren't quite there, either for quality, or often it's just a different taxonomy, that doesn't belong in the usual flora and fauna, I think – that's the best way to put it. So for me, *Sunken Garden* is in and *Wake* is out of my universe.

RHB: Yes, that's interesting – so even though there was Marinus in there, it's moved to the oubliette as you said, as the parallel universe Marinus rather than the continuous universe …

DM: Yes, yes …

RHB: It must have been really fascinating to watch a team of artists bring your words to life, both in *Wake* and *Sunken Garden*. Did you have any involvement with the set design, staging or casting for either of those?

DM: The casting with *Wake*, a little. Michel's an insider in the network and he knew his own people, so it was fine. Set design: I was shown things with a presidential veto principle. If I hated it, then I could have made a fuss and had it changed, but I don't know the first thing about designing sets, and these people are doing it for a living, and what do I know? If I didn't want to collaborate, then I wouldn't be in business writing a libretto!

RHB: Yes … Just as *Wake* memorialized the Enschede disaster, was there a similar real world event, or events, behind *Sunken Garden*?

DM: No.

RHB: Okay. Finding hope after human tragedy and music's ability to heal, I think, are very important in both of your libretti. What is it, for you, that music brings to narrative, that's otherwise lost in words alone?

[1hr 2m 55s]

DM: If I could properly answer this, then music would not need to exist. Yes, you feel it don't you; it's more viscerally melded with emotion, and possibly mind. It's the bits in a song that are just a few seconds, and they either make you literally, or mentally, go 'aaah' [sighs] and kind of catch your breath. They're consoling, and healing, and stimulating, and make you so happy to be alive, all at once. We've all got our favourite pieces of music that do this to us. It's beyond words. I can't do it – I can't answer! It's music.

RHB: Well that's a great answer in itself I think. Your work's got this lovely visual, cinematic quality to it I think, as does all of your writing …

DM: … Thank you …

RHB: … Following the libretti, would you like to write specifically for the stage or screen again?

DM: I've always said 'no, I'll stick to what I know'. Screenwriting's a different art: you start in your twenties, you write episodes of Holby City, you work up to an independent film, if that does well, you get noticed by larger studios, and then you've entered the elite twenty, thirty great screenwriters in the world. Just because I can crank out a half-decent novel on a good day, hopefully, that doesn't mean that I can then jump across the barrier. Show me anyone who's done it. Show me a well-known, or well-known-ish novelist who's done that, and it ended happily. I would argue there aren't any. In the other way, coming back, yes – the novel's a more forgiving form, it's baggier. There's nothing baggy about a well-done screenplay. They have to do so much more with so much less. It's almost like poetry, in a way. Ditto the screen.

There's overlapping things: an eye for dialogue, an ear for dialogue – we both need that. But the novel constantly holds your hand by allowing you to mask what you can't do with what you can do. Even the greats: there are areas in which Dickens is horribly weak, but because the areas in which he's strong are good, he gets away with it. Screenplays don't let you get away with it, like a poem doesn't. One duff line, and you've popped it. You might do okay with screenplays, but why bother with an okay one? So I've always said, 'no, thanks but no'. Even more so for stage, I think. Tom Stoppard can write *Shakespeare in Love* and it's brilliant, but a novelist can't write *Rosencrantz and Guildenstern* [*Are Dead*]. I mean, you can see that, can't you?

RHB: Yes …

DM: … However, I'm in a situation now where I have recently accepted a couple of offers. One may well come to nothing, because the majority of screen ventures do come to nothing. One won't come to nothing – that's happening. In these situations, what I write will be converted by a collaborator into screenplay form. Both ideas, were they not the offers they were, from the people who have made them, then I would have said no. It's just because of who they are … at the moment it's world-building, and character building. So, I'm a busy lad! It's a lot of work, but I couldn't turn down either …

RHB: Thank you so much – that's absolutely wonderful …

DM: You're really welcome – let's make this not the last!

[End of interview – 1hr 14m]

Appendix H: An Interview with David Mitchell, 2016

Interview with David Mitchell by Rose Harris-Birtill, 12.02.16.

[DM = David Mitchell; RHB = Rose Harris-Birtill]

RHB: To start off, then: Marinus, I think, is one of your most fascinating characters, particularly after seeing Claron McFadden's wonderful portrayal of her in *Sunken Garden*, and managing to spend time with her in Lyon earlier …

DM: Yes, it was really helpful that, wasn't it? It's been really helpful for me, because in my imagination, when I was writing the book, she was Claron for all intents and purposes in my head. So it was great to have a human model before I really got my teeth into the imagined version.

RHB: Absolutely – having met Claron, I can see you've based Iris Marinus on Claron's character and her portrayal from *Sunken Garden*. What was it you wanted to bring from Claron's stage Marinus – or even Claron herself – to your textual Marinus?

DM: Her self-possession. Claron's ears will be burning unaccountably hotly at the moment: 'Who's talking about me!' Her coolness under duress. I don't know Claron, really, any better than you do, so where her persona starts and her true self ends, and vice versa, I don't really know, but what I perceive Claron to be is a person with these qualities: self-possession, grace under pressure, coolness under duress, a kind of manifestation of an old soul is what I'd like to say, without being able to avoid new-age language. A manifestation of an old soul – you know you sometimes meet people and you think, you are thousands of years old … Sometimes they're kids, which is really weird. I know I'm probably projecting that on to them, and I don't really believe that they are a soul who's been alive for thousands of years, but dammit, it's as if they are. It's metaphorically true.

RHB: Yes, I know exactly what you mean – you do meet people like that every now and then, don't you …

DM: You do, don't you!

RHB: … maybe it's just a collection of life experience, but you feel like they've done a lot of living, that means they should be far older than they are.

DM: You do, you do … when I was teaching English in Japan in the early nineties there was, I think, a Brazilian guy who was being paid for by a UN department, because he was working for them now. He had been tortured in the seventies by some unpleasant people in government, or attached to the government, in Brazil. He just had this different quality – he was astonishing. I still remember him. I don't remember anything about him, I don't even remember his name, but he had that quality.

Again, one time in Japan, not a Japanese person, but I was flying back – and this was in the old days, before you could assign yourself a seat online, and it was much more dependent on the person on the counter when you queued up for your paper ticket, if you're old enough to remember those days. It was this African-American guy, and it was their job to assign people to the emergency rows next to the emergency exits – so you had a bit more legroom, but you can't have your stuff there, and you have to obviously open the door in the case of an emergency. So it was his job to look out for likely candidates in that morning's intake of people he was assigning seats for. And for whatever reason, he chose me. It was really like you'd met God or something! He was probably about 50 but he seemed 5,000 years old. He just had this effect. But they're not necessarily grown-ups. Sometimes they're kids as well. Claron also had that quality – possibly coming from stagecraft, and maybe from being an actor as well – but for whatever reason, she has it. So I thought, thanks very much! Since you're playing Marinus, this can be a two-way street: just as you're putting lots of Marinus into you onstage, I'll put some of you into Marinus.

RHB: Absolutely … that was the other thing I was going to ask: in terms of the pronunciation of 'Marinus', as I was following 'I_Bombadil' …

DM: Oh yes, you're right, yes – I've been saying it wrong for years. I've recently learnt it's 'Ma-reen-us'. The stress is on the second syllable. There was an early geographer, Marinus of Tyre, and I was listening to some specialists on that Melvyn Bragg programme, *In Our Time*, on Radio 4. I listened to that when I was signing several thousand tipping sheets for *Slade House* before Christmas. The conversation was on the classical world that week, and these scholars were all talking about 'Ma-reen-us' of Tyre. And I thought, whoops! It's 'Ma-reen-us'. So there we go!

RHB: I noticed that detail in 'I_Bombadil', and I thought it was interesting because in the interview that I did with Claron earlier, she was saying that the cast of *Sunken Garden* were all trying to equalize the pronunciation of 'Ma-rinus' or 'Ma-reen-us', because in *Sunken Garden*, Sadaqat says 'Ma-rinus' on film, whereas she was saying it was written into the score as 'Ma-reen-us', so they were trying to make it a bit more homogenized throughout. So I thought it was fascinating that you picked up on that.

DM: Yes, yes – it's nice to be corrected, even if it's a little bit embarrassing that the creator of the character has been wrong all this time! On the other hand, this confusion, this lack of homogeneity, is also pleasing, in that it's mimetic. It reflects the real world, and there are those names … just try being Irish and being called Maeve and spelling it in the traditional way from the Gaelic [Medbh]. You will be meeting ten different pronunciations of your name – all of them wrong – or at least, all of them non-canonical. It's somehow pleasing that even amongst our level of reality, that for people who have come into contact with Marinus, this fuzziness is there. That fuzziness would probably have applied to her world as well, that she or he would have his or her name pronounced one way or the other down the centuries, from the fifth century onwards, really, as it's been going on forever. So it kind of has a rightness to it that I'm continuing that tradition, and that we're having a handful of real, live human beings who know and care about this fictional character in these books by an obscure British writer. We share that tendency to inconsistency, and we also are part of that fuzziness. Which is a big, big roundabout way of saying – this will take you fifty minutes to transcribe, sorry …

RHB: No, not at all – it's a pleasure …

DM: … that I don't really mind. It's embarrassing, but there's kind of a rightness to it, as well: to having been wrong.

RHB: Absolutely, I know exactly what you mean. Marinus seems to have this special ethical role, I think, in your works as a force for good …

DM: Yes …

RHB: … and I know in your original text for *Sunken Garden* she says, 'I'd make more sense in Sanskrit, or better yet, Tibetan', which are the languages of Tibetan Buddhism. Rather than the traditional Messiah figure, which keeps haunting secular culture, Marinus seems to me a sort of secular bodhisattva – I don't know if you're familiar with the concept of the bodhisattva?

DM: Please refresh me or teach me – I'm not sure if I'm familiar with it. Go on …

RHB: It's from Mahayana Buddhism. It's one of the figures of compassion from Buddhist teaching: someone who delays reaching Enlightenment to deliberately keep coming back to help others who suffer.

DM: Oh, yes! I've been mispronouncing it all my life – bodhisattva.

RHB: You're probably more right than I am, to be fair …

DM: … I doubt it very much; but yes! I should let you finish your question before I jump in, but go on …

RHB: This figure of compassion, who is being reborn to help others around her – I think this fits perhaps both in her role as a healer, but also in her being reborn into the bodies of children that otherwise would have died, and sparing their families a lot of grief. So I wanted to ask are you familiar with this Buddhist concept of the bodhisattva, and how it fits in with Marinus' role?

DM: Yes, I am familiar, and have been familiar since my late teens, I suppose, when my reading first went in those directions. There's the same kind of figure you find in Japanese manifestations of Buddhism as well. Not all of them; as you know, it's a really fractured belief system, and different shards can believe in wholly contradictory things and yet still come under the larger umbrella of Buddhism, so we can't look for consistency there. But yes, I am familiar with the concept, and I find a beauty in it. I'm attracted to their engagement with the mess and the mud of the world. Messiahs I find unconvincing, because of their Messianic nature, because of their Manichean nature. Because you're a Messiah … and as with a cult like ISIS, you see yourself as someone who's going to purge the world of all its mess and confusion, of its greyness. And maybe one reason why these movements and cults are more persuasive to younger people who may have less experience of the inherent messiness of reality, of the built-in greyness of reality, than perhaps some older people who have already learnt this the hard way. But my problem with – let's stick to literature – but my problem with Messianic characters is, what do you do when you've gained power, what do you do when you've won? Immediately you come back to square one.

A perverse part of myself, a perverse me hopes that Trump wins because all these grey-hating, reality-denying people who voted for him – whole generations of them – will see that actually, when you get power, you can't just make the Mexicans build a fence. It was an infantile thought in the first place. How? How? Expel or keep out Muslims – well, which ones? All Muslims? According to many Sunni Muslims, Shias aren't Muslims – so whose definition of Muslim would you go for? How about Muslim diplomats: are you going to expel the entire diplomatic corps of thirty or forty countries on earth because they're Muslim? Really? If he ever won … if ever the barking dog who chases the car actually caught the car, what on earth would he do with it? This is how I feel about Messianic characters in literature, who we are expected to take seriously and believe in. They're sort of literary Trumps, cut from the same cloth.

Of much more interest to me are angels with feet of clay, I suppose – people who may be spiritually more developed than us, but they are nonetheless us, and that spiritual development just comes from bitter, hard-earned experience that we're exposed to in our lives as well. It's just that they've had more of it. In Marinus' case he's had 1,500 years more of it. They're interesting, because they aren't a different species. They're us, but just more so. They've been alive longer – that's all. That's the difference: they know more about suffering, about pain, about betrayal, about mortification, about doing stupid things and having to pay the consequences later. Not because they were born that way – not because of superior spiritual DNA. It's just because they've been through it more often.

It's analogous to a fifteen-year-old teenage male having a great connection with a grandfather who can understand where the younger man is coming from and why he might be impelled to do stupid things, but the grandfather has had the longer life, and so can … in an ideal context, the young man is wise enough at least to listen, if not to not make the mistakes, then that relationship could be a fruitful and a profitable one. The vegetarian atemporals are like these sort of wonderful wise grandparents. Even though they might be in bodies that are a lot younger than our own, their souls aren't. That's attractive, that gets me going – wow, just think of the narrative possibilities that could fly off that, is how I think. So that's my attraction to them. So yes, first identified in bodhisattvas, but co-opted for my own, in a way, more secular purposes. In the Buddhism that I've read about, they don't really feel that religious, and that's why I'm attracted to them.

[19m 30s]

RHB: Absolutely …

DM: There's a story I've almost finished – I just want to spend a weekend polishing it. It's really short, it's just 2,000 words. There's these two artists, Kai and Sunny – I deal mostly with Kai. They work together; they're graphic artists mostly, but they did my first set of matching jackets about ten years ago … we've stayed in touch. They asked me about seven years ago, they were having an exhibition called *The Flower Show* … we collaborate occasionally. When they have a show, instead of producing a page of that ghastly art-speak guff that you normally get in art exhibition programmes, that are full of words like 'epistemological' and 'conceptual' – words that you probably understand the meanings of, but most ordinary human beings don't. Instead of producing a page of art-crit stuff, they asked me to write a story. A really short one, almost like a micro-story. And I've just done a third one for them, for the show they've got next month. I try to do it in conversation with the images that they've got in the upcoming show, so they send me what they've got. They do these beautiful, mesmerizing, abstract prints, just made of lines, or patterns or forms. They did the illustrations for *The Reason I Jump* – that, in a sense, is a favour they did back my way. These meditative, strange, calming images sort of capture infinity.

This upcoming show is about time, so I had this idea: what if you lived at a twelfth of the speed of time to everyone else. So the sun still crosses the sky once for you, just the same as it does for everyone else, and that's your day. But your speed of time is twelve times slower, one-twelfth the speed of everyone else's speed of time. What would that be like? Counter-intuitively, you'd be living in a world where everyone is moving twelve times more slowly than you are. So you walk down a busy high street and everyone would be there – they would be moving, but incrementally slowly. You'd be able to walk past a car whose speedometer needle was on fifty, and it wouldn't be lying – for the people in the car, relative to them in time, they would be going at fifty. But your speed of time, because it's twelve times everyone else's, and everyone else's time is lasting twelve times longer relative to you, you'd be able to walk past it. What a world that would be! And what would you do with it …

The story is actually what happens to Richard Cheeseman when he's about to shoot Crispin Hershey in the head. From Hershey's point of view, he's closed his eyes, and said, OK, your cause is just – I did do this to you, I made you spend five years in a Columbian prison cell, and you've lost your life, you've lost your profession, you've lost your career, you've lost your money, probably. You've lost everything, so you can be judge, jury and executioner. And I don't want to die, and I don't want you to do it, but you've got the right to decide that. So that's the last of Crispin Hershey's 'Lonely Planet' section of *The Bone Clocks*, and Crispin Hershey's got his eyes clamped shut. When he opens them, Richard Cheeseman's gone. This 2,000-word story that I've done … is from his point of view. He had decided to do it, and he was holding the gun, and he was counting down from ten to zero in his head – and he got to three, and at three, the snow in the window behind Hershey's head, it slowed down to where it was hardly falling, it was almost stationary. What'd happened was that it was now moving at a twelfth of its ordinary speed.

This really old woman just came into his field of vision, and just rested her hand on his hand – on the gun hand – and the gun slowly lowered, like that. And she walked him out of the room. There was a cleaner outside, who is mentioned in the book I think, in *The Bone Clocks*, and they walk straight past her, but she didn't seem to see them. Downstairs in the lobby of the English building, there's a group of students, but they were like almost-waxworks, the students – hardly moving at all. One girl had flicked her hair back and it was moving in super-slow motion, like in a shampoo advert. Again, they didn't appear to notice them. Because of course, for them, these people are moving at twelve times their speed, so they've gone by like that superhero Flash, whose skill is to zip round super quickly.

Also, human vision … I've got a line that works: 'vision is redacted by belief'. So you see what you think is there, and not what is really there. This is apparently, in biology and neurology, this is true. We think we see a whole room, but we only have enough cones and rods in the backs of our retinas to register a very small fraction of this, 10 or 20%. Our brain is guessing what the rest of the room is doing, and what's there, and what's light. But actually, when you see is a kind of core circle at the middle of it all, and everything else is kind of made up by our brains. We human beings, we don't … I mean, this wouldn't work if you're an animal who has to live by eyesight, like a bird of prey or something. They really do need to be able to see everything. That's why so much of their brains are given over to vision, rather than the things that the human brain has to do.

So because people don't believe in these – I've called them 'meanderers' – these people who move through time at slow speeds, we don't see them. Even speech would be quite hard, and they'd be talking in a really slow voice. So when they communicate with us, it's actually by text, it's by sentences. Email is fine, because the words don't need a speed of time to exist in: they're there. Anyway, what would you do with this? What would it be for? Well, Richard Cheeseman – one of the reasons he's going to go through with shooting Hershey, and then himself, is that he's been given about eighteen months to live. He's had cancer that went undiagnosed during his long imprisonment. He's led outside the building by the old woman who says: it's really simple, you're now moving at one twelfth of the speed of everyone else – that's why. If I leave you, you can then go back to doing whatever you want, and if you want to go upstairs and commit murder then you can, but somehow I don't think it's you. Or you can come with me and find out more about my relationship with time, and this gift I have.

He's got nowhere to go, and he's got no money – he just intends to come and shoot Hershey, then himself, and that would be it. So he goes with the old woman to her cabin at some distance, some miles, through this snowy evening. It's a kind of proposed recruitment – she says: I've had my eye on you. That's the name of the story: 'My Eye On You'. It's an elongated life, and it's a solitary life, but you can actually achieve a lot of good, and this is why I'm giving this chapter and verse, really, because you're talking about bodhisattvas. If you can move at this speed you can do some Robin Hood-type redistributions. If there's a homeless person, you can walk into the supermarket next door, steal them some food, and it won't be noticed. No-one will notice you because you're moving at twelve times their speed – and you can just leave it with them. If a brutal husband is about to smack his wife, you can – without needing to be in too much of a hurry about it – you can bind his wrists together with a piece of rope. As far as he's concerned, one moment he's about to slap her, and the next his hands are tied, and he has no idea why this happened.

This is where the myth of the guardian angel has come from: it's these meanderers, doing these services for us. When they go bad, on a few occasions when they're malign rather than benign, this is where demons and poltergeists come from as well. There can't be that many of them in the world, obviously, otherwise this would be going on in the world and we'd know about it. There's just a few of them around, and the majority are benign, and this is what they do. Because they live at one-twelfth the speed of time, they have – relative to our years – twelve times the lifespan as well, so this particular old woman was born in the late Middle Ages. But it's not immortality; they do die.

Somehow – and I don't get into the mechanics of this, because it's only 2,000 words – you can pass this on, and she's chosen Richard Cheeseman, this unlikely guy. He says, firstly, I've only got eighteen months to live, and she says, that's one reason why I've chosen you. Eighteen months times twelve: you do the math. That's a couple of decades you can have if you accept this gift. Secondly, he says, I just tried to kill someone – I was just about to. How I've spent my life: I've wasted it, in a way. I'm not really guardian angel material, am I? She says something like – and this is a huge answer to your short question, sorry! – she says something like, what kind of guardian angel doesn't understand these most violent desires, these darker impulses. What kind of angel hasn't got feet of clay? They have to understand the darkness of the human heart to be able to let the light in. And I thought, hey, I've done it again – this sounds like a familiar thing.

This is interesting, for me. Angels aren't, not in the traditional sense. They have one moral alignment and they're as dull as ditchwater, narratively. Messianic protagonists aren't interesting. They're visible, and worse than that, they're dull. Where's the character development going to be for someone who is zealously righteous at the beginning, and in the middle, and at the end? The narrative could be interesting, but not because of them. Or it could be interesting in a Don Quixote way, but the joke would be on them, not on the rest of the world. The joke would be on them thinking the world is black and white, when it is tragically, comically, demonstrably, perpetually grey – morally, I mean. So, heaven only knows what question that was an answer to! Good luck Rose, sorry – just skip out the dull bits and just type up the bits that are interesting! You'll probably be spending weeks of your time when you've got more important things to do …

RHB: No, not at all – I feel very privileged. It is a pleasure to be in this position, genuinely: what wonderful stuff to be transcribing! What an amazing story. Is this just for a one-off for 'My Eye On You', or do you think you'd bring them into …

[34m 45s]

DM: Well, this is the thing, really, Rose: it's enormous! I could do a thousand-page book on this. I could do a whole Neal Stephenson job on it, couldn't I?

RHB: Absolutely …

DM: It's huge! I've crammed it into five paragraphs, with not much dialogue in it – it's mostly reported speech. So, it's theirs for the exhibition; I retain copyright. I've got eighteen stories apparently – my agent's assistant was on to me this week, saying some of my foreign publishers would like to do an anthology of short stories. I don't think any one person has read them all, but just it's just bits and pieces I've done. About a sixth, I kind of don't really want out there. Maybe three or four I don't want because they're not canonical: 'The January Man', the early version of the first chapter of *Black Swan Green* that I sent to Granta – I redid that, and that sort of knocked it out of the bed of what is canonical, and what is not. Three or four just aren't that great, and I don't really want them out because I'm not happy with them. But I've got eight or nine that are really worth it, I think – and this is another one. So, what would I do with it? I think the German *Bone Clocks* is coming out soonish. This is like a little sprig off the German *Bone Clocks* that might be really nice for a freebie giveaway at least … I've showed it to the artists; they like it, and it fits with their images. Instead of trying to cram it on one page – what they've done in the past is print the story on the same size of paper as it fits, so if you want to, you can kind of buy it framed. I'm not sure how many takers they've ever had for that in the past. People also buy their prints from the show in box set form, and the story's included in that – it's usually A3-size. But this one, because it's a bit longer, it's in five distinct paragraphs. I think the last I heard they're going to letterpress print it, with one paragraph per page, and I guess have it distributed between the pictures around the exhibition. So I just wanted the weekend to do a really close word-nerd thing on it and get the language as close to 100% as I can, and then on Monday I'll send it to them …

There's a book in the future that is part three of the Marinus trilogy. That's one reason I did *Slade House*: Marinus needs a Moriarty of his own, or her own, and it's Norah Grayer. That's a kind of human being who feels implacable hatred towards Marinus, and everything she is and stands for. *Slade House* would sort of slot in to the third Marinus trilogy book, but I think these meanderers, they should have a role. It's a beautiful idea, and their non-existence is unprovable. That's why I like them. Yet they aren't a pre-existing cliché either – the closest thing is a guardian angel. But these people are very different. They aren't divine in origin. They just have this thing, they call it a 'gift' but even that word's a bit hoary. They have this sort of lens, that they occupy this twelve-times-slower time stream to the rest of us. As far as I know, at least, in British folklore and Japanese folklore, it hasn't really been done before. It probably has been, you could find things in science fiction, but nothing really big. Nothing really well known, nothing that I know of. And that's really attractive to me. So I think meanderers are earning their berth aboard part three of the Marinus trilogy as well. You can't have got very far down your list of questions Rose! What's next?

[41m]

RHB: On the back of what you were saying, about your short stories – I've actually found twenty-two so far, that you've done …

DM: Wow, you've searched more assiduously than my agents! What's the most obscure? It might be something that I haven't heard of, which would be really funny …

RHB: The most obscure is probably 'Imaginary City', which I've classified as a short story, but it's kind of a genre-straddle between a creative essay and a short story, from when you were flying into Vancouver, and what your imaginary Vancouver was like.

DM: I remember doing that, yes!

RHB: Probably the other one that I think they might have missed would be 'Preface' for *Black Swan Green*, which was on your BlackSwanGreen.co.uk website once upon a time, but I think the website has disappeared. I've had a lot of fun searching for these – the nice thing is that because I'm doing a PhD on your works, I get to go down these rabbit holes! I would love to see a short story collection of yours out. I think they're fantastic.

DM: There are a few ropey ones Rose – I'm grateful for your kind opinion. I did one for *McSweeney's*. I think that might have involved Hugo Lamb, actually. It's really non-canonical at this point – I can't even remember the title. I keep mixing it with that Sinéad O'Connor album, *I Do Not Want What I Haven't Got* …

RHB: 'What You Do Not Know You Want' … I know the one …

DM: Yes, it seemed like a nice idea at the time. Is that the one about Mishima's sword?

RHB: Yes …

DM: I don't mind if that never sees a wider audience. They're hard. It's considered to be a beginner's form, but it's really not. When they're not working, there's nothing you can do to make them work. You can't really fix them. They're just duff stories. You can fix novels; you can go back, you can restructure, you can cannibalize what you've got. Short stories: they're somehow less formulisable, less graspable. They're more serendipitous things, I think. I don't really understand how good ones ignite into being good, and how to make a mediocre one do that. Either it does or it doesn't, and you know when it has done. 'The Massive Rat' is a good piece of work, and that can hold its head up. That's just right – it has a rightness that 'What You Do Not Know You Want' hasn't got. I can't really put my finger on that rightness and bottle it, or distil. Have you found 'The Gardener' and 'Lots of Bits of Star'?

RHB: Yes, absolutely – that was the other thing I was going to say, on the back of what you were saying earlier. I'm actually trying to build a David Mitchell collection to help other scholars at the university, and I've managed to get the department and Special Collections here to kindly put up a little bit of money. We've just acquired both box sets for 'Lots of Bits of Star' and for 'The Gardener', which is very exciting!

DM: Ah, so you know the artists I'm talking about!

RHB: Yes, I've just done a blog for the university's Special Collections on 'Lots of Bits of Star', a piece for Special Collections signposting that it's here … One of the questions that I was going to ask was about the new piece that you were doing with Kai and Sunny, as they haven't announced that yet, and Kai and Sunny very kindly sent through some pictures for 'Whirlwind of Time', which is beautiful. They're such gorgeous, hypnotic works, aren't they …

DM: Good! They're really something, aren't they? It's the first time they've used colour – aren't they great? What they remind me of are novelty biros from the 1980s that you'd buy at now long-defunct stationer's chains, with sort of metallic gold. There was a shade called Jupiter Red. They use these strange inks, these strange tones, and they're exquisite. There's one which – all art is hard to describe – has a big black dot in the middle, with coloured rays spiralling out of it. That's the one that gave me the title, 'My Eye On You', because it looks like this divine retina. 'My Eye On You': I love that phrase – good titles are often titles that have existed in the mind of the reader forever, but when you tweak them a little and take them out of context, you just sort of see the beauty of the words in a different way. It's a phrase we've used a thousand times: 'I've got my eye on you, you just watch it'. But the [phrase] 'my eye on you', and the stresses that fall on it … They're all words of one syllable, and then the 'my' and 'you'. There's two pronouns in there: one possessive and one objective. My eye on you – it's quite hard to say it, but when you stop to say it properly, it's beautiful. I love things like that.

I was really happy with 'You Dark Horse You', the chapter title in *Slade House*. How many times have we said that? If there was that thing on your phone or your laptop that says how many times you've played this piece of music since you bought it – I wish you had one of those for phrases: the number of times you go, ooh, you dark horse you. It's a friendly thing to say that's implying that the other person has hidden qualities, with perhaps a blokey, matey element to it as well. It's a warm, special, odd phrase, but just look at it for a moment – it's got the word 'you' at the beginning and the end of it: you dark horse, you. And 'dark horse' in the middle. How beautiful is that, and we never noticed.

'Lots of Bits of Star' – that one's got a good title as well. I've got a slight idea for about eight autism stories, to write very obliquely about autism. I did 'The Gardener', the dénouement of which is a ghost, and then Kai said: we really like that one, can you do a sequel to that? So I said: no, he's a ghost! He's got one photon torpedo at the end of it which is: he's a ghost, he's not real. Well, he is real, but on a ghostly plane. So how can I possibly have a sequel? But then I really liked the fact that they liked it, and I like these impossible challenges. So what would a good sequel to that possibly look like, that still had a ghost in … It's a bit like the kid in *The Sixth Sense* that can see ghosts. The kid can see his grandfather, but not know that it's his grandfather, and even not be able to say, because he's not that verbal, I've just met this guy in the garden, and he said this, and took me here, and did that. It just sort of happened … So that was the story behind 'Lots of Bits of Star'.

RHB: It's beautifully done. I love the way that there's that supernatural connection, especially because of the rareness of these stories. When I read 'Lots of Bits of Star', I thought, the grandfather's back! But it's dropped in so that you would never know there were any supernatural goings-on … it's so matter of fact. There are lots of things going on and competing for Leo's attention, and that's just another one of them. It's second nature to him, but it's only us that find it slightly sublime, if you like. You did it beautifully!

DM: … I'd like to do about eight or nine of them when I have the chance, with different members of the family. I might go back to Leo again, because he's at the heart of it. I'd like to write about autism, and that's the way I'd like to address autism. I don't want to do a memoir, it's too Crispin Hershey, somehow. As you would have worked out by now, my privacy and anonymity are important to me … I wouldn't want to write about it directly, but I know a lot of stuff about autism now, and its impact on the lives of people with autism. There's a lot I'd like to say about autism … I'd like to write a little story about this. It might be Leo's dad, or someone else close to Leo – I think she's a single mum in this story, isn't she. But say, someone who's close to Leo, or Leo's sister or something, and talk about that … Life teaches you stuff, and these little, little encounters and life-lessons rarely are labelled – they're off-the-cuff things. Something a teacher might have said to you twenty years ago, not imagining it was an important thing to say, but you still remember it, and you've still got it, and it still modifies your behaviour now. Have you got a few of those things?

RHB: Absolutely. One of them that I thought of when you were saying this was an assembly story that we had, and I think there was a book of assembly stories that a lot of British kids grew up with … I think you might have even referenced this one in one of your works somewhere: it was this one where someone wants to visit heaven and hell. They go to heaven and everybody's very well fed, sitting around a table. They've got these super-long chopsticks, and they're too long to feed yourself, but they're long enough to feed the other people around the table. So in heaven, everybody is very content because although nobody is feeding themselves, they're all feeding each other. Conversely, this character gets taken to have a look at hell, and it's exactly the same scenario, but everyone is suffering and starving because they're only trying to feed themselves …

DM: It's a great story isn't it? You're right, I think I have used that story – perhaps our teachers had the same bumper book of school assembly stories, one-a-day! It's obviously an Eastern story because of the chopsticks, but I think that's an evergreen perennial. And it is unforgettable … I want to do a few more Leo/autism stories to put forward experiences, and also to put in some ideas, and with luck, they may catch on. … This stuff matters. Words really matter. In the area of ethnicity, they really matter. In the area of gay rights, the language you choose really matters. It's not 'PC gone mad!' – it really matters, this stuff …

[1hr 5min 15s]

RHB: I completely agree with you, it's something that should be out there … I think for a lot of people reading 'The Gardener' and 'Lots of Bits of Star', particularly if they are living with family members who themselves live with autism, I think the impact on family members themselves is also something where your writing can really help a lot of people talk about something that's not talked about as much as it should be, to help move forward those perceptions. Do you know what I mean?

DM: I really do. There's a conspiracy of silence, of love … I really understand their reasons, I don't blame them, and I'd do the same. But it's not a good state of affairs. I had it in a much smaller way with my stammer, which my parents never, ever, ever referred to. Huge bloody stammering elephant in the living room if there ever was one. If I opened my mouth, it was there. They wouldn't talk about it. And it doesn't help, even if their motives are good, to not upset me. Even if I'd have sulked and said, 'I don't want to talk about it' at the time, that was because they lacked the information to know how to bring it up in a way that wouldn't provoke that reaction. Because it's still not that widespread, no-one would refer to it or knew how to bring it up. As for stammering, so for autism, on steroids, really.

I was asked a really good question in Norway, where *The Reason I Jump* was number one for four weeks, and knocked Alex Ferguson's then-most-recent book off the number one slot. Someone said, 'my neighbour has a son with autism. What can I do to help?' I wanted to kiss her! That's it – that's exactly the question. I want to write stories that answer that question. That will be the purpose of the Leo cycle. So people understand, and then understand what they can do to help.

Firstly, let's not use the adjective autistic. Let's not use the word severe. That's the first thing to do to help. Second: allow the person with autism to be as – I can use the word here, because it's describing the behaviour, not the people – they can be as autistic as they want, and it's not fazing you. That reduces the stress on the parents. So if you're in a restaurant and someone obviously – or even less obviously – with autism walks over, stumbles into your table, nicks one of your chips, puts it in his mouth and walks off: don't go nuclear until you've worked out what's going on. Now that would be an enormous help. That's how you help people with autism. Just don't jump to the assumption that this is an obnoxious brat and their parents are shite parents – because actually the reverse is true. That kid is handling things that would get you sectioned by half past four this afternoon, and the parents are fantastic parents, because they're still there and haven't given up and handed their kid in to places with padded cells that you really wouldn't want your worst enemy to be in …

It's relevant to 'Lots of Bits of Star'. 'The Gardener' earns its place, and that would be the Trojan horse to get people in. To get them to switch off their, 'I don't want to read a depressing book about how hellish life with autism is, thank-you-very-much', to sort of lull them in. 'Lots of Bits of Star' can then be part two, and then part three, I think a sister, or perhaps the mother actually … It would be just a short piece about the unintentional burden that other people add to the mix as a result of their sometimes perfectly well-meaning ignorance about autism. That would be a good two-thousand worder …

We need for these narratives to become much more common. Even if we're having a shitty day, and a hard day, and a bad day, and a tough day, and we're short-tempered and in a bad mood, and you're in a busy car park and someone's jumped into the space that you sort of felt you had dibs on because you've been waiting there longer while the previous occupant was loading up the car and driving off: let's just not get into a road rage here. Let's remember that you never know what people are dealing with. They could have had a diagnosis of cancer just now. You just never know. We assume it's selfishness and arrogance and some sort of character failing. Wouldn't it be a better world if we actually assumed the opposite first? Until we know better, let's give compassion the first vote, and if that gets its face kicked in and made a fool of, fine, then the gloves can come off. But first, let's keep the gloves on …

Everything's in flux, as a wise friend says. When things are going well, let's cherish it, because we know things are in flux. And when things aren't going well, let's take it as a source of fortitude, and hope, and strength – it won't last forever, because things are in flux. It works for me … Isn't the world amazing? Aren't relationships amazing, and aren't the interconnections between those amazing? Isn't everything one thing, and one thing everything!

RHB: Absolutely … shall I use that as a good way to segue back to Marinus then, because I think that Marinus would probably agree with that perspective …

DM: Yes, ok then!

[1hr 29m 30s]

RHB: In *The Bone Clocks*, we find out that Marinus was originally born in 640 AD as the son of a Sammarinese falconer. What was the trigger to her cycle of rebirths? Did she originally choose to keep being reborn, or is it involuntary?

DM: No, it's involuntary. When Steven Moffat, the showrunner for *Doctor Who*, is asked a question like this – a really good question that he hasn't got an answer for yet – he says, 'we'll sort it out in the Christmas Special'. And that's a question for the Christmas Special! That's part three of the Marinus trilogy. It's a fine line; if you talk about it too much you're in the realm of fantasy, and it's the whole line of *The Bone Clocks*: how can you take its politics seriously when you talk about Iraq or something if you've then got these immortals and all this magic going on? From the other side of the fence, how can you take the magic seriously if I'm also talking about British foreign policy in Iraq – what kind of a fantasist am I, anyway?

That was the matter anti-matter paradox in *The Bone Clocks* which, if you think it works, I've solved, but if you think it doesn't work, I didn't. It can be solved: the tightrope is walked in one of my favourite ever books, *The Master and Margarita*. You've got Stalin, you've got serious heavy stuff, you've got theology, Soviet politics, Jewish theology, and you have a talking cat that fires a machine gun. And yet, it's brilliant. Magical realism found ways to deal with it as well. But I think unless you're from that tradition, because magical realism became – for non-Latin-American writers who hadn't lived under brutally oppressive dictatorships – it became an excuse to do what the heck you want, and it all became a bit twee from that side. And that isn't an avenue I want to claim, or a tool box I want to say is mine. I chiefly try to do it in *The Bone Clocks* by insulation, by putting a big brick wall between the fantastical parts and the politics, say, and only hearing faint echoes with a wine-glass pressed against the wall – maybe it's not a brick wall, but maybe a plasterboard wall between them.

I'll be facing this problem when I answer your question in a future book. My feeling is that some individuals have been selected here – my friend Lana Wachowski winces and says, 'Not the chosen one! Don't make him the chosen one!' – it sounds crap but hopefully it won't be crap when I write it. Some agency, who is not human, has chosen certain individuals to have this rebirth thing, to make them essentially recording devices of the human experience. They are walking archives, rather than archivists. They store what it has been like to be a human being of all genders and ethnicities, all positions and class hierarchies down the centuries and the millennia.

They're rather like – I've been reading a lot about Antarctica for another possible project – these core samples where drills are lowered into ice that is two miles thick and tens of millions of years old. Antarctica is essentially an enormous ice dome, and it's lowered down. They've drilled down and gone to within a few feet of the bottom, and there's an ethical problem about whether they burst through into the original – there are lakes, large, large lakes underneath the ice. They've been sealed off from the rest of the ecosphere for millennia, and the ethical dilemma of whether to go in there with the drills or not is, of course, will we be contaminating it with the antifreeze drill fluid and the outside world, and what if there's something like smallpox down there that is way out of anything our medicine could handle. So they haven't gone through it. But these core samples are retrieved and they're useful for climatology, because there are air bubbles trapped in the core samples, and these are not just images or spectroscopic representations of the earth's atmosphere from ten, twenty, thirty million years ago. It is actually the air – it is the atmosphere, little pieces of the atmosphere, so you can see how much carbon was in it, and compare it with now. You can imagine the results are fairly bad news for us. The atemporals are perhaps core samples. They're recording devices. They're scientific apparati that record the human experience, and I think that's why they are what they are.

How much I go into that, how much I talk about presumably an extra-terrestrial agency that has arranged all this, how many answers I give – that's a really fine line. Give everything, and it is hardcore science fiction; don't give enough and it's slightly unsatisfying mysticism. If you give everything you get indigestion. There's just too much otherness. There's too much off-world stuff. Don't give enough then it's indigestible mysticism – it's just hinted at, and you're constantly flirting and not giving the goods. Yes, I'd have to find the right balance in the middle somewhere, and that's why almost all of these don't really work. The author hasn't quite got the balance right. As you can see, a part of my head is thinking about this book. It's about three books away. I'll be writing about it in my mid-fifties. Maybe I need to be that old to be able to do it, and sort of make sense as well. There are young writers' books, and middle-aged writers' books, and old writers' books. The trick is to write age appropriately!

[1hr 37m 35s]

RHB: I see what you mean! Where does Marinus' vocation as a healer come from? Is it that with that amount of time, and seeing that amount of suffering, she's drawn to this role as a doctor, a helping figure, or is it somewhere else that that's come from?

DM: It's by thinking and looking at other people's immortals, and looking at what they do, and how they live. Ursula Le Guin, in her sci-fi Ekumen sequence, she's got an ancient race of aliens. They live long; they're not immortals, but they are probably the original humanoid life form from which humanity and the others – it's not a densely populated universe, like *Star Trek* or something, and it's not an easily traversable universe as well. There's only near-light-speed travel, so it's suspended animation, and you will not be seeing your kids if you ever leave and come back. So she doesn't violate Einsteinian physics just because it's convenient, which gives her work some heft, I think.

There's a species, I can't remember what she calls them – essentially they were the first, and the other handful were offshoots of them. And the oldest – they're so old, they've done it all. They've done all the political systems you can imagine. They've done all the utopias, all the dystopias you can imagine. They've tried it all. They do not suffer from black-and-white, false, bright tomorrows. They know they're not there. They know all we have is very grey, murky today. They're slow-moving, and wise, and ancient, and plausible, and Taoist, really. Even more than Buddhist. There's an equilibrium which comes from the Earthsea books; her fantasy is shot through with this as well, and I find that very persuasive.

That's part one – let's park that there … Read *The Left Hand of Darkness* and read *The Dispossessed*; I cite those books as evidence of gender-bias in American publishing, in all publishing. If she was male, those books would be mid-twentieth-century American classics by now. They'd be published by Everyman, I'd maintain. But because of the gender bias, and the genre bias, they're not yet, but I think they'll be in print 1,500 years from now. They're just masterly … She's always in the corner of my vision, because she was so important in the beginning of my relationship with my imagination.

So that's there – then looking at when immortals go wrong when they go mad, when they lose it. Anne Rice, actually – *Interview with the Vampire* … When vampires age, because they should be immortal, when they become out of tune with the zeitgeist, when they're no longer walking at the same speed as the rhythm of the world, that's when they start to age, and when decrepitude catches up with them. As long as they're young and vital in spirit, they stay young in body as well. That impressed me very much. It's kind of a counterpoint to what I just said about this original species of Ursula Le Guin's who are quite old and Vulcan-like, to reference *Star Trek*, in their philosophy and outlook. Tom Cruise's character in *Interview with the Vampire* is actually the opposite. He's Peter Pan-ish, almost. So that's hovering around in how I thought I'd cast the atemporals, what I thought they'd be.

This is getting towards your point – why is Marinus a healer? Brevity of life endows life with a meaning. We're only here for a limited number of years. Christ, let's not waste them. I think this structures our minds, our outlooks, maybe what we call our souls more than we think it does: this expiry date we are born with. If that expiry date is removed, and there's no best-before date … The expiry date: if we don't have one, then where do we get a meaning of life from? What are we here for? Existential ennui wouldn't just be something we feel when we're in a melancholic French mood. It would be what kills us in the end. We would die of a lack of meaning, I feel. And this is why I come back to compassion – that's it. That's your meaning. There isn't anything else that brings you fulfilment apart from unfazed compassion. You can't even do it for the gratitude, because then people will know what you are.

On the rare occasions I've done it, when I've really done it, when I've helped someone anonymously – yes, that was it – you know in *The Guardian* recently ... there's a column called 'What I'm really thinking', and it's just three or four hundred words by – allegedly – a call-centre operator, a junior doctor, a 999-operator, the long-distance grandmother are four that come to mind. And there's one by a charity fundraiser. The charity fundraiser said something that really stuck with me: I meet lots and lots of unhappy people, unhappy because of the circumstances they're in. I meet lots and lots of rich unhappy people, who are unhappy despite the money, and not because of their chronic lack of it. People I meet who are happy are the people who are in touch just occasionally – I think he's talking about the rich people who are happy – he says, the only ones who qualify for me are, they're in touch occasionally and they give me a cheque for £100,000. I know who their names are, because their name is on the cheque, but they give it to me on the condition that it goes to this charity who I know and can assure them the money won't get frittered by African civil servants or on expensive marketing campaigns, or whatever. So it's a highly efficient charity in terms of the ratio of the donation that goes to helping the people it's supposed to help. And it's anonymous. And those are the people who are happy, this charity fundraiser said.

That really stuck with me. Somehow, if you want gratitude, if you want something named after you, if you have 'The Bill and Melissa Gates Foundation' over the door, if you've got a seat at the university named after yourself, somehow that cheapens it. You think it makes you happy, in the same way as having a good gossip, you think that makes you happy – or a big mouthful of chocolate biscuit, you think it's going to make you happy. But afterwards, actually, you don't feel that great. You might even know why, which you would with the chocolate biscuits, but not with the named public displays of mega-philanthropy.

So I thought that Marinus and his or her ilk, they're in some Buddhist ideas of hell – this idea of eternal rebirth that you can never get out of. In Zen Buddhism, the point is that it's your desires, and your impurities that keep you coming back, and the purpose is to purge yourself of those, so eventually, finally you can stop it and get off this mad carousel, escalator, rollercoaster-thing. They want to become nothing, that's the point, so they can stop the pain and they can stop the suffering that they feel when they're reborn. I part ways from that slightly ... But Marinus and their ilk, this is where they get their meaning. It's from helping people anonymously, and not even being admired for doing it anonymously. No-one knows they do what they do.

I guess this is at the front of my mind because this is how the meanderers work. They don't get thanked, and they don't even get thanked for not being thanked. They don't even get admired for not being thanked – they're absolutely anonymous. They're in favelas, and mosques, and homeless shelters, and hospitals. Wherever they're needed, that's where they are. They're sometimes in the houses of the rich and the wealthy as well. They're in prisons, and Richard Cheeseman, because he's been in prisons, specializes in prisons, just doing what he can. Yes, he makes mistakes sometimes, yes he doesn't see the whole picture, but you sense that every day of his life as a meanderer has been worth more than his whole forty years as a critic, as an arbiter of taste, as a man of letters, I suppose.

That seemed plausible to me. So that's why Marinus is a healer. He's tried everything else. Everything else he wants, or he wanted, when he was the Falconer's son – he's done it, a hundred times more. But at the end of it, what's the point? This is fulfilment: fixing something that's broken, even if it's just someone who hasn't eaten that day. Now they've got some food there. They didn't have it until you came along, and they wouldn't have had it without you, but now they have. That doesn't need anything more, and that stops them from dying of ennui.

[1hr 52m 20s]

RHB: That's really interesting, the idea of this selfless sense of giving. There's a movement for random acts of kindness, which is a similar kind of thing. You hear about these movements under different names: The New Sincerity, or that kind of thing, about this wave of people who have grown up with the cynicism, if you like, from a Beckettian generation of nihilism, and who are wanting to do good for the sake of doing good – not deconstruct it and disprove the fact that 'good' is even possible, but to reconnect with some kind of ethical, human-based good in the world, I think.

DM: Yes, I think so. I know Margaret Atwood wrote *The Handmaid's Tale* and I remember her saying there's nothing in it she made up. The whole thing about groups of people pulling the rope as someone's being hanged so there's joint responsibility, and they can't afterwards say, it was him, it was her, it was him, it was her. Surrogacy itself; mad, ferocious Christian Evangelism; theocracies: there's nothing in there she made up. She just assembled it in a new form.

For what it's worth, there's nothing in *The Bone Clocks*, nothing in the constitution of the more unseen parts of what I've called my multiverse or my über-book – there's nothing really I've made up. It's from either existing belief systems, or it's simply from the human heart. It's already there. It's in us. There is nothing in the atemporals, or indeed the antagonists in the book, that I haven't seen happening inside me, and the people around me. They're the best parts, and the worst parts. I amplify them and listen to the songs that come back. There's other belief systems where that isn't supernatural. It's simply how it works. Maybe that's the artistic rule with fantasy. It's basically not made up, it's just renamed, and maybe amplified here and there as well, or magnified.

RHB: With that idea that it's not necessarily new, it's just a renamed phenomenon, why did you choose Marinus of Tyre as Marinus' namesake?

DM: I didn't, at first. I found the name when I was looking for names for the *Jacob de Zoet* book. It was there in, I think, the public archive, or the equivalent of the parish records of Zealand, the seaboard province of the Netherlands, the chief town of which is Middelburg. Vlissingen is there, which we call Flushing, because of the war. So that's the part of the world. I was looking for names, because Jacob was going to be from there, and I just found this name amongst all these other Dutch names. It just jumped out at me: Marinus. I thought, well, that's Latin – what's a Latin surname doing amongst a load of Dutch names that are as Dutch as Gouda, with all the Vans ... what's that name doing there? It just jumped out at me, a really distinctive name that seemed out of time, and yet somehow immortal, as well. Then at some point shortly after I must have Wikipedia'd it and found Marinus of Tyre.

What if this sort of nineteenth-century Zealand whoever he or she was – if you were immortal, a serial atemporal who changed his or her body from incarnation to incarnation, you'd want to keep something. You'd want to keep one thing, in the same way that refugees might want to keep one button from their grandmother's cardigan, or something. It's a totem of who or what you were, as you go through all these lifetimes. You just want to keep something that was originally yours, long ago, and you can't. Maybe these days you could; you could rent a box, somewhere in perpetuity with a number-operated keypad that only you could get into. But for most of the last fifteen hundred years that just hasn't been an option. Marinus might have had one life in Amsterdam or something, where strongboxes might have been, but then the next eight lifetimes might have been in other parts of the world that no-one in the Netherlands knew the existence of, and where no-one knew the existence of the Netherlands.

So the only thing you've got is the name. You will be renamed, you will be entering bodies with their own names, and you may be entering a body in the part of the world that speaks a language where there is no letter 'M'. But in your own head, you've got this name, and you take it with you from life, to life, to life. And when you come of age, you want to graft it on to whatever name you land in. If you're in a society that has records, archives and passports, and has options where you can change your name by deed poll, say, then you'd want to do that. So, this is why they like to keep their names near-ish to them, and they like to incorporate it into their adult names after they've come of age, when they have the choice, or they might use it as a nickname. So that's where the name comes from, and that's why he or she keeps using it.

RHB: And why did you choose Bombadil from *Lord of the Rings* for Mark's pseudonym?

DM: It's because he would be a Tolkien nerd ... Tom Bombadil, how interesting he is. I do find him a really interesting character. That first book, *The Fellowship of the Ring* – how *au fait* are you with *Lord of the Rings*, incidentally, Rose?

RHB: Reasonably, actually – I've seen all of the films a few times, and I listened to the massive box set reading of them. We used to listen to them as kids on long car journeys with about a million tapes ...

DM: Yes, yes, done in the early eighties I think, with Michael Hordern as Gandalf. It's been cut, and it needs to be cut, because the first of three books, *The Fellowship of the Ring*, is just a dog's dinner. He didn't know what he was doing – it's all over the shop. If I handed it in to my editor they'd just throw it back at me now. It's great, but it's great for the same reason that it's all great, as a supreme imaginative feat. As the realization of a world in more detail than most worlds ever get realized in, including their linguistics. All the academic disciplines, Tolkien thought about and put in: the history, the ancient history, the languages, the geography, the politics, the economics, the ethnicity, the carbon biology, the ecology, everything. He thought about it. That's why it's got such conviction, that's why it's such a believable world.

As a writer though, my lord! With the first one, he didn't really know what he was doing. There's about a seventy-page section at the house of Tom Bombadil where he presses the pause button on the whole narrative. It's nothing to do with the ring, nothing to do with anything. It's Tom Bombadil – he's kind of a green knight figure, a green man figure. This idiosyncratic nature of the book, where it just goes off on these wild sheep chases – this is actually part of the charm, and part of the genius of the novel that you can do it and not kill the book, and in a weird way, as long as you've got the stamina, it actually enhances the book. No filmmaker, no adapter in his or her right mind could do that and not kill the film, so the Tom Bombadil section's chopped out of the films. One or two of his lines are given to Treebeard the Ent, a kind of token gesture for the cognoscenti. But it's basically gone. Isn't that a bit interesting? Isn't that a bit attractive? I feel a perverse desire to go and have a look at those places.

I feel the same about Shakespeare's oddball plays: *Cymbeline, Pericles, Timon of Athens*, one or two others that never get performed because they're basically dog's dinners. They've got some moments of beauty in them. In the Beatles canon, incidentally, in the byways and sideways of *The White Album*, it seems to happen. In some creative careers, especially where commercial success has already been achieved and proven, or it wasn't really a factor in the first place. Where neither of those are true, they get edited out, in short order. But I'm kind of attracted to them, and I'm not quite sure what to call them. They're errant genius – maybe errant is a good word. They're aberrations in some way. There are quality dips; they're not masterpieces – either the sections, or the songs, or the words. But you can still see hard, glinting, mica-like flashes of beauty, and truth, and genius in them. And they're dog's dinners. But it sort of doesn't matter. So, it just seemed really appropriate for a loner like Bombadil to give himself a name like that: 'I, Bombadil'. And there's a reference to Isaac Asimov's *I, Robot* …

RHB: Yes, of course!

DM: … 'Bombadil' was already taken, so he'd look around for something nearby, and better, and more elusive. So that's it! He's also really annoying; in the book, Tolkien gives him lots of 'Tra-la-das' and 'Hey nonny nos' and 'Hey diddle diddles', and he just sort of skips along. You'd just want to punch his lights out after five minutes in his company, really. But he's one of the necessary wrongnesses in the book that makes the whole thing right. OK, back to you! The last thing is, he's somehow the spirit of spring, and he's indomitable. He's got heritage in the green knight, which Tolkien as a Medievalist would have known much more about than most people then living – or now living, in fact. Back to you!

RHB: Thank you, that was very interesting – I was just going to ask, in *The Bone Clocks*, Marinus says, 'After a thousand years, Cupid's arrows tend to bounce off me'. Do you see this loss of love over time as inevitable for an atemporal human, or has something happened to Marinus to make her feel that way? Given everlasting life, would we lose love?

[2hr 7m 20s]

DM: I think you'd become immune to the cheap tricks of love. By cheap tricks, I mean both obvious chat-up lines, which actually, many people don't need a thousand years to become immune to. Ten years can be plenty! But also in a way that the biological cheap tricks of love, by which I mean the power that sex has over you aged, say, late-teens to early thirties – maybe especially for guys. Marinus knows that it happens, knows that it's your bodies demanding reproduction. She knows that this is how nature perpetuates itself. Yes, she feels it, she sees the hormones, but it's more, 'oh, here we are again'. And once you're able to think that, they have a lot less power over you. So I can't imagine Marinus after two or three hundred years ever falling head-over-heels with someone before, because she knows those acrobatics of those heads and those heels. She's been there, done it – multiple times – and it somehow loses that druggy, intoxicating, 'oh my god, I'm so in love!'

Even when you're in your late forties, like me, you can look back slightly wryly and see it happening in the next generation – two generations behind me now: oh, it's your turn to think that you have a unique love that no-one else in human history has ever encountered before, it's your turn to shut your eyes and actually see the image of the beloved on the inside of your eyelids. Even when you're trying to shut them out, they're there. It's your turn just to have this drug, and to be addicted to it, and it's great while it lasts, and enjoy it. Keep an eye out for the consequences, because it will try to outwit you, and make a baby happen. Yes, she's seen it, and done it. That's why she delivers that slightly world-weary line. The humanistic love is still there; she still loves people. She can still love human beings very much. I don't think their sexuality can be switched off, either. It's just they're so much more knowing and sentient about what happens, about the whole process, because they've done it so very many times.

Doctor Who is maybe the most fully realized immortal in popular culture, because of the number of hours of scripts that exist, and the canonicity that's grown up around it. So that's sort of a useful guide. A doctor is also a healer of course – maybe arrived at for the same reasons. Danny Boyle, who made that film *Sunshine* written by Alex Garland a few years ago – you don't have to have seen [it], it's a science fiction film with spacesuits, that's all you need to know – he said, when he was having the meetings about production, particularly production design, that in the room is every person who's ever had a meeting about spacesuits. How do you show the actors' bloody faces inside the spacesuits? How do you know who is who inside the spacesuits? And he said he was having this meeting, and he could feel the ghost of Stanley Kubrick there, on the other side of the room, and the ghosts of directors from other films. Every person has the same problem: once you've got actors in spacesuits, how do you know who they are? How do you show their faces?

Basically, you eliminate the smaller, less-good possibilities and you plump for some kind of mini-light inside the helmet that shines on to the face, and the name of the astronaut written in big letters on the front of the suit. There's basically not a lot else you can do. And I kind of felt the same, sort of. When you're writing an immortal, everyone who's ever written an immortal is saying: ok, what are you going to do about sexuality, what are you going to do about ennui? What are you going to do about the fact that people, if you're not ageing, will eventually notice that you're not getting any older? What can you do about this?

It's the same small number of questions that come up, and I'd like to think that the collective of writers who have thought about time lords, and the Doctor in particular, they've come to the same conclusion. The Doctor derives satisfaction from fixing broken things, and from co-opting companions' eyeballs, to see the world afresh through them. An intriguing character in the last one, who's a fabulous immortal played by the young girl from *Game of Thrones* – I've forgotten her name. She's made immortal. She's a Viking girl and the Doctor implants some alien technology to save her life, some medical technology, but it stops her ageing forever. Unfortunately, it hasn't enhanced her memory, so she's had all these lives, but she can't remember them that well, so she writes them all down in books. She's a sad, strange, beautiful, really,

really well-realized immortal. The only reason I bring this up is that I'm not quite working alone. I look at what other people have done, where they've gone wrong – which is really instructive – what I like about what they've done, what I don't like about what they've done, and use it to inform my own immortals. Over to you!

RHB: That's fantastic … Reincarnated souls, I think, have featured in your works since *Ghostwritten* had its noncorpum, and the noncorpum learns that he became disembodied as a child, and I think this is the first of the macronovel's forays into reincarnation. I noticed that there, in the text, there's a monk in a saffron robe, who wears a yellow hat that arcs forward, it's described as – which are markers of the Tibetan Buddhist tradition. He attempts to save a child's soul before execution, and that's where the noncorpum comes from: it results in his mind living on after the death of his body. What is it that you wanted to bring to your works with the exploration of reincarnation, both more generally but also with this mythology of the Tibetan or 'yellow hat sect' Buddhism that's referred to?

[2hr 15m 25s]

DM: … It's not really what I wanted to bring to it, it's what *it* brought to it. It allows the fantasist, and the comic-book geek aspect of me, free rein for death to not be death, for it to be a staging point, a roundabout, a carousel. It allows it to be things other than the end. And this can make for rich narrative possibilities that I find tasty, and nourishing. I've learnt to trust that if I do, then readers will as well. That's part one of the answer.

Part two of the answer is kind of interesting. We are sentient human beings – wouldn't it be really weird if we weren't interested in death, if we weren't curious about it, if we weren't curious about the range of possible answers to this big, bad question: what happens afterwards, if anything? It would be odd if we weren't curious about that. I think we are, I think we demonstrably are. I think that's one of the big reasons that religions get invented: to provide reassurance over this very issue, this universal, recurring, multicultural human issue – what happens afterwards. So, it's there in the world, and I'm interested in it, so in it goes!

RHB: I'd also like to ask you about the idea of cyclical time and reincarnation that keeps resurfacing – in Marinus' rebirths, and the repeated victimhood in the structure of *Slade House*, where it's through the cumulative efforts of each of the characters that are caught out that they're able to help future victims, that they're able to, together, break the cycle and make Marinus' journey into that world possible, through each generation leaving something for the one that comes after …

[2hr 17m 50s]

DM: Yes, yes …

RHB: … and the proposed era of the Anthropocene as a new marker of geological time – do you know what I mean there?

DM: Yes, yes I do – the geological era where life and the planet's ecosphere is being engineered by *Homo sapiens* …

RHB: Yes – exactly. So the proposed era of the Anthropocene is a new marker in geological time, which recognizes that human activities have got huge power to permanently change our world; to me, it seems that the Anthropocene is a kind of wake-up call that geological time is all too linear, and that damage to the earth and its species is frighteningly irreversible. By exploring reincarnation and cyclical time as an alternative approach to linear geological time, it seems to me that your works perhaps suggest the value of seeing the cyclical within the linear. So amid the threat of a long, dystopic, linear decline, our ends are still others' beginnings and change is still possible at each given moment in this endless cycle of human births, and rebirths, and experiences. What do you think?

DM: Yes! I'll take that and raise you one. The inevitability of life after the Anthropocene, that even if we wipe ourselves out as a species and take a lot of species down with us – as we've already done, heaven knows – that there will still be life, I find great solace in that. My GP was telling me about a game, I think it's called *Plague*, it's an app that's really popular. You play the role of a virus, of a human-killing microbe, and your job in the game is to wipe out humanity, which sounds revolting, right? But in a way, the beautiful part of it – and this is why my GP was impressed with it – is you can't really win it. You can take out large sections of the human race, but actually because of our immune systems, because of mutation, because of the barriers of medicine that we put up, and quarantine as well, you can't destroy every single human being; at least, in the game there's always enough people who have a natural immunity to any plague you can design to guarantee some kind of regeneration afterwards.

Similarly, whatever damage we do to the earth, even every single nuclear bomb in existence and all the damage that would do – it wouldn't be enough to wipe out everything. Come back in a billion years and just see what's flourishing here. It may come out of the lakes underneath Antarctica, for all I know. But there will always be something – and the chances are, there'd be a lot, lot more than a small something. It would be a big something that would be left after us. And that is hopeful, and a source of hope.

Raising it, I've read this lovely book, *The World Without Us*, it's an American multi-discipline science guy who wrote this book about if human beings all vanished now, what would the world look like say, in twelve hours, in twenty-four hours, in three days, in a week, in a month, in a year, in a decade, in a century, in a thousand years: what would be left of us then. What would be left of us in ten thousand years. Great ending, incidentally: the universe is spherical, so it comes back to the original point in space-time. This is a garbled, poorly remembered layman's version I'm giving you, but if you had a powerful enough telescope and pointed it in any direction, you would eventually see the back of your own head. And what would be left of humans in billions and billions and billions of years would be ever-diminishing, but never quite vanishing, signals that we sent out between the invention of radio waves and the rise of broadband and Wi-Fi which no longer is transmitting our products into outer space. What would be left is about a hundred years' worth of broadcasts and radio waves that would eventually come back to the same spot, because the universe is spherical.

Isn't that cool? Isn't that beautiful? Isn't it an antidote to the pollution, and the spilled mercury sulphate, and the albatrosses dead in oil slicks, and the Russian president's bombing citizens in Syria to provoke refugee crises to hit the economies of the countries that are punishing him with trade sanctions for having invaded the Ukraine, et cetera. Isn't it an antidote to all of that? I find it is. It's out there, so it goes in! That could be the title for your thesis: 'It's out there, so it goes in!'

RHB: Do you want to know what the title of my thesis is so far actually, just as an aside?

DM: Yes! Go on, go on …

RHB: … You can tell me if you think it's rubbish! It's called 'Mitchell's Mandalas: Mapping David Mitchell's Textual Universe'. So there you go!

DM: Oh, fantastic! Mitchell's mandala's – that could be a great backing band, couldn't it? 'And now, for one night only, Rose and Mitchell's mandalas!'

[2hrs 24m 35s]

RHB: Absolutely! Well, we'll see where it goes. So, you've mentioned the idea of your narratives as islands, which I think is a really beautiful way of describing your interlinked stories as part of this larger fictional map. But as much as islands can be interconnected, they've got distinct boundaries, and they can also be places of separation, isolation and confinement. I'm thinking in particular of the panopticon from *number9dream*, in which the first chapter is thoroughly infused with the panopticon, and panopticism. Why did you choose this structure in particular, and how and why do these imprisoning spaces and boundaries function in the macronovel?

DM: Why do I choose islands as settings for a lot of my sections, and themes for my chapters … in a weird way, you've actually answered the question in your question. They do exactly what you said: they isolate, which is where we get the word from, of course, and yet they can also exist in chains. They can also link. They isolate, but they also protect. They guarantee the integrity and the existence of the thing on them as long as they have the means to sustain themselves, as long as there's no invasion. Once they do, as I guess for the Moriori in *Cloud Atlas*, they become places you can't escape from. But it depends if you have boats, doesn't it? If you have boats, then the seas are roads, they're highways, they're motorways. They're flyovers between islands.

If you don't have boats, then they are invisible barriers that they were for the Australian aborigines, that keep them safe for tens of thousands of years, but then stops the knowledge seeping in, which it does into Japan, to Dejima. In a weird way, Dejima is – I've used the metaphor a million times, as you will remember – it's a cat flap, or a keyhole. If you don't have a cat flap, then your being an island is what will kill you in the long run, because you never get the hints, and the rumours, and the artefacts that allow you to develop muskets to defend yourself from the invaders who have got the muskets. It's out there so it goes in, he said lazily – there'll be a T-Shirt with that on before long! And isn't that true? Aren't these things true, and usable, and crackling with narrative possibilities?

What keeps you safe can also be what makes life fatal for you, potentially. It's dangerous, the fact of you being an island. Islands generate identity as well – they answer the 'who am I?' question. You're an islander, and it's called this, so you're British, or you're Japanese, or you're from the Island of Hoy …

I've been thinking a lot about islands recently, and I like them, and I like being on them. I like visiting them. They haunt the memory. They generate interesting species; because of the barrier, we can think about Darwin's finches on the Galapagos islands. I like stories about islands – we all do: *Treasure Island*, *Robinson Crusoe*, *Utopia*, *The Tempest*. I'm not the first person to think this way. When that invisible glass barrier is broken and the Vikings arrive with these kick-ass, superpower boats they had,

Marshall Court had suddenly arrived. There was no decent defence against Vikings for about a hundred, a hundred and fifty years.

And what is an island, anyway? For the aliens in *The War of the Worlds*, earth was an island, the whole planet was an island, and they arrived on it and were like the Vikings, or like the Georgian English, with gunpowder, guns and amputated consciences that led them to give smallpox-infected blankets to Aborigines, to wipe them out with bacteriological warfare as well, to exterminate large numbers of them. When that happens, when there is now a bridge – whether metaphorical, or maritime/ navigational – then you can see civilizations clash, and you can see how technology determines the fates of people. This is all rich, interesting stuff, isn't it?

RHB: Absolutely! What about the panopticon as an idea – where did that come from?

DM: You'll have to remind me, it's been years since I've read or thought about *number9dream* – so it existed in reality of course, it's in penal history. Jeremy Bentham had this idea of supervision leading to reform. How's it used in *number9dream* again? I'm really sorry, it's been years …

RHB: Not at all! So, in *number9dream*, the first chapter is called 'PanOpticon', and Eiji is sitting outside the PanOpticon building, which is where the lawyer is supposedly hiding the secret of Eiji's father's identity. So the title of the chapter is PanOpticon, the name of the building is PanOpticon, and then he goes to the cinema and he watches a movie which is called PanOpticon, which has that interesting mythology which was made into *The Voorman Problem*, the film …

DM: Ok, ok …

RHB: Yes, do you see what I mean? So it seems quite heavily invested in the panopticon and panopticism, and I was just wondering if there was any more behind that?

DM: Yes, I'm a bit vague and fuzzy, and I don't really look at my early books these days, but as I recall – I'm thinking back to me doing media at the time – every chapter of *number9dream*, as far as possible, is told through a separate estate of the mind: memory, or nightmare, or image, or historical memory. There's one or two others. This was all more persuasive at the time, so you might want to go back, if you've got the time and the patience! The first section is generally about daydream, more specifically, the imagination: what is it, what does it do. That's why there's all those Matrix-y type false starts where things are happening that aren't happening, but you think they are. My god, that's a tightrope I come perilously close to falling off! Here and there I think I do.

However, the panopticon: firstly, I liked the word. Secondly, I was interested in prison history at the time, and thirdly, just this idea that you can stand on one place and see all the possible variations that could go on. The imagination is a panopticon, and the prisoners – instead of being a prison panopticon where you can see all of the prisoners doing all of their actions, and there's no such thing as privacy, which incidentally would be quite nightmarish if they applied it to reality, I think. It's no surprise it never really caught on. What you get is *Nineteen Eighty-Four*, I suppose. That's one giant panopticon, isn't it? It's taking the same shape, and applying it to a different zone – the shape is the same. Instead of the panopticon being a prison, the panopticon is a space where you can see all possible outcomes from the centre. It could go this way, it could go that way, it could turn into that, it could go over there.

The idea that this is what the imagination is, and does – it's a point where you can see all possible thought-experiments, all possible outcomes, all possible causal chains from a course of action, without having to pay the penalties for it happening to your body, to your atoms in the physical world. Essentially *2001* was about all of this, where the ape works out that you can actually use a bone as a murder weapon, and it's the black slab that appears that sort of activates the imagination as a faculty of mind.

So there you have it: the panopticon is a metaphor for the imagination, and so many imaginings happen in that chapter because Eiji is standing at the centre of the panopticon, drinking his coffee, sitting in the centre of the panopticon looking round the different angles: it could go this way, it could go that way, it could go this way, my dad could be that, my dad could be this, my dad could be him, it could be that guy over there. It could happen this way, it could happen that way – never actually leaving his stool.

I don't think there's much profundity there, but I'm fascinated in the imagination because it's how I earn a living. I'm fascinated by it, by the evolutionary advantage it gives us. What we'd be without it – I don't think we could even think without it. And it's not just human beings – there are crows … crows get shellfish that their beaks can't get into, they fly above the road, drop it onto the tarmac and either go down and pick up bits from the shattered shell, or they drop them – when they see a bus or a car coming – in your path, so that the chances are good that you'll drive over it, and they'll pick up the bits of shellfish. They can say that crows copied other crows doing that, and that's how they know to do it. But at some point a crow worked it out. At some point, a crow – maybe it was an accident that the crow noticed, and then repeated the accident, perhaps …

RHB: That's amazing, isn't it …

DM: It's interesting, isn't it? And it's out there, so in it goes!

RHB: Wonderful! I know you mentioned in an earlier essay that you used to keep a page headed 'Unobvious Opposites' in your writers' notebook …

DM: Yes, I did, yes …

RHB: So if the entire Mitchellian worldview, the entire macronovel, had an unobvious opposite, what would it be?

DM: Unobvious opposites, they creep up on you and announce themselves. It's like thinking up a metaphor – you can't really do it on demand and be any good. So you have to work out the obvious opposite. The obvious opposite is one small, self-contained narrative that has characters in it that never appear elsewhere, and it's quite short, and has an ABCDE narrative, linear, no jiggery-pokery, no metalepsis, no nothing. So a short novella by Henry James is the obvious opposite of the multiverse! What you can do is not think about it and look at it sideways for a bit – I think I might need to come back to you on that one, Rose; I don't think I can do that on demand. If I do, then I'll come back. It will probably be something like 'Kiwi-fruit! Here's why …'. One more, and then shall we go and think about lunch?

RHB: Yes, absolutely – I was just going to ask if you were planning to attend the Time's Urgency conference in Edinburgh in June …

DM: Yes, I'm speaking at it – I'll be there … I had some interesting conversations that I think are in the public realm, conversations about the nature of times, versus time. I learnt quite a lot from it. Just the idea that linguistically time is singular, but actually it's plural – there are so many different kinds of time. There's a lifespan, there's mayfly time, there's dog year time, there's geological time, there's planetary time. I think our sun's gone nova about three times and has reformed itself into a sun, and has started up again. There's a deep time cycle; suns die, as we all know, but then the gravitational forces exert themselves and the matter of the dead sun starts to reform. So there's even sun time. There's circadian time, the course of a single day. There's dream time. There's times – and interesting things happen when they meet, when they run alongside each other.

I suppose that's what the meanderer idea is all about. There's Marinus time, there's reincarnation time. There's CERN accelerator, particle accelerator time, these tiny, tiny moments where vast things can happen. So yes, I learnt a lot from those conversations, and I accepted this kind invitation not to be the centre of attention, but because I think I'll learn stuff from them!

RHB: … I'll let you go – thank you so much for your time … it is so appreciated, and I'm very grateful.

DM: You too – and the best of luck … until next time, Rose!

[End of interview: 2hr 58m]

David Mitchell: Selected Critical Reading

This list of selected reading on David Mitchell's writing is intended to help provide researchers, teachers, students and those simply curious to find out more about the author's works with a list of useful critical reading, loosely grouped by the author's own publications. However, this list is by no means exhaustive. There are now well over 100 scholarly publications on David Mitchell's works at the time of writing, and, as such, the aim here is to provide readers with a springboard into a range of critical voices, which will themselves lead to further avenues on the author's writing. Happy reading!

Books and journal special issues

Dillon, Sarah, ed. *David Mitchell: Critical Essays*. Canterbury: Gylphi, 2011. Print.

Eve, Martin Paul. *Close Reading with Computers: Textual Scholarship, Computational Formalism, and David Mitchell's Cloud Atlas*. Stanford: Stanford UP, 2019. Print.

Harris, Paul A., ed. *SubStance: David Mitchell in the Labyrinth of Time* 44.136 (2015). Print.

Harris-Birtill, Rose, ed. *C21 Literature: David Mitchell Special Edition* 6.3 (2018). Web.

Knepper, Wendy, and Courtney Hopf, eds. *David Mitchell: Contemporary Critical Perspectives*. London: Bloomsbury Academic, forthcoming. Print.

O'Donnell, Patrick. *A Temporary Future: The Fiction of David Mitchell*. New York: Bloomsbury, 2015. Print.

Ghostwritten

Ballard, Shawn. 'Complex Systems and Global Catastrophe: Networks in David Mitchell's *Ghostwritten*'. *New Directions in Ecocriticism* (2011). Web. 22 July 2014.

Barnard, Rita. 'Fictions of the Global'. *Novel* 42.2 (2009): 207–15. Print.

Boulter, Jonathan. 'Posthuman Temporality: Mitchell's *Ghostwritten*'. *SubStance* 44.136 (2015): 18–38. Print.

Caracciolo, Marco. '"The Bagatelle of Particle Waves": Facing the Hard Problem of Consciousness in Houellebecq's *Les Particules Élémentaires* and Mitchell's *Ghostwritten*'. *Critique: Studies in Contemporary Fiction* 57.5 (2016): 487–501. Print.

Childs, Peter. 'Planetary Novels?: Cosmopolitanism and Globality in and out of a National Literature'. *East-West Cultural Passage* 1 (2011): 9–25. Print.

Dillon, Sarah. 'Chaotic Narrative: Complexity, Causality, Time, and Autopoiesis in David Mitchell's *Ghostwritten*'. *Critique: Studies in Contemporary Fiction* 52.2 (2011): 135–62. Print.

Dunlop, Nicholas. 'Speculative Fiction as Postcolonial Critique in *Ghostwritten* and *Cloud Atlas*'. *David Mitchell: Critical Essays*. Ed. Sarah Dillon. Canterbury: Gylphi, 2011. 201–23. Print. [Also discusses *Cloud Atlas*]

Edwards, Caroline. "Strange Transactions': Utopia, Transmigration and Time in *Ghostwritten* and *Cloud Atlas*'. *David Mitchell: Critical Essays*. Ed. Sarah Dillon. Canterbury: Gylphi, 2011. 177–200. Print. [Also discusses *Cloud Atlas*]

Ganguly, Debjani. 'Spectral Worlds, Networked Novel'. *This Thing Called the World: The Contemporary Novel as Global Form*. Durham: Duke University Press, 2016. 87–109. Print.

Griffiths, Philip. "'On the Fringe of Becoming"–David Mitchell's *Ghostwritten*'. *Beyond Extremes* (2004): 79–99. Print.

Schoene, Berthold. 'Tour Du Monde: David Mitchell's *Ghostwritten* and the Cosmopolitan Imagination'. *College Literature* 37.4 (2010): 42–60. Print.

Selisker, Scott. 'The Cult and the World System: The Topoi of David Mitchell's Global Novels'. *Novel: A Forum on Fiction* 47.3 (2014): 444–60. Print. [Also discusses *Cloud Atlas*]

Shaw, Kristian. "'A Multitude of Drops": The Global Imaginaries of David Mitchell'. *Cosmopolitanism in Twenty-First Century Fiction*. Cham: Palgrave Macmillan, 2017. 27–66. Print. [Also discusses *Cloud Atlas*]

Vermeulen, Pieter. 'David Mitchell's *Ghostwritten* and the "Novel of Globalization": Biopower and the Secret History of the Novel'. *Critique: Studies in Contemporary Fiction* 53.4 (2012): 381–92.

Number9dream

Bayer, Gerd. 'The Ethics of Breaking up the Family Romance in David Mitchell's *Number9dream*'. *Contemporary Trauma Narratives: Liminality and the Ethics of Form*. Eds. Jean-Michel Ganteau and Susana Onega. Abingdon: Routledge, 2014. 120–36. Print.

Harris-Birtill, Rose. "'A Row of Screaming Russian Dolls": Escaping the Panopticon in David Mitchell's *Number9dream*'. *SubStance* 44.136 (2015): 55–70. Print.

Huber, Irmtraud. 'Dreaming of Reconstruction: David Mitchell's *Number9dream*'. *Literature after Postmodernism: Reconstructive Fantasies*. Hampshire: Palgrave Macmillan, 2014. 181–214. Print.

Huber, Irmtraud. 'Interior Monologue'. *Present Tense Narration in Contemporary Fiction: A Narratological Overview*. London: Palgrave Macmillan, 2016. 55–67. Print.

Nihei, Chikako. 'Thinking outside the Chinese Box: David Mitchell and Murakami Haruki's Subversion of Stereotypes about Japan'. *NEW Voices* (2009): 86–103. Web. 5 October 2017. [Also discusses *Ghostwritten*].

Posadas, Baryon Tensor. 'Remediations of "Japan" in *Number9dream*'. *David Mitchell: Critical Essays*. Ed. Sarah Dillon. Canterbury: Gylphi, 2011. 77–103. Print.

Rosen, Jeremy. 'Everywhere at Once and Nowhere Specific: The Generic Sites of the Contemporary Global Novel'. *ASAP/Journal* 2.3 (2017): 627–52. Print.

Simpson, Kathryn. "'Or Something Like That": Coming of Age in *number9dream*'. *David Mitchell: Critical Essays*. Ed. Sarah Dillon. Canterbury: Gylphi, 2011. 49–76. Print.

Veel, Kristin. 'Digital Information Structures in Literary Fiction'. *Narrative Negotiations: Information Structures in Literary Fiction*. Göttingen: Vandenhoeck & Ruprecht, 2009. 85–177. Print.

Cloud Atlas

Baucom, Ian. '"Moving Centers": Climate Change, Critical Method, and the Historical Novel'. *Modern Language Quarterly* 76.2 (2015): 137–57. Print.

Bayer, Gerd. 'Perpetual Apocalypses: David Mitchell's *Cloud Atlas* and the Absence of Time'. *Critique: Studies in Contemporary Fiction* 56.4 (2015): 345–54. Print.

Bentley, Nick. 'Studying Form: Realism, Modernism, Postmodernism and After'. *Contemporary British Fiction*. London: Palgrave, 2018. 12–28. Print.

Danilescu, Andrada. 'Beyond the Human: Transhumanist Negotiations and Posthuman Instantiations in Aldoux Huxley's *Brave New World* and David Mitchell's *Cloud Atlas*'. *Caietele Echinox* 34 (2018): 255–74. Print.

De Cristofaro, Diletta. '"Time, No Arrow, No Boomerang, but a Concertina": *Cloud Atlas* and the Anti-Apocalyptic Critical Temporalities of the Contemporary Post-Apocalyptic Novel'. *Critique: Studies in Contemporary Fiction* (2017): 1–15. Print.

Diamant, Cristina. 'Archiva(b)l(e) Bodies and Cyber Afterlife in David Mitchell's *Cloud Atlas*'. *Caietele Echinox* 34 (2018): 218–28. Print.

Dimovitz, Scott. 'The Sound of Silence: Eschatology and the Limits of the Word in David Mitchell's *Cloud Atlas*'. *SubStance* 44.136 (2015): 71–91. Print.

Economides, Louise. 'Recycled Creatures and Rogue Genomes: Biotechnology in Mary Shelley's *Frankenstein* and David Mitchell's *Cloud Atlas*'. *Literature Compass* 6.3 (2009): 615–31. Print.

Eve, Martin Paul. 'Close Reading with Computers: Genre Signals, Parts of Speech, and David Mitchell's *Cloud Atlas*'. *SubStance* 46.3 (2017): 76–104. Print.

Eve, Martin Paul. '"You Have to Keep Track of Your Changes": The Version Variants and Publishing History of David Mitchell's *Cloud Atlas*'. *Open Library of Humanities* 2.2 (10 August 2016): 1–34. Print.

Front, Sonia. 'Eternal Recurrence and David Mitchell's *Cloud Atlas*.' *Shapes of Time in British Twenty-First Century Quantum Fiction*. Newcastle upon Tyne: Cambridge Scholars Publishing, 2015. 73–96. Print.

Gibson, Rebecca. 'More Than Merely Human: How Science Fiction Pop-Culture Influences Our Desires for the Cybernetic'. *Sexuality & Culture* 21.1 (2017): 224–46. Print.

Hicks, Heather J. '"This Time Round": David Mitchell's *Cloud Atlas* and the Apocalyptic Problem of Historicism'. *Postmodern Culture* 20.3 (2010). Web. 21 February 2014.

Hitchcock, Peter. 'On the Cultural Representation of Labor (Value)'. *Labor in Culture, or, Worker of the World(s)*. Cham: Springer, 2017. 75–100. Print.

Hopf, Courtney. 'The Stories We Tell: Discursive Identity through Narrative Form in *Cloud Atlas*'. *David Mitchell: Critical Essays*. Ed. Sarah Dillon. Canterbury: Gylphi, 2011. 105–26. Print.

Hortle, Luke. 'David Mitchell's *Cloud Atlas* and the Queer Posthuman'. *Lit: Literature Interpretation Theory* 27.4 (2016): 253–74. Print.

Jameson, Fredric. 'The Historical Novel Today, or, Is It Still Possible?' *The Antinomies of Realism*. London: Verso, 2013. 259–313. Print.

Knepper, Wendy. 'Toward a Theory of Experimental World Epic: David Mitchell's *Cloud Atlas*'. *Ariel: A Review of International English Literature* 47.1 (2016): 93–126. Print.

Parker, Jo Alyson. 'David Mitchell's Cloud Atlas of Narrative Constraints and Environmental Limits'. *Time: Limits and Constraints*. Eds. Jo Alyson Parker, Paul A. Harris and Christian Steineck. Vol. 13. Leiden: Koninklijke Brill NV, 2010. 201–18. Print.

Rickel, Jennifer. 'Practice Reading for the Apocalypse: David Mitchell's *Cloud Atlas* as Warning Text'. *South Atlantic Review* 80.12 (2016): 159–77. Print.

Shanahan, John. 'Digital Transcendentalism in David Mitchell's *Cloud Atlas*'. *Criticism* 58.1 (2016): 115–45. Print.

Shoop, Casey, and Dermot Ryan. '"Gravid with the Ancient Future": *Cloud Atlas* and the Politics of Big History'. *SubStance* 44.136 (2015): 92–106. Print.

Sims, Christopher A. 'David Mitchell's *Cloud Atlas*: Cloned AIs as Leaders of an Ontological Insurrection'. *Tech Anxiety: Artificial Intelligence and Ontological Awakening in Four Science Fiction Novels*. Jefferson: McFarland, 2013. 178–222. Print.

Wallhead, Celia, and Marie-Luise Kohlke. 'The Neo-Victorian Frame of Mitchell's *Cloud Atlas*: Temporal and Traumatic Reverberations'. *Neo-Victorian Tropes of Trauma: The Politics of Bearing after-Witness to Nineteenth-Century Suffering*. Eds. Marie-Luise Kohlke and Christian Gutleben. Amsterdam: Rodopi, 2010. 217–52. Print.

Black Swan Green

Brady, Mary. 'Afflictions Related to "Ideals" of Masculinity: Gremlins Within'. *Contemporary Psychoanalysis* 53.2 (2017): 196–208. Print.

Schmitt-Kilb, Christian. 'Gypsies and Their Representation: Louise Doughty's *Stone Cradle* and David Mitchell's *Black Swan Green*'. *Facing the East in the West: Images of Eastern Europe in British Literature, Film and Culture*. Eds. Barbara Korte, Eva Ulrike Pirker and Sissy Helff. Vol. 138. Amsterdam: Rodopi, 2010. 293–308. Print.

Larsonneur, Claire. 'Weaving Myth and History Together: Illustration as Fabrication in David Mitchell's *Black Swan Green* and *The Thousand Autumns of Jacob de Zoet*'. *Image & Narrative* 17.2 (2016): 24–33. Print. [Also discusses *The Thousand Autumns of Jacob de Zoet*]

The Thousand Autumns of Jacob de Zoet

Bayer, Gerd. 'Cannibalising the Other: David Mitchell's *The Thousand Autumns of Jacob de Zoet* and the Incorporation of "Exotic" Pasts'. *Exoticizing the Past in Contemporary Neo-Historical Fiction*. Ed. Elodie Rousselot. Basingstoke: Palgrave Macmillan, 2014. 103–19. Print.

de Waard, Marco. 'Dutch Decline Redux: Remembering New Amsterdam in the Global and Cosmopolitan Novel'. *Imagining Global Amsterdam: History, Culture, and Geography in a World City*. Ed. Marco de Waard. Amsterdam: Amsterdam University Press, 2012. 101–22. Print.

Larsonneur, Claire. 'Revisiting Dejima (Japan): From Recollections to Fiction in David Mitchell's *The Thousand Autumns of Jacob de Zoet* (2010)'. *SubStance* 44.136 (2015): 136–47. Print.

Larsonneur, Claire, and Hélène Machinal. 'Mediations: Science and Translation in *The Thousand Autumns of Jacob de Zoet* by David Mitchell'. *Études britanniques contemporaines* 45 (2013). Web. 5 October 2017.

Matz, Jesse. 'Introduction'. *Lasting Impressions: The Legacies of Impressionism in Contemporary Culture*. New York: Columbia University Press, 2017. 1–35. Print.

Wang, Ching-Chih. 'Dejima as an Imaginary Homeland: The Imag(i)nation of Gaijin in David Mitchell's *The Thousand Autumns of Jacob de Zoet*'. *Harbour Urban Studies* 8 (2013): 41–59. Print.

The Bone Clocks

Callaway, Elizabeth. 'Seeing What's Right in Front of Us: *The Bone Clocks*, Climate
   Change, and Human Attention'. *Humanities* 7.1 (2018): 1–12. Print.
Deckard, Sharae. 'Capitalism's Long Spiral: Periodicity, Temporality and the Global
   Contemporary in World Literature'. *Literature and the Global Contemporary*. Eds. Sarah
   Brouillette, Mathias Nilges and Emilio Sauri. Cham: Springer, 2017. 83–102. Print.
   [Also discusses *Cloud Atlas*]
Harris, Paul A. 'David Mitchell's Fractal Imagination: *The Bone Clocks*'. *SubStance* 44.136
   (2015): 148–53. Print.
Larsonneur, Claire. 'Archipelagos of Apocalypse: Extreme Islands in David Mitchell's
   Cloud Atlas and *The Bone Clocks*'. *Textus (Studies in Italy)*, Tilgher Genova (2016)
   XXIX: 197–211. Web. 5 October 2017. [Also discusses *Cloud Atlas*]
Metz, Joseph. 'Genre Beside Itself: David Mitchell's *The Bone Clocks*, Pulp Intrusions,
   and the Cosmic Historians' War'. *Critique: Studies in Contemporary Fiction* (2016):
   1–8. Print.
Visel, Robin. 'Reading Forward: The Fractal Texts of Doris Lessing and David Mitchell'.
   Doris Lessing Studies 34 (2016): 12–15. Print.

Slade House

Literary review essays on *Slade House* include Brian Finney's review for the *Los Angeles
Review of Books* ('The David Mitchell Übernovel: Brian Finney Reviews "Slade House"',
5 December 2015), Scarlett Thomas' review for the *New York Times* ('David Mitchell's
Slade House', 11 November 2015), Stuart Kelly's review for *The Scotsman* ('Book Review:
Slade House by David Mitchell', 25 October 2015), Liz Jensen's review for *The Guardian*
('*Slade House* by David Mitchell review – like Stephen King in a fever', 29 October 2015),
Paul Harris and Patrick O'Donnell's review of reviews on the University of Wisconsin Press
website ('Slade House in Review(s)', 25 January 2016), and Rose Harris-Birtill's review essay
for *Foundation: The International Review of Science Fiction* ('David Mitchell: *Slade House*'
45.2 (2016): 119–21).

Selected publications on multiple works by David Mitchell

Boulter, Jonathan. 'Humanizing History: David Mitchell'. *Melancholy and the Archive:
   Trauma, History and Memory in the Contemporary Novel*. London: Bloomsbury, 2011.
   101–39. Print. [Discusses *Ghostwritten, number9dream, Cloud Atlas*].
Childs, Peter. 'Food Chain: Predatory Links in the Novels of David Mitchell'. *Études
   Anglaises* 68.2 (2015): 183–95. Print. [Discusses *Ghostwritten, number9dream, Cloud
   Atlas, Black Swan Green, The Thousand Autumns, The Bone Clocks*].
Childs, Peter, and James Green. 'David Mitchell'. *Aesthetics and Ethics in Twenty-First
   Century British Novels: Zadie Smith, Nadeem Aslam, Hari Kunzru and David Mitchell*.
   London: Bloomsbury, 2013. 127–57. Print. [Discusses *Ghostwritten, number9dream,
   Cloud Atlas*]
Childs, Peter, and James Green. 'The Novels in Nine Parts'. *David Mitchell: Critical Essays*.
   Ed. Sarah Dillon. Canterbury: Gylphi, 2011. 25–47. Print. [Discusses *Ghostwritten,
   number9dream, Cloud Atlas*]

Dillon, Sarah. 'Introducing David Mitchell's Universe'. *David Mitchell: Critical Essays.* Ed. Sarah Dillon. Canterbury: Gylphi, 2011. 3–23. Print. [Discusses *Ghostwritten, number9dream, Cloud Atlas, Black Swan Green, The Thousand Autumns, Wake*]

Finney, Brian. 'David Mitchell: Global Novelist of the Twenty-First Century'. *The Contemporary British Novel since 2000.* Ed. James Acheson. Edinburgh: Edinburgh University Press, 2017. 27–36. Print. [Discusses *Ghostwritten, number9dream, Cloud Atlas, Black Swan Green, The Thousand Autumns, The Bone Clocks, Slade House*]

Harris, Paul A. 'Introduction: David Mitchell in the Labyrinth of Time'. *SubStance* 44.136 (2015): 3–7. Print. [Discusses *Ghostwritten, number9dream, Cloud Atlas, Black Swan Green, The Thousand Autumns, The Bone Clocks*]

Harris-Birtill, Rose. '"Looking down Time's Telescope at Myself": Reincarnation and Global Futures in David Mitchell's Fictional Worlds'. *KronoScope: Journal for the Study of Time* 17.2 (2017): 163–81. Print. [Discusses *Ghostwritten, number9dream, Cloud Atlas, Black Swan Green, The Thousand Autumns, The Bone Clocks, Slade House, Wake, Sunken Garden*]

McNally, Lisa. *Reading Theories in Contemporary Fiction.* London: Bloomsbury, 2013. [Discusses *Ghostwritten, Cloud Atlas* and *Black Swan Green*]

Stephenson, William. '"Moonlight Bright as a UFO Abduction": Science Fiction, Present-Future Alienation and Cognitive Mapping'. *David Mitchell: Critical Essays.* Ed. Sarah Dillon. Canterbury: Gylphi, 2011. 225–46. Print. [Discusses *Ghostwritten, Cloud Atlas* and *Black Swan Green*]

Walkowitz, Rebecca L. 'English as a Foreign Language: David Mitchell and the Born-Translated Novel'. *SubStance* 44.2 (2015): 30–46. Print. [Discusses *Ghostwritten, number9dream, Cloud Atlas, Black Swan Green, The Thousand Autumns*]

Libretti and short fictions

Andersen, Tore Rye. 'Staggered Transmissions: Twitter and the Return of Serialized Literature'. *Convergence* 23.1 (2017): 34–48. Print.

Rogers, Holly. '"The Public Will Only Believe the Truth If It Is Shot in 3D": Michel van der Aa, "Nine Years in an Ophanage" (Zenna), *Sunken Garden*, Scene 6'. [*sic*] *Cambridge Opera Journal* 28.2 (2016): 277–82. Print.

Works Cited

Abramson, Seth. 'On Literary Metamodernism'. *Huffington Post*. 20 July 2013. Web. 24 Mar. 2017.

Anand, Dibyesh. *Geopolitical Exotica: Tibet in Western Imagination*. Minneapolis: University of Minnesota Press, 2007. Print.

Asad, Talal. *Formations of the Secular: Christianity, Islam, Modernity*. Stanford: Stanford University Press, 2003. Print.

Astell, Ann W. *Divine Representations: Postmodernism and Spirituality*. Mahwah, NJ: Paulist Press, 1994. Print.

Atwood, Margaret. *MaddAddam*. London: Bloomsbury, 2013. Print.

Atwood, Margaret. *Oryx and Crake*. London: Bloomsbury, 2003. Print.

Atwood, Margaret. *The Year of the Flood*. London: Bloomsbury, 2009. Print.

Avatar. Dir. James Cameron. Perf. Sam Worthington, Zoe Saldana and Stephen Lang et al. 20th Century Fox, 2009. Film.

Aziz, Robert. *The Syndetic Paradigm: The Untrodden Path Beyond Freud and Jung*. Albany: SUNY Press, 2007. Print.

Ballard, Shawn. 'Complex Systems and Global Catastrophe: Networks in David Mitchell's *Ghostwritten*'. *New Directions in Ecocriticism* (2011). Web. 22 Jul. 2014.

Barnes, Jonathan. 'Perspectives: A Kaleidoscopic Imagination'. *The Lancet* 384 (11 Oct. 2014): 1338. *ScienceDirect*. Web. 30 Oct. 2014.

Barthes, Roland. 'The Death of the Author'. 1967. *Image Music Text*. Trans. Stephen Heath. London: Fontana Press, 1977. 142–8. Print.

Batchelor, Stephen. *Buddhism without Beliefs*. 1997. London: Bloomsbury, 1998. Print.

Batchelor, Stephen. 'The other Enlightenment Project: Buddhism, Agnosticism and Postmodernity'. *Faith and Praxis in a Postmodern Age*. Ed. Ursula King. London: Cassell, 1998. Print. 113–27.

Baudrillard, Jean. 'Radical Exoticism'. *The Transparency of Evil: Essays on Extreme Phenomena*. 1990. Trans. James Benedict. London: Verso, 2002. Print. 146–55.

Before the Dawn. Comp. Kate Bush. Hammersmith Apollo, London. Aug. 2014. Performance.

Bentham, Jeremy. *The Panopticon Writings*. 1791. London: Verso, 1995. Print.

Berlant, Lauren. 'Austerity, Precarity, Awkwardness'. *Supervalent Thought*. November 2011. Web. 7 Feb. 2018.

Berlant, Lauren. 'Compassion (and Withholding)'. *Compassion: The Culture and Politics of an Emotion*. Ed. Lauren Berlant. Abingdon: Routledge, 2004. Print. 1–14.

Berlant, Lauren. *Cruel Optimism*. Durham: Duke University Press, 2011.

Bischoff, David. *Mandala*. Berkley: Berkley Science Fiction, 1983. Print.

Boon, Marcus. 'To Live in a Glass House Is a Revolutionary Virtue Par Excellence: Marxism, Buddhism, and the Politics of Nonalignment'. *Nothing: Three Inquiries in Buddhism*. Ed. Marcus Boon, Eric Cazdyn and Timothy Morton. London: University of Chicago Press, 2015. 23–104. Print.

Boon, Marcus, Eric Cazdyn, and Timothy Morton. 'Introduction'. *Nothing: Three Inquiries in Buddhism*. London: University of Chicago Press, 2015. 1–22. Print.

Borggreve, Marco. 'Wake Nationale Reisopera'. Photographs of set design. *Paul Keogan Lighting Design*. 2010. Web. 12 Mar. 2015.

Boxall, Peter. 'A Curious Knot: Terrorism, Radicalism and the Avant-Garde'. *Twenty-First-Century Fiction*. New York: Cambridge University Press, 2013. 123–64. Print.

Boxall, Peter. 'Sovereignty, Democracy, Globalisation'. *Twenty-First-Century Fiction*. New York: Cambridge University Press, 2013. 165–209. Print.

Bradford, Richard. *The Novel Now: Contemporary British Fiction*. Oxford Blackwell, 2007. Print.

Breaking Bad. Dir. Vince Gilligan. Perf. Bryan Cranston et al. AMC, 20 Jan. 2008. Web. 22 Jan. 2017.

Brecht, Bertolt. '*Verfremdung* Effects in Chinese Acting'. 1936. Trans. Jack Davi et al. *Brecht On Theatre*. Eds. Marc Silberman, Steve Giles and Tom Kuhn. London: Bloomsbury, 2014. 151–9. Web. 5 May 2015.

Brett, R. L. *Faith and Doubt: Religion and Secularization in Literature from Wordsworth to Larkin*. Cambridge: James Clarke & Co, 1997. Print.

Brunon-Ernst, Anne. 'Deconstructing Panopticism into the Plural Panopticons'. *Beyond Foucault: New Perspectives on Bentham's Panopticon*. Ed. Anne Brunon-Ernst. Ashgate: Surrey, 2012. 17–41. Print.

Brunon-Ernst, A., and Guillaume Tusseau. 'Epilogue: The Panopticon as Contemporary Icon?' *Beyond Foucault: New Perspectives on Bentham's Panopticon*. Ed. Anne Brunon-Ernst. Ashgate: Surrey, 2012. 185–200. Print.

Bryant, Barry. *The Wheel of Time Sand Mandala: Visual Scripture of Tibetan Buddhism*. 1992. New York: HarperCollins, 1995. Print.

Burke, Seán. *The Death and Return of the Author: Criticism and Subjectivity in Barthes, Foucault and Derrida*. 1992. Edinburgh: Edinburgh UP, 2008. Print.

Burn, Stephen J. 'Reading the Multiple Drafts Novel'. *MFS Modern Fiction Studies* 58.3 (2012): 436–58. Print.

Byatt, A. S. 'Wild World of Ghostly World'. *The Mail on Sunday*. 26 Sep. 1999: 68. Print.

Calvino, Italo. *If on a Winter's Night a Traveller*. 1983. London: Vintage, 1998. Print.

Camus, Albert. 'The Myth of Sisyphus'. Trans. Justin O'Brien. *The Myth of Sisyphus and Other Essays*. 1942. New York: Vintage Books, 1991. Print.

Carruthers, Jo, and Andrew Tate, eds. *Spiritual Identities: Literature and the Post Secular Imagination*. Vol. 17. Bern: Peter Lang, 2010. Print.

Cartwright, David E. 'Schopenhauer's Compassion and Nietzsche's Pity'. *Schopenhauer Jahrbuch* 69 (1988): 557–67. Print.

Casanova, Pascale. *The World Republic of Letters*. 1999. Trans. M. B. DeBevoise. Cambridge, MA: Harvard University Press, 2004. Print.

Childs, Peter. 'Food Chain: Predatory Links in the Novels of David Mitchell'. *Études Anglaises* 68.2 (2015): 183–95. Print.

Childs, Peter, and James Green. 'David Mitchell'. *Aesthetics and Ethics in Twenty-First Century British Novels: Zadie Smith, Nadeem Aslam, Hari Kunzru and David Mitchell*. London: Bloomsbury, 2013. 127–57. Print.

Childs, Peter, and James Green. 'The Novels in Nine Parts'. *David Mitchell: Critical Essays*. Ed. Sarah Dillon. Canterbury: Gylphi, 2011. 25–47. Print.

Chuang, Rueyling. 'Tibetan Buddhism, Symbolism, and Communication Implications in the (Post)Modern World'. *Intercultural Communication Studies* 15.1 (2006): 12–23. Print.

Clark, Imogen. 'Exhibiting the Exotic, Simulating the Sacred: Tibetan Shrines at British and American Museums'. *Ateliers d'anthropologie* 43 (2016). Web. 5 Jan. 2017.

Clayton, Jay. 'Genome Time: Post-Darwinism Then and Now'. *Critical Quarterly* 55.1 (2013): 57–74. Print.

Cloud Atlas. Dir. Lana Wachowski, Tom Tykwer, and Andy Wachowski. Perf. Tom Hanks et al. Warner Bros. Entertainment, 2012. Film.

'Coca-Cola Logo'. The Coca-Cola Company: Enjoying Success in a Changing World. *JulieGilhuly.wordpress.com*. 7 Mar. 2014. Web. 28 Aug. 2015.

'Coca-Cola Theatre'. *World of Coca-Cola*. WorldOfCoca-Cola.com. N.d. Web. 26 Oct. 2016.

Collodi, Carlo. *The Adventures of Pinocchio*. 1883. Trans. Ann Lawson Lucas. Oxford: Oxford UP, 2009. Print.

de Botton, Alain. *Religion for Atheists: A Non-Believer's Guide to the Uses of Religion*. London: Penguin, 2012. Print.

De Cristofaro, Diletta. '"Time, No Arrow, No Boomerang, but a Concertina": *Cloud Atlas* and the Anti-Apocalyptic Critical Temporalities of the Contemporary Post-Apocalyptic Novel'. *Critique: Studies in Contemporary Fiction* (2017): 1–15. Print.

Deleuze, Gilles, and Félix Guattari. *A Thousand Plateaus: Capitalism and Schizophrenia*. 1980. Trans. Brian Massumi. Minneapolis: University of Minnesota Press, 1987. Print.

Dellios, Rosita. 'Mandala-Building in International Relations as a Paradigm for Peace'. *Humanities & Social Sciences papers* 99 (1996): 1–13. Print.

Dellios, Rosita. 'Mandala: From Sacred Origins to Sovereign Affairs in Traditional Southeast Asia'. *CEWCES Research Papers* 8 (2003): 1–15. Print.

Dellios, Rosita. 'Missing Mandalas: Development and Theoretical Gaps'. *Twentieth Century Development: Some Relevant Issues*. Eds. K. C. Roy and R. N. Gosh. New York: Nova Science, 2004. 303–16. Print.

de Man, Paul. *Blindness and Insight: Essays in the Rhetoric of Contemporary Criticism*. 1971. 2nd ed. London: Methuen, 1983. Print.

Derrida, Jacques. 'Faith and Knowledge'. Trans. Samuel Weber. *Acts of Religion*. 1998. Ed. Gil Anidjar. Oxfordshire: Routledge, 2002. 40–101. Print.

Derrida, Jacques. 'Letter to a Japanese Friend'. Trans. David Wood and Andrew Benjamin. *Derrida and Différence*. 1983. Eds. David Wood and Robert Bernasconi. Coventry: Parousia Press, 1985. 1–5. Print.

Derrida, Jacques. *Margins of Philosophy*. 1972. Chicago: University of Chicago Press, 1984. Print.

Derrida, Jacques. *Of Grammatology*. 1967. Trans. Gayatri Chakravorty Spivak. Baltimore: The Johns Hopkins University Press, 1997. Print.

Deudney, E. 'The Archetypal Mandala: Visions of the Self in the Poetry of Coleridge, Eliot and Breytenbach'. *Literator* 15.2 (August 1994): 159–82. Print.

Devitt, Amy J. 'Integrating Rhetorical and Literary Theories of Genre'. *College English* 62.6 (2000): 696–718. Print.

de Vries, Klaas. Interview by Rose Harris-Birtill. Personal Interview. 15 Dec. 2014.

de Waard, Marco. 'Dutch Decline Redux: Remembering New Amsterdam in the Global and Cosmopolitan Novel'. *Imagining Global Amsterdam: History, Culture, and Geography in a World City*. Ed. Marco de Waard. Amsterdam: Amsterdam University Press, 2012. 101–22. Print.

Dillon, Sarah. 'Chaotic Narrative: Complexity, Causality, Time, and Autopoiesis in David Mitchell's *Ghostwritten*'. *Critique: Studies in Contemporary Fiction* 52.2 (2011): 135–62. Print.

Dillon, Sarah, ed. *David Mitchell: Critical Essays*. Canterbury: Gylphi, 2011. Print.

Dillon, Sarah. 'Introducing David Mitchell's Universe'. *David Mitchell: Critical Essays*. Ed. Sarah Dillon. Canterbury: Gylphi, 2011. 3–23. Print.

Doctor Strange. Dir. Scott Derrickson. Perf. Benedict Cumberbatch, Chiwetel Ejiofor, Rachel McAdams et al. Walt Disney Studios Motion Pictures, 2016. Film.

Dutta, Shomit. 'Eiji, Anju, Ai and Goatwriter'. *Times Literary Supplement*. 5019 (2 Mar. 2001): 22. Web. 2 Jan. 2015.

Economides, Louise. 'Recycled Creatures and Rogue Genomes: Biotechnology in Mary Shelley's *Frankenstein* and David Mitchell's *Cloud Atlas*'. *Literature Compass* 6.3 (2009): 615–31. Print.

Edwards, Caroline. '"Strange Transactions": Utopia, Transmigration and Time in *Ghostwritten* and *Cloud Atlas*'. *David Mitchell: Critical Essays*. Ed. Sarah Dillon. Canterbury: Gylphi, 2011. 177–200. Print.

Eve, Martin Paul. 'Close Reading with Computers: Genre Signals, Parts of Speech, and David Mitchell's *Cloud Atlas*'. *SubStance* 46.3 (2017): 76–104. Print.

Eve, Martin Paul. 'Thomas Pynchon, David Foster Wallace and the Problems of "Metamodernism"'. *C21 Literature* 1.1 (2012): 7–25. Print.

Farrell, John. *The Varieties of Authorial Intention: Literary Theory Beyond the Intentional Fallacy*. Cham: Palgrave Macmillan, 2017. Print.

Fike, Matthew A. *The One Mind: C. G. Jung and the Future of Literary Criticism*. New York: Routledge, 2014. Print.

Foucault, Michel. *Discipline and Punish: The Birth of the Prison*. 1975. Trans. Alan Sheridan. London: Penguin, 1977. Print.

Foucault, Michel. 'What Is an Author?' 1969. *The Foucault Reader*. Ed. Paul Rabinow. London: Penguin, 1991. 101–20. Print.

Franklin, Ruth. 'Bursting the Thermometer'. *New Republic* 235.4 (24 Jul. 2006): 25–31. Print.

Frow, John. *Genre*. Abingdon: Routledge, 2006.

Garber, Marjorie. 'Compassion'. *Compassion: The Culture and Politics of an Emotion*. Ed. Lauren Berlant. Abingdon: Routledge, 2004. Print. 15–28.

Garland, Alex. *The Tesseract*. London: Penguin, 1998. Print.

Gessert, George. 'Cloud Atlas'. *Leonardo* 38.5 (2005): 425–45. Print.

Goss, Robert. 'Tibetan Buddhism and the Resolution of Grief: The Bardo-Thodol for the Dying and the Grieving'. *Death Studies*. 21.4 (1997): 377–95. Web. 8 Dec. 2014.

Grey, Maggie. 'The Bhavachakra or Wheel of Life Mandala as a Buddhist Paradigm for International Relations'. *Culture Mandala: The Bulletin of the Centre for East West Cultural and Economic Studies* 7.2 (Dec. 2006): 1–11. Print.

Grey, Maggie. 'Encountering the Mandala: The Mental and Political Architectures of Dependency'. *Culture Mandala: The Bulletin of the Centre for East-West Cultural and Economic Studies* 4.2 (2001): 1–13. Print.

Griffin, David Ray. *God and Religion in the Postmodern World: Essays in Postmodern Theology*. Albany: SUNY Press, 1989. Print.

Griffiths, Philip. '"On the Fringe of Becoming" – David Mitchell's *Ghostwritten*'. *Beyond Extremes* (2004): 79–99. Print.

Guerin, Wilfred L., et al., ed. *Mandala: Literature for Critical Analysis*. New York: Harper & Row, 1970. Print.

Gyatso, Janet. 'Discipline and Resistance on the Tibetan Plateau'. *Cultural Anthropology* (8 Apr. 2012). Web. 5 Oct. 2016.

Gyatso, Tenzin. 'The XIV Dalai Lama: Foreword'. *The Wheel of Time Sand Mandala: Visual Scripture of Tibetan Buddhism*. 1992. Ed. Barry Bryant. New York: HarperCollins, 1995. xi–xii. Print.

Habermas, Jürgen. 'Notes on Post-Secular Society'. *New Perspectives Quarterly* 25.4 (2008): 17–29. Print.

Harris, Clare E. *The Museum on the Roof of the World: Art, Politics, and the Representation of Tibet*. Chicago: University of Chicago Press, 2012. Print.

Harris, Paul A. 'David Mitchell's Fractal Imagination: *The Bone Clocks*'. *SubStance: David Mitchell in the Labyrinth of Time* 44.136 (2015): 148–53. Print.

Harris, Paul A. 'David Mitchell in the Labyrinth of Time'. *SubStance: David Mitchell in the Labyrinth of Time* 44.136 (2015): 3–7. Print.

Harris-Birtill, Rose. 'David Mitchell: *The Bone Clocks*'. *Foundation: The International Review of Science Fiction* 44.1 120 (2015): 131–4. Print.

Harris-Birtill Rose. 'David Mitchell: *Slade House*'. *Foundation: The International Review of Science Fiction* 45.2 124 (2016): 119–21. Print.

Harris-Birtill Rose. '"Looking down Time's Telescope at Myself": Reincarnation and Global Futures in David Mitchell's Fictional Worlds'. *KronoScope: Journal for the Study of Time* 17.2 (2017): 163–81. Print.

Harris-Birtill Rose. '"A Row of Screaming Russian Dolls": Escaping the Panopticon in David Mitchell's *number9dream*'. *SubStance: David Mitchell in the Labyrinth of Time* 44.136 (2015): 55–70. Print.

Harris-Birtill Rose. 'Voicing Tragedy in David Mitchell's Libretti: *Wake* and *Sunken Garden*'. *David Mitchell: Contemporary Critical Perspectives*. London: Bloomsbury, forthcoming. Print (in press).

Harrison, M. John. *Nova Swing*. London: Gollancz, 2006. Print.

Havel, Václav. *Disturbing the Peace: A Conversation with Karel Hvížďala*. New York: Vintage, 1990. Print.

Heninger, S. K. 'A Jungian Reading of "Kubla Khan"'. *Journal of Aesthetics and Art Criticism* 18.3 (1960): 358–67. Print.

Hicks, Heather J. '"This Time Round": David Mitchell's *Cloud Atlas* and the Apocalyptic Problem of Historicism'. *Postmodern Culture* 20.3 (2010). Web. 21 Feb. 2014.

Higashida, Naoki. *Fall Down 7 Times Get Up 8*. Trans. David Mitchell and K. A. Yoshida. London: Sceptre, 2017. Print.

Higashida, Naoki. *The Reason I Jump*. Trans. K. A. Yoshida and David Mitchell. London: Sceptre, 2013. Print.

Hoad, Phil. '*Cloud Atlas*: How Hollywood Failed to Put It on the Map'. *The Guardian* (20 Feb. 2013). Web. 22 Sep. 2014.

Hoban, Russell. *Riddley Walker*. 1980. London: Bloomsbury, 2002. Print.

Hoogenboezem, Jan, Joop Garssen, and Lenny Stoeldraijer. 'More Suicides since 2008'. *Statistics Netherlands / Centraal Bureau voor de Statistiek (CBS)*. 24 Oct. 2013. Web. 20 Apr. 2018.

Hopf, Courtney. 'The Stories We Tell: Discursive Identity through Narrative Form in *Cloud Atlas*'. *David Mitchell: Critical Essays*. Ed. Sarah Dillon. Canterbury: Gylphi, 2011. 105–26. Print.

House of Cards. Dir. Beau Willimon. Perf. Kevin Spacey et al. Netflix, 1 Feb. 2013. Web. 22 Jan. 2017.

Huber, Irmtraud. *Literature after Postmodernism: Reconstructive Fantasies*. Hampshire: Palgrave Macmillan, 2014. Print.

Huh, Jung A. 'Mandala as Telematic Design'. *Technoetic Arts* 8.1 (2010): 19–30. Print.

Iyer, Pico. 'The Concertina of Time'. *Time* 164.8 (23 Aug. 2004): 67. Print.

Jacobson, Michael F. *Liquid Candy: How Soft Drinks Are Harming Americans' Health*. Washington, DC: Center for Science in the Public Interest, 2005. Print.

James, David, and Urmila Seshagiri. 'Metamodernism: Narratives of continuity and revolution'. *PMLA* 129.1 (2014): 87–100. Print.

Jameson, Fredric. *The Antinomies of Realism*. London: Verso, 2013. Print.

Jameson, Fredric. *The Cultural Turn*. London: Verso Press, 1998. Print.

Jameson, Fredric. 'The Historical Novel Today, or, Is It Still Possible?' *The Antinomies of Realism*. London: Verso, 2013. 259–313. Print.

Jänicke, S., G. Franzini, M. F. Cheema and G. Scheuermann. 'On Close and Distant Reading in Digital Humanities: A Survey and Future Challenges'. *Eurographics Converence on Visualization*, Italy: The Eurographics Association, 2015. Web.

Jung, C. G. *The Archetypes and the Collective Unconscious*. 1959. Trans. R. F. C. Hull, 2nd ed. London: Routledge & Kegan Paul, 1969. Print.

Jung, C. G. 'The Difference between Eastern and Western Thinking'. *The Collected Works of C. G. Jung: Psychology and Religion: West and East*. Trans. R. F. C. Hull. Vol. 11. New York: Pantheon Books, 1958. 475–93. Print.

Jung, C. G. 'Psychology and Religion'. *The Collected Works of C. G. Jung: Psychology and Religion: West and East*. Trans. R. F. C. Hull. Vol. 11. New York: Pantheon Books, 1958. 3–106. Print.

King, Ursula, ed. *Faith and Praxis in a Postmodern Age*. London: Cassell, 1998. Print.

Konik, Michael. 'On Not Getting Away from It All'. *The New York Times* (1991). Web. 10 Feb. 2016.

Krippner, Stanley. 'The Role Played by Mandalas in Navajo and Tibetan Rituals'. *Anthropology of Consciousness* 8.1 (1997): 22–31. Print.

Krishnaswamy, Revathi. 'The Criticism of Culture and the Culture of Criticism: At the Intersection of Postcolonialism and Globalization Theory'. *Diacritics* 32.2 (2002): 106–26. Print.

Kulish, Nicholas, and Michael Cieply. 'Around the World in One Movie: Film Financing's Global Future'. *The New York Times* (6 Dec. 2011): A1. Web. 22 Sep. 2014.

Larson, Kay. 'Sands of Time'. *New York Magazine* (29 Aug. 1988): 64–66. Print.

The Last Mimzy. Dir. Robert Shaye. Perf. Joely Richardson. New Line Cinema, 2007. Film.

Larsonneur, Claire. 'Revisiting Dejima (Japan): From Recollections to Fiction in David Mitchell's *The Thousand Autumns of Jacob de Zoet* (2010)'. *SubStance: David Mitchell in the Labyrinth of Time* 44.136 (2015): 136–47. Print.

Le Guin, Ursula K. 'The Bone Clocks by David Mitchell – Dazzle of Narrative Fireworks'. *The Guardian* (2 Sep. 2014). Web. 24 Sep. 2014.

Lehman, Briana. 'The Colburn Orchestra Play Takemitsu – "From Me Flows What You Call Time"'. *Open Call*. 3 May 2012. Web. 12 Mar. 2015.

Leidy, Denise Patry, and Robert A. F. Thurman. *Mandala: The Architecture of Enlightenment*. Boston: Shambala, 1997. Print.

Lewis, Simon L., and Mark A. Maslin. 'Defining the Anthropocene'. *Nature* 519 (12 Mar. 2015): 171–80. Print.

Lukács, Georg. *The Theory of the Novel*. 1920. Trans. Anna Bostock. Cambridge, MA: MIT Press, 1971. Print.

Lyotard, Jean-François. *The Postmodern Condition: A Report on Knowledge*. 1979. Trans. Geoff Bennington and Brian Massumi. Manchester: Manchester University Press, 1984. Print.

Machinal, Hélène. '*Cloud Atlas*: From Postmodernity to the Posthuman'. *David Mitchell: Critical Essays*. Ed. Sarah Dillon. Canterbury: Gylphi, 2011. 127–54. Print.

Manley, Katherine. Interview by Rose Harris-Birtill. Personal interview. 11 Feb. 2015.

Manos, John K. 'Tibetan Buddhism'. *Salem Press Encyclopedia*. Ipswich: Salem Press, 2016. Web. 4 May 2016.

Martel, Yann. *Life of Pi*. Edinburgh: Canongate Books, 2002. Print.

The Matrix. Dir. Andy Wachowski and Lana Wachowski. Perf. Keanu Reeves et al. Warner Bros. Entertainment, 1999. Film.

The Matrix Reloaded. Dir. Andy Wachowski and Lana Wachowski. Perf. Keanu Reeves, et al. Warner Bros. Entertainment, 2003. Film.

The Matrix Revolutions. Dir. Andy Wachowski and Lana Wachowski. Perf. Keanu Reeves et al. Warner Bros. Entertainment, 2003. Film.

McCarthy, Cormac. *The Road*. London: Pan Macmillan, 2006. Print.

McClure, John. *Partial Faiths: Postsecular Fiction in the Age of Pynchon and Morrison*. Athens: University of Georgia Press, 2007.

McClure, John. 'Postmodern/Post-Secular: Contemporary Fiction and Spirituality'. *MFS Modern Fiction Studies* 41.1 (1995): 141–63. Print.

McEwan, Ian. *Saturday*. 2005. London: Random House, 2006. Print.

McFadden, Claron. Interview by Rose Harris-Birtill. Personal interview. 22 Feb. 2015.

McGranahan, Carole, and Ralph Litzinger. 'Self-Immolation as Protest in Tibet'. *Cultural Anthropology* (9 Apr. 2012). Web. 15 Aug. 2016.

McLagan, Meg. 'Spectacles of Difference: Cultural Activism and the Mass Mediation of Tibet'. *Media Worlds: Anthropology on New Terrain*. Eds. Faye D. Ginsburg, Lila Abu-Lughod and Brian Larkin. London: University of California Press, 2002. 90–111. Print.

McMorran, Will. ''Cloud Atlas and *If on a Winter's Night a Traveller*: Fragmentation and Integrity in the Postmodern Novel'. *David Mitchell: Critical Essays*. Ed. Sarah Dillon. Canterbury: Gylphi, 2011. 155–75. Print.

Mitchell, David. 'Acknowledgements'. *Prospect* 115 (Oct. 2005). Web. 22 Sep. 2014.

Mitchell, David. 'A Forgettable Story'. *Silkroad* (30 Jun. 2017). Web. 29 Sep. 2017.

Mitchell, David. 'All Souls Day'. *Jealous Saboteurs*. 2010. Francis Upritchard. Melbourne: Monash University Museum of Art, 2016. 78–86. Print.

Mitchell, David. 'Asia in English Literature'. *Asia's Literary Journal* 12 (Autumn 2005): 12–17. Print.

Mitchell, David. *Black Swan Green*. London: Sceptre, 2006. Print.

Mitchell, David. 'Black Swan Green Revisited'. *The British Stammering Association* (1 Mar. 2011). Web. 10 Jan. 2016.

Mitchell, David. *The Bone Clocks*. London: Sceptre, 2014. Print.

Mitchell, David. 'The Book of Revelations'. *The Guardian* (5 Feb. 2005). Web. 23 Sep. 2014.

Mitchell, David. 'Character Development'. *Freedom: Short Stories Celebrating the Universal Declaration of Human Rights*. Edinburgh: Mainstream Publishing Company, 2009. 125–35. Print.

Mitchell, David. *Cloud Atlas*. London: Sceptre, 2004. Print.

Mitchell, David. 'David Mitchell: Adventures in Opera'. *The Guardian* (8 May 2010). Web. 12 Mar. 2015.

Mitchell, David. 'David Mitchell: Almost Everything I'd Been Told About My Son's Autism Was Wrong'. *New Statesman* (8 Jul. 2017). Web. 22 Aug. 2017.

Mitchell, David. 'David Mitchell on Earthsea – a Rival to Tolkien and George RR Martin'. *The Guardian* (23 Oct. 2015). Web. 9 Jan. 2017.

Mitchell, David. 'David Mitchell on Historical Fiction'. *The Telegraph* (8 May 2010). Web. 23 Sep. 2014.

Mitchell, David. 'David Mitchell: What My Son's Autism Has Taught Me'. *The Guardian* (8 Jul. 2017). Web. 22 Aug. 2017.

Mitchell, David. 'Dénouement'. *The Guardian* (26 May 2007). Web. 10 Jan. 2016.

Mitchell, David. *Dreizehn Arten das Stottern zu betrachten.* Köln: Demosthenes, 2016. Print.

Mitchell, David. 'Earth Calling Taylor'. *Financial Times* (30 Dec. 2010). Web. 28 Aug. 2015.

Mitchell, David. 'The Earthgod and the Fox'. *McSweeney's: Multiples* 42 (2012): 59–77. Print.

Mitchell, David. 'Enter the Maze'. *The Guardian* (22 May 2004). Web. 23 Sep. 2014.

Mitchell, David. 'Foreword'. *David Mitchell: Critical Essays.* Ed. Sarah Dillon. Canterbury: Gylphi, 2011. 1–2. Print.

Mitchell, David. 'The Gardener'. *The Guardian* (6 Jun. 2011). Web. 12 Mar. 2015.

Mitchell, David. *Ghostwritten.* London: Sceptre, 1999. Print.

Mitchell, David. 'Guardian Book Club: Cloud Atlas by David Mitchell'. *The Guardian* (12 Jun. 2010). Web. 10 Jan. 2016.

Mitchell, David. 'Hangman'. *New Writing 13.* Eds. Ali Smith and Toby Litt. London: Picador, 2005. 90–105. Print.

Mitchell, David. 'I_Bombadil'. Twitter. 31 Oct. 2015. Web. 10 Jan. 2016.

Mitchell, David. 'Imaginary City'. *Geist* 80 (Spring 2011). Web. 10 Jan. 2016.

Mitchell, David. 'An Inside Job'. *Fighting Words.* Ed. Roddy Doyle. Dublin: Stoney Road Press, 2012. 35–7. Print.

Mitchell, David. Interview by Richard Beard. 'David Mitchell Interview'. *RichardBeard. info.* Tokyo University. 12 Jan. 2005. Web. 24 Sep. 2014.

Mitchell, David. Interview by Adam Begley. 'David Mitchell: The Art of Fiction No. 204'. *The Paris Review.* 2010. Web. 23 Sep. 2014.

Mitchell, David. Interview by Robert Birnbaum. 'David Mitchell'. *The Morning News.* 11 May 2006. Web. 23 Sep. 2014.

Mitchell, David. Interview by Wayne Burrows. 'An Interview with David Mitchell on Cloud Atlas, Murakami, Money and the Sinclair ZX Spectrum'. *The Big Issue in the North.* 2 Mar. 2004. Web. 24 Sep. 2014.

Mitchell, David. Interview by Edward Champion. 'David Mitchell'. *The Bat Segundo Show.* 6 Oct. 2004. Web. 10 Jan. 2016.

Mitchell, David. Interview by Edward Champion. 'David Mitchell II, Part One'. *The Bat Segundo Show.* 16 Aug. 2006. Web. 10 Jan. 2016.

Mitchell, David. Interview by Edward Champion. 'David Mitchell III'. *The Bat Segundo Show.*11 Aug. 2010. Web. 10 Jan. 2016.

Mitchell, David. Interview by Tom Cox. 'Black Swan Green'. *The Times.* TheTimes.co.uk. 16 Dec. 2006. Web. 15 Aug. 2016.

Mitchell, David. Interview by Mike Doherty. '"It's Stupid, It Shouldn't Work"'. *Maclean's* (9 Aug. 2014): 72. Web. 10 Jan. 2016.

Mitchell, David. Interview by Tishani Doshi. 'Secret Architectures'. *The Hindu.* 1 Jul. 2007. Web. 4 Dec. 2014.

Mitchell, David. Interview by Claire Fallon. '"The Bone Clocks" Author David Mitchell: Self-Described "Sucker for Punishment"'. *Huffington Post.* 18 Sep. 2014. Web. 10 Jan. 2016.

Mitchell, David. Interview by Alison Flood. '*Cloud Atlas* Author Translates Autistic Teenager's Memoir'. *The Guardian.* 26 Feb. 2013. Web. 24 Sep. 2014.

Mitchell, David. Interview by Harriet Gilbert. 'World Book Club: David Mitchell – Cloud Atlas'. *BBC World Service.* Apr. 2010. Web. 24 Sep. 2014.

Mitchell, David. Interview by Goodreads. 'Interview with David Mitchell'. *Goodreads.com.* Sep. 2014. Web. 12 Jun. 2015.

Mitchell, David. Interview by Andrew Graham-Dixon. 'Andrew Graham-Dixon Interviews David Mitchell'. Andrewgrahamdixon.com. 18 Aug. 2010. Web. 24 Sep. 2014.

Mitchell, David. Interview by Laurie Grassi. 'Best-Selling Author David Mitchell on His Biggest Wow Moment'. *Chatelaine.* Chatelaine.com. 2 Sep. 2014. Web. 10 Aug. 2016.

Mitchell, David. Interview by Paul A. Harris. 'David Mitchell in the Laboratory of Time: An Interview With the Author'. *SubStance: David Mitchell in the Labyrinth of Time.* 2015: 8–17. Print. 21 May 2015.

Mitchell, David. Interview by Rose Harris-Birtill. Personal interview. 14 Aug. 2015.

Mitchell, David. Interview by Rose Harris-Birtill. Personal interview. 12 Feb. 2016.

Mitchell, David. Interview by Herald Scotland. 'Sex, drugs and Talking Heads in writer's latest incarnation'. *Herald Scotland.* 7 Sep. 2014. Web. 20 Mar. 2018.

Mitchell, David. Interview by Ron Hogan. 'David Mitchell: "I got rid of my TV – that was the first, crucial thing"'. *Beatrice Interview.* N.d. Web. 4 Dec. 2014.

Mitchell, David. Interview by Stuart Jeffries. 'David Mitchell: "I Don't Want to Project Myself as This Great Experimenter"'. *The Guardian.* 8 Feb. 2013. Web. 24 Sep. 2014.

Mitchell, David. Interview by James Kidd. 'Time and Again: The Critically Acclaimed Novelist David Mitchell on Life, Death and Everything in Between'. *The National.* 9 Oct. 2014. Web. 12 Mar. 2015.

Mitchell, David. Interview by Elmira Kuznetsova. 'Writer David Mitchell Talks About the *Cloud Atlas* Film Subtext'. *Prime Time Russia.* Reuters. 11 Sep. 2013. Web. 23 Sep. 2014.

Mitchell, David. Interview by John Lopez. 'Q&A with David Mitchell, Literary Platypus'. *Vanity Fair.* 20 Jul. 2014. Web. 24 Sep. 2014.

Mitchell, David. Interview by Michael MacLeod. 'David Mitchell: "I Have Created My Own Middle Earth"'. *The Guardian.* 17 Aug. 2015. Web. 25 Aug. 2017.

Mitchell, David. Interview by Wyatt Mason. 'David Mitchell, the Experimentalist'. *The New York Times.* 25 Jun. 2010. Web. 23 Sep. 2014.

Mitchell, David. Interview by Simon Mayo. 'Radio 2 Book Club: David Mitchell'. *BBC Radio 2.* 8 Sep. 2015. Radio. 10 Jan. 2016.

Mitchell, David. Interview by Andrei Muchnik. 'David Mitchell Talks About Moscow, Literature and the Future'. *Moscow Times.* 13 Sep. 2013. Web. 2 Oct. 2014.

Mitchell, David. Interview by Loranne Nasir. 'David Mitchell: LibraryThing Author Interview'. *LibraryThing.com* (2015). Web. 15 Feb 2016.

Mitchell, David. Interview by David Pilling. 'Lunch with the FT: David Mitchell'. *FT Weekend Magazine.* 12. 24 Aug. 2007. Web. 24 Sep. 2014.

Mitchell, David. Interview by Jasper Rees. '10 Questions for Writer David Mitchell'. Theartsdesk.com. 10 Apr. 2013. Web. 23 Sep. 2014.

Mitchell, David. Interview by James Rocchi. 'Interview: Novelist David Mitchell of "Cloud Atlas"'. *The Hitlist: the MSN Movies Blog.* 8 Nov. 2012. Web. 24 Sep. 2014.

Mitchell, David. Interview by Zack Ruskin. '"The Blank Screen Is the Enemy": The Millions Interviews David Mitchell'. *The Millions.* TheMillions.com. 29 Oct. 2014. Web. 15 Aug. 2016.

Mitchell, David. Interview by Zahra Saeed. 'Cork-Based Cloud Atlas Author David Mitchell on Twitter, His Children, and Latest Novel'. *Irish Examiner.* IrishExaminer. com. 4 Sep. 2014. Web. 15 May 2016.

Mitchell, David. Interview by Shanghai TV. '2012 Shanghai Book Fair'. *Reading Tonight.* YouTube. 21 Aug. 2012. Web. 2 Oct. 2014.

Mitchell, David. Interview by Michael Silverblatt. 'David Mitchell on Bookworm'. *Bookworm.* KCRW, Los Angeles. 2002. Web. 4 Dec. 2014.

Mitchell, David. Interview by Boyd Tonkin. 'David Mitchell Interview: "It's High Stakes. Do It Wrong and You've Got a Broken Book"'. *The Independent.* Independent.co.uk. 5 Sep. 2014. Web. 24 Aug. 2017.

Mitchell, David. Interview by Lana Wachowski. 'David Mitchell with Lana Wachowski at the Music Box Theatre 4 of 5'. *YouTube.* 9 Nov. 2015. Web. 10 Jan. 2016.

Mitchell, David. Interview by Eleanor Wachtel. "'Cloud Atlas" with Author David Mitchell'. 2004. *CBC Radio*. 21 Nov. 2012. Radio. 10 Jan. 2016.

Mitchell, David. Interview by Erica Wagner. 'David Mitchell, the Master Builder'. *New Statesman*. NewStatesman.com. 2 Oct. 2014. 58–61. Web. 15 May 2016.

Mitchell, David. Interview by Christopher Wallace. 'The Expansive David Mitchell'. *Interview Magazine*. 1 Oct. 2014. Web. 12 Mar. 2015.

Mitchell, David. Interview by Geordie Williamson. 'David Mitchell in Conversation with Geordie Williamson'. 2011. YouTube. 2 May 2013. Web. 28 Aug. 2015.

Mitchell, David. 'In the Bike Sheds'. *The Bookseller: We Love This Book* (20 Jun. 2012). Web. 28 Aug. 2012.

Mitchell, David. 'The January Man'. *Granta: Best of Young British Novelists 3*. 81 (Spring 2003). Web. 10 Jan. 2016.

Mitchell, David. 'Japan and My Writing'. *Bold Type* 4.7 (Nov. 2000). Web. 22 Sep. 2014.

Mitchell, David. 'Judith Castle'. *The Book of Other People*. Ed. Zadie Smith. London: Hamish Hamilton, 2007. 3–18. Print.

Mitchell, David. 'Learning to Live with My Son's Autism'. *The Guardian* (29 Jun. 2013). Web. 22 Sep. 2014.

Mitchell, David. 'Let Me Speak'. *The British Stammering Association* (1 Jun. 2006). Web. 22 Sep. 2014.

Mitchell, David. 'Lost for Words'. *Prospect* (Mar. 2011). Web. 22 Sep. 2014.

Mitchell, David. 'Lots of Bits of Star'. *Caught by the Nest*. Kai Clements and Anthony Sunter. London: Kai & Sunny, 2013. Print.

Mitchell, David. 'The Massive Rat'. *The Guardian* (1 Aug. 2009). Web. 10 Jan. 2016.

Mitchell, David. 'Mongolia'. *New Writing 8*. Eds. Tibor Fischer and Lawrence Norfolk. Vol. 8. London: Vintage, 1999. 514–61. Print.

Mitchell, David. 'Muggins Here'. *The Guardian* (14 Aug. 2010). Web. 10 Jan. 2016.

Mitchell, David. 'Music for a Lost Horologist: A *Bone Clocks* Playlist'. *BBC Radio 4: Book at Bedtime*. 2014. Web. 12 Mar. 2015.

Mitchell, David. 'My Eye On You'. *Whirlwind of Time*. Kai Clements and Anthony Sunter. London: Kai & Sunny, 2016. Print.

Mitchell, David. 'My life before writing: David Mitchell on dreams of being a lighthouse keeper'. *The Guardian* (24 Jun. 2016). Web. 26 Sep. 2017.

Mitchell, David. *number9dream*. London: Sceptre, 2001. Print.

Mitchell, David. 'On Becoming a Non-Stammering Stammerer'. *BlackSwanGreen.co.uk* (9 May 2006). Web. 28 Aug. 2015.

Mitchell, David. 'Once Upon a Life: David Mitchell'. *The Guardian* (9 May 2010). Web. 10 Jan. 2016.

Mitchell, David. 'Preface'. *The Daily Telegraph* (29 Apr. 2006). *Nexis*. Web. 10 Jan. 2016.

Mitchell, David. 'The Reason I Jump – Book of the Week'. *The Radio 4 Blog* (21 Jun. 2013). Web. 10 Jan. 2016.

Mitchell, David. 'The Right Sort'. Twitter. 20 Jul. 2014. Web. 22 Sep. 2014.

Mitchell, David. 'The Siphoners'. *I'm with the Bears: Short Stories from a Damaged Planet*. Ed. Mark Martin. London: Verso, 2011. Print.

Mitchell, David. 'Six Shorts'. *Freeman's: The Best New Writing on Arrival*. Ed. John Freeman. London: Grove Press UK, 2015. 19–21. Print.

Mitchell, David. *Slade House*. London: Sceptre, 2015. Print.

Mitchell, David. 'A Sublime Search for the Ancient Sagas in Iceland'. *The Independent* (20 Jul. 2012). Web. 22 Sep. 2014.

Mitchell, David. *The Thousand Autumns of Jacob de Zoet*. London: Sceptre, 2010. Print.

Mitchell, David. 'Variations on a Theme by Mister Donut'. *Granta: Japan*. 127 (Spring 2014): 39–61. Print.

Mitchell, David. 'The View from Japan'. *The Telegraph* (14 Oct. 2007). Web. 24 Sep. 2014.

Mitchell, David. 'What Use Are Dreams in Fiction?' *Journal of European Studies* 38.4 (Dec. 2008): 431–41. Print.

Mitchell, David. 'What You Do Not Know You Want'. *McSweeney's Enchanted Chamber of Astonishing Stories*. Ed. Michael Chabon. New York: Vintage, 2004. 11–31. Print.

Mitchell, Kaye. *Intention and Text: Towards an Intentionality of Literary Form*. London: Continuum, 2008.

Moretti, Franco. 'Conjectures on World Literature'. *New Left Review* 1 (2000): 54–68. Print.

Moretti, Franco. *Distant Reading*. London: Verso, 2013. Print.

Moretti, Franco. *Graphs, Maps, Trees: Abstract Models for a Literary History*. London: Verso, 2005. Print.

Moretti, Franco. *Modern Epic: The World-System from Goethe to García Márquez*. London: Verso, 1996. Print.

Moretti, Franco. 'World-Systems Analysis, Evolutionary Theory, "Weltliteratur"'. *Review (Fernand Braudel Center)* 28.3 (2005): 217–28. Print.

Muste, John M. 'The Mandala in *Gravity's Rainbow*'. *Boundary 2* 9.2 (1981): 163–80. Print.

Ng, Lynda. 'Cannibalism, Colonialism and Apocalypse in Mitchell's Global Future'. *SubStance: David Mitchell in the Labyrinth of Time* 44.136 (2015): 107–22. Print.

Niemöller, Martin. 'First They Came for the Jews'. *Holocaust Poetry*. 1946. Ed. H. Schiff. New York: St Martin's Press, 1995. 9. Print.

Nietzsche, Friedrich. *Daybreak: Thoughts on the Prejudices of Morality*. 1881. Trans. R. J. Hollingdale. Cambridge: Cambridge University Press, 1997. Print.

Nietzsche, Friedrich. *The Gay Science*. 1882. Trans. Josefine Nauckhoff. Ed. Bernard Williams. Cambridge: Cambridge University Press, 2001. Print.

Nietzsche, Friedrich. *Thus Spoke Zarathustra*. 1883. Trans. Adrian Del Caro. Eds. Adrian Del Caro and Robert Pippin. Cambridge: Cambridge University Press, 2006. Print.

Norbu, Jamyang. *The Mandala of Sherlock Holmes*. New York: Bloomsbury, 1999. Print.

Norell, Donna. 'The Novel as Mandala: Colette's *Break of Day*'. *Women's Studies* 8 (1981): 313–33. Print.

O'Donnell, Patrick. *A Temporary Future: The Fiction of David Mitchell*. New York: Bloomsbury, 2015. Print.

Ondaatje, Michael. *Anil's Ghost*. 2000. London: Bloomsbury, 2011. Print.

Orange is the New Black. Dir. Jenji Kohan. Perf. Taylor Schilling et al. Netflix, 11 Jul. 2013. Web. 22 Jan. 2017.

Ostwalt, Conrad. *Secular Steeples: Popular Culture and the Religious Imagination*. 2nd ed. London: Bloomsbury, 2012. Print.

Ozeki, Ruth. *A Tale for the Time Being*. Edinburgh: Canongate, 2013. Print.

Packard, Edward. *The Mystery of Chimney Rock*. Choose Your Own Adventure. New York: Bantam Books, 1979. Print.

Parker, Jo Alyson. 'David Mitchell's Cloud Atlas of Narrative Constraints and Environmental Limits'. *Time: Limits and Constraints*. Eds. Jo Alyson Parker, Paul A. Harris and Christian Steineck. Vol. 13. Leiden: Koninklijke Brill NV, 2010. 201–18. Print.

Pendergrast, Mark. *For God, Country, and Coca-Cola: The Definitive History of the Great American Soft Drink and the Company That Makes It*. New York: Basic Books, 2013. Print.

Penner, Nina. 'Opera Singing and Fictional Truth'. *Journal of Aesthetics and Art Criticism* 71.1 (2013): 81–90. Print.

Pham, Andrew X. *Catfish and Mandala*. New York: Picador, 1999. Print.

Phillips, D. Z. *From Fantasy to Faith: The Philosophy of Religion and Twentieth Century Literature*. Hampshire: Macmillan, 1991. Print.

Pilgrim, Richard B. 'The Buddhist Mandala'. *Literature and Medicine* 8.1 (1989): 36–41. Print.

Pynchon, Thomas. *Gravity's Rainbow*. 1973. London: Penguin, 2006. Print.

Ratti, Manav. *The Postsecular Imagination: Postcolonialism, Religion, and Literature*. New York: Routledge, 2013. Print.

Reese, Jennifer. '"Swan" in a Million'. *Entertainment Weekly*. 872 (14 Apr. 2006): 89. Print.

Ricard, Matthieu. 'Introduction to the Purpose and Symbolism of the Mandala in Tibetan Buddhism'. *Mandala: The Architecture of Enlightenment*. Eds. Denise Patry Leidy and Robert A. F. Thurman. Boston: Shambala, 1997. 157. Print.

Rinpoche, Tulku Thondup. *Buddhist Civilization in Tibet*. London: Routledge & Kegan Paul, 1987. Print.

Robertson, Roland. *Globalization: Social Theory and Global Culture*. London: Sage, 1992. Print.

Robinson, Richard, and Willard Johnson. *The Buddhist Religion*. 4th ed. Sacramento, CA: Wadsworth Publishing Company, 1996. Print.

Rogers, Holly. '"The Public Will Only Believe the Truth If It Is Shot in 3D": Michel van der Aa, "Nine Years in an Ophanage" (Zenna), *Sunken Garden*, Scene 6'. [sic] *Cambridge Opera Journal* 28.2 (2016): 277–82. Print.

Rowland, Susan. *C. G. Jung and Literary Theory: The Challenge from Fiction*. Hampshire: Macmillan, 1999. Print.

Samsara. Dir. Ron Fricke. Perf. Ni Made Megahadi Pratiwi et al. Oscilloscope Laboratories, 2011. Film.

Samuels, Andrew. 'Foreword'. *Post-Jungian Criticism: Theory and Practice*. Eds. James S. Baumlin, Tita French Baumlin, and George H. Jensen. New York: SUNY Press, 2004. Print.

Samuels, Andrew. *Jung and the Post-Jungians*. 1985. East Sussex: Routledge, 2013. Print.

Schalansky, Judith. *Atlas of Remote Islands. Fifty Islands I have not visited and never will*. 2009. Trans. Christine Lo. London: Penguin, 2010.

Schlosser, Eric. *Fast Food Nation*. London: Penguin, 2002. Print.

Schneider, Anthony. 'Game of Tomes'. *Los Angeles Review of Books* (12 Dec. 2015). Web. 24 Oct. 2016.

Schoene, Berthold. *The Cosmopolitan Novel*. Edinburgh: Edinburgh UP, 2009. Print.

Schulz, Kathryn. 'Boundaries Are Conventions. And *The Bone Clocks* Author David Mitchell Transcends Them All'. *Vulture*. 25 Aug. 2014. Web. 10 Jan. 2016.

Scurr, Ruth. 'A Triumphant Homecoming'. *The Times* (2 Apr. 2006). Web. 24 Sep. 2014.

Self, Will. *The Book of Dave*. 2006. London: Penguin, 2007. Print.

Sense8. Dir. Lana Wachowski, Lilly Wachowski, J. Michael Straczynski et al. Netflix, 5 Jun. 2015. Web. 9 Sep. 2016.

Seven Years in Tibet. Dir. Jean-Jacques Annaud. Perf. Brad Pitt et al. TriStar Pictures, 1997. Film.

Shakya, Tsering. 'Transforming the Language of Protest'. *Cultural Anthropology* (8 Apr. 2012). Web. 5 Oct. 2016.

Shanahan, John. 'Digital Transcendentalism in David Mitchell's *Cloud Atlas*'. *Criticism* 58.1 (2016): 115–45. Print.

Shaw, Kristian. *Cosmopolitanism in Twenty-First Century Fiction*. Cham: Palgrave Macmillan, 2017. Print.

Shoop, Casey, and Dermot Ryan. "'Gravid with the Ancient Future": *Cloud Atlas* and the Politics of Big History'. *SubStance: David Mitchell in the Labyrinth of Time* 44.136 (2015): 92–106. Print.

Simpson, Kathryn. "'Or Something Like That": Coming of Age in *number9dream*'. *David Mitchell: Critical Essays*. Ed. Sarah Dillon. Canterbury: Gylphi, 2011. 49–76. Print.

Singh, Charu Sheel. *Concentric Imagination: Mandala Literary Theory*. Delhi: B. R. Publishing Corporation, 1994. Print.

Sion, Ioana. 'The Shape of the Beckettian Self: *Godot* and the Jungian Mandala'. *Consciousness, Literature and the Arts* 7.1 (2006): 1–13. Print.

Skidelsky, William. 'A World of Tricks'. *New Statesman* 133.4680 (22 Mar. 2004): 55. Print.

Smith, Ali. *Hotel World*. 2001. London: Penguin, 2002. Print.

Smith, Matthew Wilson. *The Total Work of Art*. New York: Routledge, 2007. Print.

Snelling, John. 'The Buddhist World View'. *The Buddhist Handbook: A Complete Guide to Buddhist Teaching and Practice*. London: Rider, 1987. 43–50. Print.

Snelling, John. 'The Spread of Buddhism'. *The Buddhist Handbook: A Complete Guide to Buddhist Teaching and Practice*. London: Rider, 1987. 121–222. Print.

Spivak, Gayatri Chakravorty. 'Rethinking Comparativism'. *New Literary History* 40.3 (2009): 609–26. Print.

Spivak, Gayatri Chakravorty. 'Three Women's Texts and a Critique of Imperialism'. *Critical Inquiry* 12.1 (1985): 243–61. Print.

Spivak, Gayatri Chakravorty. 'Translator's Preface'. *Of Grammatology*. 1967. By Jacques Derrida. Trans. Gayatri Chakravorty Spivak. Baltimore: The Johns Hopkins University Press, 1997. Ix–lxxxviii. Print.

Spivey, Ted R. 'The Archetype of Renewal: Mandala Symbolism in the Poetry of Wallace Stevens and Dylan Thomas'. *Interpretations* 16.1 (1985): 53–61. Print.

Steiner, George. "'Tragedy," Reconsidered'. *New Literary History* 35.1 (2004): 1–15. Print.

Stephenson, William. "'Moonlight Bright as a UFO Abduction": Science Fiction, Present-Future Alienation and Cognitive Mapping'. *David Mitchell: Critical Essays*. Ed. Sarah Dillon. Canterbury: Gylphi, 2011. 225–46. Print.

Stewart, Douglas. 'Cloud Atlas'. *Publishers Weekly* 251.26 (28 Jun. 2004): 30. Print.

Struck, Wolfgang. 'Genesis, Retold: In Search of an Atlas of the Anthropocene'. *Environmental Humanities* 5 (2014). 217–32

'Suicides in the United Kingdom, 2012 Registrations'. *Office for National Statistics*. 18 Feb. 2014. Web. 20 Apr. 2018.

Sunken Garden. Comp. Michel van der Aa. Lib. David Mitchell. English National Opera, London. 12 Apr. 2013. Performance.

Takemitsu, Toru. *From Me Flows What You Call Time*. Perf. Pacific Symphony Orchestra. Rec. 1997. Sony Music, New York, 1998. CD.

Tan, Gillian G. 'The Place of Hope in Acts of Protest and Offering'. *Cultural Anthropology* (8 Apr. 2012). Web. 5 Oct. 2016.

Taylor, Ken. 'Cultural Landscape as Open Air Museum: Borobudur World Heritage Site and Its Setting'. *Humanities Research* 10.2 (2003): 51–62. Print.

Thorsen, Leah. 'Buddhist Monks Here on Sacred Tibetan Arts Tour Made Stir on Social Media'. *St. Louis Post-Dispatch*. 22 Aug. 2014. Web. 12 Mar. 2015.

Thurman, Robert A. F. 'Mandala: The Architecture of Enlightenment'. *Mandala: The Architecture of Enlightenment*. Eds. Denise Patry Leidy and Robert A. F. Thurman. Boston: Shambala, 1997. 127–45. Print.

'Tibetan Bhavacakra'. *Uidaho.edu*. University of Idaho. 7 Mar. 2011. Web. 28 Aug. 2015.

The Tibetan Book of the Dead. Trans. Gyurme Dorje. Eds. Graham Coleman and Thupten Jinpa. London: Penguin, 2006. Print.

'Tibetan Healing Mandala'. *Freer and Sackler Galleries: The Smithsonian's Museums of Asian Art.* 7 Jan. 2004. Web. 12 Mar. 2015.

Tolkien, J. R. R. *The Adventures of Tom Bombadil.* London: Allen & Unwin, 1962. Print.

Tolkien, J. R. R. *The Fellowship of the Ring.* 1954. London: Grafton, 1991. Print.

Tolkien, J. R. R. *The Return of the King.* 1955. Boston: Houghton Mifflin, 1986. Print.

Tolkien, J. R. R. *The Two Towers.* 1954. Boston: Houghton Mifflin, 1965. Print.

Tucci, Giuseppe. *The Theory and Practice of the Mandala.* 1961. Trans. Alan Houghton Brodrick. New York: Dover Publications, 2001. Print.

Tusseau, Guillaume. 'From the Penitentiary to the Political Panoptic Paradigm'. *Beyond Foucault: New Perspectives on Bentham's Panopticon.* Ed. Anne Brunon-Ernst. Ashgate: Surrey, 2012. 115–40. Print.

van der Aa, Michel. Interview by Emma Pomfret. 'The Future of Opera Is Live, and It's in 3-D'. *The Times.* 4 Apr. 2013: 8–9. Web. 12 Mar. 2015.

Veel, Kristin. *Narrative Negotiations: Information Structures in Literary Fiction.* Göttingen: Vandenhoeck & Ruprecht, 2009. Print.

Vermeulen, Timotheus. Interview by Cher Potter. 'Timotheus Vermeulen Talks to Cher Potter'. *Tank Magazine.* Spring 2012. Web. 10 Jan. 2016.

Vermeulen, Timotheus, and Robin van den Akker. 'Notes on Metamodernism'. *Journal of Aesthetics and Culture* 2 (2010). Web. 17 Apr. 2015.

Vessantara. *Meeting the Buddhas: A Guide to Buddhas, Bodhisattvas, and Tantric Deities.* 1993. Birmingham: Windhorse Publications, 2003. Print.

Visel, Robin. 'Reading Forward: The Fractal Texts of Doris Lessing and David Mitchell'. *Doris Lessing Studies* 34 (2016): 12–15. Print.

The Voorman Problem. Dir. Gill, Mark. Perf. Freeman, Martin, Tom Hollander and Simon Griffiths. ShortsHD and Magnolia Pictures, 22 Sep. 2012. Film.

Wagner, Richard. *The Art-Work of the Future and Other Works.* 1895. Trans. William Ashton Ellis. London: University of Nebraska Press, 1993. Print.

Wake. Comp. Klaas de Vries & René Uijlenhoet. Lib. David Mitchell. Nationale Reisopera, Enschede. 13 May 2010. Performance.

Walcott, Susan M. 'Mapping from a Different Direction: Mandala as Sacred Spatial Visualization'. *Journal of Cultural Geography* 23 (2006): 71–88. Print.

Wallerstein, Immanuel. 'The Rise and Future Demise of the World Capitalist System: Concepts for Comparative Analysis'. *Comparative Studies in Society and History* 16.4 (Sep. 1974): 387–415. Print.

Wallis, Glenn. 'Mineful Response and the Rise of Corporatist Spirituality'. *Speculative Non-Buddhism* (17 Feb. 2014). Web. 15 Aug. 2016.

Waugh, Patricia. *Metafiction: The Theory and Practice of Self-Conscious Fiction.* London: Methuen, 1984. Print.

Weisenburger, Steven C. *A Gravity's Rainbow Companion: Sources and Contexts for Pynchon's Novel.* 2nd ed. Georgia: University of Georgia Press, 2006. Print.

White, Patrick. *The Solid Mandala.* 1966. London: Vintage, 1995. Print.

'Who We Are'. *Coca-Cola Journey.* Coca-ColaCompany.com. 28 Aug. 2015. Web. 28 Aug. 2015.

Williams, Holly. 'Heads Up: *Cloud Atlas*'. *The Independent* (20 Jan. 2013). Web. 22 Sep. 2014.

Williams, Roderick. Interview by Rose Harris-Birtill. Personal interview. 13 Jan. 2015.

Williamson, Rodney. *The Writing in the Stars: A Jungian Reading of the Poetry of Octavio Paz*. Toronto: University of Toronto Press, 2007. Print.

Wilson, Erin K., and Manfred B. Steger. 'Religious Globalisms in the Post-Secular Age'. *Globalizations* 10.3 (2013): 481–95. Print.

Winter, Jessica. 'Only Connect And Connect'. *The New York Village Voice* (10 Aug. 2004). Web. 24 Sep. 2014.

Wordsworth, William. 'A Slumber Did my Spirit Seal'. 1778. *William Wordsworth: The Major Works*. Ed. Stephen Gill. Oxford: Oxford UP, 2008. Print.

Yeats, William Butler. 'The Second Coming'. 1920. *The Collected Works of W. B. Yeats: The Poems*. Vol 1. 2nd ed. Ed. Richard J. Finneran. New York: Scribner, 1997. 189–90. Print.

Žižek, Slavoj. 'From Western Marxism to Western Buddhism'. *Cabinet* 2 (Spring 2001). Web. 14 Aug. 2016.

Index